COLLECTED WORKS OF JOHN STUART MILL

VOLUME XVIII

By Courtesy of the National Portrait Gallery, London

Essays on Politics and Society

by JOHN STUART MILL

Editor of the Text

J. M. ROBSON

Professor of English
Victoria College, University of Toronto

Introduction by

ALEXANDER BRADY

Professor Emeritus of Political Economy
University of Toronto

First published in Great Britain in 1977
by Routledge & Kegan Paul

Reprinted in 1996
by Routledge
2 Park Square, Milton Park, Abingdon, Oxfordshire OX14 4RN
711 Third Avenue, New York, NY 10017
First issued in paperback 2014
Routledge is an imprint of the Taylor and Francis Group, an informa company

Transferred to Digital Printing 2008

British Library Cataloguing in Publication Data
A catalogue record for this book is available from the British Library

ISBN 13: 978-0-415-14553-4 (hbk)
ISBN 13: 978-0-415-75696-9 (pbk)

This volume has been published with the assistance of a grant from the Canada
Council

Publisher's Note
The publisher has gone to great lengths to ensure the quality of this reprint but
points out that some imperfections in the original may be apparent

Contents

*

* *

Introduction

ALEXANDER BRADY

JOHN STUART MILL'S DEVELOPMENT as a political and social thinker may be divided into at least three periods, with the first two largely determining the course and character of the third. The first embraces his youthful apprenticeship in and passionate proselytizing for the utilitarianism in which from childhood he had been carefully nurtured by his father and Bentham. His career as a young and orthodox utilitarian extended to his mental crisis in 1826 at the age of twenty. The second period began with his recovery from the crisis (1826–30) and terminated with the dissolution of the Philosophic Radicals as a distinct party towards the end of the 1830s. In this crucial period of his life Mill refashioned his thinking under a variety of intellectual and emotional influences. The final period comprised the remaining thirty-three years of his career (1840–73), when he published his major works, including *A System of Logic, Principles of Political Economy, On Liberty,* and *Considerations on Representative Government.*

THE YOUNG UTILITARIAN

MILL'S OWN ACCOUNT of his extraordinary education is a classic in the intellectual history of the last century. This is not the place to describe the rigorous pedagogic experiment to which he was subjected, other than to note its apparent effectiveness in making him, as he admitted, a reasoning machine with impressive powers for analysis and a reverence for facts and principles. It was ostensibly designed by his father to enable him to think for himself, although independent thought was not its immediate result. The highly precocious boy who at sixteen (in 1822) founded the Utilitarian Society had already faithfully absorbed in his father's study and from the writings and tutelage of Bentham a philosophy of ethics and politics wherein utility was the supreme criterion. He related how he felt as a youth after reading Dumont's translation of Bentham's treatise on legislation: "When

I laid down the last volume of the Traité I had become a different being. . . .
I now had opinions; a creed, a doctrine, a philosophy; in one among the
best senses of the word, a religion; the inculcation and diffusion of which
could be made the principal outward purpose of a life."[1]

With obvious zealotry Mill was now ambitious to reform the affairs of
mankind to conform with utilitarian canons. Fired by the influence of his
father and Bentham, he engaged in a crusade to carry the torch of rationalism and utilitarianism into every sector of British life. In devotion he no less
than Karl Marx had a sense of historic mission. His obvious instrument was
journalism, which in his opinion was to modern Europe what political
oratory had been to Athens and Rome. At seventeen he began eagerly
dashing off letters and articles to newspapers and periodicals, arguing for
the specific changes that utilitarians then sought: civil and criminal law
reform, population restriction, a free press, a free economy, destruction of
monopoly wherever present, abolition of colonial slavery, parliamentary
reform, and a redress of Irish grievances. From the outset he wrote less to
earn a living than to fulfil a mission and convert a public. In 1823 his father
had secured his appointment as a clerk in the East India Company, where
in the next thirty-five years he rose to high office and enjoyed ample freedom
and adequate income to study and champion those causes to which he was
dedicated. His position in time gave him not merely an invaluable independence but a practical experience in coping with complex human situations in the sub-continent on the other side of the globe.

The empiricist here had a congenial opportunity to reinforce his theories
with a special experience of public affairs. In later life he wrote:

the occupation accustomed me to see and hear the difficulties of every course,
and the means of obviating them, stated and discussed deliberately, with a view
to execution; it gave me opportunities of perceiving when public measures, and
other political facts, did not produce the effects which had been expected of
them, and from what causes; above all it was valuable to me by making
me, in this portion of my activity, merely one wheel in a machine, the whole of
which had to work together. . . . I became practically conversant with the difficulties of moving bodies of men, the necessities of compromise, the art of sacrificing the non-essential to preserve the essential. I learnt how to obtain the best
I could, when I could not obtain everything. . . .[2]

Two years after Mill founded the Utilitarian Society, Bentham and a few
friends launched the *Westminster Review* as an official organ for utilitarian
ideas. In its first four years (1824–28) Mill, despite his youth, was a frequent
contributor on a wide range of themes, which he treated in the spirit of
utilitarian orthodoxy. He criticized the follies of aristocratic rule in Britain

[1]*Autobiography*, ed. Jack Stillinger (Boston: Houghton Mifflin, 1969), 42.
[2]*Ibid.*, 52–3.

and Ireland, the illusions of chivalry formerly associated with aristocracy, the vested interests of great landowners in corn and game laws, and the ills of a faulty journalism. He strove to liberate the English press from the trammels of an abused and arbitrary law of libel and the burden of press duties.[3] Mill like his father and other contemporary Radicals saw in the freedom of the press the essential instrument for mobilizing opinion, breaking down resistance to reform, and creating that degree of popular discontent which would compel the aristocratic government to make substantial concessions. He was naturally inspired by his father's famous essay on "Liberty of the Press," first published in 1821 as a supplement to the *Encyclopaedia Britannica*. He accepted his parent's uncompromising belief that no special laws should exist to hamper the freedom of newspapers to print facts and advance opinions to protect the people against the tyranny of a government.[4]

In 1826 when Mill was twenty he entered the shadows of a mental crisis, which lasted for months, and has been variously assessed and explained by biographers. It is easy to accept the traditional and simple view that it resulted from prolonged and excessive work. Mill had recently undertaken the prodigious task of editing the five volumes of Bentham's *Rationale of Judicial Evidence*, contributed to newspapers and journals, debated in the societies with which he was associated, tutored his brothers and sisters at home, and dealt with official duties at India House. Yet there was more involved than heavy work and physical exhaustion. In the *Autobiography* he blames a faulty education which cultivated his intellect but starved his feelings and aesthetic yearnings. His faith in the efficacy of utilitarian thought was evidently shaken, and it is symptomatic that on this, unlike other occasions, he failed to seek from his father guidance, sympathy, or compassion. He had secretly begun to rebel against certain elements in the philosophy of James Mill and Jeremy Bentham and felt compelled to work out alone an intellectual accommodation with his inheritance. A. W. Levi has advanced a Freudian explanation of the mental crisis and its disappearance.[5] Whether we accept this view or not, Mill's illness marked a milestone in his intellectual development. He awoke to deficiencies in the eighteenth-century utilitarian thought in which he had been indoctrinated, and to repair them sought guidance from other and varied sources, including

---

[3]See for his characteristic ideas at the time: "The Game Laws," *Westminster Review*, V (Jan., 1826), 1–22; "Law of Libel and Liberty of the Press," *Westminster Review*, III (April, 1825), 285–381.

[4]Joseph Hamburger in *James Mill and the Art of Revolution* (New Haven: Yale University Press, 1963), 27–33, discusses James Mill's ideas on the necessity of a free press to effect reform.

[5]A. W. Levi, "The Mental Crisis of John Stuart Mill," *The Psychoanalytic Review*, XXXII (1946), 84–101.

a constellation of new friends and new mentors. In the fourteen years after 1826 the orthodox utilitarian was transformed into an eclectic liberal who in no sense repudiated all his inheritance but modified and combined it with many fresh ideas and methods of thought demanded in a world gripped by change where truth, as he saw it, must be many-sided.

He found for depression an early antidote in Wordsworth's tranquil and contemplative poetry, which supplied something which had been lacking in his father's rigorous educational regime—a cultivation of feeling inspired by natural beauty. Yet the Wordsworthian culture of the feelings was at the time merely one of a medley of influences.[6] Even Macaulay's caustic criticism in the *Edinburgh Review* of his father's *Essay on Government* persuaded Mill that although Macaulay himself was faulty in philosophy, he scored valid points against the narrowness of his father's political thought and its neglect of significant springs in the conduct of modern man.[7]

The thinkers, very different from his father and Bentham, who gave him intellectual stimulus in the early 1830s were the Saint-Simonians, Comte, Coleridge, Carlyle, and Tocqueville. He appreciated the fact that these writers emphasized the significance of history and a philosophy of history, and endorsed the idea that each state of society and the human mind tended to produce that which succeeded it, with modifications dictated by circumstances. At the same time, the whirl of change in events and ideas impressed him with the relativity of political institutions; each different stage in human society must have different institutions. Further, as he put it, "government is always either in the hands, or passing into the hands, of whatever is the strongest power in society, and . . . what this power is, does not depend on institutions, but institutions on it. . . ."[8]

Not the least fascinating circumstance in the shaping of Mill's thought in the early 1830's was his coming under different streams of influence and endeavouring to reconcile them or to select from each some element or elements of significance. This process was admirably illustrated in the letter to John Sterling in October 1831.[9] He discussed here contemporary Toryism and Liberalism, and distinguished between the contrary types of speculative and practical Toryism, but oddly failed to recognize the significant reformism of men like Huskisson and Peel. "Practical Toryism," he said, "simply means, being *in*, and availing yourself of your comfortable position *inside* the vehicle without minding the poor devils who are freezing *outside*. . . . Such Toryism is essentially incompatible with any large and generous

---

[6]See his long letter to John Sterling, 20–22 October, 1831, in *Earlier Letters*, ed. F. E. Mineka, *Collected Works*, XII (Toronto: University of Toronto Press, 1963), 74–88 (hereafter cited as *EL, CW*, with volume and page numbers).
[7]See Textual Introduction, *System of Logic, CW*, VII, liv–lv.
[8]*Autobiography*, 97.
[9]*EL, CW*, XII, 74–88.

aspirations. . . ." Yet this is the Toryism that appealed to the privileged classes of his day, who had little faith in human improvement, unlike his friends the speculative Tories—Wordsworth, Coleridge, and Southey. These wanted an ideal Toryism, an ideal King, Lords, and Commons, the old England as opposed to the new, an England as she might be, not as she is. They represented a reverence for government in the abstract,

sensible that it is good for man to be ruled; to submit both his body & mind to the guidance of a higher intelligence & virtue. It is therefore the direct anti-thesis of liberalism, which is for making every man his own guide & sovereign master, & letting him think for himself & do exactly as he judges best for himself, giving other men leave to persuade him if they can by evidence, but forbidding him to give way to authority; and still less allowing them to constrain him more than the existence & tolerable security of every man's person and property renders indispensably necessary. It is difficult to conceive a more thorough ignorance of man's nature, & of what is necessary for his happiness or what degree of happiness & virtue he is capable of attaining than this system implies.[10]

These sentiments may seem somewhat uncharacteristic of one renowned as spokesman of British nineteenth-century liberalism. They reflect his thinking at a critical period when he was striving to assess the changing winds of current opinion. At the same time they also reflect an enduring element: his doubts about the average man's capacity unaided to cope wisely with the complex problems of citizenship.

In combining his earlier utilitarian doctrines with those of new intellectual associates, Mill saw politics as an immensely important part of the structure of society, since only through political activity could men maximize their moral and social potentiality. The institutional contrivances of the state, being interwoven with the main facets of economic and social life, were comprehensible only in the context of the whole. Politics reflected the character of economic and social systems and the ethical values men held. Culture and politics were thus inseparable, political progress and social progress interdependent. Some years later, in a letter to John Chapman, Mill expressed in general terms a view that for him had become axiomatic:

I understand by Sociology not a particular *class* of subjects included *within* Politics, but a vast field *including* it—the whole field of enquiry & speculation respecting human society & its arrangements, of which the forms of govern-ment, & the principles of the conduct of governments are but a part. And it seems to me impossible that even the politics of the day can be discussed on principle, or with a view to anything but the exigencies of the moment, unless by setting out from definite opinions respecting social questions more fundamental than what is commonly called politics.[11]

[10]*Ibid.*, 84.
[11]*Later Letters*, ed. F. E. Mineka and D. N. Lindley (Toronto: University of Toronto Press, 1972), XIV, 68 (hereafter cited as *LL*, *CW*, with volume and page numbers).

IDEAS AND ACTIVITY, 1830–40

THE VARIED INTELLECTUAL STIMULI that Mill experienced after his mental crisis helped to shape the mould of his political thought in that turbulent and confused era of the 1830s. However much he strayed from the strict path of his father's thought, he remained in agreement with the main legal and political reforms sought by James Mill and the Philosophic Radicals. In his journalism he still advocated extensive changes in the laws, the parliamentary system, and the whole system of government to reduce what, in his opinion, was the baneful influence of the aristocracy on the major aspects of British society. He endeavoured to arouse the Radicals in and out of parliament to form a powerful party that either alone or allied with progressive Whigs could shape public policies on reformist lines. In a letter to Edward Lytton Bulwer in March 1838 he summarized his political ambitions in the preceding years:

I have never had any other notion of practical policy, since the radicals were numerous enough to form a party, than that of resting on the *whole body* of radical opinion, from the whig-radicals at one extreme, to the more reasonable & practical of the working classes, & the Benthamites, on the other. I have been trying ever since the reform bill to stimulate, so far as I had an opportunity, all sections of the parliamentary radicals to organize such a union & such a system of policy....[12]

Yet despite his genuine zeal, Mill found the task of trying to achieve unity among the Radicals frustrating. They were splintered into stubborn factions, and no parliamentary leader with the requisite qualities emerged to unite them. They constituted a party of many lieutenants without a general. For a short interval Mill pinned his hopes on Lord Durham, who left the Whig ministry, undertook the Canadian mission, surrounded himself with Radical advisers like Charles Buller and Gibbon Wakefield, and produced a report that was a Radical rather than a Whig or Tory document. But Mill's hopes and designs for Durham's leadership or indeed for the future of the party were soon shattered by adverse events, including the serious illness and death of Durham and Mill's own inability to sustain much longer the heavy financial and other burdens of the *London and Westminster Review*, the organ for radical causes. By 1840 he had virtually ceased to be a leading counsellor to Radical politicians, although his interest in utilitarian reform continued unabated.

Significantly, in the 1830s Mill was not absorbed exclusively in British political ideas and activities. In contrast with his father, who disliked France

---

[12]*EL, CW*, XIII, 380. Much information on this theme is contained in Joseph Hamburger, *Intellectuals in Politics: John Stuart Mill and the Philosophic Radicals* (New Haven: Yale University Press, 1965).

and the French, he was early influenced by French thinkers and fascinated by the dialectic of French politics. In 1829 he told a Parisian friend that he admired his countrymen because they were open to ideas and more ready than the English to act on them.[13] Never perhaps was his Francophile enthusiasm more pronounced than in 1830. On the collapse of the Bourbon monarchy he hurried to Paris, mixed freely with young revolutionaries and Saint-Simonian leaders, shared the excitement and joy of his French friends in what they assumed was the triumph of revolution over aristocratic politics and ultramontane theology, and returned to England with a renewed zest for reforms.[14]

Mill's political hopes for France resembled those for Britain: a political regime on utilitarian lines, a widely representative assembly, a liberal franchise, a free press, free associations, popular education, and an enlightened public. However, the revolution of 1830 became a dismal disappointment. The monarchy of Louis Philippe, wedded to narrow commercial and financial groups, was unwilling to jeopardize for the sake of reform its powers and privileges, and at every step opposed major changes. From London Mill closely and anxiously followed events, and between 1830 and 1834 in successive articles in the *Examiner* poured out his bitterness.[15]

Mill's severe disenchantment left an imprint on his political thinking throughout the 1830s and even later. Although he did not lose liberal convictions or a belief in representative government, he now doubted that large electorates could make sound decisions without the positive leadership of enlightened minorities. An extended suffrage, however important in itself, alone could not prevent the continuance of self-interested oligarchies whether of the aristocracy or middle class. His doubts and fears at the time about representative institutions and democracy were evident in numerous articles. Seven of these are included in the present volume, beginning with the review articles on *The Use and Abuse of Some Political Terms* by George Cornewall Lewis and *Rationale of Political Representation* by Samuel Bailey.[16]

LEWIS AND BAILEY

Lewis was a man of Mill's own age, equipped with similar precocious erudition, and of utilitarian sympathies. His book dealt with the relation of

---

[13]*EL, CW*, XII, 32.

[14]See letters to his father from Paris, *ibid.*, 54–67.

[15]Iris W. Mueller examines the content of these articles in *John Stuart Mill and French Thought* (Urbana: University of Illinois Press, 1956), Chapter ii.

[16]Three other notable writings of this decade, not included in the present volume, also shed illuminating light on his political ideas: "The Spirit of the Age" (1831), "Bentham" (1838), and "Coleridge" (1840).

logic to politics, a topic in which Mill was then too deeply interested to treat casually. Two years later he confessed to Carlyle that his review was an outgrowth from his own mind and the truest he had ever written—that is, it was no mere product of an orthodox utilitarian schooling.[17] He commended Lewis's attempt to bring a lucid logic into the language of politics, since slovenly thinking and equivocal words were together the bane of political discussion. But he took strong exception to certain points, of which the most important concerned rights. Lewis, following his teacher John Austin, argued that all rights are creations of law and the will of the sovereign. To call anything a right which is not enforceable in the courts is an abuse of language. In contrast Mill emphasized the reality of moral rights. He contended that, in saying that no man has a moral right to think as he pleases, for he ought to inform himself and think justly, Dr. Johnson refers to a right Lewis evidently fails to comprehend. Yet for Mill a right in the Johnsonian sense is no abuse of terms; it is good logic and good English. Rights are the correlatives of obligations and duties, and moral as well as legal rights have a necessary and significant place in the contemporary state. It is a moral right of subjects to be well-governed and a moral duty of the sovereign to govern well. The focus of this criticism is the mischief inherent in unduly simplified and inflexible concepts. Mill reacts here against the rigidity of some utilitarian logicians. His further complaint concerned the apparent and unjustified contempt with which Lewis disposed of Locke and Rousseau for assuming an unhistorical and fictitious state of nature and a social contract. Mill believed that it was inconsequential whether anything like a state of nature existed. The real issue was the extent to which as an hypothesis it shed light on the fact of a morality outside the law to which men could appeal. To Mill as to Locke such morality was important. Independent states in relations with one another remained in a state of nature, without a common superior, but responsive to moral obligations and duties. However unskilfully formulated, the old theories of the social contract and the inalienable rights of man in Mill's opinion had a rightful place in the evolution of political liberty and justice by indicating a pragmatic limit on the power of the sovereign. He concluded his review of Lewis's book by emphasizing the necessity of recognizing, despite all the linguistic differences, the close relationship between ideas of different political thinkers, and also the possibility of combining them into a whole.

In reviewing Samuel Bailey's *Rationale of Political Representation*, Mill in effect summarized his own ideas on the subject. Sharing the views of the Sheffield Radical, he employed the book to illustrate what for him were the requisites of sound representative government. In his argument he reverted

[17]*EL, CW,* XII, 205.

to the cherished utilitarian dogma of his father that in politics it was essential
to achieve the closest possible identification of interest between rulers and
ruled. But this, he thought, was feasible only if decisions were made, not
by the uninstructed multitude, but by a carefully selected body commanding
special knowledge and techniques and accountable to the public. Strict
accountability would help to ensure that rulers pursued the interests of the
people rather than their own. Admittedly the task of overcoming the inbred
chicanery and low cunning of politicians was difficult. It could not be
accomplished simply by institutional machinery without a massive and prolonged public enlightenment. His fear of a sudden flood of new and ignorant
voters made him cautious about any rapid extension of the franchise: "no
one is disposed," he wrote, "to deny that we ought cautiously to feel our
way, and watch well the consequences of each extension of the suffrage
before venturing upon another" (32). (This and subsequent parenthetical
references are to the text of the present edition.) This caution extended even
to his favourite cause of women's enfranchisement. Despite a passionate
belief in female suffrage, he thought in 1835 that its public advocacy would
serve no practical purpose (29n).

Although wary about changes in the franchise, Mill supported many
reforms in political machinery in harmony with orthodox Philosophic
Radicalism: the secret ballot, triennial parliaments, publicity for parliamentary proceedings, payment of members and their professionalization,
reduction in the size of the House of Commons to render it more efficient,
and the creation of strong local government which he assumed would reduce
the burdens of the national parliament. He also proposed a radical change
in the House of Lords to destroy it as a rigid barrier to reforms fashioned in
the Commons. He would abolish its hereditary principle and select its
membership from the lower house. By such changes he hoped to transform
Britain's government from an aristocracy into a special kind of democracy
led by an enlightened few.[18]

He said little about the enlightened few beyond emphasizing that they
consist of those specially endowed with public spirit and educated to conduct
a thoughtful direction of national affairs: the fittest persons whom the existing society could produce. He believed that since 1688 the landed aristocracy had governed England badly: it reflected the attitudes of unimagina-
tive dilettantes incapable of the rigorous intellect that government needed,
and it was fettered by its own enormous wealth and special privileges.
Anxious to protect its own position, it could do little to bridge the chasm
between the social classes, which increasingly endangered a Britain subject
to the new powerful pressures of nineteenth-century industrialism. To Mill

---

[18]See J. S. Mill, "The House of Lords," *Globe*, 16 October, 1836, 2; and "The Close
of the Session," *London Review*, II (October, 1835), 271–2.

its strength and effectiveness seemed inferior to those of the aristocracy of
Prussia (23–4).

Through his reform programme Mill hoped to create a new and independent ruling class of paid and professional parliamentarians freed from
electoral pledges. He believed that unpaid legislators and magistrates sustained the monopoly power of the aristocracy because aristocrats could
usually afford to serve without pay (35). Among the Radicals the issue of
pledges provoked acrimonious debate. In 1832 Mill had irritated some in
arguing that, although in cases of constitutional change pledges might sometimes be justified, they were in general bad. "The sovereignty of the people,"
he wrote, "is essentially a delegated sovereignty. Government must be performed by the few, for the benefit of the many. . . ."[19] The same view he
repeated in the "Rationale of Representation," contending that electors are
obligated to select representatives fully qualified to form sound decisions
on public matters. They must not expect that those they elect should act
slavishly in parliament according to popular judgment any more than
patients expect a physician to cure their ills according to their own chosen
ideas of medicine (40). For Mill, pledges conflicted with the essence of
representative government. Voters were free to reward or punish, by re-elec-
tion or rejection, a representative at the end of his term, but to shackle him
from the outset with inflexible instructions would cripple his powers of initiative and responsibility.

AMERICA, TOCQUEVILLE, AND DEMOCRACY

As a British radical, Mill from youth was profoundly interested in the
United States. For him and most of his fellow utilitarians the republic was
a unique experiment of a democracy in action, and hence important for all
European liberals. Unlike the Tory writers of the *Quarterly Review*, they
looked to America to demonstrate the virtues of democracy, and abundant
praise of the United States became their orthodox practice. They admired
it for experimenting with new social ideas, rejecting an established church,
extending franchise laws, promoting popular education, recognizing a free
press, and believing in a free economy. Such was Jeremy Bentham's
enthusiasm for America that to Andrew Jackson he described himself as
"more of a United Statesman than an Englishman." For him and his
disciples the republic seemed to apply the principle of utility more assiduously than did Britain.

It is hardly surprising, therefore, that between 1835 and 1840 Mill wrote
three leading articles on America: two lengthy reviews in 1835 and 1840

[19]*Examiner*, 1 July, 1832, 417. See also a similar argument two years earlier in
"Prospects of France," *Examiner*, 10 October, 1830, 642.

on the separate parts of Tocqueville's *Democracy in America* and in 1836 an essay on the state of American society as depicted in five contemporary volumes. In these essays he endeavoured not merely to illustrate the work of a new and major political thinker, but also to portray the democratic society of the United States compared with the aristocratic regimes of Europe. In doing this under the weighty influence of Tocqueville, he clarified and matured his own thought on the merits and faults of democracy. Hence his two essays on Tocqueville are highly significant in the evolution of his thinking.

Almost the same age, although of different social backgrounds, the two men had much in common. Both were convinced that the new industrial age was destined to affect profoundly society and politics. Both were interested in the shape of things to come, in the trend to equality, and in democracy as almost an inevitable force of nature that must be adjusted to human circumstances and needs. Both believed that it alone could diffuse the spirit of a vigorous citizenship and sense of community throughout the whole national state. Yet they were also deeply concerned about its inherent defects and anxious to remedy them. "Man cannot turn back the rivers to their source," wrote Mill, "but it rests with himself whether they shall fertilize or lay waste his fields" (158).

Tocqueville's idea of democracy was more loosely defined than Mill's. He referred to it less often as a particular form of government than as an equality of social conditions, without elements of aristocracy and privilege, the kind of equality which was best exemplified in the United States. Equality of conditions might exist under an absolute ruler, and Tocqueville feared that in some countries, including his own France, it might emerge solely in that form. Mill, on the other hand, applied the term democracy more consistently to a form of government in which the people constitutionally exercised a dominant sway. He was fully aware, however, that democratic government had wide social implications, and a large measure of social equality was a natural accompaniment.

In his two reviews Mill welcomed Tocqueville's book as a landmark in the literature of politics, hailing the first part as among "the most remarkable productions of our time" (57). He saw its author, in his wide-ranging thought, as comparable to Montesquieu. His praise for the second part was equally enthusiastic. It was "the first philosophical book ever written on Democracy, as it manifests itself in modern society."[20] The reasons for this laudation are found in the grand sweep of Tocqueville's sociological description and perception and his penetrating comments on democracy,

---

[20]De Tocqueville on Democracy in America [II]," 156. See also Mill's laudatory remarks in a letter to the author after he had read the second part, *EL, CW*, XIII, 433–5 (referred to in the Textual Introduction, lxxvi–lxxvii below).

its mixed properties and tendencies, the dangers it confronted, and the different demands it made on mankind. For Mill method was hardly less important than content. In Tocqueville he saw the new kind of political scientist he was ambitious to be himself, quick to probe the varied social forces that mould man's political conduct, skilful in combining deduction and induction, and adept in applying comparative methods to the facts of society and government.

In his first essay, especially, Mill employed long quotations to illustrate Tocqueville's views on American democracy and society and on the operation of its institutions. He acted like a modest chairman, briefly introducing a speaker and giving him abundant time to elaborate his theme, confident in the speaker's mastery of the subject. But his quotations in both essays indicate his deep interest in certain aspects of Tocqueville's account, especially the role of a numerical majority and its influences on individual and national life. Anxiously he scrutinized how far in practice Americans respected the principle of true democracy as defined in "The Rationale of Representation." He was hardly encouraged by his findings. The people often directly governed rather than merely exerting an ultimate control over government. He learned from Tocqueville how widely delegation had replaced representation (74). Electors, however poorly informed, often laid down conditions that their representatives were compelled to respect. The majority was unmistakably dominant, constantly and aggressively asserted its will, shaped the character of opinion, and lived in perpetual adoration of itself. It was little comfort for Mill to read Tocqueville's verdict that he knew of no country with less independence of mind and less real freedom of discussion than the United States (81). No monarch had such power over opinion as the popular majority. Tocqueville admitted that the majority refrained from attacking the property and material interests of the rich minority, but it otherwise imposed a despotic yoke on public opinion, on independent thought, and hence on individuality of character.

In view of his previous generous admiration for America, Mill doubtless wished that the evidence was different, but could not escape the compelling force of Tocqueville's critical picture. Yet, although he accepted most of Tocqueville's strictures on American institutions, he sometimes tried to moderate and excuse them. In the first part of his work Tocqueville concluded that the American electors were disposed to choose mediocrities rather than able candidates, owing partly to their own limited education and understanding and partly to the insatiable envy that most men had for their superiors. Mill feared that this charge, if true, meant that his own belief in a talented élite to guide and instruct the democracy was unlikely to be justified. He thought he found, however, in the facts furnished by Tocqueville a situation less discouraging than had at first appeared. In critical times able Americans assumed a positive leadership. In ordinary times, un- fortunately, the range of public activity was too restricted to attract men of ambition and talent. Mill believed that this situation would eventually improve with the advance of education, general enlightenment, and the social needs of America.[21] He was much less pessimistic than Tocqueville about democracy's falling under the control of the mediocre.

In his first review Mill also questioned Tocqueville's assertion that aris- tocracy had qualities of prudence and steadiness absent in democracy. The steadiness of an aristocracy, he said, was commonly expressed in a tenacious grip on its own cherished privileges. Its strength of will, as English history illustrated, was shaped by its class interests, and its opinions tended to fluc- tuate with its immediate impulses and needs (77–9).

Mill's main criticism in his second essay was well taken: Tocqueville, in failing to define democracy with precision, sometimes confused its effects with those of a commercial civilization in general. As a nation progresses in industry and wealth, its manufactures expand, its capital grows, its class structure changes, and the intermediate group between poor and rich, com- prised of artisans and middle class, multiplies. This may seem to make, as Tocqueville believed, a trend to equalization, but it could be merely one of many consequences from augmented industry and wealth, which created a highly complex society without necessarily furthering political freedom and democratic equality. Mill doubted whether in itself a commercial civiliza- tion, aside from other influences, necessarily equalized conditions among men. At any rate it failed to do so in Britain. There, he wrote, "The extremes of wealth and poverty are wider apart, and there is a more numerous body of persons at each extreme, than in any other commercial community" (193). Owing to their abundant children, the poor remained poor, while the laws tended to keep large concentrations of capital together, and hence the rich remained rich. Great fortunes were accumulated and seldom distributed. In this respect, Mill thought, Britain stood in contrast to the United States, although in commercial prosperity and industrial growth she was similar.

However ready to accept Tocqueville's belief in the passion for equality as a dynamic factor in modern industrial nations, Mill in comparing Britain and the United States saw and illustrated other influences. He agreed with Tocqueville that in the two countries the middle classes were remarkably alike in structure and aspirations. Both experienced social instability, the restless drive of individuals to improve their lot, the ceaseless pursuit of wealth, and the enlargement of the middle class through constant recruit- ment from below. But in one respect they differed. Britain, unlike America,

---

[21]"De Tocqueville on Democracy in America [I]," 76–7. In 1840 he told Macvey Napier that he did not differ strongly from Tocqueville on this issue (*EL, CW*, XIII, 444).

had a governing and landed aristocracy, and also a leisured class and a learned class, larger and more significant in influence than their counterparts in the republic. Such class features produced between the two countries differences in the quality of political life. Mill admitted that in Britain profound changes then occurring narrowed the divergences. The strongholds of aristocratic powers were weakening. The House of Lords, for all its pretensions and authority, failed to defeat the Reform Bill. Peers were now influenced by bourgeois opinion and even taste. The edifice of government might still rest on an impressive aristocratic base, but its transformation had begun, and Mill and the Philosophic Radicals were determined that it must be carried to ultimate success.

It is needless to dwell on differences in opinion between Mill and Tocqueville, since the dissimilarities are less important than what the men shared in common. Mill saw Tocqueville as he saw himself—a leader in the great transition of thought between the eighteenth and nineteenth centuries and a contributor of social insights and ideas to those who desired for Europe a new liberal age. In his *Autobiography* he described how Tocqueville more effectively than any other contemporary depicted the virtues of democracy as well as its perils. He admitted that his French friend reinforced his own fears about the political tyranny of popular opinion and influenced him in shifting his ideal from that of pure democracy to its modified form later presented in *Considerations on Representative Government*.[22] Both men observed in America harsh forms of popular tyranny, not in laws, but in what Mill called the dispensing power over all law. "The people of Massachusetts," he remarked, "passed no law prohibiting Roman Catholic schools, or exempting Protestants from the penalties of incendiarism; they contented themselves with burning the Ursuline convent to the ground, aware that no jury would be found to redress the injury" (177). In these cases popular tyranny was expressed not merely in the action of mobs, incited by the passions of religion, party, or race, but by the inability of the administrative and judicial organs to work effectively owing to their direct dependence on popular opinion.

Mill, like Tocqueville, saw in the democratic majority perennial threats to what for both were supreme values: individuality, intellectual variety, effective minority opinions, and the spontaneous initiatives derived from individuals and groups. For Mill these values remained an enduring element in his liberal philosophy and pervaded *On Liberty*. Their implications for national development were manifest. But no single rule or set of concepts could determine the same development for all nations. Each nation must pursue a course appropriate to the varied interests, circumstances, and temperament of its citizens. Years before Mill had criticized Comte's folly in

[22]*Autobiography*, 115–16.

assuming a single law of evolution for all nations, a criticism he never retracted.[23]

Mill no less than Tocqueville was eager to recognize the main political corollaries of these liberal ideas. He emphasized the importance for individuals of fostering and preserving combinations or associations to promote mutual protection and common causes, such as political unions, antislavery societies, and the like. He saw the freedom of combination as intimately joined to that of the press. "The real Political Unions of England," he wrote, "are the Newspapers. It is these which tell every person what all other persons are feeling, and in what manner they are ready to act." (165.) He evidently did not foresee that sometimes newspapers might also become the instruments of a democratic despotism.

He likewise agreed with Tocqueville in extolling the value of local government as a means for extending among the people the management of public business, training them in self-rule, and enlarging their scope for political freedom. He here reflected his faith that under democracy politics becomes a form of adult education. He was hardly less confident than Tocqueville that the spirit and habit of local autonomy was a primary source of American freedom and would no less promote freedom in other democracies.

Finally, in his second article on Tocqueville he also expressed the conviction that in a mass democracy, whether in Europe or America, it was essential to bolster influences that countervailed those of the mass. For him the evil was not the preponderance of a democratic class in itself, but of any class, especially when it lacked intellectual cultivation (196). He believed with Tocqueville that the overwhelming dominance of a single class would always predispose it to establish a deadening uniformity in the style and texture of life for the whole society. This would mean an intellectually static community resembling that of China as understood in Europe at the time.

Mill, like Tocqueville, remained apprehensive that in an industrial and commercial age democracy would impoverish the national culture by imposing on it a single and inflexible set of mass values. Although he admitted that public opinion must rule, he speculated that to form

the best public opinion, there should exist somewhere a great social support for opinions and sentiments different from those of the mass. The shape which that support may best assume is a question of time, place, and circumstance; but (in a commercial country, and in an age when, happily for mankind, the military spirit is gone by) there can be no doubt about the elements which must compose it: they are, an agricultural class, a leisured class, and a learned class. (199.)

These sentiments, tinged with Coleridgean conservatism, may have seemed strange and unwelcome to some fellow Philosophic Radicals, but by 1840

[23]Letter to Gustave d'Eichthal, *EL, CW*, XII, 37 (8/10/29).

his associates in the movement had learned that his Benthamite orthodoxy had long since disappeared.

It may be added that Mill did not remain convinced that the existence of a leisured class was of pre-eminent importance. In 1847 he wrote to John Austin:

I have even ceased to think that a leisured class, in the ordinary sense of the term, is an essential constituent of the best form of society. What does seem to me essential is that society at large should not be overworked, nor over-anxious about the means of subsistence, for which we must look to the grand source of improvement, repression of population, combined with laws or customs of inheritance which shall favour the diffusion of property instead of its accumulation in masses.[24]

At this time Mill was working on his *Principles of Political Economy*, and the healing virtues of the stationary state were fresh and vivid in his mind.

In his essay on the "State of Society in America" Mill expressed not merely some additional reflections on the American experiment, but also briefly raised questions on how environment determines a nation's politics, how nations could benefit from one another's experience through a science of comparative institutions, and how American society was judged by European observers in the doubtful light of their own prejudices, especially hostility to popular rule. He was strongly convinced that the American form of democracy must be directly related to the special character of American society, moulded by a wide variety of forces: abundant natural wealth, a fast growing population, a remarkable opportunity for all classes to raise their standards of living, the absence of aggressive neighbours, the lack of a leisured class except in the southern states, and the inheritance of a language and culture from a parent nation three thousand miles away. Its experiment in politics was scarcely comprehensible apart from the interplay of these numerous influences, all of which, although seldom the product of government, impinged directly on government. They were not all favourable to the success of democracy. To Mill the United States was a classic demonstration of the intimate bonds between social circumstances and political forms.

Characteristic is the sentence: "High wages and universal reading are the two elements of democracy; where they co-exist, all government, except the government of public opinion, is impossible" (99). Mill held that the high premium on labour in North America meant that the common man was not merely well remunerated but also had to be consulted about his government. Likewise the general literacy of the Puritans, originally cherished as a means for reading Holy Writ, had become the invaluable medium for political and forensic debates whereby the Americans established and

[24]*EL, CW*, XIII, 713.

sustained their freedoms. Thus with the strokes of a broad brush Mill explained to readers in the *London Review* American democracy in terms of environment, history, and social conditions. He may have provided an unduly simplified version of reality, but it was well calculated to correct the partisan bias of the many itinerant writers who came and went across the Atlantic.

"CIVILIZATION"

Mill's long essay, "Civilization," is closely related to those on America and the ideas of Tocqueville. It reflects the same concern over certain profound changes then occurring or about to occur in society and their significance for the individual and his government.

Alexander Bain thought Mill's definition of civilization inadequate and much of his article merely a Philosophic Radical's criticism of contemporary British society.[25] Mill explicitly restricted use of the term to institutions and practices different from those of the savage. "Whatever be the characteristics of what we call savage life," he wrote, "the contrary of these, or the qualities which society puts on as it throws off these, constitute civilization" (120). A modern anthropologist may be even less likely than Bain to feel satisfied with this definition. Yet whatever its deficiency it in no way hampered Mill in discussing that in which he was principally interested—certain aspects of contemporary Britain on which he had strong opinions. He advocated reform in many established institutions, ideas, and prejudices. He recognized that in every country civilization exhibits ill as well as salutary traits, and both he scrutinized.

Civilized men, unlike savages, have clustered in great and fixed concentrations, acted together in large bodies for common purposes, and proceeded from one material achievement to another. They have created populous cities, developed specialized industries, accepted fully the division of labour, expanded channels of trade, improvised techniques of production, and applied science to the cultivation of the soil. Thus they have augmented their material comforts and satisfactions as well as their pleasures in social intercourse. Mill welcomed the general results of this onward thrust of civilization, but was disturbed by some of its features, and especially by the passing of power increasingly from individuals and small groups of individuals to the masses, whose importance grew while that of individuals shrank. The characteristic product of modern material civilization has been a mass society, which Mill no less than Tocqueville feared. "When the masses become powerful," he wrote, "an individual, or a small band of

[25]Alexander Bain, *John Stuart Mill: A Criticism with Personal Recollections* (London: Longmans, 1882), 48.

individuals, can accomplish nothing considerable except by influencing the masses; and to do this becomes daily more difficult, from the constantly increasing number of those who are vying with one another to attract public attention" (126).

Not the least interesting part of his essay is a sketch of the possible strategy whereby the literate and educated elements of the population might guide the masses or create a rival power to them. He believed that an effective civilization is possible only through the capacity of individuals to combine for common ends. Combination, as in trade unions and benefit societies, had already made the workers more powerful. Combination and compromise also could enlarge the influence of the literate middle class, demolish old barriers between all classes, and extend the range of law and justice. English educational institutions were imperfectly organized for their task, and he feared the advent of democracy before the people were sufficiently educated and ready to shoulder their responsibilities. He censured the ancient English universities for failing to make the present rulers grasp what had to be done in reform to avoid the worst features of mass domination. In pursuing narrow sectarian ends, as in the exclusion of Dissenters, the universities were ignoring political realities.[26] They must moreover extend their scope to serve a larger proportion of the population, and at the same time sponsor more through research in the manner of the German universities.

In his targets for criticism Mill included the Established Church. For this ancient instrument of national religion and culture he had little reverence, partly because he was not a believer, and partly because its intimate alliance with the aristocracy had bolstered conservative forces hostile to reform. Evident throughout his essay is what Matthew Arnold called Mill's insensitivity to religion, especially dogmatic religion. On this subject he was explicit: "The principle itself of dogmatic religion, dogmatic morality, dogmatic philosophy, is what requires to be rooted out" (144). For him the Establishment in particular was too sectarian, too protective of its own institutional monopoly, and too much a prop of the existing social order. With satisfaction he witnessed the shrinkage of its power as other religious bodies secured a greater public freedom. In 1829 he described to Gustave d'Eichthal the immense significance of Catholic emancipation. "It forms an era in civilization. It is one of those great events, which periodically occur, by which the institutions of a country are brought into harmony with the better part of the mind of that country. . . ."[27] He was gratified that the Established

---

[26]In 1859 Mill added a footnote to his original article admitting that his criticisms were now less justified because of recent university reforms.

[27]*EL, CW,* XII, 27.

Church and its ally the aristocracy had suffered a defeat, for he felt the emancipation had dealt a fatal blow in general to exclusion from political rights on grounds of religion. As a sequel to this event, Mill was inclined in the early 1830s to predict an imminent collapse of the power of the Church. Here his perception failed him. He greatly underestimated the Church's resilience, vitality, and capacity for change and survival, as he also misunderstood the human feelings that helped to sustain it.

In turning from the general aspects of contemporary civilization to its moral effects, Mill generalized freely about the imponderables in individual conduct. He thought that civilization relaxed individual energy and tended to focus it within the narrow sphere of the individual's money-getting pursuits. He believed that in the civilized milieu the individual received so many elements of security and protection for himself, family, and property, that he depended less on his own unaided initiatives and exertions. This profound change in man's spirit and temper was illustrated in all phases of society, including literature and the arts, which now tended to lose their older distinct and enduring standards. As literacy spread, good literature diminished. The influence of superior minds over the multitude weakened. "The individual," wrote Mill, "becomes so lost in the crowd, that though he depends more and more upon opinion, he is apt to depend less and less upon well-grounded opinion; upon the opinion of those who know him. An established character becomes at once more difficult to gain, and more easily to be dispensed with" (132). In Mill's view it was now only in small communities that the valuable influence of public opinion could be demonstrated.

In discussing the advance of civilization Mill attempted no confident and systematic balance-sheet of gains and losses for mankind. In his own age of transition he evidently felt that his chief task as a utilitarian reformer was to concentrate on augmenting the gains and minimizing the losses in the best way possible. To this end his reformist recommendations were directed.

"ESSAYS ON GOVERNMENT"

The one remaining selection in this volume illustrative of Mill's political ideas in the decade 1830–40 is a brief review of *Essays on Government* (1840). The author of this slender volume was an anonymous radical who believed in republican government, universal suffrage, the ballot, and rule by a natural aristocracy composed of those with wisdom and virtue whom the community selected in contrast to the existing aristocracy of birth and wealth. Mill found in the book no deep or original thought, but simply some rather naïve current thinking about democracy. The machinery constituted for choosing a natural aristocracy does not necessarily secure one. Unlike the author, Mill was not confident that the people would either know where to find natural aristocrats or select them as rulers when they found them.

Further he saw in the book contradictions between the principal prerequisites for good government. It insisted that the government must conform to the opinion of the governed, and also that the rulers must be the wisest and best persons in the community. Would the wise ones consent to rule in conformity with the opinions of the less wise? Dissatisfied with the book's ambiguities, Mill summed up his own position:

We think that democracy *can* govern: it can make its legislators its mere delegates, to carry into effect *its* preconceived opinions. We do not say that it *will* do so. Whether it will, appears to us the great question which futurity has to resolve; and on the solution of which it depends whether democracy will be that social regeneration which its partisans expect, or merely a new form of bad government, perhaps somewhat better, perhaps somewhat worse, than those which preceded it. (152.)

MATURE VIEWS, 1840–73

TWO RELATED THEMES dominated Mill's political thought from 1840 to his death: the invention and maintenance of institutions that would efficiently express the sanction of citizens for what rulers did in their name; and the appropriate role of the state in furthering human betterment in a Britain hurrying deeper into the industrial age. On the first theme his *Considerations on Representative Government* summarized most of his thinking over many years and became his chief classic in political science, providing a practical and liberal guide to nineteenth-century man searching for stable and competent government. On his second theme, however, Mill produced no equivalent single volume, although of cardinal importance were his *On Liberty* and his *Principles of Political Economy* in its successive editions. Illuminating also on this subject are his occasional writings and speeches, especially those on Ireland. In the last century some Englishmen viewed Ireland as a social laboratory where it was necessary to try special experiments not tolerable at home. Mill in particular was ready to enlarge greatly the agenda of government to combat Ireland's indigenous and lingering poverty.

CIVIL SERVICE REFORM

In the seven years before *Considerations on Representative Government* appeared, Mill produced some papers that foreshadowed the arguments in his major essay. First in time was the submission, requested by Sir Charles Trevelyan, then Assistant Secretary to the Treasury, which strongly commended the Northcote-Trevelyan Report for advocating the recruitment of civil servants, not by the casual methods of political patronage, but by open competitive examinations. For Mill this genuine reform harmonized with his long-held conviction that representative government could be efficient only if conducted by the country's best-educated and orderly minds. On reading the report he quickly dispatched a characteristic comment to Harriet: "it is as direct, uncompromising, & to the point, without reservation, as if we had written it."[28] Apart from placing administration under the control of competent and professional officials, he hoped that the new mode of recruitment would strengthen existing political institutions by opening public positions to the competition of all classes and persons, thus diminishing the traditional sway of the aristocracy and privileged classes. This in turn, he thought, would extend intellectual cultivation and encourage talented individuals.

Sir Charles Trevelyan, an unshakably determined man, was not content simply to submit a report. To overcome troublesome opposition he carefully primed the press, solicited the opinions of influential individuals likely to support it (Mill being one), and printed them in a special blue book, *Papers on the Reorganisation of the Civil Service.* Yet his effort won little immediate success. The proposals were bitterly resisted, and their supporters had to be content with piecemeal reforms until their final triumph under Gladstone in 1870.[29]

PARLIAMENTARY REFORM

It is evident from Mill's correspondence that throughout the 1850s he thought frequently about the contentious issue of parliamentary reform. The outcome was a pamphlet and a major article, both published in 1859: *Thoughts on Parliamentary Reform* and "Recent Writers on Reform." The first of these was largely written in 1853 with subsequent revisions and additions. In it he argued that since the Reform Bill British opinion had profoundly changed. A new and restless public came to believe that a further improvement in parliamentary representation was a national necessity. An unremitting trial of strength between the progressive and stationary forces confronted all party leaders, who were compelled to recognize that out of

[28]*LL, CW*, XIV, 175.
[29]See Edward Hughes, "Sir Charles Trevelyan and Civil Service Reform 1853–55," *English Historical Review*, LXIV (1949), 64. A comprehensive and lucid review of the controversy concerning the Northcote-Trevelyan Report is contained in J. B. Conacher, *The Aberdeen Coalition, 1852–1855* (Cambridge: Cambridge University Press, 1968), 312–32.

the ceaseless dialectic of debate change must come. For them the main issue was its extent and timing.

In the light of this situation, Mill in his pamphlet attempted to formulate his own electoral programme in seven main proposals: grouping of small boroughs into districts, gradual steps to universal male and female suffrage, electioneering reform to free candidates from expenses amounting to a burdensome property qualification, a minimal educational requirement for the franchise, plural voting based on educational attainments, representation of minorities through the cumulative vote, and rejection of the ballot, which had not yet become a part of British electoral law.

Some of these topics naturally figured more prominently in public discussion than others, and it is needless here to examine Mill's arguments on all of them. His proposal to protect the views of minorities through the cumulative vote became obsolete a month after the publication of *Thoughts on Parliamentary Reform*, with the appearance of Thomas Hare's *Election of Representatives*. Hare's book, discussed below, promptly convinced Mill. In March 1859 he enthusiastically wrote to its author: "You appear to me to have exactly, and for the first time, solved the difficulty of popular representation; and by doing so, to have raised up the cloud of gloom and uncertainty which hung over the futurity of representative government and therefore of civilization."[30] Henceforth he was committed to Hare's scheme of electoral reform, with its preferential and transferable vote, calculated quota, and transformation of the country into a single constituency. To him it seemed the best protection for minorities that parliament could provide.

Mill's proposals in *Thoughts on Parliamentary Reform* had in the preceding years evolved through prolonged discussions with his wife, who then greatly influenced his thinking. His suggested educational qualification for the franchise, and his rejection of the secret ballot provoked much controversy. On the first of these, he argued that a minimal education test must accompany a universal franchise. In view of the high value he consistently placed on a trained intelligence, he found it impossible to accept the equality of educated and uneducated electors.

If it is asserted that all persons ought to be equal in every description of right recognized by society, I answer, not until all are equal in worth as human beings. It is the fact, that one person is *not* as good as another; and it is reversing all the rules of rational conduct, to attempt to raise a political fabric on a supposition which is at variance with fact. Putting aside for the present the consideration of moral worth, . . . a person who cannot read, is not as good, for the purpose of human life, as one who can. (323.)

Taking off from a premise that rejected the old radical dogma of "one man one vote," Mill argued that all adult men and women who passed an

[30]*LL, CW*, XV, 598–9.

education test should be enfranchised, but those with superior training should receive plural or extra voting power, even to the extent of some individuals having three or more votes. In this Mill's logic may have been impeccable, but the political practicability of his proposal was a different matter. The passion for equality that Tocqueville saw as part and parcel of the democratic movement was unlikely to render possible the kind of voting that Mill described. He himself appeared to have doubts. In the same year he admitted to John Elliot Cairnes that his proposal for plural voting on the basis of intellectual qualification was intended "not as an immediately practical measure but as a standard of theoretical excellence."[31] Yet on the same matter he commented to Alexander Bain: "One must never suppose what is good in itself to be visionary because it may be far off. . . . We must remember too that the numerical majority are not the politically strongest force yet. The point to be decided is, how much power is to be yielded to them; & justice always affords the best basis for a compromise, which even if only temporary may be eminently useful."[32]

On the issue of the ballot, Mill in *Thoughts on Parliamentary Reform* publicly expressed for the first time his volte-face from a position stoutly held in the 1830s. In the earlier period, he, like other Philosophic Radicals, had extolled the ballot as scarcely less important than an extended franchise in overthrowing the ruling oligarchy in Britain. Without it the franchise might mean little. For him and his associates it became virtually a symbol of their radicalism. Secret voting, once established, was expected to demolish the political power of the aristocracy and privileged classes, and hence open the road for the march of the Radical party. It would protect tenants from coercion by landlords, customers from coercion by shopkeepers and vice versa, employees from coercion by employers, and the general public from coercion by miscellaneous and often sinister interests of every kind. It would benefit the people in that comprehensive way so dear to the Radicals. In 1837 Mill told Tocqueville with simplistic assurance that with the ballot "reform will have finally triumphed: the aristocratical principle will be completely annihilated, & we shall enter into a new era of government."[33] He then believed that in the country there was a deep radicalism which without the ballot was repressed. Two years later, in a letter to John M. Kemble, he wrote in more moderate terms, but still considered the ballot essential for the success of the radical cause.[34]

In defending his change of mind in the 1850s, Mill argued that when earlier he and the Philosophic Radicals had first advocated the ballot they were justified by the circumstances of the time. Many voters were then artfully manipulated by landlords and employers, and unable to declare their

[31]*Ibid.*, 596.
[33]*EL, CW*, XII, 317.
[32]*Ibid.*, 606.
[34]*EL, CW*, XIII, 410.

real convictions in an open election. Twenty-five years later, however, the conditions were different. No longer were the rich the masters of the country. The middle classes and workers were less subservient to those above them, felt their own strength, and resented attempts by others to coerce them. In the larger electorates the real evil now lay in the selfish partialities of the voter himself, which reduced his concern for the general interest. Open voting, Mill thought, might best correct this egocentric attitude, foster a wholesome sense of public responsibility, and emphasize the vote as a trust for which the voter was accountable to the community.

Social circumstances had unquestionably changed, but for most Liberals the changes had failed to diminish the practical advantages of the ballot as a means for moderating the influences of wealth and power. Mill and his wife thus fell singularly out of step with the main army of reformers, who persistently advocated this change until its final triumph under Gladstone in 1872. Competent studies of the electoral system in this period seem to support the practical utility of the ballot.[35]

The few remaining active Philosophic Radicals, like George Grote and Francis Place, deplored Mill's change of view. Place, often critical of Mill, was specially irritated by his pronounced shift of opinion on the ballot. "If James Mill," he wrote bitterly, "could have anticipated that his son John Stuart should preach so abominable a heresy . . . he would have cracked his skull."[36] Place charged Mill with a shocking inconsistency, but on his part Mill thought mere consistency a minor virtue. Where circumstances change a situation, he would argue, then it is only common sense to alter one's view of it.

In "Recent Writers on Reform" Mill examined the ideas of three contemporary writers on parliamentary institutions in the 1850s, selected for their distinction and the importance of their ideas: John Austin, James Lorimer, and Thomas Hare. Austin had been one of Mill's oldest friends, under whom as a youth he had studied law, and whose ability he greatly admired. Yet Austin, although a disciple of Bentham, had in later years become conservative and estranged from Mill, who in particular was disturbed by his vehement criticism of the French revolutionary government of 1848. In his *Plea for the Constitution* Austin displayed a hostility to further parliamentary reform in the conviction that it was likely to destroy the delicate balance of the existing constitution and the appropriate attitudes of mind which facilitated its operation. The constitution, he believed,

---

[35]See H. J. Hanham, *Elections and Party Management: Politics in the Time of Disraeli and Gladstone* (London: Longmans, 1959); Charles Seymour, *Electoral Reform in England and Wales: The Development and Operation of the Parliamentary Franchise, 1832–1885* (New Haven: Yale University Press, 1915), 432. In Ireland the ballot had its greatest effect, because intimidation was more common there.

[36]Quoted from the Chadwick Papers by Hamburger, *Intellectuals in Politics*, 274.

combined democratic and aristocratic elements. The electors were a democratic body, while the elected in the main constituted a remarkably skilled, devoted, and aristocratic governing class, who throughout a long span of time had acquired and were still able to apply the arts of ruling a country they understood.

This version of the British system combined with a laudation of the governing aristocracy was something that since the 1820s Mill had consistently condemned. On finding it in the pages of Austin he criticized it afresh, although, evidently out of respect for his old friend, his condemnation was moderate. He was content to show that the aristocratic classes, who had an opportunity to become instructed and trained statesmen, had frittered away their opportunities. Historically, they were less effective than the open aristocracy of Rome or the closed aristocracy of Venice. He noted Austin's point that parliamentary reform was needless because the existing elected members of the lower house were already fully alert to the requirements of sound legislation and able to draft it. But Mill replied that, aside from law-making, parliament had another role. The House of Commons as the grand council of the entire nation must contain spokesmen to discuss the critical issues that divide the community and reflect the diverse shades of opinion in all classes. The most numerous class in the kingdom, that of the workers, had a moral right to representation to avoid having its affairs disposed of in its absence. He did not believe that recognizing this right of the workers and shopkeepers would produce all the disastrous social consequences that Austin took for granted.

By contrast, Mill had some reason for satisfaction with James Lorimer's *Political Progress Not Necessarily Democratic*, for Lorimer was hardly less hostile than himself to the domination of the majority, accepted universal suffrage, but also favoured plural votes for certain citizens, although his criterion for them differed from Mill's. He thought that a man's social status, whether that of a peer or a labourer, should determine his voting power. This thesis Mill rejected as a dangerous sophistry, since it assumed that society must bend to forces created by itself, whereas he was convicted that men must intelligently try to mould society into something better, and his proposal for plural votes was intended to help the educated in doing so. In Lorimer's work he was specially gratified with one feature: the rejection of current demands for the representation of interests. Mill expressed his own characteristic view that whenever interests are not identical with the general interest, the less they are represented the better. "What is wanted is a representation, not of men's differences of interest, but of the differences in their intellectual points of view. Shipowners are to be desired in Parliament, because they can instruct us about ships, not because they are interested in having protecting duties." (358.) Mill had no intention of suggesting that ideas can always be divorced from interests. As a reformer of society he knew better. He was trying to emphasize, as he did frequently, the necessity for cultivating an overriding and dispassionate sense of a public interest, which in his opinion was the prime purpose of a representative government.

The most important part of Mill's article dealt with Thomas Hare's book and the electoral mechanism it recommended to ensure for minorities a parliamentary voice equal to their strength. Hare appeared to solve a problem in representation that had worried Mill for a quarter of a century: how the domination by an electoral majority could be mitigated and a real image of the nation's varied groups be expressed. It was only by solving this problem that true rather than false democracy could be achieved. He unhesitantly welcomed Hare's departure from the principle of strict territorial representation, hitherto dominant in the constitution of the Commons. No longer would it be necessary for a candidate to gain or keep his seat by those "time-serving arts, and sacrifices of his convictions to the local or class prejudices and interests of any given set of electors" (366). Through the transferable vote he could appeal to a wider electorate, while on their part electors could enjoy a larger range in the choice of candidates, and thus achieve, as Mill said, a more personal rather than local representation. He expected that the quality of candidates would greatly improve, the tone of public debate rise, and the inducements of a parliamentary career for talented men increase. He enthusiastically wrote to Hare in December, 1859: "If the Americans would but adopt your plan (which I fear they never will) the bad side of their government and institutions, namely the practical exclusion of all the best minds from political influence, would soon cease. Let us hope that in the old country (thanks to you) democracy will come in this better form."[37]

Mill was confident that with the implementation of Hare's proposals any ill consequences of universal suffrage would be greatly diminished and even the plural voting he had recommended might become unnecessary. He hoped that the system could be accepted without prolonged delay, for reasons he confided to Henry Fawcett in February 1860: "It is an uphill race, and a race against time, for if the American form of democracy overtakes us first, the majority will no more relax their despotism than a single despot would."[38]

Mill's hopes for an early acceptance of the new principles were singularly unrealistic. Yet for the remainder of his life he continued to be an undaunted advocate of the single transferable vote and constantly encouraged and helped his friends like Hare and Fawcett in their efforts. Although women's suffrage and the Hare system of electoral reform were not the sole

[37]*LL*, *CW*, XV, 654.
[38]*Ibid.*, 672.

practical causes that occupied him in the 1860s, they were pre-eminent in appeal, and when in the House of Commons he strove to further both. Despite his efforts parliament never took the action he wanted, and the reasons are not far to seek. At the time when Mill was advocating a new electoral system, party managers gradually began to remould the organization of the two major parties to render them more disciplined and effective instruments for shaping policies and winning elections. For them the Hare-Mill electoral ideas seemed too revolutionary, too complicated, and their effects on party fortunes too uncertain to be acceptable. Hence, except for some of their members, they showed little interest in proportional representation of the type that Mill supported and were unwilling to incorporate it as an essential element in their political plans. Gladstone, for example, although in some reforms he was evidently influenced by Mill, rejected proportional representation when he considered electoral changes. This is not to say, however, that Mill's ideas lacked influence. Even into the twentieth century, his basic idea, as stated in *Representative Government*, continued to incite the interest of many: in a democracy, any and every section must be represented, not disproportionately, but proportionately. A majority of the electors should always have a majority of the representatives; a minority of electors should always have a minority of representatives.

"CONSIDERATIONS ON REPRESENTATIVE GOVERNMENT"

Considerations on Representative Government brings together many of Mill's views expressed in earlier writings, especially those on the domination of majorities, the proposals of Thomas Hare, the folly of extracting pledges from parliamentarians, the superiority of public voting, the equity of female suffrage, and the desirability of plural votes for the educated.[39] But the book is more than a résumé of previous opinions. It contains some of the author's most effective arguments on political liberalism and it assesses the liabilities no less than the assets of what for Mill was the best form of government. It has usually been rated as one of the most influential appraisals of the subject written in Victorian England, though to a modern political analyst it has some deficiencies. It says little about the social and economic environment in which the institutions are expected to operate, although Mill was well aware of social forces and class struggles. Another work of the same decade, the *English Constitution* by Walter Bagehot, has perhaps since received more profuse acclaim, especially for elegance of style, but, except on the subject of Crown and parliament, Bagehot's range

---

[39]Though *On Liberty* was written and published before *Considerations on Representative Government*, the latter is here discussed first, because it provides a fuller treatment of the views of Mill just outlined.

was narrower and his probing of problems less profound and original.[40]

It is not proposed here to examine and evaluate in detail the contents of its eighteen chapters, but merely to comment on salient features. At the outset Mill attempts to distinguish the two contemporary forms of political speculation. The first postulated politics as a practical art, the product of invention and contrivance, concerned with means and ends and the devices for persuading citizens to accept them. It considered government a machine and a matter of rational choice, an opinion congenial to many British utilitarians. The second viewed government as less a machine than a living social organism, evolving like organisms in natural history. Emerging from simple situations, it grows spontaneously under the shaping influences of environment and the habits, instincts, and unconscious wants and desires of mankind. This theory was much cherished by Conservatives in Britain.

Mill believes that neither theory alone explains the nature of politics. Each has elements of truth; each in itself can mislead. But both together help to further political comprehension. For him the essential fact is that political institutions, as the work of men, depend on will and thought, and are subject to the errors as well as the wisdom of human judgment. Unlike trees, which once planted grow while men sleep, they are controlled by the constant decisions and participation of individuals, exposed to a host of influences. "It is what men think, that determines how they act" (382). He rejects the idea that any people is capable of operating any type of political system. A bewildering medley of circumstances usually determines the nature and outlook of a country's government. For a system to be successful, the people must be willing to accept it, do whatever ensures its survival, and strive to fulfil its purposes. Representative government makes heavy demands on the energy and initiative of citizens, requiring in particular self-discipline, moderation, and a spirit of compromise. It can succeed only when, in a favourable environment, the citizens have the qualities requisite to operate it. Mill admits that until relatively recent times a free and popular government was rarely possible outside a city community because physical conditions failed to permit the emergence and propagation of a cohesive public opinion. These views were not new to him in the 1860s. In his *Autobiography* he relates that some thirty years earlier he had seen representative democracy as a question of time, place, and circumstance.[41]

Mill viewed government as primarily an instrument to further the im-

[40]For an argument that Bagehot was heavily indebted to Mill, see T. H. Ford, "Bagehot and Mill as Theorists of Comparative Politics," *Comparative Politics*, II (January, 1970), 309–24. A. H. Birch lauds *Considerations on Representative Government* as "the most systematic attempt ever made in Britain to set out a theory of the purpose and proper organization of representative institutions" (*Representative and Responsible Government* [Toronto: University of Toronto Press, 1964], 57).

[41]*Autobiography*, 102.

provement of mankind, and to this end representative institutions are ideally the best, although hitherto human progress has often been served by efficient regimes that did not represent the people. An autocracy which successfully curbs a lawless and turbulent populace may for an interval provide an essential prerequisite for the order and progress of civilization: the ingrained habits and spirit of obedience to law. At critical times enlightened despots can achieve concrete social advances that may be less feasible under representative institutions, which permit powerful vested interests to block reform.

Nevertheless, for Mill the most desirable form of government, provided the people are willing and able to fulfil its conditions, is representative, because it offers the maximum opportunity for fostering men's intelligence, virtue, and happiness. But at the same time he admits that where the people are morally and mentally unfit for this demanding form of rule, it may become an instrument of tyranny, and popular elections less a security against misgovernment than an additional wheel in its machinery (378). Even in the progressive democracies many men are content to be passive in public affairs. Absorbed in private cares and satisfactions, they patiently endure social evils and surrender to the pressure of circumstances. Usually present, however, are an energetic and active few who express thought, advocate innovations, and encourage provocative debate, thus making progress possible. Representative institutions enable these few to thrash out differences and reach workable agreements for the common good. With characteristic sober optimism Mill describes the competitive and restless spirit of liberal society as he perceives it in the nineteenth century: "All intellectual superiority is the fruit of active effort. Enterprise, the desire to keep moving, to be trying and accomplishing new things for our own benefit or that of others, is the parent even of speculative, and much more of practical, talent. . . . The character which improves human life is that which struggles with natural powers and tendencies, not that which gives way to them." (407.)

Electoral Machinery, Responsibility, and Expertise

In *Representative Government*, Mill is principally concerned with three institutional features: the electoral machinery, the structure of a responsible national government, and the paramount role of a professional and expert class in administration and law-making.

The first of these themes, which he had earlier explored in articles, emphasizes his distinction between true and false democracy. True democracy represents all, and not merely the majority. In it the different interests, opinions, and grades of intellect are heard, and by weight of character and strength of argument influence the rest.[42] This democracy is achieved by

[42]P. 467. In the year after publishing *Considerations on Representative Government*

reforming the electoral system according to the proposals of Thomas Hare, by ensuring that everyone, male and female alike, has a voice (although not an equal voice) in the voting process, and by fostering education from infancy through life. Mill believes that the expansion of democratic rights in itself exerts a pervasive educational influence. He accepts Tocqueville's belief that American democracy fostered both a robust patriotism and an active intelligence. "No such wide diffusion of the ideas, tastes, and sentiments of educated minds," he writes, "has ever been seen elsewhere, or even conceived as attainable" (468). He strongly holds this view, although in earlier essays on the United States he also acknowledged in the American electorate a narrow and intolerant mentality. Although Mill at times fluctuates between trust and distrust of democracy, he always believes in its potentiality to improve men. Active citizenship can usually nourish the qualities that good citizenship demands, draw out human resources otherwise dormant, and advance the lot of mankind.

In discussing the executive in the representative system, Mill is the empiricist and Benthamite, who is eager to accept innovations but clearly places a high value on what has been tested by experience. He sanctions the parliamentary executive, which the British developed through common sense and the accidents of a long history. Indeed, he gives scant attention to any other system except the American, which affords him merely a basis for contrasts. With brevity and acumen he discusses precepts that must govern a responsible and effective executive. "It should be apparent to all the world, who did everything, and through whose default anything was left undone. Responsibility is null when nobody knows who is responsible." (520.) But it is equally true that in many counsellors there is wisdom. A single individual even in his own business seldom judges right, and still less in that of the public. These and related points, he thinks, are woven into the fabric of British parliamentary practice.

Distinguishing between policy and administration, he is anxious that in the latter highly trained minds should save democracy from errors. He fears that the popular tolerance of mediocrity impairs the competence and quality of the state. In defending the Northcote-Trevelyan Report on the civil service he had advocated the recruitment of officials through competitive examinations from the ablest brains in the country, irrespective of social class. This case he confidently argues afresh in *Representative Government* (529–33) and defends it for every democratic state. In 1869 he writes to an American correspondent that "the appointments to office, without regard

---

Mill wrote to Henry S. Chapman that Australian democracy, as described by Chapman, confirmed his fears about false democracy (*LL, CW*, XV, 764–5). See also R. S. Neale, "John Stuart Mill on Australia: A Note," *Historical Studies Australia and New Zealand*, XIII (April, 1968), 242–4.

to qualifications, are the worst side of American institutions: the main cause
of what is justly complained of in their practical operation, and the principal
hindrance to the correction of what is amiss; as well as a cause of ill-repute
to democratic institutions all over the world."[43]

Even in Britain he saw a too common inclination to ignore in officials the
need for special qualifications: "Unless a man is fit for the gallows, he is
thought to be about as fit as other people for almost anything" (427).
Critical of British complacency and aristocratic casualness, he constantly
extols the professional and the expert above the amateur and the dilettante.

His zeal for professional skills extends from administration to law-
making. In his opinion a large and unwieldy parliament can no more legislate than administer. His Benthamite conscience was hurt by the haphazard
and often dilatory manner in which British laws were made, with little
concern for whether they fitted logically into the existing legal structure. His
remedy was a legislative commission, composed of those who from assiduous
study and long experience acquired an expertise in drafting bills which parliament could pass, reject, or return for further consideration (430–2). A
legislature in Mill's opinion should not itself draft law, but merely ensure its
competent drafting. He suggests that on their appointment members of the
commission should become life peers and thus enlarge the element of expertise in the House of Lords. In his chapter on second chambers, however,
he emphasizes that the House of Lords should not be considered the main
instrument for tempering the ascendancy of the majority in the lower house,
a task better achieved through the electoral reforms that he and Thomas
Hare advocated. As a drafting body, Mill's legislative commission resembled
the Parliamentary Counsel to the Treasury established by Gladstone in 1869,
but Mill would have given to permanent experts more power than any
House of Commons was ever likely to concede. His sympathy always seemed
stronger for the men in Whitehall than for those in Westminster, for the
officials rather than the politicians.

More than a quarter of *Representative Government* is devoted to four
topics that may seem somewhat marginal to the main subject of the book.
But because for Mill they are important and illustrate cardinal features of
his liberalism they merit separate discussion.

Local Government

In both *On Liberty* and *Representative Government* Mill extols local institutions as essential for the welfare and education of the people. They permit
citizens to acquire invaluable experience in working for common ends, introduce them to the skills and ethics of collaboration, and are an indispensable preparatory school for the democratic state. In Britain, moreover, such

[43]*LL, CW*, XVII, 1572.

institutions are a necessary auxiliary to the national parliament itself, which otherwise would become harassed and strained by tasks better left to local bodies, visible and sensitive to local electorates and directly accountable to them. A robust municipal system, Mill believed, would nourish a responsible public spirit and foster among the citizenry the political enlightenment essential for an extended franchise and a viable democracy.

In these views Mill was faithful to the utilitarian and radical tradition, drawing inspiration from Bentham who had emphasized the inherent value of local government and the necessity for its overhaul in England. He shared an early and lifelong friendship with Edwin Chadwick, a zealous and energetic Benthamite and the chief architect of municipal reform in the 1830s and 1840s. In 1833 he saw Chadwick as "one of the most remarkable men of our time in the practical art of Government. . . ."[44] He had ample reasons for praising his friend, although Chadwick incurred much unpopularity for an apparently uncompassionate attitude towards the administration of the Poor Law and for centralist prejudices. The two men freely consulted, exchanged general ideas, and usually agreed on policy. Mill supported the major innovations that were deeply indebted to Chadwick's utilitarian thought and ingenuity; in particular the Poor Law Amendment Act of 1834, the Corporations Act of 1835, and the Public Health Act of 1848, each of which was a conspicuous landmark in the evolution of new forms of local administration and service.

When in 1861 Mill came to write his chapter on local government he surveyed a scene of increasing complexity and baffling confusion. The rapid growth of industry and population had created massive urban concentrations of people clamouring for new and varied services. The different municipal bodies launched in the 1830s and 1840s were busily trying to cope with the problems of a social cauldron. The Boards of Poor Law Guardians, the borough councils, and the numerous *ad hoc* boards and commissions responsible for specific services all attempted to give a new meaning to municipal rule in a changing society. But in the counties the ancient system of appointed justices of the peace meeting in Quarter Sessions still survived. On this institution Mill as a faithful Radical is caustic:

The mode of formation of these bodies is most anomalous, they being neither elected, nor, in any proper sense of the term, nominated, but holding their important functions, like the feudal lords to whom they succeeded, virtually by right of their acres. . . . The institution is the most aristocratic in principle which now remains in England; far more so than the House of Lords, for it grants public money and disposes of important public interests, not in conjunction with a popular assembly, but alone. (537.)

[44]*EL, CW*, XII, 211. See also *LL, CW*, XVI, 1431–2. For an account of the abilities and weaknesses of this exceptional man, see S. E. Finer, *The Life and Times of Sir Edwin Chadwick* (London: Methuen, 1952).

He would correct the deficiencies of county government through elected county councils to replace the Quarter Sessions, a reform not achieved until 1888.

Mill also attacks the cluttering proliferation of boards and commissions which needlessly fragmented and confused English civic life. He anticipates the Royal Sanitary Commission's Report of 1871 and the critical verdict that England suffered from a chaos of local authorities and a chaos of local rates.[45] He advocates consolidation of the existing services (such as paving, lighting, water supply, and drainage) under a single elected council rather than leaving them under separate *ad hoc* commissions. In brief, he recommends for all the local business of a town one body, whose members should be chosen only by ratepayers. He criticizes the subdivision of London into several independent units, each jealously clinging to responsibility for providing the same services, and thus preventing co-operation. Like other of Mill's ideas in *Representative Government*, this one played a practical part in his parliamentary career when, a few years later, he introduced the first proposal for a London Corporation.[46]

Mill had pronounced convictions on the relations of central and local governments, believing that the central authority's principal task was to give instructions and that of the local authority to apply them. Action must be localized, though knowledge, to be useful to all citizens in the kingdom, should be centralized. In the public interest a close partnership between the two levels of government is imperative. The central government should designate a specific department to act as a responsible guardian, adviser, and critic, scrutinizing everything done in local areas and making its fund of special knowledge available to those who need it. It should in particular supervise those matters of national interest left to local administration, but its power should be limited to compelling local officers to obey the laws enacted for their guidance. His chief example for this type of supervision is that of the Poor Law Board over the Local Guardians.

In their standard work on local government, Josef Redlich and Francis Hirst remark that Bentham's "idea of centralisation was interpreted, modified, and adapted to English needs by Mill and not till it was adapted by Mill was it fully adopted by England."[47] His influence on local government clearly asserted itself in the years after 1871 with the organization of an efficient central authority for doing what he had long advocated, supervising municipal rule. In these ideas he demonstrates his type of utilitarian thought

[45]Harold J. Laski, *et al.*, *A Century of Municipal Progress, 1835–1935* (London: Allen and Unwin, 1935), 48.
[46]*Hansard's Parliamentary Debates*, 3rd ser., CXCI, cols. 1859–63 (5 May, 1868). See also *LL, CW,* XVI, 1501–2, and XVII, 1555–6.
[47]Josef Redlich and Francis Hirst, *Local Government in England* (London: Macmillan, 1903), I, 180.

at its best, especially in taking traditional English institutions and adapting them to the necessities of a new industrial age.

Nationality

Mill's discussion of nationality, unlike his discussion of local government, might at the time have seemed of little relevance to Britain's domestic politics. But in the wider perspective of her relations with continental Europe it was important. The idea of a self-conscious nationality emerged as a revolutionary force in transforming European politics after the French Revolution, and in Mill's opinion Britain could not elude its wide-ranging effects.

His chapter on the subject is brief, little more than half the length of that on local government, perhaps too brief for him to render full justice to the magnitude and complexity of the theme. In "Coleridge" and *A System of Logic* he had viewed nationality as an essential condition for a stable political society, but emphasized that he did not mean nationality in the vulgar sense.[48] In the interval between these writings and the appearance of *Representative Government* Mill saw nationality in Europe grow stronger in influence, more militant, and more uncompromising. It was manifested in a people through a powerful sense of community and an anxiety to live under one government. It was fostered by a variety of influences, such as identity of race, a common homeland, common language, common religion, and a common sense of history. "But the strongest of all is identity of political antecedents: the possession of a national history, and consequent community of recollections; collective pride and humiliation, pleasure and regret, connected with the same incidents in the past" (546). This passage has been quoted and requoted. Yet in his brief sketch Mill does not explain precisely how, why, and when the actual unifying sense of a common national history arises, especially in cases like Germany and Italy, where for generations deep political divergences expressed in a plethora of small states seemed more conspicuous than unity.[49]

Mill took a definite position on the relations of nationality to democracy. "Where the sentiment of nationality exists in any force, there is a *primâ facie* case for uniting all the members of the nationality under the same government, and a government to themselves apart. This is merely saying that the question of government ought to be decided by the governed." To this remark he adds another no less revealing: "Free institutions are next to impossible in a country made up of different nationalities" (547). In brief,

[48]"Coleridge," *Collected Works*, X (Toronto: University of Toronto Press, 1969), 135–6, 504–8 (henceforth cited as *CW*, X); and *A System of Logic, Collected Works*, VIII (Toronto: University of Toronto Press, 1973), 923 (henceforth cited as *CW*, VII or VIII as appropriate).

[49]See a criticism of Mill's view in Boyd C. Shafer, *Nationalism: Myth and Reality* (New York: Harcourt Brace and World, 1955), 53.

democracy works best in a uni-national state of like-minded people. He contends that different nationalities, speaking different languages, would hamper the crystallizing of public opinion on which successful representative institutions depend. Social fragmentation and divisiveness would result from the presence of separate leaders of different nationalities. The same books, newspapers, pamphlets, and speeches would fail to circulate throughout all sectors of the society. Each nationality would thus differently assess facts and differently express opinions. Such differences, when sharp enough, would favour despotism rather than freedom. Politicians for their own advantage and power would exploit mutual antipathies.

Mill makes two far-reaching qualifications to his principle that the boundaries of state and nation should coincide. First, circumstances may sometimes render it difficult or impossible to implement: for example, in parts of Europe, notably the Austrian Empire, nationalities were so intricately intermingled as to make separate national states impracticable. In such cases the people affected must make a virtue of necessity and tolerantly accept life together under regimes of equal rights and equal laws. Second, it is often socially advantageous for a small nationality, rather than pursuing political independence, to merge in a larger one. He thinks it preferable for a Breton or Basque to become a part of the richly-endowed French nation than "to sulk on his own rocks, the half-savage relic of past times, revolving in his own little mental orbit, without participation or interest in the general movement of the world" (549). He believes that this also applies to the Welshman and the Scottish Highlander. Whatever his sympathy for such small nations, he is confident that their members would reap cultural benefits from close association with the larger nation, and in return confer benefits. In this type of situation it is essential for the weaker to receive not only equal justice but equal consideration, and thus help to blend qualities inherent in the different nationalities to the advantage of mankind.

Mill's qualifications to his main thesis on state and nation are often forgotten while his general thesis is remembered. They are manifest in his treatment of the contentious national problem of Ireland. This Mill discussed in a sparse single paragraph in *Representative Government*, but in subsequent writings he said much on the subject, and notably in his pamphlet *England and Ireland*.[50]

Mill recognizes that the nationality of the Irish had never been absorbed in the larger nationality of Britain, as Bretons and Alsatians had been absorbed in that of France. For this result he gives two reasons: the Irish are numerous enough to constitute in themselves a respectable nationality and had for generations nursed a deep enduring enmity towards England

[50]John Stuart Mill, *England and Ireland* (London: Longmans, 1868). See also his *Chapters and Speeches on the Irish Land Question* (London: Longmans, 1870).

because of its harsh methods of rule. His comments in *Representative Government* suggest that Mill believed that recent improvements in British policy had reduced Irish hostility, and in the future even more harmonious relations between the two countries might be expected. Hence he omits discussion of whether Ireland's distinct nationality requires a separate statehood, as his general principle would imply. Seven years later, however, in *England and Ireland*, he is more pessimistic. In the interval a severe agrarian depression and Irish agitations for land reform had failed to win an adequate response from the British parliament. The consequent rise of a revolutionary Fenian movement committed to tactics of violence to achieve independence worsened and embittered relations between the two countries. Mill now wrote a sombre criticism of British rulers: "What seems to them the causelessness of the Irish repugnance to our rule, is the proof that they have almost let pass the last opportunity they are ever likely to have of setting it right. They have allowed what once was indignation against particular wrongs, to harden into a passionate determination to be no longer ruled on any terms by those to whom they ascribe all their evils. Rebellions are never really unconquerable until they have become rebellions for an idea."[51]

Nevertheless, despite the inflamed sense of Irish nationality, Mill desires that the two countries should remain united. Their affairs are intimately intertwined in trade, population movements, and international security. Geography makes it easier for them to exist within one state rather than two. But the imperative condition for doing so successfully is that English rulers radically change their attitude towards Ireland. In making laws for that island they must resolve to recognize Irish circumstances and satisfy Irish interests no less than their own.

In particular, Mill argues, they should introduce sweeping agrarian reforms, leaving Irish peasants in permanent possession of their land, subject to fixed charges. In 1867, he told a correspondent that his guiding principle was: "To declare openly on all suitable occasions that England is bound either to govern Ireland so that Ireland shall be satisfied with her government, or to set Ireland free to govern herself."[52] He still hoped that it would be unnecessary to apply to Ireland the principle of one state for one nation, but, if English rulers failed in their duty, this would be inescapable.

Mill's association of nationality with the idea of democratic and free government has held a prominent place in the literature of modern nationalism. Koppel S. Pinson asserts that *Representative Government*, translated into the language of subject nationalities, "had a tremendous influence on

[51]*England and Ireland*, 7.
[52]*LL, CW*, XVI, 1328.

the shaping of nationalist ideology."[53] Mill seems to have less fear than Lord Acton that a sense of nationality fosters political forces hostile to democracy, although he did see the danger in multi-national states where anti-liberal governments may play off one nationality against another. In such a state, Mill believes, an army composed of different nationalities could readily be the executioner of liberty (548). For this reason he prefers whenever feasible the uni-national state, confident that it gives richer promise for free government.

Even in a uni-national state, however, a spirit of aggressive nationality may destroy democratic liberties whenever the power and prestige of the nation are threatened. A nationalist is not necessarily a liberal or a democrat. He may support any form of government that satisfies the ambition and interests of his nation. On this matter Mill attempts no direct argument, but from the nature of his general philosophy we can deduce his views. Primarily concerned as he is with individual liberty and human progress, he nowhere suggests that the claims of nationality are superior to those of liberalism.

Federalism

Mill's chapter on federal government has been less influential and significant than that on nationality. Federalism he extols as an invaluable instrument to achieve a larger and more fruitful collaboration in defence and social development between communities endowed with many mutual interests, but separately weak and often absorbed in petty rivalries. He discusses with acumen the conditions necessary to render a federation acceptable and feasible, the different modes of organizing it, the institutions such as a supreme court essential to fulfil its purposes, and the broad beneficial consequences flowing from its success. In federal states he sees decisive advantages similar to those conferred by other practical modes of co-operation wherein persuasion replaces command and for certain purposes the weak meet on equal terms with the strong. For him in some degree the federal principle is implicit in every truly free state.

Although most of Mill's remarks are hardly less relevant today than when he wrote, he was clearly handicapped by the paucity of existing federations from which to draw illustrations, the only two of importance being the United States and Switzerland. This fact partly explains his conclusion that a federal government had inadequate authority to conduct effectively any war except one in self-defence. In the American case he had some evidence to support this opinion, but scarcely sufficient on which to rest a firm and enduring generalisation. Hence, although his principal remarks on federal-

[53]Koppel S. Pinson, *Bibliographical Introduction to Nationalism* (New York: Columbia University Press, 1935), 13.

ism reflect shrewd intuitions, he lacked adequate data for the full play of his characteristically empirical thinking. He made no attempt to probe the history of federal ideas in such thinkers as Jean Bodin and the German jurists. His chief inspiration and guidance came directly from the American Federalist Papers and the wealth of American practical experience. He looked to concrete political experiments as a guide. Writing on the eve of the Civil War he thought that American federalism had already achieved something valuable in limiting the tyranny of majorities, protecting territorial groups, and creating a judicial arbiter supreme over all the governments, both state and federal, and able to declare invalid any law made by them in violation of the constitution.

The Government of Dependencies

Mill's chapter on the rule of dependencies draws on his life-long interest in colonies and empire. As a servant of the East India Company for thirty-five years, he was constantly preoccupied with imperial issues. He also became closely associated with those Philosophic Radicals who in the 1830s advocated colonial reform in general and systematic colonization in particular: notably Charles Buller, William Molesworth, Edward Gibbon Wakefield, and the enigmatic Lord Durham. Wakefield's seminal if erratic mind fed the group with ideas on the economics of colonial development. Mill freely admitted his debt to Wakefield.[54] He turned aside from the anti-imperial concepts of his father and Bentham, expressed in Bentham's pamphlet *Emancipate Your Colonies*. For him the old mercantilist empire was near death, and not to be mourned, but a renovated and vigorous empire could be established on the mutual interests of self-governing colonies and the metropolis. This cause made him actively interested in the National Colonization Society, launched by Wakefield and his associates to create a new colonial society on liberal principles, built on British capital and British labour. The new empire was expected to ensure markets and sources of supply for Britain and relieve her population pressures, economic stagnation, and the miseries of an industrial society.[55]

Mill's enduring interest in the dependencies, evident in *Representative Government*, was heavily indebted to his earlier absorption in the imperial issues of the 1830s and especially his part in the discussions provoked by the Canadian Rebellion of 1837–38. He was elated in January 1838 by the

[54]See, e.g., *EL, CW*, XIII, 642, 660, 687, and 737.

[55]The founding of South Australia benefited from the zealous efforts of the National Colonization Society and other groups which received Mill's blessing. See Douglas Pike, *The Paradise of Dissent* (Melbourne: Melbourne University Press, 1957), and Donald Winch, *Classical Political Economy and Colonies* (Cambridge, Mass.: Harvard University Press, 1965), especially Chapter vi. Mill extolled the plans for establishing South Australia in *Examiner*, 20 July, 1834, 453–4.

appointment of Lord Durham as High Commissioner and Governor General of British North America, because this event provided an unparalleled opportunity for the Philosophic Radicals to prescribe for a critical colonial situation. If Durham succeeded, the Radical party no less than the Empire would immediately benefit. Durham took with him to Canada Buller and Wakefield, both of whom substantially contributed to the contents and character of the famous report, including its recommendation for colonial autonomy. Mill for his part promptly employed the *London and Westminster Review* to defend Durham and his mission.[56] From this action he derived unusual satisfaction, telling a friend in 1840 "that, as far as such things can ever be said, I saved Lord Durham—as he himself, with much feeling, acknowledged to me. . . ."[57]

In 1861 his praise of Durham's Report remained confident and forcible. It began, he wrote, "A new era in the colonial policy of nations" and remained an imperishable memorial to its author's courage, patriotism, and liberality, as well as to the intellect and sagacity of his associates Wakefield and Buller (563). Such a generous assessment was far from acceptable to all the contemporary Radicals. Roebuck in particular was forthright in criticizing Durham, especially for his contemptuous attitude to the French Canadians and their nationality. Although Mill praised Durham's Report for advocating the general principle of colonial autonomy, he nowhere subjects it to a detailed and public analysis or meets the legitimate criticisms lodged against it at the time, especially those directed against the apparent impracticability of the formal terms for colonial autonomy.[58]

In the wake of triumphant free trade in Britain and responsible government in Canada certain members in the Liberal camp were openly hostile to colonies and empire. Spokesmen for the Manchester School and a few veteran Benthamites, like Place, wrote of colonies as expensive and needless encumbrances. Since trade was everywhere free or becoming so, the burdens and perils of a permanent colonial connection were unacceptable. The most polished and influential exponent of this view was Goldwin Smith, Regius Professor of Modern History at Oxford, who in *The Empire* argues that the self-governing colonies contribute nothing to Britain, and threaten to involve her in conflicts with other major powers.[59] Mill rejects Smith's thesis. In

[56]Consult in particular *London and Westminster Review*, XXVIII (January, 1838), 502–33; *ibid.*, XXIV (August, 1838), 507–12 (2nd ed. only); and *ibid.*, XXXII (December, 1838), 241–60.

[57]*EL, CW,* XIII, 426.

[58]The issues involved here have been critically examined by Ged Martin, *The Durham Report and British Policy* (Cambridge: Cambridge University Press, 1972), 42–74.

[59]Goldwin Smith, *The Empire* (Oxford and London: Parker, 1863). Consult also R. S. Neale, "Roebuck's Constitution and the Durham Proposals," *Historical Studies Australia and New Zealand,* XV (1971), 579–90.

Representative Government he contends that Britain and her colonies had so many interests in common that a severance of formal ties would be a mistake (565–6). The empire could survive by consent. For him colonization, despite its numerous problems, is justified by its ultimate and enduring benefits. The imperial society preserves peace among its scattered territories, pursues a civilizing mission, furnishes an opportunity for invaluable co-operation between young communities and the mature metropolis, and helps to keep their markets open to one another, immune from exclusion by hostile tariffs. On the last point Mill reflects a sanguine belief, then current among British Liberals, but soon shattered by events, that the free trade so recently introduced must naturally appeal to the overseas segments of empire.

Mill moreover considered that a continuance of imperial ties augmented the moral stature and influence of Britain in the councils of the world. In a special expression of national pride he lauds Britain as the power that best understands liberty, and that in dealings with foreigners is more responsive to conscience and moral principle than any other great nation (565). Such qualities were consonant with his deep respect for the imperial links. In 1862 he wrote to his friend, John E. Cairnes:

... I think it very undesirable that anything should be done which would hasten the separation of our colonies. I believe the preservation of as much connexion as now exists to be a great good to them; and though the direct benefit to England is extremely small, beyond what would exist after a friendly separation, any separation would greatly diminish the prestige of England, which prestige I believe to be, in the present state of the world, a very great advantage to mankind.[60]

Although he favoured the maintenance of the colonial connection, Mill rejected as unrealistic the idea of a federation of Britain and its colonies, which was then occasionally mooted, especially in the form of direct colonial representation in the parliament at Westminster:

Countries separated by half the globe do not present the natural conditions for being under one government, or even members of one federation. If they had sufficiently the same interests, they have not, and never can have, a sufficient habit of taking counsel together. They are not part of the same public; they do not discuss and deliberate in the same arena, but apart, and have only a most imperfect knowledge of what passes in the minds of one another. They neither know each other's objects, nor have confidence in each other's principles of conduct. (564.)

The conditions essential for a genuine federation did not exist, and to assume otherwise would be folly. As late as January, 1870, Mill expressed similar views to a friend in New Zealand.[61]

[60]*LL, CW,* XV, 784; cf. 965.
[61]*LL, CW,* XVII, 1685.

Mill advocated, however, one proposal designed to consolidate the sense of imperial unity. He would open the public service in all departments and in every part of the empire on equal terms to the inhabitants of the colonies. He commended his old radical friend Sir William Molesworth for setting an excellent example in appointing Francis Hincks, a Canadian politician, to the governorship of a West Indian Island (566).

In the concluding pages of his chapter on dependencies Mill presents his mature opinions on governing India. In his last years as a high official of the East India Company he had taken a significant part in the struggle against the company's extinction by the British parliament, and in the preparation of several papers, two being of major importance: *Report on the Two Bills now Before Parliament Relating to the Government of India* and *Memorandum on the Improvements in the Administration of India during the Last Thirty Years*.[62] He saw India as an immense tradition-bound land with many and vast disparities, acute problems, widely conflicting cultures and religions, and hence as unfit for immediate self-rule.[63] Nowhere does he suggest a willingness to apply the full teachings of *Liberty* and *Representative Government* to the India of his day. Instead he believed that it needed for a prolonged period enlightened governance by those with high administrative competence and a profound grasp of its special difficulties. In his opinion the best available vehicle under the Crown for applying sound utilitarian principles was the East India Company, with its large and unique stock of knowledge and experience. More effectively than any other institution the Company could act as a trustee and guardian for the Indian people.

In 1834 the Company had concluded its role as trader. Henceforth the welfare of subjects, rather than the dividends of shareholders, was its paramount concern. In 1858, however, parliament transferred the Company's ruling authority directly to the Crown, to be exercised by a Secretary of State, responsible to parliament and advised by a Council of India sitting in London. In *Representative Government* Mill criticized this fundamental change on the ground that a British politician would usually be ignorant of the country, seldom hold office long enough to acquire an intelligent grasp of the subject, and naturally be more responsive to considerations of party advantage in Britain than of social progress in India (573). Since a Secretary of State must constantly be answerable to the British people, his authority could hardly serve the best interests of Indians, whom he was unable to see, hear, or know, and whose votes he had no need to solicit. The parliament and public to which he was accountable were even less likely

[62]These papers were published for the East India Company by Cox and Wyman, London, 1858.

[63]See George D. Bearce, "John Stuart Mill and India," *Journal of the Bombay Branch of the Royal Asiatic Society*, XXVII (December, 1954), 67–80. A useful general study is Eric Stokes, *The English Utilitarians and India* (Oxford, 1959).

than himself to understand Indian affairs. In its ignorance it would be unable to judge whether and to what extent he abused his powers.

Mill admits that any system whereby one people attempts to rule another is defective, for alien rulers usually misjudge and despise subject populations; they do not and cannot feel with the people. But political systems differ in the amount of wrong they commit. He feared that in 1858 Britain had selected the worst possible system (573). So intense were his convictions that he twice refused an invitation to serve on the new Council of India.

A major issue confronting the British in India was to formulate proper policies for education, language, and culture, and at the India House Mill had to deal with these. He witnessed with disapproval the attempt of Lord Bentinck and Thomas Macaulay to downgrade the study of Oriental languages and philosophy and exalt that of English literature, thought, and science. Bentinck and Macaulay desired to impose on India an unmistakable English image, and in particular emphasized the necessity of useful knowledge. On these matters Mill followed a moderate course, free from much of the dogmatism of his father and utilitarian friends. He thought that education for Indians as for Englishmen should foster the self-development and social progress integral to his concept of liberty. Since the state must play a positive part in promoting the country's material advances, an educated Indian élite must be developed, who would help the English to govern India, interpret western ideas to its many millions, create equality under the law, eradicate racial discrimination, and establish a foundation for the society's material and intellectual progress. In principle Mill opposed any aggressive cultural imperialism, such as attempts to discard India's scholarship and ignore its learned class.[64] He saw no reason for Indians to jettison their entire cultural tradition and inheritance and doubted that they could be induced to do so. Their vernacular languages must be respected and cultivated as the indispensable means whereby the bulk of the people could assimilate useful ideas from Britain and Europe. He had little sympathy for missionaries who wanted to proselytize India or impose practices repugnant to the religious feelings of its people (570).

Mill was confident that Britain had conferred on India solid benefits, including greater peace, order, and unity under law than the country had ever enjoyed before and than any native despot seemed able to ensure. It had introduced the vitalizing influence of highly trained and competent administrators who furthered social progress and prepared for the time,

[64]Abram L. Harris, "John Stuart Mill: Servant of the East India Company," *Canadian Journal of Economics and Political Science*, XXX (May, 1964), 196. See also Gerald Sirkin and Natalie Robinson Sirkin, "Mill in India House: A Little Bureaucratic Tale in Two Letters," *Mill News Letter*, IX (Summer, 1974), 3–7. This article contains references to other relevant articles by Gerald Sirkin and Natalie Robinson Sirkin.

however remote, when India would rule itself. Although Mill accepted the superiority of British culture, he denied that cultural differences were due to racial differences. A variety of influences, such as education, state enactments, and special social and historical circumstances were more important than race. Nowhere is he more explicit on this subject than in his *Principles of Political Economy*: "Of all vulgar modes of escaping from the consideration of the effect of social and moral influences on the human mind, the most vulgar is that of attributing the diversities of conduct and character to inherent natural differences."[65] Donald Winch reminds us that Mill shared this view with other members of the liberal and classical school of political economy, who derived it from eighteenth-century thinkers.[66] They assumed that human nature was the same wherever found and that it could always be elevated in the scale of civilization by effective government and assiduous education. They also assumed that it was Britain's inescapable obligation to accomplish this goal in India.

"ON LIBERTY": INDIVIDUAL, SOCIETY, AND STATE

The relations between individual, society, and state is a theme constantly pursued throughout Mill's writings, a theme which achieves a special and impressive focus in *On Liberty*, a classic much misunderstood and the most controversial of all his works.[67] Mill's broad aim is to establish the primacy of the individual and the freedom essential for the abundant growth of his inherent powers. This task, as he conceived it, was compelling because of the circumstances in a critical age of transition, which witnessed the emer-

[65]*Principles of Political Economy, Collected Works*, II (Toronto: University of Toronto Press, 1965), 319.

[66]Donald Winch, *Classical Political Economy and Colonies*, 168.

[67]From the outset the book provoked controversy. J. S. Rees, *Mill and His Early Critics* (Leicester: Leicester University College, 1956), discusses certain reviews of it between 1859 and Mill's death in 1873 which were critical, among other things, of its individualistic assumptions and concept of liberty. A modern writer, Gertrude Himmelfarb, examines Mill's main argument in *On Liberty and Liberalism: The Case of John Stuart Mill* (New York: Alfred A. Knopf, 1974) and contends that it runs counter to his position in other writings. Carl J. Friedrich, ed., *Nomos IV, Liberty* (New York: Atherton Press, 1966), collects a series of reflective studies commemorating the centennial of Mill's work, and useful in this connection is one by David Spitz, "Freedom and Individuality: Mill's Liberty in Retrospect." Richard B. Friedman examines Mill's argument afresh in "A New Exploration of Mill's Essay on Liberty," *Political Studies*, XIV (October, 1966), 281–304. Maurice Cowling in *Mill and Liberalism* (Cambridge: Cambridge University Press, 1963) presents a novel and relentless criticism of Mill as an authoritarian bent on establishing a new religion of humanity on the basis of social science. The book and the reaction to it among scholars illustrate the wide range of controversial opinion that *On Liberty* can still provoke. For a selection of other interesting commentaries see Peter Radcliff, ed., *Limits of Liberty: Studies of Mill's On Liberty* (Belmont, California: Wodsworth Publishing Company, 1966). A British jurist's views on Mill and morals are reflected in Patrick Devlin, *The Enforcement of Morals* (London: Oxford University Press, 1965), Chap. vi.

gence of democracy, improved and enlarged media for expressing opinions, the threatened tyranny of the majority, and the active presence of reformers like Auguste Comte hostile to the principle of individual liberty.

In no sense is *On Liberty* isolated from Mill's other writings. It selects, refines, and develops certain elements from earlier essays that advocated religious tolerance, free discussion for testing ideas and sifting truth from error, and a free press to promote public enlightenment and responsible government. Early friendships and associations, especially those with Thomas Carlyle, Alexis de Tocqueville, the Saint-Simonians, and notably Harriet Taylor, influenced his conceptions of freedom.[68] So pervasive indeed in his own opinion was the intellectual assistance and guidance of his wife that he regarded her as virtually a joint author. Some commentators, most notably Gertrude Himmelfarb, attribute to Harriet's persuasion certain divergences in Mill's ideas from those he earlier expressed. In addition, the social environment, Britain's flexible constitution, and the general moods and attitudes of the country in the middle of the last century exerted on this book a subtle and profound influence. It is easy to agree with Noel Annan that Mill's *On Liberty* rests on the unconscious assumption that the British Navy ruled the seas and no fifth column could take root in England, the only major power in Europe where pacifism was then able to flourish.[69] It rests also on Mill's supremely confident faith in man's rationality.

In the introduction Mill remarks that his object

is to assert one simple principle, as entitled to govern absolutely the dealings of society with the individual in the way of compulsion and control, whether the means used be physical force in the form of legal penalties, or the moral coercion of public opinion. That principle is, that the sole end for which mankind are warranted, indirectly or collectively, in interfering with the liberty of action of any of their number, is self-protection. That the only purpose for which power can be rightfully exercised over any member of a civilised community, against his will, is to prevent harm to others. His own good, either physical or moral, is not a sufficient warrant. (223.)

This general formula is supplemented by an argument that the independence of an individual in whatever concerns merely himself should be absolute. From the outset the broadness of this formula made it subject to varied interpretations. For Mill it implies an individual utility, since liberty is an unfailing source of personal development, and also a social utility, since ultimately society must benefit from whatever sustains a diverse and rich individual life. Progress for all depends on liberty for each.

[68]J. C. Rees attempts to assess these influences in "A Phase in the Development of Mill's Ideas on Liberty," *Political Studies*, VI (February, 1958), 33–44.
[69]Noel Annan, *The Curious Strength of Positivism in English Political Thought* (London: Oxford University Press, 1959), 16.

The chief terms of Mill's liberty are inapplicable either to children or to undeveloped societies where free and equal discussion is not feasible. His liberal principle is thus not an absolute ethic, irrespective of time or place, but related to changing circumstances affecting the conduct of man as a progressive being (224). Despotism rather than liberty is a legitimate rule for primitive societies, provided it aids their development to the ultimate stage where they can benefit from liberty. The appropriate domain of liberty comprises that of conscience, thought, opinion, and all the tastes and pursuits of an individual pursuing his own good in his own way and at his own risk. Included also are voluntary combinations of individuals for purposes involving no harm to others.

In Mill's argument for liberty certain elements merit special emphasis. His initial and main interpretation of the concept is in the British empirical tradition, which equates liberty with an absence of external coercion over an individual's thought and activity. Men are free when they can act according to their desires (294). Their liberty consists in expressing views they want to express and doing what they want to do without injuring others. To such liberty the principal threat has hitherto come from unresponsible and despotic governments, which to satisfy their own ambitions and interests encroached on the customary areas of individual liberty. Hence the early liberal movement sought to resolve the conflict between authority and liberty by making rulers accountable to the people through constitutions and bills of rights. These endeavours brought to Western Europe a major era of political liberalism and democracy, which people hoped would foster their interests and protect their liberties. At the outset Mill shared their hopes, but, influenced partly by Tocqueville and American experience, he soon perceived in democracy an implicit element of tyranny—that of the majority, or those who accepted themselves as the majority, threatening the liberties of individuals and minorities (218–19).

He also saw that increasingly in the democratic age the chief menace to liberty is derived, not from public officials and the penalties of law, but from society itself through the inescapable pressures of social usage, popular prejudice, and public opinion. Society, in exercising power, executes its own mandates and over the individual asserts a pervasive compulsion hardly less relentless and even more capricious than that of law. "In our times," Mill writes in his third chapter, "from the highest class of society down to the lowest, every one lives as under the eye of a hostile and dreaded censorship" (264). Under such strict public surveillance individuals and families shape their conduct less by what they think it ought to be than by what the circumstances of the society seem to demand. Their inclination is to conform with custom, public opinion, and established norms. They become lost in the crowd: "by dint of not following their own nature, they have no nature to follow" (265). In the modern state mass emotions have a larger opportunity for expression and dominance. To Mill this fact undermines the opportunity for variety in man's nature and originality in his thinking.[70] Hitherto the human race had benefitted immensely from men of genius who had rendered progress possible. He feared, however, that the emergence of mass domination would destroy the atmosphere of freedom and tolerance necessary for a lonely genius to develop and exert influence.

The ultimate phase of social tyranny occurs when the majority desert or renounce liberty by failing to make judgments and choices. They thus frankly "do not desire liberty, and would not avail themselves of it" (267). As individuals they lose the capacity to determine their own fate. In his *Autobiography* Mill saw this as a degeneration of society "into the only despotism of which in the modern world there is real danger—the absolute rule of the head of the executive over a congregation of isolated individuals, all equals but all slaves."[71]

Fears about current social tendencies explain the fervour with which Mill formulated a plan to protect men from what seemed to him a dismal fate. Rules of conduct must encourage the individual to explore abundantly the ends and qualities of life to his own advantage and that of mankind. In Chapter ii he extols liberty to exchange ideas as cardinal to other liberal values. It enables a society to know and to reform itself. "Wrong opinions and practices gradually yield to fact and argument" (231). Mill rejects out of hand the claim made in some nations that a government is entitled to interfere with a free press when the public so demands (229). The best government is no more entitled than the worst either to dictate or silence opinion. Although for him freedom of discussion is not a natural right, it is a supreme priority in the life of a progressive society.

This freedom provides, not merely protection against tyrannical and corrupt rulers, but helps also to foster understanding among citizens about themselves and their society, to resolve social conflicts, and to establish truth as the ideal if elusive aim of human inquiry. Mill assumes that the collision of adverse opinions is an instrument of enlightenment. Truth may suffer from silencing a single dissenter. "Complete liberty of contradicting and disproving our opinion, is the very condition which justifies us in assuming its truth for purposes of action; and on no other terms can a being with human faculties have any rational assurance of being right" (231). This hopeful view was not supported by all his contemporary adherents. Leonard

[70]David Riesman, Reuel Denney, and Nathan Glazer in *The Lonely Crowd* (New Haven: Yale University Press, 1950), 301, pay tribute to Mill for foreshadowing the arguments of modern sociologists on social conformity and the subtle effects of public opinion in a democracy. See also Sheldon S. Wolin, *Politics and Vision* (Boston: Little, Brown and Company, 1960), 349–50.

[71]*Autobiography*, 116.

Courtney doubted that truth was to be found half-way between two anti-thetical theories. Such a doctrine might be a plausible weapon in combatting dogmatism, but "its value ceases when from a sword of offence and contro-versy it is beaten into a ploughshare of peace and domestic economy."[72]

The opinions Mill confidently expressed on the virtues of free discussion were not those he had hitherto invariably approved. Nor did they contain reservations one might expect him to make. In the 1830s in "The Spirit of the Age," in "Civilization," and in "Coleridge," he confessed fears about unlimited free debate.[73] He then doubted that magnifying discussion would necessarily magnify political wisdom or strengthen public judgment, especi-ally when it affected the fundamental principles underlying the authority of the national state. He believed that it was the quality, rather than the quan-tity, of discussion that counted. In 1833 he told Carlyle: "I have not any great notion of the advantage of what the 'free discussion' men, call the 'col-lision of opinions,' it being my creed that Truth is *sown* and germinates in the mind itself, and is not to be struck *out* suddenly like fire from a flint by knocking another hard body against it. . . ."[74]

These reservations are explained by differences in time and circum-stances. Mill's ruling ambition was to be a philosopher-teacher for the British public. Under different circumstances and in different periods he frankly bared his mind on important matters, but what he wrote sometimes failed to coincide with what he said when circumstances and his own think-ing were different. This variance is particularly evident in his treatment of free discussion in relation to authority, where he leaves many questions unanswered. Yet there is no ignoring the firmness of his convictions and assurance of his language in Chapter ii of *On Liberty*. However inconsistent with earlier writings, it clearly reads as his genuine and unamended testa-ment.

In the third chapter Mill argues on lines parallel to those in the second. In one he contends for freedom of discussion to discover social truth and in the other for liberty of action to achieve a vital individuality. In some respects this is the most distinctive part of his essay, because the concept of individuality contributes to his liberalism a more original and more conten-tious element than the older and long-extolled liberty of speech. His great liberal forbears, like Milton and Locke, never attempted to annex so large

[72]W. L. Courtney, *Life and Writings of John Stuart Mill* (London: Walter Scott Publishing Co., 1889), 126-7. Courtney also quotes Caroline Fox on "that terrible book of John Mill's on Liberty, clear and calm and cold, he lays it on as a tremendous duty to get oneself well contradicted and admit always a devil's advocate into the presence of your dearest, most sacred truths" (*ibid.*, 125).

[73]Gertrude Himmelfarb in *On Liberty and Liberalism*, 36–56, discusses some of Mill's contradictions.

[74]*EL, CW*, XII, 153.

and uncertain a territory for the free and autonomous self. Mill's argument adds a dimension to his view of an open society, and reflects his debt to the German, Wilhelm von Humboldt, whose words form the epigraph to this essay.[75] From Humboldt Mill takes the precept that men must direct their efforts to the "individuality of power and development," including a necessary scope for freedom and variety in human life (261).

When he describes human development as strictly synonymous with the cultivation of individuality he reflects Humboldt's spirit. The potential aggregate of qualities in the individual must be fostered as an antidote to the ills of a drab social uniformity, whereby people are cast in the same mould. As an innovative force individuality is assumed to express itself in a ready originality, in differences of conduct and practice, in diverse displays of spontaneity and energy, and in distinct styles of living. Indeed, Mill believes that eccentricity in itself is significant in helping to destroy the yoke of mass attitudes and opinions. He assumes that "Eccentricity has always abounded when and where strength of character has abounded; and the amount of eccentricity in a society has generally been proportional to the amount of genius, mental vigour, and moral courage which it contained" (269). The inventor and innovator, he thinks, are likely to be regarded by others as eccentric. In all this Mill fails to admit what Leslie Stephen later recognized, that eccentricity is not invariably a virtue: it may be positively bad when it wastes individual energy and expends itself on trifles.[76] A modern critic remarks that Mill "looked to liberty as a means of achieving the highest reaches of the human spirit; he did not take seriously enough the possibility that men would also be free to explore the depths of depravity. He saw individuality as a welcome release of energy and ingenuity, as if individuals cannot be as energetic and ingenious in pursuing ignoble ends as noble ones."[77]

Mill, however, makes the reservation that men must never undervalue human tradition and experience: "it would be absurd to pretend that people ought to live as if nothing whatever had been known in the world before they came into it; as if experience had as yet done nothing towards showing that one mode of existence, or of conduct, is preferable to another" (262). Yet it was imperative that they should be free to interpret experience in their own way and according to their own circumstances.

In supporting his plea for individuality Mill deplores any set of beliefs, like that of Calvinism, which in his opinion views human nature as corrupt and self-will as a source of evil. Strict Calvinism, by inculcating rigid submis-

---

[75]Mill read von Humboldt's work, *The Sphere and Duties of Government*, after its appearance in an English translation in 1854.

[76]Leslie Stephen, *The English Utilitarians* (London: Duckworth and Co., 1900), III, 269.

[77]Himmelfarb, *On Liberty and Liberalism*, 321.

sion to the will of God, thereby numbs the independence of the individual (265). Mill does not extol obedience over will and self-denial over self-assertion. He finds more attractive the Greek ideal of self-development, which recognizes human nature as suitable for purposes other than merely abnegation. He is particularly disturbed by the tendency of modern creeds to consolidate into a massive uniformity all that is distinctly individual instead of fostering it within bounds set by the rights and interests of others.

For the remainder of this chapter Mill continues to praise the merits of the distinct individual, whose development confers immeasurable benefits on the human race: "whatever crushes individuality is despotism, by whatever name it may be called, and whether it professes to be enforcing the will of God or the injunctions of men" (266). He fears that to its own loss society is getting the better of individuality. More active life in individuals would mean more real life in the mass. Those endowed with originality and genius can help their fellows to reduce the deadening ascendency of mediocrity. Mill evidently here, in contrast to what he says elsewhere, trusts the capacity of the average man to recognize and accept the initiative of the gifted (267).

In the last two chapters of his essay he examines how his libertarian principle may be reasonably interpreted and applied. In limited space he tried to explore a vast subject with wide moral and social ramifications. To make this endeavour manageable he attempts to assign one part of life to individuality and another to society, a venture in logic that creates difficulties and confusions which critics have long stressed. It is not feasible in this introduction to traverse the wide range of the argument. But it may be useful to note some instances where he applies his principle to concrete human situations: to the indulgence of an individual in alcohol, drugs, and gambling; to the provision of education; to economic life; and to the governance of the state.

Mill's preference is to leave the individual free to exercise autonomy in all matters concerning his personal life, since presumably he knows better than anyone else his own wants and needs. But he admits that to do so poses difficult problems, because no man is isolated from society. An individual, for example, should be free to consume alcoholic beverages according to his inclination, even though he becomes drunk. He should not be punished by society for intoxication in itself, but only if it has ill consequences for others. A soldier or a policeman must certainly be punished for drunkenness on duty, for thus he commits an other-regarding act of positive or potential peril to his fellow citizens. Where others drink to excess and harm themselves and their families, they should at least be subject to moral disapprobation, and in some circumstances to legal penalties. In general, whenever personal vices lead to acts injurious to others, these must be taken from the realm of liberty and made subject either to morality or to law.

Mill comments on the gravity of the issues:

If protection against themselves is confessedly due to children and persons under age, is not society equally bound to afford it to persons of mature years who are equally incapable of self-government? If gambling, or drunkenness, or incontinence, or idleness, or uncleanliness, are as injurious to happiness, and as great a hindrance to improvement, as many or most of the acts prohibited by law, why (it may be asked) should not law, so far as is consistent with practicability and social convenience, endeavour to repress these also? And as a supplement to the unavoidable imperfections of law, ought not opinion at least to organize a powerful police against these vices, and visit rigidly with social penalties those who are known to practise them? (280-1.)

Such measures in no way prevent the flowering of individuality or cramp new and venturesome experiments in personal living. They merely deal with practices long condemned by the judgment of the world. Alcohol also affects another issue on which Mill has strong views: temperance societies sought to reduce the consumption of liquor by prohibiting its sale. Drinking is mainly a private matter, whereas selling is a social act. Any interference with sales would, in Mill's opinion, violate the liberty of prospective buyers and consumers. But the campaign for prohibition was supported by those who alleged that their social rights were violated by merchants who trafficked in liquor. In the transient victories of American temperance societies Mill, with much indignation, finds a classic example of pressure groups which ignore the liberty of others in using the machinery of democracy to achieve their own ends (287-8). He likewise rejects sabbatarian legislation, which also reflects the religious prejudices of a part of the population who coerce the remainder into its acceptance.

Liberty, Mill remarks, is often granted where it should be withheld, and withheld where it should be granted (301). Education is an example. When he wrote it was still common, in the name of liberty, for a father to have exclusive power to determine the instruction of his children, a practice Mill criticises as unjust. For him it is self-evident that a nation has a major stake in the welfare of its children, whether rich or poor. It must, in particular, ensure that they are all educated up to a prescribed standard, that parents guarantee they reach this, and that the costs for educating the poor are publicly defrayed.

Mill, because of his rationalism, has an extravagant confidence in education as a meliorative force, including it with population control as one of two major remedies for existing social ills. Yet he repudiates the idea that the state should provide instruction. Here he apparently makes a concession to parents who for many reasons, usually religious, hold diverse views on the substance of education and the values it should inculcate. In any case, however, he has his own pronounced reason for rejecting state instruction.

He fears it as a ready instrument for moulding citizens to be exactly alike, thus shattering his ambition for the proper cultivation of individuality. A common mould would be created for the convenience and advantage of the dominant power, whether an absolute monarch, a priesthood, an aristocracy, or a majority in a democracy. "An education established and controlled by the State," he writes, "should only exist, if it exists at all, as one among many competing experiments, carried on for the purpose of example and stimulus, to keep the others up to a certain standard of excellence" (302). To this rule he makes one exception: if the society is so backward and impoverished that citizens cannot afford a proper education, then the government must provide it.

In *On Liberty* Mill attempts no extensive discussion of liberty in economic life, for he had already treated it at length in his *Principles of Political Economy*, first published in 1848 and revised four times before 1859, when *On Liberty* appeared. But he makes clear his attachment to the concept of a free market. It was once, Mill observes, the responsibility of governments to fix market prices and regulate manufacturing processes (293). But long experience has demonstrated that the quality, quantity, and cheapness of goods are best achieved by a free market of buyers and sellers, from which society in general benefits even though some individuals suffer. This basic concept of the market as an instrument of liberty he tries to preserve, even in such commodities as alcohol and poisons which can be abused or put to destructive purposes.

He recognizes, however, that no less firmly rooted in experience is the need for the state at times to interfere in the market process to secure among other things a balance of public and private interests, prevention of fraud, exposure of adulteration in food, and protection of workers in dangerous occupations. Mill adheres to the idea of the free market except when the results are obviously bad; then he approves of intervention, permitting expediency to replace liberty. For him it is usually better to leave people alone than to control them, but at times it is imperative to control them in the general interest.

From the late 1840s Mill's interest in state intervention was greatly strengthened by the compelling influence of events: the impoverished plight of Ireland in the famine years, its continuing and baffling land problem, the critical social issues of industrial Britain, the explosion of Chartism, and above all the French Revolution of 1848 and the emergence of the socialists with proposals for profound changes. The revolution in Paris struck Mill with the same forcible effect as the earlier events of 1830. Less than a week after the proclamation of the French Republic in February 1848 he writes to Henry S. Chapman: "I am hardly yet out of breath from reading and thinking about it. Nothing can possibly exceed the importance of it to the world or the immensity of the interests which are at stake on its success."[78]

What most impressed Mill in the revolution was the effectiveness of the socialists in raising the issue of a government's role in economic and social life, especially in reducing economic inequalities which breed bitter dissension and undermine the stability and security of the state. He was convinced that in both England and France private property was so seriously threatened that ways had to be found to remedy existing abuses. This aspect of his reformist ideas is reflected in successive editions of his *Principles of Political Economy*, notably the third in 1852. Although he rejects certain elements in the socialist argument he has more sympathy for it than hitherto. In November, 1848, he writes to an American correspondent, John Jay: "I have expressed temperately and argumentatively my objections to the particular plans proposed by Socialists for dispensing with private property; but on many other important points I agree with them, and on none do I feel towards them anything but respect, thinking, on the contrary, that they are the greatest element of improvement in the present state of mankind."[79]

Lord Robbins believes that in a part of his mind Mill had sympathy for socialism, and in another part was critical. He concludes that Mill was "unsettled about the fundamental basis of society; in spite of his belief in progress, he was afraid of the future; he did not feel confident that he knew where we were going; what is more he did not feel quite confident that he knew where he wanted us to go."[80] Some may question whether Mill is as uncertain and negative as Lord Robbins suggests but, at any rate, his thinking on the issue of socialism remained in a state of flux. In 1849 he had writen that "Socialism is the modern form of the protest, which has been raised, more or less, in all ages of any mental activity, against the unjust distribution of social advantages."[81] He continues to consider it an invaluable movement of protest, but doubts that conditions in society are yet suitable to make it an acceptable substitute for a system of private property. Considerable moral and educational progress is essential before socialism is practicable. To a German professor in 1852 he complains of "the unprepared state of the labouring classes & their extreme moral unfitness at present for the rights which Socialism would confer & the duties it would impose."[82]

[78]*EL, CW*, XIII, 731. See Mill's extensive defence of the revolution in the *Westminster Review*, LI (April, 1849), republished in *Dissertations and Discussions*, II, 335–410.

[79]*EL, CW*, XIII, 740–1.

[80]Lionel Robbins, *The Theory of Economic Policy in English Classical Political Economy* (London: Macmillan, 1952), 143.

[81]*Dissertations and Discussions*, II, 388.

[82]*LL, CW*, XIV, 85. See also his views in another letter of the same year, *ibid.*, 87.

Mill's increased sympathy for socialism is not evident in *On Liberty*. Since this work is strongly intended to foster individuality, it is perhaps hardly to be expected that it would pay tribute to the collectivist idea. In the last part of the essay he summarizes his principal objections to government intervention, apart from cases where it is intended to protect the liberty of individuals (305–10). He opposes it in matters which can be managed more effectively by private individuals than by the government, because they have a deeper interest in the outcome. He also opposes it when individuals may be less competent than public servants, but can acquire an invaluable public education in providing the service. Thus they strengthen their faculties, their judgment, and their grasp of joint and diverse interests that deeply concern themselves and society. He finds examples of these in jury service, participation in local administration, and conduct of voluntary philanthropic or industrial activities. Without such practical experience and education, no people can be adequately equipped for success in political freedom. It is the role of the central government, not to engage directly in these activities, but to act for them as a central depository, diffusing the diverse experience gathered in the many experiments of civic activity.

For Mill not the least important reason for opposing the undue intervention of the central government is to avoid the evil of excessively augmenting its power. The greater this power, the less scope remains for independent initiative by individuals and groups.

If the roads, the railways, the banks, the insurance offices, the great joint-stock companies, the universities, and the public charities, were all of them branches of the government; if, in addition, the municipal corporations and local boards, with all that now devolves on them, became departments of the central administration; if the employés of all these different enterprises were appointed and paid by the government, and looked to the government for every rise in life; not all the freedom of the press and popular constitution of the legislature would make this or any other country free otherwise than in name (306).

Here certainly is no advocate of a centralized state socialism.

Among the many themes discussed in the final chapter of *On Liberty*, the last is bureaucracy. As noted earlier, Mill was a devoted advocate of recruiting brilliant talent to the British civil service. Although on this matter he does not alter his views, he argues that in the interest of political liberty no civil service must monopolize all the distinguished brains and skills of the nation. He thinks it essential to ensure outside the service a countervailing intellectual influence, in no degree inferior to that within, in order to prevent bureaucracy from dominating the government and stifling intelligent criticism. He fears for political freedom if the multitude looks exclusively to the bureaucracy for direction and dictation, or if the able and ambitious mainly depend on it for personal advancement. Indeed, its own competence is likely to be undermined unless it is kept, in Mill's words, under "the watchful criticism of equal ability outside the body" (308). Otherwise it will fall victim to its traditional failings: a slavish attachment to rigid rules and a ready acquiescence in indolent routine. It may also commit errors of a different kind. Leaders of the corps may pursue half-examined and over-sanguine ventures of policy that political chiefs too easily accept and an innocent public too patiently tolerates.

Mill's argument throughout is shrewd, but couched in general terms. His dicta on bureaucratic traits appear to have been derived mainly from what he had learned from the history and experience of European states. He attributes no specific abuses to the bureaucratic power in either the United States or Britain. Indeed, his lavish praise for the New England system of local government and his glowing admiration for American civic capacity suggest that he is not complaining of bureaucratic ills in the republic. His obvious intention is to offer a solemn warning that bureaucracy can imperil the liberty of individuals whenever two necessary safeguards are absent or neglected: the presence of an alert and critical public that keeps it under a constant and intelligent scrutiny; and a wide diffusion of political power throughout the nation, which enables individuals and groups to be effective elements in the body politic. For Mill the ills of bureaucracy and centralism are intertwined and inseparable. The best protection against both is to ensure the maximum amount of local government consistent with national unity.

"CENTRALISATION"

Mill carries the themes of centralisation and bureaucracy from *On Liberty* into his essay on centralisation which, under the guise of reviewing the ideas of two French writers, presents an acute comparison of French and English political thought and institutions. The first of the authors, M. Odilon Barrot, has opinions readily defined and in harmony with Mill's own. A severe critic of the current centralism of France under Napoleon III, he condemns its confusion of spiritual and temporal powers, its petty interferences with the privacy of individuals, and its restrictions on the rights of communes to manage their local affairs and appoint their local officials. He complains that the central authority, with an insatiable appetite for power, forbids the communes to convene their councils without its permission, prescribes their annual estimates, and compels them at their expense to employ its own engineers and architects.

Mill readily accepts Odilon Barrot's criticism of despotic structures and policies in the Second Empire. To him the elaborate citadel of centralized power in Paris is repellant. In his review, however, he deals principally with the wide-ranging discussions of Dupont-White on individual, state, and centralism.

Writing in a France torn by class warfare and ideological conflict, Dupont-White assumes that with the evolution of society the selfishness of individuals and classes becomes sharper and more pervasive, and that a powerful centralized government is needed to control the manifestations of friction and conflict. Without it, society is likely to be dismembered by bitter hatreds. The state, as the chief instrument of stability and progress, is obligated to protect the weak from the strong, a task that grows ever larger and more complex with an expanding industrial society. State interference in economic life, far from being an evil, is an unavoidable result of social progress and a requisite for continued progress.

These speculations greatly interest Mill, and with many of the conclusions he has sympathy. But, as might be expected, he rejects Dupont-White's pronounced bias for centralism and his easy faith that it can always accomplish great things, including a reduction in the natural inequalities among men. For him the French writer's convictions serve to illustrate a sharp contrast between France's political culture and that of England and the United States. Frenchmen cling to centralism as a splendid achievement of the Revolution and a continuing necessity for the greatness of their country. Those in active politics invariably have a vested interest in the centralist regime, even when critical of it. Tocqueville once remarked: "Most of those people in France who speak against centralisation do not really wish to see it abolished; some because they hold power, others because they expect to hold it."[83] They ignore Tocqueville's testimony, based on studies of England and America, that decentralized government is an invaluable school of freedom.

Mill's view of what centralism means for France is clear: it fails to give adequate scope to the practical enterprise and public spirit of individuals and groups throughout the nation (582, 601). Private initiative, compared with that in England, is shackled and weakened by the excessive interference of government. Mill says of Dupont-White:

Our author, having pointed out many needful things which would never be done by the mere self-interest of individuals, does not seem to be aware that anything can be expected from their public spirit: apparently because public spirit in this form is almost entirely stifled in the countries with which he is most familiar, by the centralisation which he applauds. But in our uncentralised country, even such a public want as that of life-boats is supplied by private liberality, through the agency of a voluntary association. (603.)

Among the principal faults of the centralist system in Mill's opinion is the massive patronage it creates and the major power that the bureaucracy

[83]Quoted in J. P. Mayer, *Prophet of the Mass Age* (London: Dent, 1939), 20.

constantly exercises at the expense of popular liberty. A centralized executive, equipped to give or withhold many favours, dominates the elections
and controls the legislature. It turns the electorate into a vast tribe of place
hunters (608–9). Hence its management of public affairs is difficult to challenge successfully, except in times of crisis, and then, as in 1830 and 1848,
the result is likely to be revolutionary violence. Indeed, an overcentralized
regime may be amenable to no effective check short of revolution.

Disturbing to Mill is the manner whereby the system fosters a supine
attitude towards officials. French citizens almost universally appear to
tremble before every petty bureaucrat, a circumstance which Mill thinks
makes them incapable of much liberty. "How should they not be slavish,
when everyone wearing a Government uniform . . . can domineer at will
over all the rest . . . ?" (587.) To him it seems evident that hitherto no French
government, whatever its liberal professions, has been able to divest itself
of the exclusive right to be a judge in its own cause.

In drawing a contrast with French practice Mill comments on the greater
degree of genuine decentralization in the institutions and procedures of the
English state, beginning with the parish vestries at the bottom. Not merely
have the local authorities in England provided a training ground for political
skill and initiative, they have also tempered any tendencies to despotism at
either level of government. Local bodies have considerable independence,
but can operate only within the areas prescribed for them by parliament.
Through experience they have generally learned to conduct themselves
with reasonable competence. Their vitality adds to that of the state in general, whereas in France the local units are too numerous and too weak to
contribute a valuable balance.

Mill is provoked to discuss the special character of British empirical col-
lectivism by Dupont-White's confident case for state interventionism in
France. Englishmen, he asserts, naturally distrust government and any extension of its powers (609). They employ it only when other means, especially the free market, fail to achieve what in general the community wants.
National grants for education were adopted only after private associations
for many years had tried their hand and demonstrated how little they could
accomplish. Government regulation of emigrant ships came only when its
absence had created sordid conditions that became a public scandal. In
this instance the free market had allowed the shipowners to profit from the
poverty, ignorance, and recklessness of emigrants (592). The Poor Law
Board was established after the old laws created a situation no longer tolerable to the public.

In citing these and other cases Mill on the whole defends the English
conservative temper and attitudes of mind that they reflect. He appears to
believe that a voluntary instrument should usually be tried before govern-

ment action is attempted. Yet he also agrees with Dupont-White that the state is obligated to regulate or supervise whenever large and complicated enterprises are run by individuals or private corporations. Railways can be built and operated by private companies, but the state may usefully limit fares, impose safety rules, protect commercial interests, and insure shareholders against reckless or fraudulent managers (593). The steady growth of business directed by individuals and corporations must necessarily enlarge rather than diminish the regulating activity of modern government.

Mill shares with Dupont-White the conviction that a growing social conscience, responding to the ethical requirements of mankind, significantly augments the activity of government, making it at times the unpaid agent of the poor and underprivileged. Partly under this influence the British parliament had regulated the hours of labour, prohibited the employment of children under a certain age, prevented employment of women and children in mines, and compelled manufacturers to maintain in factories those conditions that reduce accidents and lessen hazards to health. Thus in England a network of practical arrangements and compromises were fashioned between state and individual, between state and corporation, and between central and local authority, with what Mill regarded as salutary consequences for the body politic and for the kind of liberty he extolled.

It is conspicuous how little formal ideology, least of all an egalitarian ideology, figured in these developments of the Victorian age. A year before the publication of *On Liberty* Mill gave to Giuseppe Mazzini impressions of his countrymen:

The English, of all ranks and classes, are at bottom, in all their feelings, aristocrats. They have some conception of liberty, & set some value on it, but the very idea of equality is strange & offensive to them. They do not dislike to have many people above them as long as they have some below them. And therefore they have never sympathized & in their present state of mind never will sympathize with any really democratic or republican party in other countries. They keep what sympathy they have for those whom they look upon as imitators of English institutions—Continental Whigs who desire to introduce constitutional forms & some securities against personal oppression—leaving in other respects the old order of things with all its inequalities & social injustices and any people who are not willing to content themselves with this, are thought unfit for liberty.[84]

CONCLUSION

MILL'S WRITINGS in the present volume illustrate the wide range of his political thoughts and insights. He touched on most aspects of political

[84]*LL, CW*, XV, 553.

speculation important in his age, although his principal interest was the emergence of representative and democratic government and its implications for the individual. Never simply a dispassionate analyst, he was constantly engaged in a reform polemic in harmony with the liberalism that he himself fashioned out of the ideas of Bentham and his father. His reform proposals were mainly a concrete product of a conscious effort to revise and interpret Benthamism in the interests of a broader humanity.

From the perspective of a century it is not difficult to cite the more salient ideas of Mill's political thinking. Along with his theory of liberty he is deeply anxious to elicit and develop in every phase of government man's rational faculty. This endeavour is a consistent strand in his discussions on representative institutions. He wants to see men governed by reasoned purpose to a far greater extent than they have ever been in the past, and to this end institutions must be designed. The paradox in Mill's position is clear enough. He believes that a majority should rule, but thinks that only a minority is likely to have the requisite wisdom. As a reluctant democrat he seeks to select for public service those few with a cultivated and eminent intelligence. All his discussions on representation and the franchise are intended to protect individual and minority interests and ensure the maximum recognition for educated minds. He assumes that respect for intellectual distinction is unnatural to the democratic spirit, but in the interest of democracy everything possible must quickly be done to cultivate it. The act of voting should be emphasized as a rational decision made by people determined that reason has to prevail.

No less cardinal in his thought is a related concern for achieving a balance amongst the powerful and contending interests in the modern state. To him industrial society appears to be a fierce struggle of classes and groups for diverse ends. In view of this struggle, democracy can only provide the best form of government when it is "so organized that no class, not even the most numerous, shall be able to reduce all but itself to political insignificance . . ." (467). It must operate in such a way as to sustain a workable plurality of interests that prevent the domination of any one over all the others. Much of what he says about political machinery concerns instruments, often complicated, that are intended to protect society from the monopoly of power by a single interest. To the end of his days he remained convinced that the presence of countervailing interests is essential for the survival of political liberty.

Less precise and much harder to summarize is Mill's view of the economic roles of the contemporary state. On this theme his thinking after 1848 underwent pronounced changes in response to transformations in society and the currents of European opinion. It was the ethos of his philosophy to further the full and free development of every human individual. He doubted, however, whether the existing industrial society offered the best environment for such development, since sometimes it failed to permit even the most harsh and exhausting labour to earn the bare necessaries of life. It fostered inequalities between groups, gave advantages to some, and imposed impediments on others. He believed that in existing society remedies for man's plight must be sought through a variety of institutions: co-operative industrial associations might replace the wage system, reformed proprietorship might replace land monopoly, and restrictions on the right of inheritance might reduce the general extent of inequality. Many new and untried instruments of economic control are possible and must be employed under the direct or indirect initiative of the state.

These and other related ideas put Mill on the road leading to a liberal and co-operative form of socialism like that championed by the early Fabians, who indeed built on his thought and were glad to admit their indebtedness.[85] Like him they saw in socialism the economic side of the democratic ideal and justified it only if it remained democratic. Yet the extent to which Mill travelled or hoped to travel the road of socialism remains wrapped in some doubt because he still continued to believe that in contemporary society private property and the competitive principle were necessary for effective production and indispensable for material progress.

It is more accurate to think of him as an empirical collectivist rather than a socialist, and as such he moved in harmony with the currents of the time and his own country. For him the new industrial society demanded extensions in the agenda of government. But he never ceased to emphasize that in any country the role of government must depend on the peculiar necessities of its economy and society. Some countries require more government than others, especially when poor, underdeveloped, and lacking in the special attitudes and institutions that nourish private enterprise. Mill abundantly illustrated this point in his discussions on Ireland and India. The major problem of Ireland, for example, was poverty, the result of bad government over generations, harsh class domination, and the gross mismanagement of its land. The remedy must be drastic action by the government to ensure a peasant proprietorship, which in Mill's opinion was best able to protect the soil and foster in the cultivators forethought, frugality, self-restraint, and the other solid qualities needed for their material progress and welfare. There was no other stimulus comparable to the ownership of the land by those who tilled it. The necessary steps proposed by Mill to ensure this end startled and annoyed the contemporary upholders of the

---

[85]There are many references to Mill in Bernard Shaw, ed., *Fabian Essays in Socialism* (London: Walter Scott, 1899). In this book Sidney Webb pays a special tribute to Mill (on page 58). There are also many references to Mill in Sidney and Beatrice Webb, *Industrial Democracy*, 2nd ed. (London: Longmans, 1898).

rights of property because they involved something alien to English custom, the control of rents by law rather than by market forces. But for Mill Ireland was not England, and a free market was not an inflexible dogma. He rejected the idea that English practice should be a norm for Irish policy. Irish circumstances and the land situation were such that only state action could remedy them, and bring to the country order and prosperity.

Mill's continuing interest in future social change made him aware of the continental exponents of revolutionary socialism, who dramatically appeared in 1848 and became enemies of both capitalism and liberalism. He did not sympathize with either their theories or their methods. The concept of a dictatorship of the proletariat with the physical force to assert its claims would obviously conflict with all his long-cherished principles. He told William R. Cremer, a trade unionist and a one-time secretary of the British section of the International Working Men's Association, that only two situations justified violent revolution: acute personal oppression and suffering; and a system of government which does not permit the redress of grievances by peaceful and legal means. In his opinion neither existed in England,[86] nor, we may infer, in other European countries under genuine constitutional regimes. On this aspect of his thought there is no equivocation and no uncertainty.

Five years after his comment to Cremer, Mill told Thomas Smith, Secretary of the International Working Men's Association of Nottingham, how much he welcomed the general principles of the Association, especially its acceptance of goals that he himself had long sought, such as equal rights for women and protection of minorities.[87] But he strongly cautioned against use of the term "Revolution" in the French style. For him revolution meant solely a change of government effected by force. He regretted that the Association relied on the vague French political language that dealt in abstractions. "It proceeds from an infirmity of the French mind which has been one main cause of the miscarriages of the French nation in its pursuit of liberty & progress; that of being led away by phrases & treating abstractions as if they were realities. . . ." He feared that these verbal practices and French ideas would have adverse effects: confuse issues, foster misunderstanding, and range men under different banners as friends or enemies of "the Revolution," without reference to the real worth of specific measures advantageous to all and accepted by all. In these views Mill was the liberal empiricist, protesting against an attempt to establish a revolutionary ideology among British workers. His appeal at the time would doubtless command

[86]LL, CW, XVI, 1248. See also a letter to Georg Brandes on 4 March, 1872, in LL, CW, XVII, 1874–5, which discusses the First International.
[87]LL, CW, XVII, 1910–12 (4/10/72).

a ready response from the bulk of British labour leaders.[88] The political ferment and social convulsions of the 1830s and 1840s were past. By 1867 the British skilled craftsmen had acquired the franchise and at the same time were busily engaged in the sober task of creating trade unions to become powerful pressure groups, furthering the material interests of their members. They also helped to build and sustain in the Liberal party a political bridge between the workers and the middle class. During the remainder of the century the Liberal-labour alliance, deeply influenced by evangelical religion, was to dominate union spokesmen, and to them Mill's form of utilitarianism was unquestionably more appealing than the revolutionary rhetoric and intricate strategies of class warfare sponsored by Marx and Engels.

Mill's ideas in time won an impressive position. It is a common and acceptable verdict that in Victorian England his was the most influential voice of liberalism. No one else produced so many substantial and readable texts, running through successive editions, and supplemented by scores of articles in periodicals and newspapers setting forth the proper principles of economics and politics in harmony with liberal philosophy. By the 1860s his authority reached its peak.[89] His writings then appealed to a wide range of readers: parliamentarians, a new and growing generation of students in the universities, middle-class elements in the towns interested in practical reform, and leaders and spokesmen among the workers. He was not the sole liberal prophet, and many who read him disagreed with him. *On Liberty*, for example, produced a chorus of criticism as well as of praise. Yet for all its controversial features, it reformulated boldly the problem of freedom in the environment of the nineteenth century and thus contributed richly to the contemporary ferment of liberal thinking. It was a distinguished liberal of the period who wrote that *On Liberty* "belongs to the rare books that after hostile criticism has done its best are still found to have somehow added a cubit to man's stature."[90]

This was the tribute of a devoted disciple, whose thinking was shaped by Mill. Yet many twentieth-century readers would still endorse it. They have continued to find enduring value in the tenets of *On Liberty*. They cherish almost as much as did John Morley a book that protests against the infalli-

[88]Henry Collins and Chimen Abramsky, *Karl Marx and the British Labour Movement: Years of the First International* (London: Macmillan, 1965), 269, cite references on the response to Mill's letter. See also Lewis S. Feuer, "John Stuart Mill and Marxian Socialism," *Journal of the History of Ideas*, X (1949), 297–303.

[89]A modern assessment is that by John Vincent, *The Formation of the Liberal Party, 1857–1868* (London: Constable, 1966). For the marked influence of Mill on John Morley and other leading liberals of the time see Frances Wentworth Knickerbocker, *Free Minds, John Morley and His Friends* (Cambridge: Harvard Press, 1943).

[90]John Morley, *Recollections* (Toronto: Macmillan, 1971), I, 61.

bility of public opinion and the arrogance of majorities. They accept Mill's distrust of centralised power and admire his ideals of individual liberty and a free state, although they may admit the increased difficulties in achieving them. They welcome his admonition that liberty and intellectual progress, insecure and fragile things, demand constant cultivation. But they would also emphasize that Mill had other valuable thoughts to express outside the pages of *On Liberty*. His writings and discussions as a whole must be considered in any genuine assessment of his worth as a social thinker. In them one view was conspicuous. He believed that political ideas and structures must change with a changing society. For him all institutional arrangements are provisional. If we imagined him living into the present century, we can conceive him still busily engaged in revising his liberal thought, in response to altered circumstances and fresh currents of opinion. He would still be feverishly absorbed in trying to reach the most reliable balance between his individualist and collectivist convictions. He would of course remain the rationalist, confident that social change could be effected by the art of persuasion and by the simple fact that men would learn from bitter experiences.

Textual Introduction

JOHN M. ROBSON

THE ESSAYS IN THIS VOLUME comprise the main body of Mill's writings specifically on political and social theory, including *On Liberty* and *Considerations on Representative Government*, his most valued contributions to this area. Given his abiding interest in the application of theory to experience, and the testing of theory by experience, and given also his view of the "consensus" that obtains in social states, it is impossible to isolate essays that deal only with political and social theory, or to include in one volume (or even in several) all his essays that touch on such matters. Perhaps the most obviously necessary exclusions in a' volume of this kind are the final Books of the *System of Logic* and the *Principles of Political Economy*, both of which are essential to an understanding of Mill's ideas. The decision to include or exclude particular essays is in large measure a pragmatic one, and students of Mill's political and social thought will want to refer, *inter alia*, to some of his essays and newspaper writings on economics, on particular political and social events, and on law and equality, which will be found in other volumes of the *Collected Works*. The main characteristics determining the selection of the essays in this volume are the focus on abiding and theoretical questions, and thematic interdependence.[1]

While the themes and purposes of these essays show much similarity, their provenances, comparative weights, and histories are diverse. Two of them, *On Liberty* and *Considerations on Representative Government*, are separate monographs, the former of which went through, in Mill's lifetime, four Library Editions and the latter, three; each also appeared in often-reprinted inexpensive People's Editions. Both of these have, it need hardly be said, earned a lasting place in discussions of British political thought. Of the other eleven items (excluding the Appendices), one, *Thoughts on*

---

[1]Fuller comment on the principles of inclusion and exclusion, and of editing procedures in these volumes, will be found in the Textual Introduction to *Collected Works* (henceforth indicated as *CW*), IV (*Essays on Economics and Society*), xliii ff., and in my "Principles and Methods in the Collected Edition of John Stuart Mill," in John M. Robson, ed., *Editing Nineteenth-Century Texts* (Toronto: University of Toronto Press, 1967), 96–122.

Parliamentary Reform, first appeared as a pamphlet, which went through two editions and then was republished in Volume III of Mill's *Dissertations and Discussions*; and another is a solicited paper in support of competitive civil service examinations, which was first published in *Parliamentary Papers* and then reprinted as a pamphlet.

The other nine items are articles: one (the earliest) from *Tait's Edinburgh Magazine*; five from the *Westminster Review* (including three from the *London Review* before it merged, in April, 1836, with the *Westminster*); two from the *Edinburgh Review*; and one from *Fraser's Magazine*. Of these nine, three were republished in *Dissertations and Discussions*: these are "Civilization" (the only one which is not actually a review) from the *Westminster*, the second review of Tocqueville on democracy in America from the *Edinburgh*, and "Recent Writers on Reform" from *Fraser's*. Such republication indicates, of course, the relative importance he attached to these essays,[2] and so one must note that both "Rationale of Political Representation" and the first review of Tocqueville (both from the *Westminster*) are represented in *Dissertations and Discussions* by the lengthy excerpts that make up the "Appendix" to Volume I (here reprinted as Appendix B). None of the others (including the review of Taylor's *Statesman*, contributed to the *London and Westminster* by George Grote and Mill, which here appears as Appendix A) was republished by Mill.[3]

The background, composition, and publishing history of these essays, spread as they are over Mill's most active years of authorship, from the early 1830s to the 1860s, provide valuable insights into his intellectual history and influence. After he and his father had virtually severed relations with the *Westminster Review* in the late 1820s, the younger Mill wrote voluminously for newspapers, especially the *Examiner*, and sought out avenues for longer essays, since the major reviews, the *Edinburgh*, *Quarterly*, and *Blackwood's*, were closed to him on political grounds. His main outlet was in the Unitarian *Monthly Repository*, but four of his articles, the first of which was his review of George Cornewall Lewis's *Use and Abuse of Political Terms* (the first essay in this volume), appeared in the short-lived *Tait's Edinburgh Magazine*. His review of Lewis's book (which he had commented on a month earlier in the *Examiner* of 22 April, 1832) shows

[2]Mill discusses the question briefly in the "Preface" to *Dissertations and Discussions*, reprinted in *CW*, X, 493–4; there are no specific references therein to the essays here reprinted.

[3]Specific details about the provenance and publishing history of the essays are given in individual headnotes to each. When Mill entitled an article, his title is of course used, but when, as is common in the Reviews of the period, the essays were not headed by titles, the running titles are used; to distinguish between the two reviews of Tocqueville's *Democracy in America*, "[I]" and "[II]" have been added to their titles; and a descriptive title has been added to Mill's letter on civil service examinations.

clearly his growing interest in logic,[4] particularly in the language of political and ethical speculation, which came to maturity not in these essays, but in the *System of Logic*. Though he does not refer to the essay in his *Autobiography*,[5] his correspondence indicates something of his view of his writings at that time. On 23 May, 1832, Mill wrote to the proprietor of the magazine, William Tait: "Since you have thought my article worthy of insertion it is very probable that I may place another or others at your disposal. . . ."[6] Six days later, in a letter to Thomas Carlyle, he refers to this review, along with his recent writings in the *Examiner* (including the shorter notice of Lewis's book), as probably having no interest for Carlyle, except as coming from Mill. "On the whole," he says, "the opinions I have put forth in these different articles are, I think, rather not inconsistent with yours, than exactly corresponding to them; & are expressed so coldly and unimpressively that I can scarcely bear to look back upon such poor stuff" (*EL, CW*, XII, 105). Later, however, he returned to the matter in another letter to Carlyle (12 January, 1834), saying:

Do you remember a paper I wrote in an early number of Tait, reviewing a book by a Mr. Lewis (a man of considerable worth, of whom I shall have something more to say yet). That paper paints exactly the state of my mind & feelings at that time. It was the truest paper I had ever written, for it was the most completely an outgrowth of my own mind & character: not that what is there taught, was the best I even then had to teach; nor perhaps did I even think it so; but it contained what was *uppermost* in me at that time; and differed from most else that I knew in having *emanated from* me, not, with more or less perfect assimilation, merely *worked* itself *into* me. (*Ibid.*, 205.)

Meanwhile the matter of the review had been in his mind for, in what must be a reference to the passage on 13 below, he wrote to Tait on 24 September, 1833: "I have not given up the idea of those 'Essays on the Ambiguities of the Moral Sciences' but for the present I see no chance of my having time for it" (*ibid.*, 179)—again, only in the *System of Logic* did he return to this question.

---

[4]The relation is demonstrated in his quoting from both reviews of Lewis in his *System of Logic* (see *CW*, VII, 153n–154n, VIII, 818).

[5]He merely mentions "several papers" he contributed to *Tait's* in 1832 (actually two appeared in 1832, and two in 1833). See *Autobiography*, ed. Jack Stillinger (Boston: Houghton Mifflin, 1969), 109. (Subsequent references to the *Autobiography* are to this edition, and are given, when practicable, in the text.)

[6]*Later Letters*, ed. Francis E. Mineka and Dwight N. Lindley, *CW*, XVII (Toronto: University of Toronto Press, 1972), 1957. Subsequent references to the four volumes of *Later Letters* (including some earlier letters, such as this one, discovered after the appearance of the earlier volumes), as well as to the two volumes of *Earlier Letters* (ed. Mineka [Toronto: University of Toronto Press, 1963]), are given (when practicable, in the text) simply by *EL* (for *Earlier Letters*) or *LL* (for *Later Letters*), and *CW*, with the volume and page number, and, where necessary, the date in short form (23/5/32 means 23 May, 1832).

Towards the end of the review of Lewis, Mill proposes "a more comprehensive view" that "would unite all the exclusive and one-sided systems, so long the bane of true philosophy . . ." (13). This aim is, of course, a theme he explores most notably in *On Liberty*; more particularly, he expressly tried to fulfil it personally in the next few years, as is shown in the essays he wrote in the 1830s.

"Rationale of Representation," "De Tocqueville on Democracy in America [I]," "State of Society in America," and "Civilization," the next four essays in this volume, form a coherent group. The actual circumstances of their publication give them an evident persuasive purpose that is not fully consonant with the retrospective account in his *Autobiography*, where he says of this period in his development:

> If I am asked what system of political philosophy I substituted for that which, as a philosophy, I had abandoned, I answer, no system: only a conviction, that the true system was something much more complex and many sided than I had previously had any idea of, and that its office was to supply, not a set of model institutions, but principles from which the institutions suitable to any given circumstances might be deduced (97).

And he adds (98) that he would willingly have taken Goethe's "device, 'many-sidedness,' " as his own. These comments would seem to apply to the years just before the founding in 1835 of the *London Review*, of which Mill was "the real," if not "the ostensible, editor" (*Autobiography*, 120), and are consistent with his account of his editorial aims, where "many-sidedness" is implied. It was, however, predominantly a Radical many-sidedness, and was further limited, as he indicates, by the need to represent strongly the Philosophic Radicals' viewpoints, especially those congenial to James Mill. So, the "old Westminster Review doctrines, but little modified . . . formed the staple of the review" (*ibid.*), and, though Mill does not say so, the party polemic also appears strongly—though not solely—in his own early articles, most obviously in those, not here included, dealing with specific political questions, but also in the four here collected. Only one of them, "Civilization," it may again be noted, was republished in full by Mill,[7]

---

[7]The parts of "Rationale of Representation" and "De Tocqueville on Democracy in America [I]" that were republished as "Appendix" in the first volume of *Dissertations and Discussions* have been cited frequently by commentators on Mill's political views, especially on his alleged elitism. It will be noted that Mill made some changes in their texts in the reprinted versions (ten in the first essay, twenty in the second); he also altered slightly (three changes) the passage from "Remarks on Bentham's Philosophy" that he quotes in "Rationale of Representation," and the passages (eight changes) from "De Tocqueville on Democracy in America [I]" that he incorporated in "De Tocqueville on Democracy in America [II]" for the version in *Dissertations and Discussions* (the passages do not appear in the periodical version). While most of these variants are of a minor kind, some of them, especially in the context of other changes made for *Dissertations and Discussions*, are not without interest: see, e.g., 23*e–e*, 72*h–h, i–i, k–k*.

because, in his own view, the others suffered from one or more of the characteristics he lists in the Preface to *Dissertations and Discussions*: the excluded essays "were either of too little value at any time, or what value they might have was too exclusively temporary, or the thoughts they contained were inextricably mixed up with comments, now totally uninteresting, on passing events, or on some book not generally known; or lastly, any utility they may have possessed has since been superseded by other and more mature writings of the author."[8]

Looking at only the last of these characteristics,[9] one may say, in justification of republication, that our view of utility includes an opportunity to assess the development of the views expressed in the "more mature writings" here included. At the very least, these essays were important to Mill when they were written and reveal some of his attitudes towards contemporary opinions, and also towards the purposes of a radical review. For example, in a letter of 15 April, 1835, Mill asked Joseph Blanco White to tell James Martineau, who had offered to review Bailey's *Rationale of Representation*, that "after a good deal of deliberation among the three or four persons who take most share in the conduct of the review, it has appeared to us that a subject involving so directly and comprehensively all the political principles of the review, should be retained in the hands of the conductors themselves . . ." (*EL, CW*, XII, 258; cf. 263).

Alexander Bain says of this article: "Bailey's view being in close accordance with his own, [Mill] chiefly uses the work as an enforcement of the radical creed. After Bentham and the Mills, no man of their generation was better grounded in logical methods, or more thorough in his method of grappling with political and other questions, than Samuel Bailey."[10]

Unlike Bailey, an old ally of the Philosophic Radicals, Tocqueville, the author of the work reviewed in the next article here printed, represented the new influences flooding in on Mill in this period. His subject, the workings of democracy in the United States, was, however, of great interest to all British Radicals, who looked to the American system as a model, either ideal or experimental, on which to found their arguments for reform. And Tocqueville's views held special importance, as coming from a Frenchman with the background of the great Continental Revolution, the other main foreign *topos* for political discussion. In fact, these two exemplars were used by political and social writers of all shades of blue as well as red.

The great importance to Mill of Tocqueville's work is brought out in his *Autobiography* (115), where he comments on the "shifting" of his "political

[8]*CW*, X, 493.
[9]The others are briefly commented on in the Textual Introduction to *CW*, IV, xliv–xlv.
[10]*John Stuart Mill* (London: Longmans, 1882), 46–7. Mill's next review of Bailey, on a non-political subject, Berkeley's theory of vision, was unfavourable; see *CW*, XI.

ideal from pure democracy, as commonly understood by its partisans, to the modified form of it," set forth in *Considerations on Representative Government*. This gradual change, he says, which began with his reading of Tocqueville, may be seen by comparing his two reviews of *Democracy in America* with one another and with *Considerations on Representative Government*.

On hearing of Tocqueville's book from Nassau Senior, Mill initially offered it, in February, 1835, to Blanco White for review in the second (July) number of the *London Review*.[11] When he had himself read it, however, he quickly developed an admiration for it and sought information about its author, and when in May Blanco White decided not to write the review, Mill took on the task for the third (October) number.[12] He met Tocqueville later that spring, and began (partly with a view to securing him as a contributor to the *London Review*) an extremely interesting and mutually laudatory correspondence with him that casts important light on the political and methodological views of both.[13]

Mill's esteem, which continued and grew, led to his second review of *Democracy in America* in 1840; in the meantime, probably stimulated by his reading of Tocqueville's book, he contributed to the next number of the *London Review* (January, 1836) a review of five works on the United States, entitled "State of Society in America." The particular line of argument adopted, based on the value of comparative studies of states of society, reminds one that this was a period of gestation for the last Book of the *Logic*, and justifies Bain's remark that the essay "may be called one of his minor sociological studies."[14]

The next article in this volume, "Civilization," appeared in the first number of the amalgamated *London and Westminster Review* (April, 1836) and further develops his sociological and cultural themes. In his *Autobiography* (121), Mill mentions that his father, then in the final year of his life, approved of this article, into which, he says, ". . . I threw many of my new opinions, and criticized rather emphatically the mental and moral tendencies of the time, on grounds and in a manner which I certainly had not learnt from him."[15]

---

[11]*EL, CW*, XII, 249.

[12]See *ibid.*, 259, 261, 263. That Mill had read the book before the July number appeared is shown by the reference at 18n below. His review was "nearly finished" in September (*ibid.*, 272).

[13]See especially *ibid.*, 265, 272, 283–4, 287–8, 300; Tocqueville, *Correspondance anglaise*, Vol. VI of *Œuvres, Papiers et Correspondances*, ed. J.-P. Mayer (12 vols. Paris: Gallimard, 1951–70), 302–4; and also, for James Mill's reaction, *Autobiography*, 121. A later judgment by Mill of Tocqueville's too harsh view of democracy is seen in *LL, CW*, XVI, 1055 (24/5/65).

[14]*John Stuart Mill*, 48.

[15]In the *Early Draft* (ed. Jack Stillinger [Urbana: University of Illinois Press, 1961]), 159, the words "and moral" do not appear.

Light on Mill's reasons for republishing this article in *Dissertations and Discussions* is thrown by his comments in a letter to George Cornewall Lewis two years after its first appearance. There he declines Lewis's article on authority in matters of belief because it is "suited only for students, & not for the public." Believing now that, as a "popular periodical," the *London and Westminster* should not publish such essays, Mill says that if this policy had been in effect earlier, neither his "Civilization" nor his "On the Definition of Political Economy" would have been published there.[16]

There are over one hundred and fifty substantive variants between the first version of this essay and that reprinted below, all but nine of them introduced in the first edition of *Dissertations and Discussions*. (In general, as would be expected, the earlier of the essays in those volumes were more rewritten by Mill than the later ones; cf. *Collected Works*, Vol. X, p. cxxii, and see also Vol. IV, p. xlvi.) Of these variants, about 15 per cent reflect a change of opinion (often minor), correction of information, or the passage of time and the altered provenance; the others are about equally divided between qualifications (of judgment and tone) and minor verbal alterations (including changes in capitalization and italicization). Various interesting examples may be cited, as illustrative of the changes found not only in this essay, but in others reprinted in *Dissertations and Discussions*. For instance, at 131^{s-s}, referring to the "refined classes" in England, Mill in 1835 said: "When an evil *comes to* them, they can sometimes bear it with tolerable patience, (though nobody is less patient when they can entertain the slightest hope that by raising an outcry they may compel somebody else to make an effort to relieve them)." In 1859 he substituted this less condemnatory sentence: "The same causes which render them sluggish and unenterprising, make them, it is true, for the most part, stoical under inevitable evils." Sometimes a seemingly minor variant disguises a significant (if occasionally enigmatic) change, such as that at 145^k, where, describing the place history should play in education, he said in 1835 that he accorded it importance "not under the puerile notion that political wisdom can be founded upon it"; this remark was excised in the republished version a quarter of a century later. One sentence on 127 will serve to illustrate three different kinds of change: the first, altered usage over time; the second, a minor verbal change; and the third, Mill's typical kind of qualification. Originally the sentence read: "With Conservatives of this sort, all Radicals of corresponding enlargement of view, could fraternize as frankly and cordially as with many of their own friends . . ."; in 1859 "democrats" replaced "Radicals", "aims" replaced "view" (and the comma was dropped), and "many" became "most". The type of variant reflecting changed provenance and/or

---

[16]*EL, CW*, XII, 360 (24/11/37). "On the Definition of Political Economy" was also republished, in his *Essays on Some Unsettled Questions of Political Economy* (1844).

passage of time may be illustrated by those in which attribution is altered, as at 134^{l-l}, where Mill deleted the specific reference in quoting from a paper by himself, and at 138^{z-z}, where, in the version of 1859, Carlyle is identified as the source of a comment (cf. the references to Maurice and Hamilton at 140^{f-f} and 142^{p-p}). Finally, as an example of Mill's sensitivity to the unintentionally ludicrous, one may refer to 122^{t-t}, where the paragraph beginning "Consider the savage" had, in 1835, a more direct invitation, "Look at the savage" (cf. 122^{x-x}).

The next item in this volume, Mill's short review of a work entitled *Essays on Government*, was not republished, and may here be treated in brief compass. It appeared in September, 1840, after the termination of his editorial relation with the *Westminster Review* (which now dropped *London* from its title), but may reflect a commitment earlier entered into. While slight, it touches on many issues central to radical politics at the time.

Mill's separation (not a total severance) from the *Westminster* in 1840 was of great significance for him, as symbolizing the end of his direct adherence to the party politics of his youth.[17] His last article during his editorship was the celebrated essay on Coleridge; his first major essay subsequently was his second review of Tocqueville's *Democracy in America* (now completed), which appeared in that full-throated organ of Whiggism, the *Edinburgh Review*, second only to the Tory *Quarterly Review* as the target of the early Philosophic Radicals' excoriating analysis.[18] That his switch was for him an end and a beginning is indicated, at least slightly, by his mention of the second Tocqueville review and its provenance in the concluding sentence of Chapter v of the *Autobiography*, Chapter vi being "General Review of the Remainder of My Life." The move (which led to his impressive series of essays on French historians) caused him some uneasiness, however, as is implied in a letter to Tocqueville announcing that his review will appear:

When I last wrote to you I lamented that from having terminated my connection with the London & Westminster Review I should not have the opportunity of reviewing your book there, but I have now the pleasure of telling you that I am to have the reviewing of it in the Edinburgh Review which as you know is much more read, and which has never had a review of your First Part—I suppose none of the writers dared venture upon it, and I cannot blame them, for that review is the most perfect representative of the 18th century to be found in our day, & that is not the point of view for judging of your book. But I & some others

[17]Bain remarks (*John Stuart Mill*, 55), with some justification, if one is thinking of the period up to Harriet's death at the end of 1858, that Mill's "Reorganization of the Reform Party," which appeared in the *London and Westminster* for April, 1839, was his farewell to political agitation. It was not, of course, a farewell to political thought, even during those years.

[18]See, for example, the satiric treatment in the essays by the two Mills in the first and second numbers of the *Westminster* (1824).

who are going to write in the Ed. Review now, shall perhaps succeed in infusing some young blood into it. They have given me till October for this article. (*EL, CW*, XIII, 435; 11/5/40.)

During the interval (1835–40) between the two parts of Tocqueville's work, Mill had of course not anticipated his giving up the *Westminster* connection, and had been continuing his efforts to get Tocqueville to contribute to the *Review*. As early as 1836 he had reconciled himself, for the moment, to Tocqueville's not having time to write more than one article, because his book was absorbing his time; and in January, 1837, hoping that the *London and Westminster* would be the first British review to notice the second part of *Democracy in America*, he asked Tocqueville if he could have advance sheets of the work (*EL, CW*, XIII, 316). When it finally appeared in 1840, Mill's anticipations were more than met, and once more the correspondence is full of mutual esteem.[19]

When Mill republished this second review in his *Dissertations and Discussions*, he interpolated passages from his first review of *Democracy in America*[20] and added a section from his "Duveyrier's Political Views of French Affairs," which had appeared in the *Edinburgh* in 1846. While there are 101 substantive variants in the text between the versions of 1840 and 1859 (nine more appear in the version of 1867),[21] few are of significance on their own. Apart from the kinds illustrated above in the discussion of "Civilization," there are two types that deserve mention. In one type, of more interest to textual than other scholars, there is evidence of Mill's preparatory editing: see 163^{t-t} and 164^{w-w}, where a correction and a tentative rewording are found in Mill's own copy (Somerville College, Oxford) of the 1840 article. The other type will prove of interest to those concerned with nuances and shading in Mill's political thought; they are not trivial in cumulative effect, especially when seen in conjunction with the changes that Mill made in reproducing Reeve's translation of Tocqueville (see 162^q and the collation of the translation in the Bibliographic Appendix). Some of these are merely changes in initial capitalization, but (and the same is true in *On Liberty* and *Considerations on Representative Government*) the hints they give, in sum, justify their indication in this volume as substantive

[19]*EL, CW*, XIII, 433–4 (the letter continues with the passage quoted above, concerning Mill's switch of allegiance to the *Edinburgh*), 457–8; and Tocqueville, *Œuvres*, VI, 330.

[20]Undoubtedly Mill would agree with Bain's comment (*John Stuart Mill*, 47) that the first "may be considered as superseded" by the second; but the articles are quite different in approach, and it should be noted that not only the interpolated passages but also the latter half of the "Appendix" to Vol. I of *Dissertations and Discussions* gave further currency to parts of the first review (see Appendix B, 650–3 below).

[21]There are also six variants (excluding those simply relating to the convenience of quotation) from the original text of the passage quoted from his first review of Tocqueville, and five from that of the passage quoted from his review of Duveyrier.

variants: see, for example, 170^{c-c} to $^{f-f}$, where the words involved are "democracy," "democratic," "society," and "state."

The following decade, marked by the publication of Mill's first books—the *System of Logic* (1843), *Essays on Some Unsettled Questions of Political Economy* (1844), and the *Principles of Political Economy* (1848)—as well as the series of essays on the French historians and many newspaper articles, saw no separate major articles by Mill on political and social theory, though those writings contain much material relevant to these areas. And in the 1850s, the decade of his marriage, he published very little of any kind, being occupied, with Harriet's collaboration, in the composition of many of his later works.

By the 50s, however, Mill was very widely known as a philosopher with practical interests,[22] and so his approbation was solicited by Trevelyan for the proposed reform of entrance to the civil service. Mill, who was enthusiastic about the similar reform of 1853 in the Indian civil service, had already praised the proposal in a letter to his wife, noting that the "grand complaint" about it was that it would "bring low people into the offices! as, of course, gentlemen's sons cannot be expected to be as clever as low people" (*LL, CW*, XIV, 147, 175 [2/2/54, 3/3/54]). He was therefore pleased by Trevelyan's request of 8 March, 1854, to comment on the plan, and in response hailed it as "one of the greatest improvements in public affairs ever proposed by a government. If the examination be so contrived as to be a real test of mental superiority, it is difficult to set limits to the effect which will be produced in raising the character not only of the public service but of Society itself." And he offered to write further in support at a later time (*ibid.*, 178–9). Gratified at the response by Trevelyan and in the House of Commons and the press to the announcement of his approval (*ibid.*, 184, 187–8), he sent the paper here printed as a letter to the Chancellor of the Exchequer, and subsequently yielded, with "great regret," to Trevelyan's request for the softening of the wording of a sentence concerning religious tests.[23]

Among the works that Mill wrote in the 1850s,[24] with Harriet's aid, is the best known of all his writings, *On Liberty*. In the *Autobiography* (144) he says: "I had first planned and written it as a short essay, in 1854. It was in mounting the steps of the Capitol, in January 1855, that the thought first

---

[22]See, e.g., the five extracts of his evidence before Parliamentary committees, dating from this period, that are printed in Vol. V of the *Collected Works*.

[23]*LL, CW*, XIV, 184, 187–8, 205–7. The sentence referred to is almost certainly that on 209–10 where Mill attacks Jowett's suggestions; what the earlier version was is not known, as Trevelyan marked it on a proof copy that has not been found.

Mill's continued enthusiasm for such measures may be seen in a letter of 1869 recommending open competition for offices in the United States (*ibid.*, XVII, 1572).

[24]For comments on the others, see the Textual Introduction, *CW*, X, cxxii–cxxix.

arose of converting it into a volume." The contemporary evidence, unfortunately, does not quite bear out this retrospective account. Mill, travelling in southern Europe for his health from December 1854 till June 1855, wrote almost daily to Harriet about his thoughts and experiences, and it is clear that the idea struck him some days before he actually visited the Capitol. He may, however, be forgiven the attractive, if mistaken, collation of events. "On my way here [from Viterbo to Rome]," he comments to her on 15 January, 1855, "cogitating" on the effect of the Italian sights in taking off "my nascent velleity of writing,"

... I came back to an idea we have talked about & thought that the best thing to write & publish at present would be a volume on Liberty. So many things might be brought into it & nothing seems to me more needed—it is a growing need too, for opinion tends to encroach more & more on liberty, & almost all the projects of social reformers in these days are really *liberticide*—Comte, particularly so. I wish I had brought with me here the paper on Liberty that I wrote for our volume of Essays—perhaps my dearest will kindly read it through & tell me whether it will do as the foundation of one part of the volume in question—If she thinks so I will try to write & publish it in 1856 if my health permits as I hope it will.[25]

It is very unlikely that Harriet sent the earlier manuscript to him, but she did approve his turning to the subject, which he said he would "think seriously about,"[26] and, heartened by the effect he believed his evidence on limited liability in partnerships before a Parliamentary committee was having, he wrote again to her on the subject:

We have got a power of which we must try to make a good use during the few years of life we have left. The more I think of the plan of a volume on Liberty, the more likely it seems to me that it will be read & make a sensation. The title itself with any known name to it would sell an edition. We must cram into it as much as possible of what we wish not to leave unsaid. (*Ibid.*, 332 [17/2/55].)

The note struck here, of approaching death, is characteristic of his correspondence with his wife in these years, and explains much of their attitude towards their self-imposed task of reform through writing.[27] The revised plan for a separate volume on liberty did not fit into their earlier

[25]*LL, CW*, XIV, 294. Cf. his comment to her four days later: "With returning health & the pleasure of this place [Rome] I find my activity of mind greater than it has been since I set out & I think I shall be able & disposed to write a very good volume on Liberty, if we decide that that is to be the subject" (*ibid.*, 300). Apparently he still had not spent time on the Capitol, which he mentions in a letter of 24 Jan., five further days later (*ibid.*, 307).

[26]*Ibid.*, 320 (9/2/55), from Naples.

[27]See his diary note for 19 Jan., 1854: "I feel bitterly how I have procrastinated in the sacred duty of fixing in writing, so that it may not die with me, everything that I have in my mind which is capable of assisting the destruction of error and prejudice and the growth of just feelings and true opinions" (Hugh S. R. Elliot, ed., *The Letters of John Stuart Mill* [London: Longmans, Green, 1910], II, 361).

scheme, which was for a volume of republished essays and another posthumous volume (or volumes) of new essays, the latter including the previously composed and briefer discussion of liberty and the "Life" (that is,
what became the *Autobiography*).[28] The strategy of publication concerned
them; Mill, considering again the collection of republished essays that they
had thought of as early as 1839,[29] wrote to his wife: "Above all, it is not
at all desirable to come before the public with two books nearly together,
so if not done now it cannot be done till some time after the volume on
Liberty—but by that time, I hope there will be a volume ready of much better Essays, or something as good. . . ."[30]

The period after his return to England in mid-1855 until Harriet's death
in late 1858 is very thin in evidence about writing, and he published very
little. His responsibilities at the India House increased in 1856 when he
became head of the Examiner's Office, and his intense involvement in the
East India Company's resistance to the government's assumption of full
control included the drafting of their petition and the writing of several
pamphlets in which, as Bain says, "he brought to bear all his resources in
the theory and practice of politics."[31] Nevertheless, it is certain that he
wrote and rewrote *On Liberty* during these years, as well as preparing new
editions of his *Logic* and *Principles*. The revision of the latter for its 5th
edition (1857) gives us the best evidence we have that he had worked on
the *Liberty* early in this period, for he writes to Parker on 16 December,
1856: "I am engaged about a new book (in one smaller volume [than the
Principles]) which I think I could finish in time for publication in May,
and I am not so certain of being able to do so if I put it aside to revise the
Pol. Economy."[32] He did not, however, finish it then, for he wrote to Theo-
dor Gomperz on 5 October, 1857, almost a year later, saying: "I have
nearly finished an Essay on 'Liberty' which I hope to publish next winter."

[28]See *LL, CW*, XIV, 142 (29/1/54), to Harriet.
[29]See *EL, CW*, XIII, 411 (4/11/39), to John Sterling. The revived notion may well
partly derive from Mill's reading of Macaulay's *Essays* at this time (see *ibid.*, XIV,
332 [17/2/55], to Harriet), as the original idea may have come from the publication of
Carlyle's.
[30]*LL, CW*, XIV, 348 (25/2/55), from Palermo. In the event, other factors outweighed this consideration, and Mill offered Parker *On Liberty* and *Dissertations and
Discussions* at the same time, though suggesting (as actually happened, *On Liberty*
appearing in February, and *Dissertations and Discussions* in April, 1859) that the
latter be published "somewhat later in the season" (*ibid.*, XV, 579 [30/11/58]).
[31]*John Stuart Mill*, 95.
[32]*LL, CW*, XV, 519. Actually the year does not appear on this letter, but its being
dated from India House rules out any later edition of the *Principles*, and the other
information rules out earlier ones.
Internal evidence shows that at least part of the text of Chap. iv was composed after
the beginning of October, 1856 (see 287n), and one footnote was added as late as 1858,
presumably after the text had taken substantially its final form (see 228n); it might be
inferred that those at 231n, and 240n (after mid-1857) were added at the same time.

And—surely most authors will sympathize—more than another year went by before he could write to Gomperz, on 4 December, 1858, to say: "My small volume on Liberty will be published early this winter" (*LL, CW,* XV, 539, 581). The arrangement had just been made with Parker, to whom Mill had offered the book on 30 November, saying: "You can have my little book 'On Liberty' for publication this season. The manuscript is ready; but you will probably desire to look through it, or to have it looked through by some one in whom you confide, as there are some things in it which may give offence to prejudices."[33]

The offer was not prompted, however, by a feeling that the manuscript was finally in its best form; rather, the death of Harriet, on 3 November, 1858, drove Mill to consider it almost as a memorial to her that should never be altered by revision. As he says in the *Autobiography* (144):

> During the two years which immediately preceded the cessation of my official life [in October, 1858], my wife and I were working together at the "Liberty." . . . None of my writings have been either so carefully composed, or so sedulously corrected as this. After it had been written as usual twice over, we kept it by us, bringing it out from time to time and going through it *de novo*, reading, weighing and criticizing every sentence. Its final revision was to have been a work of the winter of 1858/59, the first after my retirement, which we had arranged to pass in the South of Europe. That hope and every other were frustrated by the most unexpected and bitter calamity of her death. . . .

His full account of the work, a few pages later in the *Autobiography* (149–52), should be consulted, not only as giving his testimony to his wife's importance on this aspect of his thought, but also as revealing his assessment of its value in the present and the future. He also comments on the question of the originality of *On Liberty*,[34] and concludes the account by returning to the circumstances of its publication: "After my irreparable loss one of my earliest cares was to print and publish the treatise, so much of which was the work of her whom I had lost, and consecrate it to her memory. I have made no alteration or addition to it, nor shall I ever. Though it wants the last touch of her hand, no substitute for that touch shall ever be attempted by mine."[35]

[33]*Ibid.*, 578–9. The letter, which includes also the offer of *Dissertations and Discussions* (with a list of contents), proposes that the payment for *On Liberty* be on the same terms as for the *Principles,* that is, "one edition at half profit," with renegotiation for later editions. When a second edition was called for (it appeared in August, 1859), he wrote to Parker to say that he thought he could "fairly ask for £200 for the edition," if 2000 copies were printed (*ibid.*, 630).

[34]He omits what he might well have mentioned, the place the work has in the Philosophic Radical tradition (cf. Bain, *John Stuart Mill*, 104), and his own previous arguments for freedom of thought and action. (For a useful gathering of early texts, see Bernard Wishy, ed., *Prefaces to Liberty: Selected Writings of John Stuart Mill* [Boston: Beacon Press, 1959].)

[35]*Autobiography*, 152. Cf. the dedication to Harriet, 216 below, and his response to

This promise has been taken at face value, but, as is the case in all of Mill's major works, there was some revision, though in this instance very slight, and not of much consequence. *On Liberty* went through four Library Editions, two in 1859, a third in 1864, and a fourth in 1869, as well as a People's Edition in 1865 (see n37 below). Only three variants were introduced in the 2nd edition;[36] twenty-eight changes, however, were made for the 3rd edition. Except for the transposition of two words (252^{e-e}), none of these involves more than one word, and many are simply initial capitalization (e.g., of "State" four times on 303–4). One may mention that the mistake in the title of Comte's *Système de politique positive* (identified as his *Traité* in the 1st edition) was corrected by Mill (227^{c-c}). The most important revisions are those such as 242^{c-c}, where "genuine principles" was changed to "general principles" (and here perhaps a printer's error was involved). In the 4th edition only two minor changes were made, the movement of quotation marks at 234^{b-b}, and the substitution of "When" for "Where" at 243^{d-d}. In short, Mill's statement is not strictly accurate, for there are substantive changes, but *On Liberty* is, by a significant margin, the least revised of his works, and his homage to Harriet is not damaged by the textual evidence.

In spite of its popularity and controversiality, and Mill's increased reputation in the 1860s, *On Liberty*, as mentioned above, after the issuance of a 2nd edition in the year of first publication, went through only two further Library Editions (both now rare), in 1864 and 1869. The explanation is that Mill agreed to the publishing in 1865 of a cheap People's Edition of *On Liberty* (and of his *Principles* and *Considerations on Representative Government*)[37] by Longmans (who had taken over Parker's business).

Frederick Furnivall's approbation of the work and especially of its dedication which, Mill says, "caused me a still deeper feeling. I did not for a moment think of doing any good by those few words of preface, but only of expressing some insignificant fraction of what I feel to the noblest and wisest being I have known. But I could do nothing more useful with the rest of my life than devote it to making the world know and understand what she was, if it were possible to do it." (*LL, CW*, XV, 615 [4/4/59].)

An early indication of his resolution not to revise *On Liberty* is shown in his letter to Parker concerning the second edition: "I do not propose to make any additions or alterations" (*ibid.*, 630 [18/7/59]).

[36]It would appear that most pages of the 2nd edition were reprinted from a second state of the first edition. All the accidentals (six, three of which are unique to the 2nd edition) as well as the three substantives (which are continued in the 3rd and 4th editions) occur in Chapter v, between pp. 177 and 192 of the original (where probably the text was reset). That Mill did not pay much heed to the 2nd edition is indicated by his failure in it to correct the title of Comte's work (227^{c-c}), mentioned in the text immediately below.

[37]The fourth of his works to appear in a People's Edition was the *Logic*, which was published posthumously in 1884 (see *Collected Works*, VII, lxxxvi). After the issuance of the People's Editions, no further Library Editions of *Representative Government* were called for, and only one each of *On Liberty* (1869) and the *Principles* (1871),

Thousands of these inexpensive copies of *On Liberty* were sold in the next few years, at a considerable pecuniary sacrifice resulting from both the low price and the reduced sales of the Library Edition;[38] the accessibility of his thoughts to a broad and less affluent public clearly more than compensated him for the sacrifice.

Thoughts on Parliamentary Reform, the next item in this volume, had, like *On Liberty*, lain fallow for some years before it appeared in February, 1859, but, it being a more occasional piece, the timing of its publication, as of its composition, was determined by political events. In the Prefatory Note (see 313*a* below) he says:

Nearly the whole of this pamphlet, including the argument on the Ballot, was written five years ago, in anticipation of the Reform Bill of Lord Aberdeen's Government [in 1854]. The causes which at that period kept back the question itself prevented the publication of these remarks upon it. Subsequent reflection has only strengthened the opinions there expressed. They are now published, because it is at the present time, if ever, that their publication can have any chance of being useful.

As the pamphlet was completed in 1858, the "five years" takes one back to 1853, and a letter to Harriet of 9 January, 1854, confirms that it was drafted by then. There Mill refers to an article by W. R. Greg in the October, 1853, number of the *Edinburgh*, in which he notes an extraordinary parallel to the ideas on the ballot expressed in their "unpublished pamphlet" (*LL*, *CW*, XIV, 126). The next reference in the correspondence, on 24 June, 1854, is to "the political pamphlet that was to have been" (*ibid.*, 218, to Harriet); the appropriate occasion had by then gone by, with the withdrawal of the Bill put forward by Russell during the Aberdeen administration, and another did not arise until Derby's proposal of 1859, the expectation of which aroused considerable discussion. So, even at the height of his grief at Harriet's death, and while *On Liberty* was going through the press,

---

while there were two more of the *Logic* (1868 and 1872), which had already gone through six Library Editions (the first in 1843), compared to five of the *Principles* (the first in 1848), three of *On Liberty* (the first in 1859), and three of *Representative Government* (the first in 1861).

Our policy in this edition is to accept the final Library Edition in Mill's lifetime as copy-text, and not to record in the usual fashion substantive variants occurring uniquely in the People's Editions; however, in the case of *On Liberty* and *Representative Government*, the widespread use of the People's Editions (and of reprints from them) suggested the propriety of listing the substantive variants, as is done in Appendices D and E. Attention may be called to one of these in *On Liberty*, both because the passage in which it occurs is frequently quoted, and because it has more importance than might at first appear: at 224.32 the People's Edition reads "of a man" rather than "of man". (Concerning *Representative Government*, see also lxxxvi–lxxxvii below.)

[38]See *Autobiography*, 165. For the financial arrangements, which were confused by an error in advertised price, see *LL*, *CW*, XV, 921, 964; XVI, 1035, 1040–1, 1044; XVII, 1815, 1819, 1820.

he was able to respond to a suggestion from Chadwick that he contribute to the debate, referring to the pamphlet "written several years ago" and now adapted "to the present time" (*ibid.*, XV, 584). The necessary adaptation, the addition of a suggested plurality of votes for some electors based on "proved superiority of education,"[39] is mentioned in Mill's account in the *Autobiography* (152–3), where he also dwells on the other two features of the pamphlet that from a Radical point of view would be viewed as "heresies"[40]—the rejection of the secret ballot, and support for minority representation.

Unlike plural voting, the argument against the ballot not only had his wife's approval but had originated with her. One piece of inferential evidence, a revision of the text of the *Logic*,[41] suggests that the change of opinion (in which, as he says, Harriet preceded him), came as early as 1851. That she was more eager than he to make known their abandonment of this part of the Radical credo appears in his letters to her in June, 1854; indeed, one can easily sense his prudent reserve about offending allies and giving comfort to enemies.[42]

Concerning minority representation it is worth noting that, while he approved of Garth Marshall's proposal for cumulative votes when *Thoughts on Parliamentary Reform* was published (as he had in 1853 when the pamphlet was drafted), it very quickly lost in importance for him when Thomas Hare's scheme for Personal Representation came to his attention. In his account in the *Autobiography* (153–5) he indicates that had he known of it earlier, he certainly would have included Hare's proposal in *Thoughts on Parliamentary Reform*, and mentions his almost immediately subsequent treatment of it in "Recent Writers on Reform" (the next essay in this volume). Actually this account disguises one further step in his propagandism for Hare's scheme. By 3 March, 1859, just after the first publication of *Thoughts on Parliamentary Reform*, Mill had read Hare's *Treatise*, and must soon have written his review of it, Austin's *Plea*, and Lorimer's *Polit-*

---

[39]Plural voting, about which he had not consulted Harriet (*Autobiography*, 153), was never as important to him as the other proposals in *Thoughts on Parliamentary Reform*, though he continued to hold by it. See *LL, CW*, XV, 606 (17/3/59, to Bain), and *ibid.*, 596 and 597 (2/3/59, to John E. Cairnes and to Holyoake); in the letter to Cairnes the question of double voting (*élection à deux degrés*) is examined as a substitute. Fuller discussion of all these matters is found in *Considerations on Representative Government*.

[40]See the letter to Bain cited in the previous note.

[41]See John M. Robson, " 'Joint Authorship' Again: The Evidence in the Third Edition of Mill's *Logic*," *Mill News Letter*, VI (Spring, 1971), 18–19.

[42]See *LL, CW*, XIV, 218 (24/6/54) and 222 (30/6/54). Cf. *ibid.*, XV, 559, 592, 601, 667, and also 619 (14/5/59), when, probably referring mainly to *On Liberty* and to "Enfranchisement of Women," in *Dissertations and Discussions*, II, Mill may also have had in mind the rejection of the secret ballot, in writing to Harriet's brother, Arthur Hardy: "I have been publishing some of her opinions. . . ."

ical Progress, for by 29 March he was able to tell Hare that it would appear in *Fraser's Magazine*, as it did in April.[43] But later in 1859, when a second edition of *Thoughts on Parliamentary Reform* was called for, he appended to it a long section from "Recent Writers on Reform" dealing with Hare's plan.[44] When the two essays appeared in the third volume of *Dissertations and Discussions* (1867)—the form in which *Thoughts on Parliamentary Reform* is usually read—there was, of course, no need to append the section, since it was included in "Recent Writers on Reform."[45]

All of the matters discussed in *Thoughts on Parliamentary Reform* and "Recent Writers on Reform" are treated at greater length in Mill's main treatise devoted to political theory, *Considerations on Representative Government*,[46] the next item in this volume, which was written in the following year, 1860. Mill wrote to Henry Fawcett on 24 December of that year that he had completed two works, "one of them a considerable volume" (the other was *Utilitarianism*, which appeared in serial form in *Fraser's* late in 1861), and made "good progress with a third" (the *Subjection*).[47] Little is known of the details of composition, though it would appear from letters to Charles Dupont-White that much of the work was completed by April of 1860, and it was in the press in early March of 1861.[48] The first edition was soon exhausted, and Mill revised the work in early summer by, as usual, "des changemens purement verbaux," and adding a note to Chapter xiv and several pages in defence of Hare's scheme to Chapter vii.[49] A third edition

---

[43]See *LL, CW*, XV, 598–9, 613.

[44]See *ibid.*, 656 (21/12/59), to Charles Dupont-White, and 339^k below.

[45]Like other essays reprinted in the third volume of *Dissertations and Discussions*, these two reveal very few substantive changes, there being eleven in *Thoughts on Parliamentary Reform* and thirteen (including those in self-quotations) in "Recent Writers on Reform." Of the former, two merit mention here: 339^k, where Mill introduced reference to Hare's scheme for proportional representation in the second pamphlet edition (a passage excised from the reprint in *Dissertations and Discussions*, as mentioned above); and 332^{j-j}, where (arguing against the secret ballot) in 1867 Mill identifies as his father the "philosopher who did more than any other man of his generation towards making Ballot the creed of Parliamentary Reformers." None of the variants in "Recent Writers on Reform" calls for special comment.

[46]In fact, he quotes from both essays in Chapter x, "Of the Mode of Voting," which incorporates the discussion of the ballot in *Thoughts on Parliamentary Reform* (see 491–5 below). His discussion of *Considerations on Representative Government* in the *Autobiography* (157–8) gives, like most of his comments on his writings, an overview, though many of the detailed questions not mentioned there are touched on in other sections of the *Autobiography* to which references have been given above.

[47]*LL, CW*, XV, 716; cf. Bain, *John Stuart Mill*, 116. Cf. also *Autobiography*, 157, where he refers to his work in 1860–61, and mentions *The Subjection of Women* (not published until 1869).

[48]*Ibid.*, 690 (6/4/60) and 721 (4/3/61).

[49]*Ibid.*, 730 (5/7/61), to Hare, and 737 (8/8/61), to Dupont-White, the latter indicating that the second edition was about to appear. For the major variants, see 462^{r-r} and 528n below.

being called for three years later, Mill finished the revision by 6 November, 1864,[50] and the edition appeared in February, 1865.

At the end of the Preface, Mill introduced in the 2nd edition a comment (see 373^a) that, apart from the pages added to defend Hare's scheme (462^{r-r465}), and a short note (528n), the only changes introduced were "purely verbal." (Cf. his comments to correspondents cited above.) In fact, he made 105 substantive changes (including another added footnote), of which about one-half involve at least a minor qualification. There is no prefatory indication in the 3rd edition of the further eighty-eight substantive variants (including four added footnotes) there introduced. (There are in addition seventeen variants in the self-quotations from *Thoughts on Parliamentary Reform* and "Recent Writers on Reform," some of them more important than might be expected.) Only a few of these may here be mentioned, though many are of more than passing interest, especially because popular reprints are often based on the 1st edition. Those mentioned in the Preface to the 2nd edition should of course be studied (that at 528n contains a further correction of fact in the 3rd edition), as should those mentioned in letters by Mill (465n, on Personal Representation, and 534–5^{b-b}, on the democratic institutions of the New England States),[51] and that in the closing paragraph of Chapter ix, on indirect election (486–7^{f-f}). The qualifications for senatorial office are interestingly modified, in the second edition at 517^{i-i}, and (of special note for academics) in the third at 517^{k-k}. There are quite a few variants reflecting changed circumstances in other countries—for example, the emancipation of the serfs in Russia (382^h), the revolution in Greece (415n), and the Civil War in the United States (553^{a-a} to $^{c-c}$, 557^{g-g} to $^{i-i}$). A kind of minor change, noted above in other contexts as having significance in cumulative effect, which might escape notice, is illustrated at 403^{c-c}, where in 1865 "a people" was changed to "the people." And finally, passing by more important matters that the attentive reader will note, two oddities may be mentioned: at 473^{g-g}, the change in the 2nd edition from "the" to "a" somewhat disguises a probable allusion to Swift; and at 497^{u-u}, the change in the 3rd edition from "euphonious" to "euphemistic" calls attention to what would appear to be an unusual lapse on Mill's part rather than a printer's error.

Among the People's Editions of Mill's works, that of *Representative Government* is unique in having some claim to textual authority, in that the variants, substantive and accidental, suggest that it was prepared from the text of the final Library Edition in Mill's lifetime (both were published in 1865).[52] The number of typographical errors in the People's Edition, how-

[50]*Ibid.*, 964, to William Longman.

[51]*Ibid.*, 969 (1/12/64), to Hare, and XVI, 992 (9/2/65), to Joseph Henry Allen.

[52]It sold for 2*s.*, though 2/6 was the price first agreed on. See *ibid.*, 921 (24/2/64), 964 (6/11/64); XVI, 1035 (17/4/65) and 1040 (30/4/65). For a further issue, see XVII, 1819 (15/5/71).

ever, and the problems of deciding among the accidentals (which are few and trivial), make it unwise to depart from our policy of using the final Library Editions as copy-text; the substantive variants between the People's and Library Editions are given in Appendix E.

It should be mentioned that more editions of Mill's works appeared in 1865 than in any other year: in addition to the two editions of *Representative Government*, the fifth editions of both the *Logic* and the *Principles*, the People's Editions of *On Liberty* and the *Principles*, the periodical and first book editions of *Auguste Comte and Positivism*, and the first and second editions of the *Examination of Sir William Hamilton's Philosophy*. The sale of all these, and his public reputation, were enhanced by his unusual and successful candidacy for Westminster in this same year.

The final item in this volume, "Centralisation," which appeared in the *Edinburgh Review* for April, 1862, explores, through its review of works by Dupont-White and Odilon Barrot, a theme long on Mill's mind, one not examined as thoroughly as might be expected in *Representative Government*, which he had presumably just completed before reading Dupont-White's *Centralisation*.[53] The article itself is not referred to in the *Autobiography* (few of Mill's late articles are), but the importance of the theme is developed at length in his homage to Tocqueville (115–16), which concludes with a reference to his "serious study" of the problems of centralization. This study included the reading of Dupont-White's *L'Individu et l'Etat* in 1858, when the two began a fairly extensive correspondence that shows Mill steering his course between extremes, but certainly closer to his own shore than Dupont-White's. Their relations were cemented by the latter's translations of *On Liberty* (1860) and *Representative Government* (1862), and Mill was attracted towards giving an account of the Frenchman's ideas after reading his *Centralisation*, a continuation of *L'Individu et l'Etat*.[54] He therefore wrote, on 1 May, 1861, to Henry Reeve, editor of the *Edinburgh*, proposing a review to be completed during the summer or autumn, and including mention of Odilon Barrot's book.[55] Although Reeve was himself writing on centralization (in education) for the July, 1861, number of the *Edinburgh*, Mill's suggestion was taken up. Having written the review after his return from Avignon in June, he reported on 4 December to Dupont-White that he had sent the review to Reeve; although Mill thought it might be too long, it was accepted, and appeared in April, 1862.[56]

This article would be better known had Mill chosen to republish it in the third volume of *Dissertations and Discussions* (1867). In fact, he would seem to have planned to include it, for his library in Somerville College

[53]See *ibid.*, XV, 715 (24/12/60), to Dupont-White.
[54]See *ibid.*, and 721 (4/3/61).
[55]*Ibid.*, 725–6; cf. his letter to Dupont-White on the same day, 724.
[56]See *ibid.*, 729 (26/5/61), 753 (4/12/61), 761 (10/1/62), and 764 (12/1/62, to Grote).

includes, among articles cut from reviews, "Centralisation," prepared like the others for republication.[57] There is no evident reason for his excluding it, especially as Volume III (which includes essays up to 1866), is slimmer than the first two volumes.

This essay of 1862, though it is the latest in this volume, does not, of course, mark the end of Mill's interest in political and social questions. But henceforth his published opinions were more closely attached to particular events, or have their main focus elsewhere, especially during his parliamentary career from 1865 to 1868.

TEXTUAL PRINCIPLES AND METHODS

AS THROUGHOUT THIS EDITION, the copy-text for each item is that of the final version supervised by Mill.[58] There are, it is to be regretted, no extant manuscripts for any of the essays here included. Details concerning revisions are given in the headnotes to each item and in the discussion above.

Method of indicating variants. All the substantive variants are governed by the principles enunciated below; "substantive" here means all changes of text except spelling, hyphenation, punctuation, demonstrable typographical errors, and such printing-house concerns as type size, etc. There being few cases of changed initial capitalization, and some of them having at least suggestive significance, these are given as substantives. All substantive variants are indicated, except the substitution of "on" for "upon" (twenty-one instances). The variants are of three kinds: addition of a word or words, substitution of a word or words, deletion of a word or words. The following illustrative examples are drawn, except as indicated, from "De Tocqueville on Democracy in America [II]."

Addition of a word or words: see 157[b-b]. In the text, the passage "will, in general, longest hesitate" appears as "will [b], in general,[b] longest hesitate"; the variant note reads "[b-b]+67". Here the plus sign indicates the edition of this particular text in which the addition appears. The editions are always indicated by the last two numbers of the year of publication: here 67 = 1867 (the 2nd edition of Volumes I and II of *Dissertations and Discussions*). Information explaining the use of these abbreviations is given in each headnote, as required. Any added editorial comment is enclosed in square brackets and italicized.

Placing this example in context, the interpretation is that when first

[57]See Editor's Note, 580 below.

[58]The argument for this practice is given in my "Principles and Methods in the Collected Edition of John Stuart Mill," in John M. Robson, ed., *Editing Nineteenth-Century Texts* (Toronto: University of Toronto Press, 1967), 96–122.

published (1840) the reading was "will longest hesitate"; this reading was retained in 1859 (the 1st edition of Volumes I and II of *Dissertations and Discussions*); but in 1867 the reading became "will, in general, longest hesitate".

Substitution of a word or words: see 157^{c-c}. In the text the passage "he has of necessity left much undone, and" appears as "he has ^{c}of necessity left much undone,^{c} and"; the variant note reads "$^{c-c}$40   left much undone, as who could possibly avoid?" Here the words following the edition indicator are those for which "of necessity left much undone" were substituted; applying the same rules and putting the variant in context, the interpretation is that when first published (1840) the reading was "he has left much undone, as who could possibly avoid? and"; in 1859 this was altered to "he has of necessity left much undone, and"; and the reading of 1859 (as is clear in the text) was retained in 1867.

In this volume there are very few examples of passages that were altered more than once: an illustrative instance is found in *Considerations on Representative Government* at 456^{k-k}. The text reads "^{k}or who could not succeed in carrying the local candidate they preferred, would have the power to^k fill up"; the variant note reads "$^{k-k}$61^1 would]   61^2 would have the power to". Here the different readings, in chronological order, are separated by a square bracket. The interpretation is that the reading in the 1st edition (1861), "would fill up", was altered in the 2nd edition (also 1861) to "would have the power to fill up", and in the 3rd edition (1865, the copy-text) to "or who could not succeed in carrying the local candidate they preferred, would have the power to fill up".

Deletion of a word or words: see 157^e and 23^{g-g}. The first of these is typical, representing the most convenient way of indicating deletions in a later edition. In the text at 157^e a *single* superscript ^{e} appears *centred* between "second" and "is"; the variant note reads "^{e}40   (published only this year)". Here the words following the edition indicator are the ones deleted; applying the same rules and putting the variant in context, the interpretation is that when first published (1840) the reading was "second (published only this year) is"; in 1859 the parenthesis was deleted, and the reading of 1859 (as is clear in the text) was retained in 1867.

The second example (23^{g-g}) illustrates the method used in the volume to cover more conveniently deletions when portions of the copy-text were later reprinted, as in the case of "Rationale of Representation," part of which was republished in the "Appendix" to *Dissertations and Discussions*, Volume I. (That is, there is here, exceptionally, a later version of part of the copy-text, whereas normally the copy-text is the latest version.) In the text the words "a most powerfully" appear as "a ^{g}most^g powerfully"; the variant note reads "$^{g-g}$−67." The minus sign indicates that in the edition signified the word enclosed was deleted; putting the example in context the interpretation is that when first published (1835) the reading was (as is clear in the text) "a most powerfully"; this reading was retained in 1859, but in 1867 it was altered to "a powerfully".

Dates of footnotes: see 164n. Here the practice is to place immediately after the footnote indicator, in square brackets, the figures indicating the edition in which Mill's footnote first appeared. In the example cited, "[59]" signifies that the note was added in 1859 (and retained in 1867). If no such indication appears, the note is in all versions.

Punctuation and spelling. In general, changes between versions in punctuation and spelling are ignored. Those changes that occur as part of a substantive variant are included in that variant, and the superscript letters in the text are placed exactly with reference to punctuation. Changes between italic and roman type are treated as substantive variants and are therefore shown, except in foreign phrases and titles of works.

Other textual liberties. Some of the titles have been modified or added, as explained above; the full titles in their various forms will be found in the headnotes. The dates added to the titles are those of first publication. When footnotes to the titles gave bibliographic information, these have been deleted, and the information given in the headnotes. In two places a line space has been inserted between paragraphs where there is a page break in the copy-text; in both cases the space is justified by other editions and parallel cases.[59] On 200, where Mill added part of another essay, a series of asterisks replaces a rule; square brackets are deleted; and the explanatory paragraph is raised to normal type size. (In the same essay, at 176.9, "first part" is altered to "First Part" to conform to earlier and adjacent usage.)

Typographical errors have been silently corrected in the text; the note below lists them.[60] In the headnotes the quotations from Mill's bibliography,

[59]See 243 and 358; for the first, cf. 252 and 257, for the second, 352.

[60]Typographical errors in earlier versions are ignored. The following are corrected (the erroneous reading is given first, followed by the corrected reading in square brackets):

4.36 King— [King.]
25.38 constitueney [constituency]
102.25 sym [sym-] [*dropped character*]
111.24 " ['] [*this edition restyles quotation marks*]
141.3 distinterestedly [disinterestedly]
146.30 [*line space omitted in* 67; *added as in* 36,59]
155.11 channel [Channel] [*as in* 40,75]
156.26 M [M.]
161.42 Is it [It is] [*as in* 40,59]
196.16 country, [country.]
201.2 govern [govern-] [*dropped character*]

256.12 been [being]
269.13 individuasl [individuals]
302.34 generation [generation,] [*as in* 59[1],59[2]]
320.3 parliament [Parliament] [*as in same paragraph, and in* 59[2]]
387.23 permanence [Permanence] [*as in* 61[1],61[2]]
393.18 it [it.]
402.42 racalcitrant [recalcitrant]
417.1 upo [upon]
419.22 mentioned [mentioned.]
432.14 acts: [acts;] [*as in* 61[1]]

the manuscript of which is a scribal copy, are also silently corrected; again, the note below lists them.[61] While the punctuation and spelling of each item are retained, the style has been made uniform: for example, periods are deleted after references to monarchs (e.g., "Louis XIV.,"), dashes are deleted when combined with other punctuation before a quotation or reference, and italic punctuation after italic passages has been made roman. Indications of ellipsis have been normalized to three dots plus, when necessary, terminal punctuation. The positioning of footnote indicators has been normalized so that they always appear after adjacent punctuation marks; in some cases references have been moved from the beginning to the end of quotations for consistency.

Also, in accordance with modern practice, all long quotations have been reduced in type size and the quotation marks removed. In consequence, it has occasionally been necessary to add square brackets around Mill's words in quotations; there is little opportunity for confusion, as there are no editorial insertions except page references. Double quotation marks replace single, and titles of works originally published separately are given in italics. Mill's references to sources, and additional editorial references (in square brackets), have been normalized. When necessary his references have been silently corrected; a list of the corrections and alterations is given in the note below.[62]

464.23 candidates [candidates.]
470.31 bu [but]
494.26 kind [kind.]
514.40–1 overagainst [over against] [as in People's Edition]
549.11 non German [non-German] [as in 61¹,61²]

576.31–2 equally and [equally unknown and] [as in 61¹,61²]
635.n1 T. [J.] [correctly given in Source]
641.n1 ἥκιστα [ἥκιστα]
641.n3 ἀρχόντας [ἄρχοντας]
647.6 von [van]

[61]In a few cases my reading of the manuscript differs from that in the edition by Ney MacMinn, J. M. McCrimmon, and J. R. Hainds, *Bibliography of the Published Writings of J. S. Mill* (Evanston: Northwestern University Press, 1945), to which page references (as MacMinn) are given in the headnotes. The corrected scribal errors (the erroneous reading first, with the corrected one following in square brackets) are:

92.18 entitled [entitled]
92.18 America, [America,"]
118.5–6 entituled [entitled]
206.4–5 hereupon [thereupon]
206.5 1844/5 [1854/5]

214.4 past [post]
342.13 Austen [Austin]
372.4 Representable [Representative]
580.7 Bant's [Barrot's]

[62]Following the page and line notation, the first reference is to JSM's identification; the corrected identification (that which appears in the present text) follows in square brackets. There is no indication of the places where a dash has been substituted for a comma to indicate adjacent pages, where "P." or "Pp." replaces "p." or "pp." (or the reverse), or where the volume number has been added to the reference. In "De Tocqueville on Democracy in America [I]," where appropriate, page references to the French original are added, and "Reeve" inserted before the references given by Mill.

76.13 p. 58 [pp. 58–9]
76.n1 p. 313 [pp. 313–14]

102.34 p. 284, *notes* [pp. 284–6]
105.n11 p. 268, *notes* [pp. 268–9]

Appendices. Two items have been taken out of the normal chronological order and appended, but otherwise treated uniformly with the main text: Appendix A, the review of Taylor's *Statesman*, is placed here because it was jointly authored by George Grote and Mill and the precise contribution of each is not known; Appendix B, the "Appendix" to Volume I of *Dissertations and Discussions*, is here relegated because it combines portions of "Rationale of Representation" and "De Tocqueville on Democracy in America[I]," both of which are fully reprinted in the text.

Appendix C consists of an extract from a letter from Benjamin Jowett on the proposed competitive examinations for the Civil Service that contains opinions criticized by Mill in his submission on the same topic, and a footnote editorially appended to Mill's own submission, containing Jowett's reply to Mill's criticism. These materials are included because they give context to Mill's remarks, and because the footnote appears in the pamphlet version of Mill's submission.

Appendices D and E, for reasons given above, list, respectively, the substantive variants between the People's Editions of *On Liberty* and *Considerations on Representative Government* and the last Library Editions of those works in Mill's lifetime.

Appendix F, the Bibliographic Appendix, provides a guide to Mill's references and quotations, with notes concerning the separate entries, and a list of substantive variants between his quotations and their sources. The items in this volume contain references to over 160 publications (excluding Statutes and Parliamentary Papers, and unidentified anonymous quotations, but including classical tags, and references that occur in quotations from others). Mill quotes from over one-half of these, including the sixteen works he reviews. He quotes from nine of his own writings, and refers to

---

107.41 67 [47]
112.8–9 p. 252–263 [pp. 252–3, 261–3]
113.n5 p. 9 [pp. 9–10]
173.13–14 *Ibid.* [Reeve, Vol. II, pp. 118–19; Tocqueville, Vol. II, pp. 111–13.]
261.n2 11–13 [11,13]
346.37 p. 13 [Pp. 13–14] [*reference moved to end of quoted passage*]
350.41 p. 23 [Pp. 23–5] [*reference moved to end of quoted passage*]
355.32 p. 17 [Pp. 17–18]
369.26 p. 126 [Pp. 126–7]
495.n1 32–36 [31–7]
496.n3 p. 39 [pp. 39–40]
497.n12–13 26 and 32 [32 and 26]
596.22 p. 268 [pp. 267–8]
597.3 297–9 [298–9]
598.36 p. 277 [pp. 277–8]
608.19 p. 586 [pp. 586–7]
610.17 p. xxi [pp. xxi–xxii]

611.8 127 [126]
612.18 P. xxix [Pp. xxix–xxx]
612.26 P. 361 [Pp. 360–1]
612.39 15 [15–16]
622.32 p. 263 [Pp. 263–5]
626.20 p. 13 [Pp. 13–16]
626.36 p. 162 [Pp. 162–3]
629.33 p. 156 [Pp. 156–9] [*transferred from 628.43 for clarity*]
635.33–4 p. 60 [Pp. 60–1]
636.23 p. 65 [Pp. 63–5]
641.11 p. 132 [Pp. 132–3]
642.6 p. 36 [Pp. 36–7]
643.38 p. 54 [Pp. 53–6]
644.14 p. 21 [Pp. 21–2]
644.32 p. 30 [Pp. 30–1]
645.21 p. 37 [Pp. 37–8]
645.37 p. 144 [Pp. 144–5]
646.11 p. 220 [Pp. 220–1]
646.37 p. 233 [Pp. 233–5]

six more. (There are also quotations from three of his father's writings, and references to three others.) The most extensive quotation is, as one would expect, from reviewed works; a large number of the shorter quotations (some of which are indirect) are undoubtedly taken from memory, with no explicit references being given, and the identification of some of these is inescapably inferential. It will be noted that Mill habitually translates from the French. Except for the standard classical authors, few important references are made to standard works in the history of political thought. In this context, one may refer (without predicting the effect of the reference) to Mill's praise of Lewis (5n below) for having "spared himself the ostentatious candour of mentioning the authors to whom he was indebted, they being mostly writers of established reputation" whose "truths . . . are the common property of mankind"; the contrary practice implies "either that the author cares, and expects the reader to care, more about the ownership of an idea than about its value; or else that he designs to pass himself off as the first promulgator of every thought which he does not expressly assign to the true discoverer." Whatever view one may take of Mill's attitude towards real property, he evidently was not, in 1832, an advocate of pedant proprietorship.

Because Appendix F serves as an index to persons, writings, and statutes, references to them do not appear in the Index proper, which has been prepared by Dr. Bruce Kinzer.

ACKNOWLEDGMENTS

TO THE MEMBERS of the Editorial Committee, and especially Alexander Brady and J. B. Conacher, to the editorial and printing staff of the University of Toronto Press, and especially the copy-editor, Rosemary Shipton, and to my research assistant, Judith Le Goff, my most sincere appreciation and thanks. I am deeply indebted to the staffs of various libraries, including the British Library, the University of Toronto Library, the Victoria University Library, the University of London Library, the British Library of Political and Economic Science, the London Library, and (a special thanks for prompt and ever-courteous aid) the library of Somerville College, Oxford. Among others who have helped in various ways, and to whom this mention is insufficient reward, are C. J. Allen, John Anton, Joan Bigwood, Frank Collins, Roland Hall, William J. Hyde, Patricia Kennedy, L. M. Kenny, Michael Laine, Jane Millgate, Ann Christine, John, and William Robson, Flora Roy, James P. Scanlan, Francis Sparshott, James Steintrager, and Kenneth Thompson. And, last and foremost, to my wife who, society and politics notwithstanding, has aided me cheerfully and expertly, my reiterated but still heartfelt gratitude.

USE AND ABUSE OF POLITICAL TERMS

1832

EDITOR'S NOTE

Tait's Edinburgh Magazine, I (May, 1832), 164–72. Unsigned. Not republished. The title is footnoted: "Use and Abuse of Political Terms. By George Cornwall [*sic*] Lewis, Esq. Student of Christ Church, Oxford. London: Fellowes, 1832." Identified in JSM's bibliography as "A review of Geo. Cornewall Lewis's Remarks on the Use and Abuse of Political Terms, in the second number of Tait's Edinburgh Magazine (May, 1832.)" (MacMinn, 21.) The copy in Somerville College, on which JSM has written "From Tait's Magazine for May 1832", has no corrections or emendations. For JSM's contemporary attitude to the essay, see the Textual Introduction, lxx–lxxii above.

JSM quotes part of this review (see 9–10 below) in his *Logic*, producing variant readings, which are footnoted. In the variant notes the editions of the *Logic* are indicated by the last two figures of their dates of publication: e.g., "51—72" means that the reading given is that of the 3rd (1851) to 8th (1872) editions; "MS—72" means that the reading is that from the manuscript through the 8th edition.

Use and Abuse of Political Terms

MR. LEWIS IS KNOWN in society as the son of the Right Hon. T. Frankland Lewis, and in literature, as the translator, jointly with Mr. Henry Tufnell, of two erudite and interesting works on classical antiquity, Muller's Dorians, and Bockh's Public Economy of Athens.[*] Mr. Lewis is also the author of a little work on logic;[†] to which subject, stimulated like many others of the Oxford youth, by the precepts and example of Dr. Whately, he has devoted more than common attention, and was so far peculiarly qualified for writing such a work as the volume before us professes to be. This alone should entitle him to no slight praise; for such is the present state of the human mind, in some important departments, that it is often highly meritorious to have written a book, in itself of no extraordinary merit, if the work afford proof that any one of the requisites for writing a good book on the same subject is possessed in an eminent degree.

Certain it is, that there scarcely ever was a period when logic was so little studied, systematically, and in a scientific manner, as of late years; while, perhaps, no generation ever had less to plead in extenuation of neglecting it. For if, in order to reason well, it were only necessary to be destitute of every spark of fancy and poetic imagination, the world of letters and thought might boast, just now, of containing few besides good reasoners; people to whom, one would imagine, that logic must be all in all, if we did not, to our astonishment, find that they despise it. But the most prosaic matter-of-fact person in the world must not flatter himself that he is able to reason because he is fit for nothing else. Reasoning, like all other mental excellencies, comes by appropriate culture; not by exterminating the opposite good quality, the other half of a perfect character. Perhaps the mere reasoners, with whom the world abounds, would be considerably less numerous, if men really took the pains to learn to reason. It is a sign of a weak judgment, as of a weak virtue, to take to flight at the approach of every thing which

[*Carl Otfried Mueller, *The History and Antiquities of the Doric Race*, 2 vols. (Oxford: Murray, 1830); August Boeckh, *The Public Economy of Athens*, 2 vols. (London: Murray, 1828).]

[†*An Examination of Some Passages in Dr. Whately's Elements of Logic* (Oxford: Parker, 1829).]

can, by any remote possibility, lead it astray. Men who, for want of cultivation, have the intellects of dwarfs, are of course the slaves of their imagination, if they have any, as they are the slaves of their sensations, if they have not; and it is partly, perhaps, because the systematic culture of the thinking faculty is in little repute, that imagination also is in such bad odour; there being no solidity and vigour of intellect to resist it where it tends to mislead. The sublimest of English poets composed an elementary book of logic for the schools;[*] but our puny rhymsters think logic, forsooth, too dry for them;* and our logicians, from that and other causes, very commonly say with M. Casimir Perier, *A quoi un poëte est-il bon?*

In undertaking to treat of the use and abuse of the leading terms of political philosophy, Mr. Lewis has set before himself a task to which no one but a logician could be competent, and one of the most important to which logic could be applied. If, however, we were disposed for minute criticism, we might find some scope for it in the very title-page. We might ask, what is meant by an abuse of terms; and whether a man is not at liberty to employ terms in any way which enables him to deliver himself of his own ideas the most intelligibly; to bring home to the minds of others, in the greatest completeness, the impression which exists in his own? This question, though it has a considerable bearing upon many parts of Mr. Lewis's book, throws, however, no doubt upon the importance of the object he aims at. His end is, to prevent *things* essentially different, from being confounded, because they happen to be called by the same *name*. It is past doubt that this, like all other modes of false and slovenly thinking, might be copiously exemplified from the field of politics; and Mr. Lewis has not been unhappy in his choice of examples. The instances, in which the confusion of language is the consequence, and not the cause, of the erroneous train of thought (which we believe to be generally the more common case,) are equally worthy of Mr. Lewis's attention, and will, no doubt, in time receive an equal share of it.

Some notion of the extent of ground over which our author travels may be gathered from his table of contents; which, with that view, we transcribe:

1. Government.   2. Constitution—Constitutional.   3. Right—Duty—Wrong —Rightful—Wrongful—Justice.   4. Law—Lawful—Unlawful.   5. Sovereign —Sovereignty—Division of Forms of Government.   6. Monarchy—Royalty— King.   7. Commonwealth—Republic—Republican.   8. Aristocracy—Oligarchy —Nobility.   9. Democracy.   10. Mixed Government—Balance of Powers.

[*John Milton, *Artis Logicæ* (London: Hickman, 1672).]

*The greatest English poet of our own times lays no claim to this glorious independence of any obligation to pay regard to the laws of thought. Those whom Mr. Wordsworth honours with his acquaintance, know it to be one of his favourite opinions, that want of proper intellectual culture, much more than the rarity of genius, is the cause why there are so few true poets; the foundation of poetry, as

11. People—Community.   12. Representation—Representative—Representative Government.   13. Rich—Middle Class—Poor.   14. Nature—Natural—Unnatural—State of Nature.   15. Liberty—Freedom—Free.   16. Free Government—Arbitrary Government—Tyranny—Despotism—Anarchy.   17. Power—Authority—Force.   18. Public—Private—Political—Civil—Municipal.   19. Property—Possession—Estate—Estates of Parliament.   20. Community of Goods.

To explain thoroughly the various senses of any one of these terms, would require, possibly, as much space, as Mr. Lewis has devoted to them all. His observations, however, are those of an instructed and intelligent mind. They contain, perhaps, not much that is absolutely new; except that ideas, which the mind has made completely its own, always come out in a form more or less different from that in which they went in, and are, in that sense, always original. Moreover, any one who can look straight into a thing itself, and not merely at its image mirrored in another man's mind, can also look at things, upon occasion, when there is no other man to point them out.*

Yet, highly as we think of this work, and still more highly of the author's capabilities, we will not pretend that he has realized all our conceptions of what such a work ought to be. We do not think he is fully conscious of what his subject requires of him. The most that he ever seems to accomplish, is to make out that something is wrong, but not how that which is wrong may be made right. He may say, that this is all he aimed at; and so, indeed, it is. But it may always be questioned, whether one has indeed cut down to the

---

of all other productions of man's reason, being logic. By logic, he does not mean syllogisms in mode and figure, but justness of thought and precision of language; and, above all, knowing accurately your own meaning.

While we are on this subject, we must be permitted to express our regret, that a poet who has meditated as profoundly on the theory of his art, as he has laboured assiduously in its practice, should have put forth nothing which can convey any adequate notion to posterity of his merits in this department; and that philosophical speculations on the subject of poetry, with which it would be folly to compare any others existing in our language, have profited only to a few private friends.

*Mr. Lewis has very properly, in our opinion, spared himself the ostentatious candour of mentioning the authors to whom he was indebted, they being mostly writers of established reputation. Such studious honesty in disclaiming any private right to truths which are the common property of mankind, generally implies either that the author cares, and expects the reader to care, more about the ownership of an idea than about its value; or else that he designs to pass himself off as the first promulgator of every thought which he does not expressly assign to the true discoverer. This is one of the thousand forms of that commonest of egotisms, egotism under a shew of modesty. The only obligations which Mr. Lewis with a just discrimination stops to acknowledge, are to a philosopher who is not yet so well known as he deserves to be, Mr. Austin, Professor of Jurisprudence in the University of London.

very root of an error, who leaves no truth planted in its stead. Mr. Lewis, at least, continually leaves the mind under the unsatisfactory impression, that the matter has not been probed to the bottom, and that underneath almost every thing which he sees, there lies something deeper which he does not see. If in this we should be deemed hypercritical, we would say in our defence, that we should never think of ranging Mr. Lewis in the class of those, from whom we take thankfully and without asking questions, any trifling matter, which is all they have to bestow. The author of such a work as the present, is entitled to be tried by the same standard as the highest order of intellect; to be compared not with the small productions of small minds, but with ideal perfection.

Mankind have many ideas, and but few words. This truth should never be absent from the mind of one who takes upon him to decide if another man's language is philosophical or the reverse. Two consequences follow from it; one, that a certain laxity in the use of language must be borne with, if a writer makes himself understood; the other, that, to understand a writer who is obliged to use the same words as a vehicle for different ideas, requires a vigorous effort of co-operation on the part of the reader. These unavoidable ambiguities render it easier, we admit, for confusion of ideas to pass undetected: but they also render it more difficult for any man's ideas to be so expressed that they shall not appear confused; particularly when viewed with that habitual contempt with which men of clear ideas generally regard those, any of whose ideas are not clear, and with that disposition which contempt, like every other passion, commonly carries with it, to presume the existence of its object. It should be recollected, too, that many a man has a mind teeming with important thoughts, who is quite incapable of putting them into words which shall not be liable to any metaphysical objection; that when this is the case, the logical incoherence or incongruity of the expression, is commonly the very first thing which strikes the mind, and that which there is least merit in perceiving. The man of superior intellect, in that case, is not he who can only see that the proposition precisely as stated, is not true; but he who, not overlooking the incorrectness at the surface, does, nevertheless, discern that there is truth at the bottom. The logical defect, on the other hand, is the only thing which strikes the eye of the mere logician. The proper office, we should have conceived, of a clear thinker, would be to make other men's thoughts clear for them, if they cannot do it for themselves, and to give words to the man of genius, fitted to express his ideas with philosophical accuracy. Socrates, in the beautiful dialogue called the *Phædrus*, describes his own vocation as that of a mental midwife:[*] not so Mr. A. or B., who, perhaps, owes the advantage of clear

[*The reference is mistaken. See, rather, Plato, *Theaetetus*, in *Theaetetus and Sophist* (Greek and English), trans. H. N. Fowler (London: Heinemann; New York: Putnam's Sons, 1921), p. 30 (149a-b); cf. p. 76 (161e).]

ideas to the fact of his having no ideas which it is at all difficult to make clear. The use of logic, it would seem, to such a person, is not to help others, but to privilege himself against being required to listen to them. He will not think it worth his while to examine what a man has to say, unless it is put to him in such a manner that it shall cost him no trouble at all to make it out. If you come to him needing help, you may learn from him that you are a fool; but you certainly will not be made wise.

It would be grossly unjust to Mr. Lewis to accuse him of any thing approaching to this; but we could have wished that his work could have been more decidedly cited as an example of the opposite quality. We desiderate in it somewhat more of what becomes all men, but, most of all, a young man, to whom the struggles of life are only in their commencement, and whose spirit cannot yet have been wounded, or his temper embittered by hostile collision with the world, but which, in young men more especially, is apt to be wanting—a slowness to condemn. A man must now learn, by experience, what once came almost by nature to those who had any faculty of seeing; to look upon all things with a benevolent, but upon great men and their works with a reverential spirit; rather to seek in them for what *he* may learn from *them*, than for opportunities of shewing what they might have learned from him; to give such men the benefit of every possibility of their having spoken with a rational meaning; not easily or hastily to persuade himself that men like Plato, and Locke, and Rousseau, and Bentham, gave themselves a world of trouble in running after something which they thought was a reality, but which he Mr. A. B. can clearly see to be an unsubstantial phantom; to exhaust every other hypothesis, before supposing himself wiser than they; and even then to examine, with good will and without prejudice, if their error do not contain some germ of truth; and if any conclusion, such as a philosopher can adopt, may even yet be built upon the foundation on which they, it may be, have reared nothing but an edifice of sand.

Such men are not refuted because they are convicted of using words occasionally with no very definite meaning, or even of founding an argument upon an ambiguity. The substance of correct reasoning may still be there, although there be a deficiency in the forms. A vague term, which they may never have given themselves the trouble to define, may yet, on each particular occasion, have excited in their minds precisely the ideas it should excite. The leading word in an argument may be ambiguous; but between its two meanings there is often a secret link of connexion, unobserved by the critic but felt by the author, though perhaps he may not have given himself a strictly logical account of it; and the conclusion may turn not upon what is different in the two meanings, but upon what they have in common, or at least analogous.

Until logicians know these things, and act as if they knew them, they must not expect that a logician and a captious man will cease to be, in common apprehension, nearly synonymous. How, in fact, can it be otherwise in the mind of a person, who knows not very clearly what logic is, but who finds that he can in no way give utterance to his conviction without infringing logical rules, while he is conscious all the time that the real grounds of the conviction have not been touched in the slightest degree?

It is only in a very qualified sense that these admonitions can be applied to Mr. Lewis; but there are so few persons of our time to whom they do not apply more or less, (and perhaps there have been but few at any time,) that we are not surprised to find them even in his case far from superfluous. It remains for us to establish this by particular instances.

Mr. Lewis, under the word *right*, gives a definition of legal rights, and then lays it down that all rights are the creatures of law, that is, of the will of the sovereign; that the sovereign himself has no rights, nor can any one have rights as against the sovereign; because, being sovereign, he is by that supposition exempt from legal obligation, or legal responsibility. So far, so good. Mr. Lewis then says, that to call any thing a right which cannot be enforced by law, is an abuse of language. We answer,—Not until mankind have consented to be bound by Mr. Lewis's definition. For example, when Dr. Johnson says[*] that a man has not a *moral right* to think as he pleases, "because he ought to inform himself, and think justly," Mr. Lewis says [p. 21] he must mean *legal* right; and adds other observations, proving that he has not even caught a glimpse of Johnson's drift. Again, according to him, whoever asserts that no man can have a *right* to do that which is *wrong*, founds an argument upon a mere ambiguity, confounding *a* right with the adjective *right*: and this ambiguity is "mischievous, because it serves as an inducement to error, and confounds things as well as words." [P. xv.]

Now, we contend that Mr. Lewis is here censuring what he does not thoroughly understand, and that the use of the word *right*, in both these cases, is as good logic and as good English as his own. *Right* is the correlative of *duty*, or *obligation*; and (with some limitations) is co-extensive with those terms. Whatever any man is under an obligation to give you, or to do for you, to that you have a right. There are legal obligations, and there are consequently legal rights. There are also *moral* obligations; and no one, that we know of considers this phrase an abuse of language, or proposes that it should be dispensed with. It seems, therefore, but an adherence to the established usage of our language, to speak of moral rights; which stand in the same relation to moral obligations as legal rights do to legal obligations. All that is necessary is to settle distinctly with ourselves, and make it intelligible to those whom we are addressing, which kind of rights it is that we mean; if we fail in which, we become justly liable to Mr. Lewis's censure. It has not

[*James Boswell, *Life of Johnson*, ed. G. B. Hill and L. F. Powell, 6 vols. (Oxford: Clarendon Press, 1934–50), Vol. II, p. 249 (7/5/73).]

totally escaped Mr. Lewis that there may be some meaning in the phrase, moral rights; but he has, by no means, correctly hit that meaning. He expounds it thus, "claims recommended by views of justice or public policy;" the sort of claim a man may be said to have to anything which you think it *desirable* that he should possess. [P. 8.] No such thing. No man in his sound senses considers himself to be *wronged* every time he does not get what he *desires*; every man distinguishes between what he thinks another man *morally bound* to do, and what he merely *would like* to see him do; between what is morally criminal, a fit subject for complaint or reproach, and what excites only regrets, and a wish that the act had been abstained from. No system of moral philosophy or metaphysics that we ever heard of, denies this distinction; though several have undertaken to account for it, and to place it upon the right footing.

If you may say that it is the moral duty of subjects to obey their government, you may also express this by saying that government has a moral *right* to their obedience. If you may say that it is the moral duty of sovereigns to govern well, or else to abdicate, you may say that subjects have a right to be well governed. If you may say, that it is morally culpable in a government to attempt to retain its authority, contrary to the inclinations of its subjects; you may say, that the people have a right to change their government. All this, without any logical inaccuracy, or "abuse of language." We are not defending this phraseology as the best that can be employed; the language of *right* and the language of *duty*, are logically equivalent, and the latter has, in many respects, the advantage. We are only contending, that, whoever uses the word *right* shall not be adjudged guilty of nonsense, until it has been tried whether this mode of interpreting his meaning will make it sense. And this we complain that Mr. Lewis has not done.

To explain what we meant by saying that almost everything which Mr. Lewis sees has something lying under it which he does not see, we have now to shew, that, in catching at an imaginary ambiguity near the surface, he has missed the deeper and less obvious ambiguities by which men are really misled. Two of these we shall briefly set forth.

*a*Speaking morally, you are said to have a right to do a thing, if all persons are morally bound not to hinder you from doing it. But, in another sense, to have a right to do a thing, is the opposite of having *no* right to do it,—*b*viz.*b* of being under a moral obligation to forbear *c*from*c* doing it. In this sense, to say that you have a right to do a thing, means that you may do it without any breach of duty on your part; that other persons not only ought not to hinder you, but have no cause to think *d*the*d* worse of you for doing it. This is a

---

a-a [quoted in JSM's *Logic, Collected Works*, Vol. VIII, p. 818]
*b-b*51—72   *i.e.*
c-c—51—72   *d-d*—51—72

perfectly distinct proposition from the preceding. The *right* which you have by virtue of a duty incumbent upon other persons, is obviously quite a different thing from a right consisting in the absence of any duty incumbent upon yourself. Yet the two things are perpetually confounded. Thus a man will say he has a right to publish his opinions; which may be true in this sense, that it would be a breach of duty in any other person to interfere and prevent the publication:—but he assumes thereupon, that in publishing his opinions, he himself violates no duty; which may either be true or false, depending, as it does, upon his having taken due pains to satisfy himself, first, that the opinions are true, and next, that their publication in this manner, and at this particular juncture, will probably be beneficial to the interests of truth, on the whole. *In this sense of the word, a man has no *right* to do that which is *wrong*, though it may often happen that nobody has a right to *prevent* him from doing it.*

The second ambiguity is that of confounding a right, of any kind, with a right to enforce that right by resisting or punishing a violation of it. *Men* will say, for example, that they have a right to *a* good government; which is undeniably true, it being the moral duty of their governors to govern them well. But in granting this, you are supposed to have admitted their right or liberty to turn out their governors, and perhaps to punish them, for having failed in the performance of this duty; which, far from being the same thing, is by no means universally true, but depends upon an immense number of varying circumstances,*a* and is, perhaps, altogether the knottiest question in practical ethics. This example involves *both* the ambiguities which we have mentioned.

We have dwelt longer on this one topic than the reader perhaps will approve. We shall pass more slightly over the remainder.

Our author treats with unqualified contempt all that has been written by Locke and others, concerning a state of nature and the social compact. [Pp. 185ff.] In this we cannot altogether agree with him. The state of society contemplated by Rousseau, in which mankind lived together without government, may never have existed, and it is of no consequence whether it did so or not. The question is not whether it ever existed, but whether there is any advantage in supposing it hypothetically; as we assume in argument all kinds of cases which never occur, in order to illustrate those which do. All discussions respecting a state of nature are inquiries what morality would be if there were no law. This is the real scope of Locke's *Essay on Government*,[*] rightly understood: whatever is objectionable in the details did not

---

[*John Locke, *Two Treatises on Government*, in *Works*, 10 vols. (London: Tegg *et al.*, 1823), Vol. V, pp. 209–485.]

*e-e*MS—46   right   *f-f*—MS—72
*g-g*51—72   People   *h-h*—62—72

arise from the nature of the inquiry, but from a certain wavering and obscurity in his notion of the grounds of morality itself. Nor is this mode of viewing the subject, we conceive, without its advantages, in an enlarged view, either of morality or law. Not to mention that, as is observed by Locke himself, all independent *governments*, in relation to one another, are actually in a state of nature, subject to moral duties but obeying no common superior;[*] so that the speculations which Mr. Lewis despises, tend, in international morality at least, to a direct practical application.

Even the social compact, (though a pure fiction, upon which no valid argument can consequently be founded,) and the doctrine connected with it, of the inalienable and imprescriptible rights of man, had this good in them, that they were suggested by a sense, that the power of the sovereign, although, of course, incapable of any legal limitation, has a moral limit, since a government ought not to take from any of its subjects more than it gives. Whatever obligation any man would lie under in a state of nature, not to inflict evil upon another for the sake of good to himself, that same obligation lies upon society towards every one of its members. If he injure or molest any of his fellow-citizens, the consequences of whatever they may be obliged to do in self-defence, must fall upon himself; but otherwise, the government fails of its duty, if on any plea of doing good to the community in the aggregate, it reduces him to such a state, that he is on the whole a loser by living in a state of government, and would have been better off if it did not exist. This is the truth which was dimly shadowed forth, in howsoever rude and unskilful a manner, in the theories of the social compact and of the rights of man. It was felt, that a man's voluntary consent to live under a government, was the surest proof he could give of his feeling it to be beneficial to him; and so great was the importance attached to this sort of assurance, that where an express consent was out of the question, some circumstance was fixed upon, from which, by stretching a few points, a consent might be presumed. But the test is real, where, as in imperfectly settled countries, the forest is open to the man who is not contented with his lot.

Notwithstanding the length to which our remarks have extended, we cannot overlook one or two passages, less remarkable for their importance, than as proofs of the haste with which Mr. Lewis must have examined the authors and even the passages he has criticised.

Thus, where Mr. Bentham recommends *natural* procedure in the administration of justice, in opposition to *technical*, Mr. Lewis observes, that as it is impossible to suppose that any mode of judicial procedure should be left to the discretion of the judge guided by no rules, the word *natural*, in this case, "seems to be a vague term of praise, signifying that system which, to the writer, seems most expedient." [Pp. 182–3.] It shews but little knowledge

[*Ibid., p. 346 (Bk. II, Chap. ii, §14).]

of Mr. Bentham's habits of mind, to account in *this* way, of all others, for any phraseology he may think proper to adopt. The fact is, as has been explained a hundred times by Mr. Bentham himself,—that by *natural* procedure, he means what he also calls *domestic* procedure; viz. the simple and direct mode of getting at the truth which suggests itself *naturally*,—that is, readily and invariably, to all men who are inquiring in good earnest into any matter which, happening to concern *themselves*, they are really desirous to ascertain. That the technical methods of our own, and all other systems of law, are bad in proportion as they deviate from this, is what Mr. Bentham affirms, and, we will add, proves.

Again, when Mr. Mill speaks of the *corruptive operation*[*] of what are called the advantages of fortune, Mr. Lewis comments [pp. 184n–185n] upon the strangeness of this sentiment from the writer of a treatise on Political Economy;[†] that is, on the production and accumulation of wealth; and hints, that the work in question must have been composed with an object similar to that of a treatise on poisons. Did it never occur to Mr. Lewis, that Mr. Mill's meaning might be, not that a people are corrupted by the amount of the wealth which they possess in the aggregate, but that the inequalities in the distribution of it have a tendency to corrupt those who obtain the large masses, especially when these come to them by descent, and not by merit, or any kind of exertion employed in earning them?

To add one instance more, Mr. Lewis falls foul of the often quoted sentence of Tacitus, "that the most degenerate states have the greatest number of laws; *in corruptissimâ republicâ plurimæ leges*;[‡] a position not only not true, but the very reverse of the truth, as the effect of the progress of civilization is to multiply enactments, in order to suit the extended relations, and the more refined and diversified forms of property, introduced by the improvement of society." [P. 205.] Mr. Lewis is a scholar, and understands the *words* of Tacitus, but, in this case, it is clear, he has not understood the ideas. He has committed what he himself would call an *ignoratio elenchi*. By a corrupt society, Tacitus (we will take upon ourselves to assert) did not mean a *rude* society. The author was speaking of the decline of a nation's morality, and the critic talks to you of the improvement of its industry. Tacitus meant, that, in the most *immoral* society, there is the most frequent occasion for the interposition of the legislator; and we venture to agree with him, thinking it very clear, that the less you are able to rely upon conscience and opinion, the

[*James Mill, *Government* (London: Traveller Office, 1821), p. 31.]

[†James Mill, *Elements of Political Economy*, 3rd ed. (London: Baldwin, Cradock, and Joy, 1826).]

[‡Tacitus, *The Annals*, in *The Histories and the Annals* (Latin and English), trans. Clifford Moore and John Jackson, 4 vols. (London: Heinemann; New York: Putnam's Sons, 1925–37), Vol. II, p. 566 (III, xxviii).]

more you are obliged to do by means of the law—a truth which is not only not the opposite of Mr. Lewis's position, but stands in no logical relation to it at all, more than to the binomial theorem.

These are the blemishes of Mr. Lewis's work. Yet they do not induce us to qualify our high opinion, both of the book and of its author. It is an able, and a useful publication; only, it is not a sufficient dissertation on the use and abuse of the leading political terms.

We have often thought, that a really philosophical Treatise on the Ambiguities of the Moral Sciences would be one of the most valuable scientific contributions which a man of first-rate intellectual ability could confer upon his age, and upon posterity. But it would not be so much a book of criticism as of inquiry. Its main end would be, not to set people right in their use of words, which you never can be qualified to do, so long as their *thoughts*, on the subject treated of, are in any way different from yours; but to get at their thoughts through their words, and to see what sort of a view of truth can be got, by looking at it in their way. It would then be seen, how multifarious are the properties and distinctions to be marked, and how few the words to mark them with, so that one word is sometimes all we have to denote a dozen different ideas, and that men go wrong less often than Mr. Lewis supposes, from using a word in many senses, but more frequently from using it only in one, the distinctions which it serves to mark in its other acceptations not being adverted to at all. Such a book would enable all kinds of thinkers, who are now at daggers-drawn, because they are speaking different dialects and know it not, to understand one another, and to perceive that, with the proper explanations, their doctrines are reconcilable; and would unite all the exclusive and one-sided systems, so long the bane of true philosophy, by placing before each man a more comprehensive view, in which the whole of what is affirmative in his own view would be included.

This is the larger and nobler design which Mr. Lewis should set before himself, and which, we believe, his abilities to be equal to, did he but feel that this is the only task worthy of them. He might thus contribute a large part to what is probably destined to be the great philosophical achievement of the era, of which many signs already announce the commencement; viz. to unite all half-truths, which have been fighting against one another ever since the creation, and blend them in one harmonious whole.

RATIONALE OF REPRESENTATION

1835

EDITOR'S NOTE

London Review, I (July, 1835), 341–71 (equivalent to *Westminster Review,* XXX); headed: "Art. IV. *The Rationale of Political Representation.* By the Author of 'Essays on the Formation of Opinions,' &c. &c. [Samuel Bailey.] London, 1835. Hunter. 8vo., pp. 436." Signed "A"; republished in part as first section of "Appendix," *Dissertations and Discussions*, I, 467–70. Running title: "Rationale of Representation." Identified in JSM's bibliography as "A review of Bailey's 'Rationale, of Political Representation' in the second number of the London Review (July 1835.)" (MacMinn, 44.) The copy of this article in the Somerville College Library has no corrections or emendations. Also in Somerville is a sewn, uncut offprint, without title, numbered 1–31, and signed "A". (In the offprint, parts of which are reset, there are no corrections; some accidental variants appear [these are not accepted in the present text], the typographical error at 25.38 is retained, and two more are introduced.) The review is not mentioned in the *Autobiography*. For comment on the circumstances of its publication, see the Textual Introduction, lxxii–lxxiii above.

In selecting a portion of this review for republication in "Appendix," *D&D*, I, JSM made a few revisions (see 22–4 below). In the variant notes, "59" indicates *D&D*, 1st ed., 1859, "67" indicates *ibid.*, 2nd ed., 1867. JSM also quotes from his "Remarks on Bentham's Philosophy" (see 42–3 below); the changes are shown as variants, in which "33" indicates "Remarks on Bentham's Philosophy."

Rationale of Representation

THIS IS THE WORK of a writer who, in the difficult art of making philosophy popular, has excelled most of his contemporaries; and his present is not inferior to the best of his former productions.

The theoretical grounds of Representative Government, and the solutions of the more momentous of its practical problems, are laid down by our author, in the spirit which is now nearly universal among the more advanced thinkers on the subject, but with a felicity of adaptation to the wants of the most numerous class of readers, which is peculiarly his own. In addition to this, several popular fallacies, of most extensive prevalence, and infecting the very elements of political speculation, are refuted, conclusively and forcibly, and with as much depth of philosophy as the purpose required. The thoughts succeed one another in the most lucid order. The style is perspicuity itself. To a practised student in abstract speculation, it will appear diffuse; but this, in a book intended for popularity, is far from being a defect. To common readers a condensed style is always cramped and obscure: they want a manner of writing which shall detain them long enough upon each thought to give it time to sink into their minds. Our author is not, indeed, entitled to the transcendant praise due to those who, like Hobbes or Bacon, employ at pleasure either the power of condensation or that of enlargement; dwelling on the idea until it has made its way into the understanding, and then clenching it by one of those striking images, or of those pregnant and apophthegmatic expressions, which sum up whole paragraphs in a line, and engrave the meaning as with a burning steel upon the imagination. But if our author's style does not come up to this exalted standard, it is easy, flowing, always unaffected, and has the greatest of merits, that to which all other excellencies of manner are merely subsidiary—that of perfectly expressing whatever he has occasion to express by it.

The work consists of an Introduction, and six Chapters: "On the proper Object and Province of Government;" "On the Grounds of Preference for a Representative Government;" "On the Representative Body;" "On the Electoral Body;" "On Elections;" and "On the Introduction of Changes in Political Institutions;" with two supplementary essays "On Political Equality," and "On Rights."

This *programme* gives a correct indication of the scope and purpose of the book. It is rightly termed "The Rationale of Political Representation," not "The Rationale of Government." It attempts an outline of a part only of the philosophy of government, not the whole. The philosophy of government, a most extensive and complicated science, would comprise a complete view of the influences of political institutions; not only their direct, but what are in general so little attended to, their indirect and remote influences: how they affect the national character, and all the social relations of a people; and reciprocally, how the state of society, and of the human mind, aids, counteracts, or modifies the effects of a form of government, and promotes or impairs its stability. Such is not the design of this work; and, considered in this comprehensive sense, the science itself is in its infancy.* But the advantages of a representative government, and the principles on which it must be constructed in order to realise those advantages, form a branch of the subject, the theory of which, so far as one branch can be considered separately from the rest, may be regarded as nearly perfect; and to the exposition of this, the work before us is dedicated.

It must be admitted also, that this one branch of the inquiry runs parallel, for a considerable distance, to the main trunk. The reasons for having a representative government, and the reasons for having a government at all, are, to a very considerable extent, identical. The ends or uses of government are indeed multifarious, since we may include among them all benefits, of whatever kind, to the existence of which government is indispensable; but the first and most fundamental of all, the only one the importance of which literally amounts to necessity, is to enable mankind to live in society without oppressing and injuring one another. And the need of a representative government rests upon precisely the same basis. As mankind, in a state of society, have need of government, because, without it, every strong man would oppress his weaker neighbour; so mankind, in a state of government, have need

*The most important contribution which has been made for many years to the Philosophy of Government, in this extensive sense of the term, is the recent work of M. Alexis de Tocqueville, *De la Démocratie en Amérique* [2 vols. Paris: Gosselin, 1835]; a book, the publication of which constitutes an epoch in the kind of writing to which it belongs. A minute analysis of this admirable work will be given in our next Number. [J. S. Mill, "De Tocqueville on Democracy in America [I]," *London Review*, I (Oct., 1835), 85–129. Printed below, pp. 47–90.] The Tory writers have already, we perceive, attempted to press it into their service, as an attack upon Democracy: in opposition both to the author's avowed opinions, and to his purpose expressly declared in the work itself. M. de Tocqueville's views are eminently favourable to Democracy, though his picture, like every true picture of anything, exhibits the shadows as well as the bright side; and as it keeps back nothing, supplies materials from which Democracy may, as suits the purpose of a writer, be either attacked or defended, and, we may add, *better* attacked and *better* defended than it could ever have been before.

of popular representation, because, without it, those who wielded the powers of government would oppress the rest.

Of this fundamental truth an acute sense is manifested by our author. He rests the necessity of a popular government upon one primary axiom: "That men will, in the majority of cases, prefer their own interest to that of others, when the two are placed in competition." (P. 68.) Whoever denies this, denies the principle on which, it is most certain, he himself habitually acts, when the interest at stake happens to be his own. It is the principle which all persons, when at liberty to follow their inclinations, uniformly observe in the guardianship of their own property. They do not appoint an agent, with liberty to do as he pleases, and without reserving the power of instantaneous dismissal. If they did, they would expect that the obligations of his trust would be disregarded, when in competition either with the interest of his pocket or with that of his ease.

"From this principle," says our author, "that men will prefer their own interest to that of others, when the two are placed in competition, it follows, that the interest of the community at large will be uniformly consulted only when they have the regulation of their own affairs." [P. 69.]

But since government cannot be performed by the community *en masse*; since "it is implied in the very notion of government, that a few are invested with authority over the rest; since, from the nature of the case, the legislative power must be lodged in the hands of a few; and as the few possessing it will be tempted in a thousand ways to sacrifice the public good to their own private interest;" [pp. 69, 70–1] here is but one resource:

It becomes essentially requisite *to place them in such a position that their own interest, and the public good, shall be identified.* The simple expedient which meets this is to make the office of legislator dependent on the will of the people. If his power were irresponsible, if it were subject to no direct control, if the improper exercise of it were not followed by evil consequences to the possessor, it would be inevitably abused; the public good would be neglected, and his own habitually preferred; but by the simple expedient of *rendering the continuance of his power dependent on his constituents, his interest is forced into coincidence with theirs.* Any sinister advantage which he might derive from the power intrusted to him would cease with the loss of the office, and he would have no inducement to pursue an advantage of that kind, if by so doing he unavoidably subjected himself to dismissal. Such is the general theory of political representation. An individual, under the title of a representative, is delegated by the people to do that which they cannot do in their own persons, and *he is determined in his acts to consult the public good, by the power which they retain of dismissing him from the office.* (P. 71.)

One might have imagined, that if any propositions on public affairs deserved the character of maxims of common sense, these did. Views of human affairs more practical and business-like, more in accordance with the received rules of prudence in private life, it would be difficult to find. These doctrines, nevertheless, or at least the possibility of drawing any conclusions from them, have met with questioners. That human beings will commonly prefer their own interests to those of other people, and that the way to secure fidelity to a trust is to make the trustee's interest coincide with his duty, have been classed among propositions which are either not true, or, if true at all, only in a sense in which they are insignificant and unmeaning. Nor has the assertion been made of these doctrines alone, but of all propositions relating to the motives of human actions. "When we pass," it has been said, "beyond maxims which it is impossible to deny without a contradiction in terms, and which therefore do not enable us to advance a single step in practical knowledge, it is not possible to lay down a single general rule respecting the motives which influence human actions."[*] Such was the doctrine maintained in a memorable article in the *Edinburgh Review*, by a writer, all whose ingenuity and brilliancy would not have made his subsequent fortunes what they have been, but for the grateful acceptance which this doctrine found in influential quarters.

Our author has no great difficulty in disposing of this theory:

Nothing [says he] can be more extraordinary than an assertion of this kind, in an age when, at all events, the nature of moral inquiries is better understood than formerly, however insignificant may have been our progress in the inquiries themselves. It is extraordinary, too, as having appeared in a work which is in the habit of favouring its readers with articles of distinguished ability on political economy, a science founded on "general rules respecting the motives which influence human actions," and which is, further, in the habit of drawing out long deductions from such general rules. Whoever turns over its pages may find inferences constantly made from propositions like the following: "commercial countries will resort to the cheapest market;" "high duties on imported articles inevitably cause smuggling;" "unusually large profits in any trade attract capital to it;" "a rise in the price of corn forces capital on inferior soils."

It would almost seem as if the reviewer was not aware that all these are general rules respecting the actions of men. To take the last proposition: we might conclude from his own doctrine, that he regarded the high price of corn as a physical agent propelling a material substance, called capital, upon a sterile field; and had forgotten that the proposition is an elliptical expression, under which is couched a law respecting human motives, and which virtually asserts, that when men become willing to give more money for corn, other men will be willing to grow it on land before uncultivated.

Political economy abounds with such laws; the common business of life abounds with them; every trade, every profession, legislation itself, abounds with them. Is not the whole system of penal legislation founded on the general rule, that if a punishment is denounced against any given act, there will be fewer instances of the commission of that act than if no penalty were annexed to it? Can

[*Thomas Babington Macaulay, "Mill's Essay on Government," *Edinburgh Review*, XLIX (March, 1829), 186–7.]

there be a proposition which comes more decidedly under the designation of a general rule respecting the motives which influence human actions? Can there be a more certain law in physics, and can there be one more fertile in practical consequences? The very term, efficacy of punishment, is only an abridged expression of this law of human nature; it implies a general rule respecting the motives which influence human actions, and a rule on which all mankind unhesitatingly and habitually proceed, both in national legislation and private management. (Pp. 16–18.)

He then shows, by copious examples, what it is strange should require to be exemplified in order to be understood—that a general proposition may be of the greatest practical moment, although not absolutely true without a single exception; and that in managing the affairs of great aggregations of human beings, we must adapt our rules to the nine hundred and ninety-nine cases, and not to the thousandth extraordinary case. " 'Tis certain," says Hume (in a remarkable passage quoted by our author), "that general principles, however intricate they may seem, must always, if they are just and sound, prevail in the general course of things, though they may fail in particular cases; and it is the chief business of philosophers to regard the general course of things. I may add, that it is also the chief business of politicians, especially in the domestic government of the state, when the public good, which is or ought to be their object, depends on the concurrence of a multitude of causes—not as in foreign politics, upon accidents and chances, and the caprices of a few persons."[*]

"The views of political reasoning here advocated," continues our author, "might be confirmed by an appeal to some of our ablest writers;" and among other apt quotations, he adds two from Burke, whom Conservatives of all denominations glorify as an oracle, because on one great occasion his prejudices coincided with theirs, but for whose authority they have not a shadow of respect when it tells against their vulgar errors.

Far [says our author] from regarding deductions from human nature as vain or frivolous, or leading to what are usually honoured by the designation of wild theories, he considers such deductions as opposed to speculative views, and as proceeding on experience. Thus, in his Letter to the Sheriffs of Bristol, speaking of the plan of pacification pursued in 1776, in reference to our colonies, he says, "That plan being built *on the nature of man*, and the circumstances and habits of the two countries, and not on any *visionary speculations*, perfectly answered its end."[†] And in his Speech on Economical Reform he tells the House, "I propose to economize by *principle*; that is, I propose to put affairs into that train, which

[*David Hume, "Of Commerce," in *Essays and Treatises on Several Subjects*, 2 vols. (London: Cadell, 1793), Vol. I, p. 251.]

[†Edmund Burke, "A Letter to John Farr and John Harris, Esqs. Sheriffs of the City of Bristol, on the Affairs of America," in *Works*, 8 vols. (London: Dodsley and Rivington, 1792–1827), Vol. II, p. 145.]

experience points out as the most effectual from the *nature of things,* and from *the constitution of the human mind.*"[*](Pp. 30–1.)

If principles of politics cannot be founded, as Burke says, "on the nature of man," on what can they be founded? On history? But is there a single fact in history which can be interpreted but by means of principles drawn from human nature? We will suppose your fact made out: the thing happened (we will admit) as you affirm it did; but who shall tell what produced it?— the only question you want answered. On this subject our author has some instructive remarks, which we regret that our limits do not permit us to quote, as well as to corroborate by some others which we think necessary to complete the analysis of the subject. It is well worthy to be treated in a separate article.

It may be interesting to collate with our author's refutation of the Edinburgh Reviewer, what the writer, who was the principal object of the reviewer's attack, has deemed it needful to say in his defence. This is to be found in pp. 277 to 292 of a recent volume, entitled *A Fragment on Mackintosh,*[†] where it is shown that the necessity of identification of interest between the rulers and the ruled, and the probability (amounting practically to certainty) that, in so far as that identification is incomplete, the rulers will pursue their separate interest, to the detriment of the ruled, has been recognised as the foundation of political wisdom by almost all its greatest masters, ancient and modern. Well may the writer exclaim—"It is mortifying to find one's self under the necessity of vindicating the wisdom of ages" against what he calls (not too severely) "pitiful objections."[‡]

*a*From *b*this*b* principle, of the necessity of identifying the interest of the government with that of the people, most of the practical maxims of a representative government are corollaries. All popular institutions are means towards rendering the identity of interest more complete. We say *more* complete, because (and this it is important to remark) perfectly complete it can never be. An approximation is all that is, in the nature of things, possible. By pushing to its utmost extent the accountability of governments to the people, you indeed take away from them the power of prosecuting their own interests at the expense of the people by force, but you leave to them the whole range and compass of fraud. An attorney is accountable to his

[*Edmund Burke, "Speech on . . . a plan for the better security of the independence of Parliament, and the oeconomical reformation of the Civil and other establishments," in *Works,* Vol. II, p. 217.]

[†James Mill, *A Fragment on Mackintosh* (London: Baldwin and Cradock, 1835).]

[‡*Ibid.,* pp. 288–9.]

*a–a*24 [*reprinted as first part of* "Appendix," *Dissertations and Discussions,* I, 467–70; below, pp. 648–50].
*b–b*59,67   the

client, and removable at his client's pleasure; but we should scarcely say that his interest is identical with that of his client. When the accountability is perfect, the interest of rulers approximates more and more to identity with that of the people, in proportion as the people are more enlightened. The identity would be perfect, only if the people were so wise, that it should no longer be practicable to employ deceit as an instrument of government: a point of advancement only one stage below that at which they could do without government altogether; at least, without force, and penal sanctions, not (of course) without guidance, and organized co-operation.

Identification of interest between the rulers and the ruled, being, therefore, in a literal sense, impossible to be realized, *c*must not*c* be spoken of as a condition which a government must absolutely fulfil; but as an end to be incessantly aimed at, and approximated to as nearly as circumstances render possible, and as is compatible with the regard due to other ends. For *d*the*d* identity of interest, even if it were wholly attainable, not being the sole requisite of good government, expediency may require that we should sacrifice some portion of it, or (to speak more precisely) content ourselves with a somewhat less approximation to it than might possibly be attainable, for the sake of some other end.

The only end, liable occasionally to conflict with that which we have been insisting on, and at all comparable to it in importance—the only other condition essential to good government—is this: That it be government by a select body, not by the *e*people*e* collectively: That political questions be not decided by an appeal, either direct or indirect, to the judgment or will of an uninstructed mass, whether of gentlemen or of clowns; but by the deliberately-formed opinions of a comparatively few, specially educated for the task. This is an element of good government which has existed, in a greater or less degree, in some aristocracies, though unhappily not in our own; and has been the cause of whatever reputation for prudent and skilful administration those governments have enjoyed. It has seldom been found in any aristocracies but those which were avowedly such. Aristocracies in the guise of monarchies (such as those of England and France) have very generally been aristocracies of idlers; while the others (such as Rome, Venice, and Holland) might partially be considered as aristocracies of experienced and laborious men. *f*But of all governments, ancient or modern*f*, the one by which this excellence is possessed in the most eminent degree is the government of Prussia—a *g*most*g* powerfully and *h*skilfully organized aristocracy of all*h* the most highly educated men in the kingdom. The British government in India partakes (with considerable modifications) of the same character.

*c-c*59,67	ought not to	*d-d*59,67	this
*e-e*59,67	public	*f-f*59,67	Of all modern governments, however
g-g—67		*h-h*59,67	strongly organized aristocracy of

Where this principle has been combined with other fortunate circumstances, and particularly (as in Prussia) with circumstances rendering the popularity of the government almost a necessary condition of its security, a very considerable degree of good government has occasionally been produced, *even* without any express accountability to the people. Such fortunate circumstances, however, are seldom to be reckoned upon. But though the principle of government by persons specially brought up to it will not suffice to produce good government, good government cannot be had without it; and the grand difficulty in politics will for a long time be, how best to conciliate the two great elements on which good government depends; to combine the greatest amount of the advantage derived from the independent judgment of a specially instructed *k*Few, with the greatest degree of the security for rectitude of purpose derived from rendering those Few responsible to the Many.

What is necessary, however, to make the two ends perfectly reconcilable, is a smaller matter than might at first sight be supposed. It is not necessary that the Many*k* should themselves be perfectly wise; it is sufficient, if they be duly sensible of the value of superior wisdom. It is sufficient if they be aware, that the majority of political questions turn upon considerations of which they, and all persons not trained for the purpose, must necessarily be very imperfect judges; and that their judgment must in general be exercised rather upon the characters and talents of the persons whom they appoint to decide these questions for them, than upon the questions themselves. They would then select as their representatives those whom the general voice of the instructed pointed out as the *most* instructed; and would retain them, so long as no symptom was manifested in their conduct of being under the influence of interests or of feelings at variance with the public welfare. This implies no greater wisdom in the people than the very ordinary wisdom, of knowing what things they are and are not sufficient judges of. If the bulk of any nation possess a fair share of this wisdom, the argument for universal suffrage, so far as respects that people, is irresistible: for, the experience of ages, and especially of all great national emergencies, bears out the assertion, that whenever the multitude are really alive to the necessity of superior intellect, they rarely fail to distinguish those who possess it.*a*

The opinions which we have been stating are substantially those of our author: from whose pages we now proceed to exemplify their application.

From the principle that the interest of the ruling body should be as closely as possible identified with that of the people, follow most of the conclusions respecting the constitution of the supreme legislature, which are commonly

*i-i*59,67   When
j-j—59,67
*k-k*59,67   few . . . few . . . many . . . many

contended for by the thorough reformers. Such are—first, that the utmost possible publicity should be given to the proceedings of parliament: secondly, that its members should be elected at stated periods: thirdly, that these periods should be short; sufficiently so, to render the sense of responsibility a perpetual, not an occasional feeling. Our author thinks, with most of the complete reformers, that three years are "the longest period consistent with a salutary sense of accountableness." (P. 203.) Fourthly, the votes at elections must be so taken, as to express the real sentiments of the electors, and not the sentiments merely of some person who has the means of bribing or of coercing them. This, where there are great inequalities of fortune, and where the majority of all classes but the richest are more or less in a dependent condition, requires that the votes be taken in secret. All these topics are handled in our author's best manner. We shall quote one passage from near the end of the discussion on the ballot; and should have extended our quotation, had not the subject been so recently and so fully treated by ourselves.[*] After replying to some of the common objections on the ballot, our author says—

The great opposition to secret voting does not, however, arise from the consideration of its being unmanly or un-English, or leading to insincerity and deception, but from a deeper source—from a feeling which many who entertain it perhaps would not avow even to themselves, although others make no scruple of publicly declaring it. The higher classes fear to commit the election of legislators to the genuine sentiments of the people. They have so long exercised a power over the community, by means of the brute force of rank and riches applied to the hopes and fears of those below them, that they have accustomed themselves to regard it as a salutary and even necessary control. It has relieved them too from a great part of the trouble of being intelligent, active, and virtuous. They have found it much easier to arrive at the office of legislator, by throwing away a few thousand pounds for a seat, or ejecting a few miserable tenants as a terror to the rest, than by winning affection through their virtues, or commanding esteem by their superior intelligence and well-directed activity. To men accustomed to domineer over the wills of their fellow-creatures, it is intolerably irksome to be reduced to the necessity of appealing to their understandings. Having been obliged to concede, nevertheless, a more popular system of representation, having been reduced to the necessity of ostensibly yielding the elective franchise to those who never before possessed it, they are unwilling to trust the real exercise of it to the parties on whom it is conferred by law. They consent to confide the privilege to a popular constituency, but only as instruments to receive a direction from a higher guidance. They cannot bear the idea for a moment of trusting the machinery to work by its own inherent power. They therefore oppose a system of voting which would snatch this domination out of their hands—which would really give to the people what the law professes to bestow upon them, which would effect what has never yet been effected in this country, that the issue of the elections should express the genuine sense of the constituent body. Here indeed

[*See James Mill, "The Ballot—A Dialogue," *London Review*, I (April, 1835), 201–53.]

would be an end to all the despotic sway of rank and riches; by this would be established the fatal necessity of combining them with moral and intellectual excellence: on this system there would be a lamentable predominance conferred on talents and virtues. Those therefore do perfectly right to oppose the ballot, who fear that it would annihilate that unjust influence in elections which they have hitherto enjoyed from mere wealth and station; who are apprehensive that to maintain themselves on the vantage-ground where they have been set down by fortune, they would have to task all their faculties: who recoil from the labour of thought, and shrink from the hardship of being useful. All those, in a word, who wish to retain any unfair domination over others in the business of elections, should rouse themselves to resist the adoption of the ballot, as utterly destructive of the object of their desires. (Pp. 296–8.)

We believe this to be a true picture of the feelings of at least the most powerful class among the enemies of popular institutions. Experience proves but too truly, that "to men accustomed to domineer over the wills of their fellow-creatures, it is intolerably irksome to be reduced to the necessity of appealing to their understandings." The hands which have ruled by force will not submit to rule by persuasion. A generation at least must elapse, before an aristocracy will consent to seek by fair means the power they have been used to exercise by foul. And yet, their portion of importance under popular institutions is no niggardly one, unless made so by their own perverseness. In every country where there are rich and poor, the administration of public affairs would, even under the most democratic constitution, be mainly in the hands of the rich; as has been the case in all the republics of the old world, ancient and modern. Not only have the wealthy and leisured classes ten times the means of acquiring personal influence, ten times the means of acquiring intellectual cultivation, which any other person can bring into competition with them; but the very jealousies, supposed to be characteristic of democracy, conspire to the same result. Men are more jealous of being commanded by their equals in fortune and condition, than by their superiors. Political power will generally be the rich man's privilege, as heretofore; but it will no longer be born with him, nor come to him, as heretofore, while he is asleep. He must not only resign all corrupt advantage from its possession, but he must pay the price for it of a life of labour. More than this: he must consent to associate with his poorer fellow-citizens, as if there existed between him and them something like human feelings, and must give over treating them as if they were a race to be kept coldly at a distance—a sort of beings connected with him by a less tie of sympathy than the brute animals of his household. Under really popular institutions, the higher classes must give up either this anti-social and inhuman feeling, or their political influence. Surely no good, hardly even any rational person, to whom the alternative was offered, would hesitate about the choice.

Is it not, then, a melancholy reflection, that in England (and in England, we believe, alone, among the great European nations) the youth of the aristocratic classes are even more intensely aristocratic than their fathers—more wedded to all that is most noxious in the privileges of their class—animated by a more violent hostility to those tendencies of their age, in accommodating themselves to which lies their sole chance of either being at ease in it, or exercising any beneficial influence over it? And how deeply ought this thought to impress upon us the necessity, the pressing and immediate necessity, of a radical reform in those institutions of education, which mould these youthful minds, and cherish, when they ought to counteract, the baneful influences exercised over them by the accident of their social position?

The question, Who should compose the constituency? is the next which presents itself. This is rather a more complicated question than any of the preceding, having to be decided by a compromise between conflicting considerations.

By making the members of the sovereign legislature elective, by sending them back to their constituents at short intervals, and by taking the votes in secret, we provide for the identity of their interest with that of the electors. But what if the interest of the electors differs from that of the community? We have then only an oligarchy of electors, instead of an oligarchy of senators. There is not the slightest reason for supposing that the former oligarchy will be less tenacious of its separate interest than the other, or less ready to sacrifice the public interest to it. Not only must the interest of the representatives be made, so far as possible, coincident with that of the electors, but the interest of the electors must be made coincident with the interest of the whole people.

If this principle were to be followed out, without limitation from any other principle, it would, we conceive, lead to universal suffrage. Imposing authorities, it is true, have held that a portion of the people may be found, much less than the whole, whose interest, so far as government is concerned, is identical with that of the whole. A portion might undoubtedly be found, less than the whole, whose interest would generally lie in good government, and only occasionally in bad. But complete identity of interest appears to us to be unattainable: (we are speaking, of course, as our argument requires, of *selfish* interest.)* The identity which is contended for cannot be identity

*Take, for instance, the strongest of all cases, and one in which nobody ever doubted the propriety of the exclusion—the case of children. Is it true that their interest is completely identical with that of their parents? Certainly not: the child is interested in being secured, in so far as security is attainable, against the parent's cruelty, the parent's caprice, the parent's weak indulgence, the parent's avarice, and, in at least nine cases out of ten, the parent's indolence and negligence, which disregards the child's good when in competition with the parent's ease. It may be said, that all these kinds of misconduct are inconsistent with the real

in all things, but only in those which properly fall within the province of government. The payers of wages, for instance, and the receivers, have opposite interests on the question of high or low wages; but as this is a question in which the interference of government cannot be really beneficial to either, the interest of both, so far as relates to the purposes of government, is (it may be contended) the same. Admitting, however (which is more than we are prepared to admit), that there exists no mode in which the middle classes could really benefit their selfish interests at the expense of the poorer class, by means of their exclusive possession of the government; still, when there is a real diversity of interest between two parties, although confined to matters with which law cannot beneficially interfere, and the powers of law are in the hands of one party, it is rarely that we do not witness some

---

happiness of the parent, and that the parent's interest, rightly understood, and the child's, are the same. And so also has it been said, that the true interest of kings is the same with that of their subjects. There is as much truth in the one doctrine as in the other. Both are true in a certain sense: both kings and parents would enjoy greater happiness on the whole, if they could learn to find it in the happiness of those under their charge. But this is a capacity seldom acquired after an early age; and those who have not acquired it, would not gain the pleasures of benevolence, even were they to forego those of selfishness. If a father be by character a bad and selfish man, it is not true that his happiness may not be promoted by tyrannizing over his children. We by no means seek to infer that parents in general treat their children no better than kings treat their subjects, or that there is not a far greater coincidence of interest. We only deny that the coincidence is anything like perfect. But if it be not perfect between parents and children, still less can it be so in any other case.

On this principle, our author characterizes the exclusion of women from the elective franchise as indefensible in principle, and standing on no better ground than any other arbitrary disqualification.

"The legitimate object of all government—namely, the happiness of the community—comprehends alike male and female, as alike susceptible of pain and pleasure; and the principle, that power will be uniformly exercised for the good of the parties subject to it, only when it is under their control, or the control of persons who have an identity of interests with themselves, is equally applicable in the case of both sexes. The exclusion of the female sex from the electoral privilege can therefore be consistently contended for only by showing two things; first, that their interests are so closely allied with those of the male sex, and allied in such a manner, as to render the two nearly identical; secondly, that the female sex are incompetent, from want of intelligence, to make a choice for their own good, and that, on this account, it would be to the advantage of the community, on the whole, to leave the selection of representatives to the stronger part of the human race, the disadvantages arising from any want of perfect identity of interests being more than compensated by the advantages of that superior discernment which the male sex would bring to the task. Let us examine, for a moment, the force of these allegations. The interests of the female sex are so far from being identified with those of the male sex, that the latter half of the human species have almost universally used their power to oppress the former. By the

attempt, well or ill advised, to make those powers instrumental to the peculiar purposes of the one party; and if these purposes are not thereby compassed, yet the interests of the other party often suffer exceedingly by the means used to compass them. Such, for example, were the laws against combinations of workmen;[*] and the laws which have existed at some periods of our history, fixing a maximum of wages. Nor is the evil annihilated although the excluded be a minority: the small number of the oppressed diminishes the profits of oppression, but does not always weaken the feelings which lead to it. Is the interest of the free blacks in the northern states of America the same with that of the whites? If so, why are they a kind of outcasts? So long, therefore, as any person capable of an independent will is excluded from the elective franchise, we cannot think that the evils of

---

present regulations of society, men wield over women, to a certain extent, irresponsible power; and one of the fundamental maxims on which representative government is founded is, that irresponsible power will be abused. The case before us presents no exception: the power of man over woman is constantly misemployed; and it may be doubted whether the relation of the sexes to each other will ever be placed on a just and proper footing, until they have both their share of control over the enactments of the legislature. If none of these regulations applied specifically to women as women, and to men as men, and to the circumstances arising from their peculiar connexion with each other, their interests might perhaps be considered as identified; but in the actual relative position in which by nature the sexes stand, and must always remain, as two parties marked by peculiar and indelible differences, separate interests cannot fail to grow up between them, and numerous laws must be directed to the regulation of their respective rights and duties. If the enactment of these laws concerning two parties who have distinct interests is solely under the control of one party, we know the consequence." (Pp. 236–8.)

If any exemplification be necessary of these last words, an obvious one may be found in the disgraceful state of the English law respecting the property of married women. If women had votes, could laws ever have existed by which a husband, who perhaps derives from his wife all he has, is entitled to the absolute and exclusive control of it the moment it comes into her hands? As to the other objection which our author anticipates, "incompetency from ignorance," (a strange objection in a country which has produced Queen Elizabeth,) of that ignorance the exclusion itself is the main cause. Was it to be expected that women should frequently feel any interest in acquiring a knowledge of politics, when they are pronounced by law incompetent to hold even the smallest political function, and when the opinion of the stronger sex discountenances their meddling with the subject, as a departure from their proper sphere?

Into the reasons of any other kind, which may be given for the exclusion of women, we shall not enter; not because we think any of them valid, but because the subject (though in a philosophical treatise on representation it could not have been passed over in silence) is not one which, in the present state of the public mind, could be made a topic of popular discussion with any prospect of practical advantage. [See "De Tocqueville on Democracy in America [I]," p. 55n below.]

[*See 39 & 40 George III, c. 106 (1800).]

misgovernment, in so far as liable to arise from a diversity of interest between the ruling body and the community, are entirely guarded against.

There are, however, other evils to be contended with, besides those arising from diversity of interest; and granting, that, by the exclusion of one class from the suffrage, something must be given up of the identity of interest between the constituency and the entire community, yet if some purpose of more than equivalent utility be attained by the sacrifice, it may still be advisable. And this, in our author's opinion, is the case. He proposes that a certain portion of identity of interest should be sacrificed, for the sake of obtaining a higher average degree of intelligence. That this is an object worth attaining at some cost, nobody will deny. A certain measure of intelligence in the electors is manifestly indispensable: a much larger measure would be eminently desirable; and if any test, even an approximative one, could be obtained of its existence, without trenching too much upon the identity of interest, the exclusion from the franchise of all who could not pass that test would add to the securities for good government. But when our author contends that such an approximative test may be found in the possession of a certain amount of property, we can only partially agree with him. It is but fair to quote the passage.

We must admit at once, that it [the possession of property] is a very inexact criterion [of knowledge;] and in regard to some classes, no criterion at all. It is not true that knowledge is in proportion to wealth. A man of 50,000*l.* a year would probably be found less intelligent and capable of discrimination than a man of 1000*l.* Great wealth relaxes the motives to exertion, and efficient knowledge is not to be attained without labour. Place a man in boundless affluence, and (to use a phrase of a masterly writer) you shelter and weather-fend him from the elements of experience.[*]

When, however, we descend lower in the scale, we find a different result. People who are raised above the necessity of manual toil can afford to cultivate their minds, and have time and motives for giving some attention to the acquisition of knowledge. One of the first effects of wealth on those who acquire it, is a desire to bestow a liberal education on their children, which of itself tends to maintain a superiority on the side of the rich. Knowledge, like many other things, is an article not readily acquired without pecuniary expense, nor yet without leisure; and, as a general rule, those who can afford to make the necessary outlay of time and money will have the greatest quantity of the commodity. Thus, people of two hundred a year will be found on the average to possess more extensive knowledge than people of fifty pounds a year, and the possessors of two thousand more than those of two hundred. Numerous exceptions to this rule will present themselves; but it is sufficient that it prevails on the whole, and affords the best criterion which we can obtain. If it holds on the whole, it will be practically useful. (Pp. 231–2.)

[*Samuel Taylor Coleridge, "Pitt," in James Gillman, *The Life of Samuel Taylor Coleridge*, 2 vols. (London: Pickering, 1838), Vol. I, p. 199.]

These propositions must, we think, be greatly qualified. They are true until we rise above the class which cannot read, or which never does read, and consequently takes no interest in political affairs; for though the intelligence of many people does not come to them by reading, the habit of applying that intelligence to public matters commonly does. But when, ascending in the scale, we reach a class which habitually reads, especially which reads newspapers, we suspect that we attain as high an average of intelligence as is to be found in any class not expressly bred and educated for some intellectual profession. We are speaking, of course, of England: in any country possessing a really national education, both for rich and poor, the case, we allow, would be different. But in this country, and at this time, between an average Birmingham gun-maker, an average London shopkeeper, and an average country gentleman, we suspect the differences of intelligence are more apparent than real. The land-holder, we find, has just as little foresight of the consequences of his actions; miscalculates as egregiously in his own conduct, both public and private; hates just as intensely all who, from however patriotic motives, set themselves against any of the things which he likes; despises as sincerely, under the name of theorists and visionaries, all who see farther than himself; is as incapable of feeling the force of any arguments which conflict with his own opinion of his immediate and direct interest. These are the tests of intelligence, and not the being able to repeat *Propria quœ maribus*.[*] If the bulk of our operative manufacturers are to be excluded from the suffrage, it must be, we suspect, on quite other grounds than inferiority of intelligence to those who are permitted to exercise it.

We have never been able to understand why, if the real object in excluding poverty were to exclude ignorance and vice, the test should not be applied to ignorance and vice directly, and not to something which is a mere presumption of their existence. It would be easy to exclude all who cannot read, write, and cipher. If a higher test be desirable, there would be no great difficulty in contriving it. If there were here (as there are in Prussia, and as there would be in every country where the good of the people was cared for) schools for all, under the superintendence of the state, the test might be a certificate from the teacher at the public or some other school, of having passed creditably through it. A test of morality would, in the present state of society, be not so easy to devise; something, however, might be done towards it. To have been seen drunk, during the year previous, might be a disqualification at the annual registry. To have received parish relief during

[*The rubric for the section on masculine nouns in traditional grammars. See, e.g., *An Introduction to the Latin Tongue* (Eton: Pote and Williams, 1806), p. 63.]

the same time, might be equally so. Conviction for any criminal offence might disqualify for a longer period, or for ever.

The most rational argument which we can conceive, for the exclusion of those who are called persons of no property, would be founded, not on inferiority of intellect, but on difference in apparent interest. All classes (it might be said) are in a most imperfect state of intelligence and knowledge; so much so, that they cannot be expected to be, and, as experience shows, hardly ever are, accessible to any views of their own ultimate interest which rest upon a train of reasoning. Since, then, it is certain that those who enjoy the franchise will exercise it in the manner dictated, not by their real and distant, but by their apparent and immediate interest, let us at least select, as the depositaries of power, those whose apparent and immediate interest is allied with the great principles on which society rests, the security of property, and the maintenance of the authority of law. These, we are sure, are safe in the hands of the possessors of property: an equal regard for them on the part of those without property would suppose a much higher degree of intelligence, since the latter benefit by them so much less obviously and directly, though not less really, than the former.

This places the question on a distinct and tangible issue; namely, whether the body of the operatives, or that portion of the body whom the rest follow, do in fact entertain opinions or feelings at variance with any of the primary principles of good government. This is a question not of argument, but of fact; and as such we think the question of universal suffrage ought always to be considered. That the prevalence of such mischievous opinions and feelings, and the difficulty of eradicating them where they exist, are vastly exaggerated, we have good reason to be assured: to what extent they really are entertained, we have no means of accurately knowing; and our belief is, that almost all persons of what are called the educated classes, if they have any opinion on the point, have it without evidence.

Happily there is no necessity for a speedy decision of the question. Many important things are yet to be done, before universal suffrage can even be brought seriously into discussion; and it will probably never be introduced, unless preceded by such improvements in popular education as will greatly weaken the apprehensions at present entertained of it. The middle classes, too, if freed from the coercive power of the rich, have an interest absolutely identical with that of the community on all the questions likely to engage much of the attention of parliament for many years to come; and no one is disposed to deny that we ought cautiously to feel our way, and watch well the consequences of each extension of the suffrage before venturing upon another. With a people like the English, whose feelings are not apt to be kindled by an abstract principle, but only by a practical grievance, very ordinary prudence would enable us to stop short at the point where good government is practically attained.

We return to the volume before us, from which we shall not again permit ourselves to stray so far.

Our author brings forward, with the prominence which justly belongs to them, several of the requisites of a well-constituted representative government, the importance of which is still far from being adequately felt. One is, that the supreme legislature should be relieved from the weight of purely local business which now oppresses it, by the establishment of subordinate representative assemblies.

Every district, [says he,] would not only send representatives to the supreme assembly, but have its own domestic legislature for provincial purposes; in which all matters relating to its roads, bridges, prisons, court-houses, and assessments, and other points concerning itself alone, might be determined. In England, at present, large sums are collected under the name of county rates, and expended (frequently with lavish profusion) under the control of the magistrates at quarter-sessions, who virtually do part of what is here assigned to a district assembly; while of the rest, some is neglected, and some is done in a hasty and slovenly manner by Parliament.

Such a district assembly would be the proper body to take cognizance of all projects for canals, rail-roads, gas-works, water-works, and other undertakings, which, on account of trespassing on private property, could not be executed without the authority of the law. Every one must see at a glance how great would be the relief to the national legislature, if all these minor matters were resigned to other bodies more competent to deal with them. *Nec deus intersit nisi dignus vindice nodus,*[*] should be the principle of the supreme assembly. It should rigorously abstain from doing what can be done as well or better without its interference, and direct its undivided energies to those points which involve the welfare of the whole empire, or which subordinate powers are incompetent to effect.

On all the subjects mentioned as the proper business of subordinate authorities, the supreme legislature might pass general regulations in strict accordance with the principle here maintained. It might enact, for instance, certain general provisions in regard to the making of canals; but whether a particular canal should be made between two towns in Yorkshire, might be left for Yorkshire itself to decide. The supreme legislature would also determine the objects and define the powers of the subordinate legislatures, and be the ultimate court of appeal in all cases of difference and difficulty amongst them.

It is evidently one of the worst possible arrangements, that the time of the supreme legislative assembly, which would find ample occupation in the preparation and perfecting of general enactments, should be taken up with matters of only local interest, and sometimes of merely individual concern; that it should be occupied with bills for changing names, alienating estates, supplying towns with water and lighting them by gas. While this continues to be the case, it is both morally and physically impossible there can be that degree of excellence in

[*Horace, *Ars Poetica*, in *Satires, Epistles, and Ars Poetica*. Ed. H. Rushton Fairclough (London: Heinemann; New York: Putnam's Sons, 1926), p. 466 (l. 191).]

legislation, which the present state of knowledge admits. It is a system which acts injuriously in both directions; a system on which neither enactments of a local nor those of a national kind can possibly be of the same beneficial character as if the preparation of them were devolved on separate assemblies. (Pp. 93–5.)

On this question, which has already occupied ourselves, and to which we shall return again and again, this is not the place to enlarge.

Another change for which our author earnestly contends, is a large reduction in the numbers of the House of Commons. This had already been advocated by Mr. Bulwer, in his *England and the English*, [*] and was one of the many points in which that valuable work was in advance of the public mind. "Large assemblies," our author justly observes [p. 161], "are unfit for deliberation;" and the immense consumption of the time of parliament, and neglect of the real business of the nation, which arises from the struggles of several hundred men, of few ideas and many words, to give their vocabulary an airing, is gradually forcing upon thinking persons the conviction, that, as our author proposes, the House should be reduced to one-half or one-third of its present numbers. A step, though but a small one, was made towards this important improvement by the first Reform Bill,[†] which broke in upon the magical number, 658; and it is to be regretted that the principle was given up, in deference to the most hypocritical clamour ever raised by Tories under the false pretence of zeal for popular rights. To diminish the number of the members of the House of Commons was treated as diminishing the amount of popular representation! As well might it be said, that the Spartans had twice as much government as we have, because they had two kings, while we have but one. Popular government does not consist in having the work done by more hands than are necessary to do it, but in having those hands, whether few or many, subject to popular control.

To the other strong reasons for reducing the numbers of the House, will sooner or later be added one of economy. We mean, of course, when the members are paid—a change to which we shall certainly come, and of which our author is a warm advocate:

This expedient, [says he,] seems to be required at all events, in order to secure the services of the ablest men, and to give the greatest intensity to the motives which impel the mind of the legislator to apply itself to the difficulties of the task, as well as to enhance the vigilance of the constituent body, by teaching them the value of his services, and of their own suffrages, in a way which the dullest amongst them can understand. Under such an arrangement, men of energetic and comprehensive minds, trained to vigorous personal and intellectual exertion, but who are obliged to devote themselves to pursuits yielding a profitable return, and are consequently at present either excluded from the legislature, or are mere

[*Edward Lytton Bulwer, *England and the English*. 2 vols. (London: Bentley, 1833).]
[†See 2 & 3 William IV, c. 45 (1832).]

cyphers in it, would be, with all their faculties, at the command of the public. Men of this description, so gifted, and so placed above private cares, would be invaluable; for instead of giving that lazy gentlemanly attention to public questions, which, in their own apprehension at least, is all that can be reasonably expected from unpaid representatives living in luxurious opulence; or that casual and intermitting, and brief attendance on their duties, which is all that professional practitioners can bestow, they would make their legislative functions the business of their lives. Strenuous intellectual exertion, except in the case of a few extraordinary minds to which it is a pleasure, as severe corporeal exercise is to a man of great muscular strength, is irksome, and seldom habitually undertaken without a powerful external motive. It is surely policy in a nation to furnish this motive for due application to national affairs. (Pp. 193–4.)

In nearly all ages and countries, popular governments have found it for their interest that all the functionaries whom they employ should be paid. The unpaid is apt to become the self-paid, and to cost dearest of all: his work, at the best, is *dilettante* work, and is put aside from the smallest call of business or pleasure. Moreover, an unpaid legislature and an unpaid magistracy are institutions essentially aristocratic: contrivances for keeping legislation and judicature in the hands exclusively of those who can afford to serve without pay. This in itself may seem but a small consideration: the important matter is not *by whom* we are governed, but *how*:—with due securities for their being properly qualified, we should not complain, although the whole legislature were composed of *millionnaires*. But those securities are themselves weakened, by narrowing the range of the people's choice. It is matter of general remark, how few able men have appeared of late years in parliament. What wonder? when, of the able men whom the country produces, nine-tenths at least are of the class who cannot serve without pay; and, for the first time since the constitution assumed its modern form, the members of the House of Commons are now practically unpaid. The rich have advantages in their leisure, and command of the means of instruction, which will render it easy for them, whenever they exert themselves, to be the ablest men in the community. That they do not take this trouble, is precisely because they are not exposed to the competition of the non-rich. Let in that competition upon them, if you would have them improve. In political, as in all other occupations, if you would stimulate exertion, you must throw open all monopolies.

If the members of the legislature were paid, legislation would become—what, to be well discharged, it must become—a profession: the study and the occupation of a laborious life. On this point our author's remarks are well worthy of an attentive perusal:

While the current of life flows on smoothly, the interest which each individual has in good government evidently makes little impression on his imagination: it consists, for the most part, of small fractions of benefit scarcely appreciable; of protection from evils, to which, as they are prevented from occurring, he is insensible; of advantages, which, to a superficial view, accrue to him only under particular circumstances, such as redress of wrong when he has occasion to appeal to the law. Most people are therefore supine and indifferent as to the general course of domestic policy, and especially indifferent as to the intellectual qualifications and conduct of their representatives. Their minds want awakening to the difficulty and importance of sound and accurate and systematic legislation. They may rest assured, that, in our complicated state of society, it is a business which requires as long and assiduous preparation as any profession which can be named; and as entire devotion to it, when its duties are once undertaken, as the calling of a lawyer or a physician, a merchant or an engineer. One chief reason why there are so many needless, blundering, crude, mischievous, and unintelligible enactments, is, that men have not dedicated themselves to legislation as a separate study or profession, but have considered it to be a business which might be played with in their hours of leisure from pursuits requiring intense exertion. (Pp. 186–7.)

Political science is perhaps that department of intellectual exertion which requires the greatest powers of mind, and the intensest application. Its facts are multifarious and complicated, often anomalous and contradictory, and demanding the guidance of clear principles: its principles are many of them abstruse, and to be developed only by long and close processes of reasoning; and the application of these principles requires the sagacity of quick observation and long experience. The whole business calls for that familiarity of mind with the subject, which can be the result of nothing but habitual daily devotion to it.

In making laws, too, not only is there a demand for powers of mind to cope with the disorder and complication of facts, and the abstruseness of reasoning, but there ought to be also a complete mastery of language, that nice and delicate instrument of thought and communication, by the clumsy handling of which so much confusion and uncertainty is yearly produced in legislative enactments. Every word in a law is of importance; every sentence ought to exhibit that perfectness of expression which is to be looked for only from the skill and caution of undistracted minds. Well might Bentham observe, that the words of a law ought to be weighed like diamonds.

Is this, then, a matter to be dealt with by an exhausted professional man in what should be his hours of recreation? Can such a one be competent to a task hard enough for the mind which comes to it every day with all its vigour fresh, all its perspicacity undimmed, its spirit of activity unworn, and its feelings of interest unabsorbed? Is the refuse of an individual's time and abilities what a people are to be content with, from a representative to whom they confide the determination of measures in which their prosperity is deeply implicated? Is this sufficient for governing the destinies of a great nation? (Pp. 184–6.)

Our author carries the practical application of this doctrine so far, as to propose (though, as he says, with some diffidence) that freedom from other business or professional avocation should be an indispensable qualification for being chosen a member of parliament. There is no doubt that it ought to be a strong recommendation, but we would not exact it by express law. It will occasionally happen, though, under a better system, much less often than at present, that half the time of one competitor is of more value than the whole time of another; and when the electoral body is rightly constituted, we know not why its choice should be fettered. We would not give power by handfuls with one hand, and take it back in spoonfuls with the other. If the people can be trusted at all, it is not in the estimation of these obvious grounds of disqualification that they are likely to be found deficient.* In the present state of society, the effect of the provision which our author desires to introduce would, we fear, be seriously mischievous: it would throw the whole business of legislation, and of control over the executive, into the hands of the idlers; excluding from parliament almost the only persons who bring habits of application and capacity for business into it. This objection, no doubt, would not exist, or at least not in the same degree, under the increased responsibility to the people which our author's argument contemplates.

Neither would we, with our author [p. 181], require as a legal qualification "maturity of years," beyond that which is now required. It will not, we suppose, be denied that a young man *may* render good service in Parliament; and if so, it may be that you have no other person who will render it as well. It might be proper enough to treat youth as a disqualification, if we were sure of finding old men suitable to our purpose: but considering the scarcity of fit men at any age, and the abundance of unfit men at all ages, we would not risk depriving ourselves of even one of the former for the sake of shutting out myriads of the latter. If your electors are likely persons to choose an unfit man, no sweeping rule of exclusion will prevent them from finding one. Nor do we see in so strong a light as our author the danger to be guarded against. It is not probable that, under any system but one of private nomination, very young men would ever compose any considerable proportion of the legislature: already the Reform Bill is understood to have excluded from the House most of the idle young men of family who formerly composed so large a portion of it: when, too, provincial assemblies, properly representative of the people, shall have been established, young men will serve their apprenticeship to public business there rather than in parliament. Those who

*In the impressive words of our author's argument on the ballot, "If the electoral body is not to be trusted, there must be something wrong in its composition; for if it is rightly constituted, the more faithfully the votes represent its sentiments the better: but on the supposition that it is wrongly constituted, the course of true policy is clear. The right way of correcting an evil is, if practicable, to remove its cause, and not to resort to some expedient for counteracting the mischief as it is continually evolved from its unmolested source. If the electoral body is composed of such unsuitable elements, that, if left to itself, the perpetual result would be the election of improper representatives, and consequent bad legislation, there cannot be a simpler or more effectual plan than altering the constitution of that body." (Pp. 281–2.)

are chosen in spite of so strong a ground of just prejudice, are likely to be among the ablest of their years; and, at least in an age of movement, it is not among young men that the greatest measure of political incapacity is usually found. It is true, as our author says, that "in legislation, as in other arts, there is a tact, a nicety of judgment, an intuitive apprehension of the relations of things, a wisdom which age, indeed, does not always bring, but which age alone can bestow." [P. 180.] But the young members will not be called upon to be the actual framers of laws: they will only assist in judging of them. The general spirit and direction of the proceedings of the House will be determined by that immense majority of its members who will always be persons of mature years; and it would not be altogether useless to counteract the apathy and prejudice of age by a small infusion even of the conceit and dogmatism of youth. Age is naturally conservative, and unless some weight be placed in the other scale, there will be danger lest the timid and sluggish should give too much of their character to the entire mass.

Our author strongly condemns the degrading practice of canvassing. In a healthy state of moral feeling, to solicit an elector would be deemed an exactly similar insult to that of soliciting a juror.

If the moral sentiments of the community had not been debased on this point by the long prevalence of a corrupt practice, they would feel that there was something not only degrading but ludicrous in the procedure of a candidate, who circulates himself from house to house for the purpose of soliciting votes from electors as so many gracious boons. On the supposition that the candidate happens to be really the best man for the office, it is asking them to have the condescension and kindness to consult their own interest out of pure favour to him. On the supposition that he is otherwise, it is craving them to be so exceedingly liberal and obliging as to disregard their own interest, and give a preference to his. In the one case, the request bears no mark of wisdom; in the other, none of modesty: in both cases, it is utterly inconsistent with manly independence.

It is true, that what is called canvassing does not necessarily assume this form. A candidate, when personally visiting the electors at their own homes, may limit himself to an explanation of his opinions, and to a proper and dignified exposition of his qualifications for the office, without stooping to the ludicrousness or servility of craving as a boon what ought to be either withheld, or given because it is the interest at once and the duty of the elector to give it. But even in this case, mark the inefficiency, the uselessness, of a personal visit; consider in what degree the candidate can set forth his pretensions in the few minutes which he can dedicate to the task of enlightening the minds of the individual electors on the subject of his merits and opinions. How degrading soever the procedure may be, there is some purpose answered by visiting a man, even for a few minutes, with the view of prevailing on him to give a promise; a few minutes may suffice for obtaining from him a yes or a no: but to devote to him only so brief a period, with the view of enabling him to form a judgment of the qualifications of the candidate, is a fruitless sacrifice of time and labour, for a purpose which can be effectually accomplished by public addresses. Of this folly few, it may be presumed, are guilty. The usual object of a personal canvass is to sway the will, not to guide or enlighten the judgment; and it must be admitted to produce in general a considerable effect. The more servile the candidate shows himself to be, the freer from scruples, from dignity, and self-respect, the fuller of artifices in adapting himself to the feelings and prejudices of the electors, so much the greater is his success likely to prove.

In every way in which the system of canvassing can be regarded, it is evil: there is nothing to recommend it; and if it prevails in any country where public sentiment does not promise to put it down, it perhaps might be put down with advantage by a legal prohibition. The experiment of prohibiting candidates and their friends from canvassing has been tried by some public charitable institutions in the election of their officers, and has proved decidedly beneficial in the few instances which have occurred since the adoption of the rule. (Pp. 305–8.)

We can add nothing to this masterly exposure.

Our author is no less decided in his condemnation of the practice of giving instructions to representatives, and of requiring pledges from candidates. We fully concur in his sentiments. The business of the constituency is to select as their representative the person best qualified, morally and intellectually, to form a sound judgment of his own on political questions; and having done this, they are not to require him to act according to *their* judgment, any more than they require a physician to prescribe for them according to their own notions of medicine.

Whenever we employ a man to do what his superior knowledge enables him to do better than ourselves, it is because the superiority of his knowledge, combined with his weaker disposition to promote our interest, will, on the whole, produce a better result than our inferior knowledge, coupled with our stronger disposition. So it is when we appoint a political deputy: we can obtain the benefit of his services only by encountering the risk of trusting him. The advantage we look for at his hands is incompatible with retaining the direction of his conduct. (P. 127.)

It is not, then, to the power of instructing their representative, that constituents are to look for an assurance that his efforts will be faithfully applied to the public service, for that would be inconsistent with the most enlightened legislation; but it is to the power of reducing him from the elevation to which their suffrages have raised him. What properly belongs to them is not a power of directing, but of checking; not a power of previous dictation, but a power of reward and punishment on a review of what he has done. The object to be obtained is not to compel the representative to decide agreeably to the opinions of his constituents, for that would be compelling him often to decide against his better judgment; but it is to force him to decide with a single view to the public good, and, at the same time, to obtain the full benefit of his intelligence. It is by leaving him unshackled with positive instructions, while he is subject to the ultimate tribunal of the opinion of his constituents, that the end in view is to be accomplished, of bringing into action, in the proceedings of the legislature, the greatest practicable quantity of intelligence, under the guidance of the purest disposition to promote the welfare of the community.

The relation between a representative and his constituents may be illustrated by a reference to the analogical relation which exists, and to which we have already slightly adverted, in the mutual circumstances of the physician and his patients. The security which patients have for the best application of the physician's skill does not arise from any ability of theirs to direct his practice, but from the circumstance of having in their own hands the power of choice. In the nature of the case they must place great confidence in his conduct, if they would obtain the benefit of his knowledge. When they select him, they are guided by such evidence as is within their reach respecting his qualifications. They may not always make the wisest choice; because, not being competent judges of the science, they must depend, in a great measure, on collateral facts, or evidence of an indirect character, and are sometimes swayed by irrelevant motives; but the power of selection and dismissal is the most effectual means of securing the best services of those whom they choose; and there can be little doubt that, on the system of each individual selecting his own medical attendant, and trusting to his discretion, patients fare better than on any other plan. And although they cannot antecedently judge of the medical treatment necessary in their case, nor direct the curative process, yet after recovery they can frequently form a tolerable estimate of the skill which has been evinced, and can always appreciate the care and attention of the practitioner; whence there are evidently strong inducements acting on his mind to please and benefit his patients. (Pp. 129–31.)

We consider this point, as we have intimated in a former passage, to be fundamental; and to constitute, in reality, the test whether a people be ripe for the sound exercise of the power of complete control over their governors, or not. The parallel holds exactly between the legislator and the physician. The people themselves, whether of the high or the low classes, are, or might be, sufficiently qualified to judge, by the evidence which might be brought before them, of the merits of different physicians, whether for the body politic or natural; but it is utterly impossible that they should be competent judges of different modes of treatment. They can tell that they are ill; and that is as much as can rationally be expected from them. Intellects specially educated for the task are necessary to discover and apply the remedy.

But though the principle that electors are to judge of men, and representatives of measures (as a king or a minister appoints a general, but does not instruct him when and how to fight) is of the very essence of a representative government, we cannot dissemble the fact, that it is a principle almost entirely inapplicable to the peculiar situation of this kingdom at the present moment. How can electors be required to repose in their representatives any trust which they can possibly withhold, when, for the purpose of purifying a political system which swarms with abuses, the circumstances of society oblige them to employ as their agents men of the very classes for whose benefit all abuses exist, and of whose disposition to reform any one particle of those abuses which it is possible to preserve they feel the most well-grounded doubts? Who can blame the exaction of pledges from such a man as the honorable member for St. Andrew's,[*] under the circumstances

[*Andrew Johnston.]

in which those pledges were exacted?* We assume, of course, that the constituency had not the option of electing a better man. If they had, they have themselves to blame for not making use of it. For, in the words of a passage quoted by our author from Roscommon's *Letters for the Press*—"When we have to employ our fellow-creatures in any office, we should in general act more wisely were we to choose those who possess qualities adapted to it, than were we to attempt to bend unsuitable qualities to our purposes, by the force of motives applied for the occasion."[*] "There is one general consideration," says our author, "which deserves to be urged on electors, in their choice of a representative: they must take the trouble to choose a fit man, and not expect a man to become fit for the situation by being placed in it." (P. 427.)

In the chapter "On the Introduction of Changes in Political Institutions," our author takes the opportunity of combating the celebrated doctrine of Lord Holland and Sir James Mackintosh, that "governments are not made, but grow."[†] This maxim was probably suggested by the numerous examples of political reformers whose institutions have been ephemeral, for want of having a sufficient hold upon the respect of the people to command steady obedience, or upon their affections, to be defended with any zeal against assault. But because governments, like other works of human contrivance, may be constructed with insufficient foresight and skill, does it follow that foresight and skill are utterly unavailing, and that no governments can hope for the support of the people's affections in times of civilization, but those produced by the fortuitous concourse of atoms in ages of barbarism? The doctrine is not only philosophically, but even historically false. The laws of Moses, those of Mahomet, were made, and did not grow: they had, it is true,

---

*The long duration of parliaments, which renders it impossible to discard an unfaithful representative when found out, is also an important consideration.

"A liberal confidence should be, and naturally will be, given to a faithful trustee, to execute the trust according to his own judgment; but if he has time to ruin you long before it is in your power to get rid of him, you will trust him with nothing that you can by possibility keep in your own hands. A man who is his own physician generally has a fool for his patient; but it is better that he prescribe for himself than obey a physician whom he believes to have been bribed by his heir." [J. S. Mill, "Pledges," *Examiner*, 1 July, 1832, p. 418.]

We quote this passage from the *Examiner* (1st July, 1832), which, with the fearlessness with which it has always thrown itself into the breach when what it deemed to be essentials of good government were assailed even by its own friends, has taken a most decided part in opposition to the exaction of pledges. See also a succeeding article, 15th of the same month. [J. S. Mill, "Pledges," *ibid.*, pp. 449–51.]

[*Francis Roscommon (pseud.), *Letters for the Press; on the Feelings, Passions, Manners, and Pursuits of Men* (London: Wilson, 1832), p. 82.]

[†See, e.g., Sir James Mackintosh, *The History of England*. 10 vols. (London: Longman, Rees, Orme, Brown, & Green, 1830–40), Vol. I, p. 72.]

the direct sanction of religious faith; but the laws of Lycurgus, the laws of Solon, were *made*, and were as durable as any laws which *grew* have hitherto been found. Those of Lycurgus, indeed, stand in history a *monumentum ære perennius*[*] of the practicability of Utopianism. Each of the North American colonies made a government: the whole of them confederated have also made a government—no bad example hitherto of adaptation to the wants of the people who live under it. Frederic of Prussia *made* a whole system of institutions, which still exists, and an excellent one. Bonaparte made another, which also in substance still exists, though an abominable one. All these governments, in so far as they have have had any stability, had it because they were adapted to the circumstances and wants of their age. That such adaptation can be made by preconceived and systematic design, every one of them is an example.

All that there is of truth in the favourite doctrine of Sir James Mackintosh amounts to a truism, which in theory has never been overlooked, howsoever in practice it may have been disregarded: That legislators and political reformers must understand their own age: That they must consider, not only what is best in itself, but what the people will bear; not only what laws to make, but how to make the people obey them: That they must forbear to establish any thing which, to make it work, requires the continued and strenuous support of the people themselves, unless, either in the ancient habits of the people, or at least in their durable and strenuous convictions, a principle exists which can be enlisted in favour of the new institution, and induce them to give it that hearty assistance without which it must speedily become inoperative. What has usually been wanting to the due observance of this maxim has been, not the recognition of it, but a sufficient practical sense, how great an element of stability that government wants which has not the authority of time:

*l*How*l* very much of the really wonderful acquiescence of mankind in any government which they find established is the effect of mere habit and imagination, and therefore depends upon the preservation of something like continuity of existence in the institutions, and identity in their outward forms; cannot transfer itself easily to new institutions, even though in themselves preferable; and is greatly shaken when there occurs anything like a break in the line of historical duration—anything which can be termed the end of the old constitution and the beginning of a new one. *m* The very fact that a certain set of political institutions already

[*Horace, "Carmina Liber III, xxx," in *Odes and Epodes* (Latin and English). Trans. C. E. Bennett (London: Heinemann; New York: Macmillan, 1914), p. 278 (l. 1).]

*l-l*33   He [Bentham] was not, I am persuaded, aware, how
*m*33   [*paragraph*] The constitutional writers of our own country, anterior to Mr. Bentham, had carried feelings of this kind to the height of a superstition; they never

exist, have long existed, and have become associated with all the historical recollections of a people, is in itself, as far as it goes, a property which adapts them to that people, and gives them a great advantage over any new institutions in obtaining that ready and willing resignation to what has once been decided by lawful authority, which alone renders possible those innumerable compromises between adverse interests and expectations, without which no government could be carried on *n* a year, and with difficulty even for a week.*

It is scarcely necessary to say that, in this country, and at this time, the danger is not lest such considerations as the above should have too little, but lest they should have too much, weight.

In the supplementary discourses of our author, on Political Equality, and on Rights, there are many just observations on the confusion which has been introduced into political reasoning by the use of vague and declamatory expressions as substitutes for a distinct appeal to the good of the community. Our author, however, while proposing to banish the words "natural rights" from philosophical discussion, makes an attempt, in which we do not think him quite successful, to discover a rational meaning for the phrase. Without doubt, as in the case of all other phrases which mankind use, there is something in their minds which they are endeavouring to express by it; but we hardly think that our author is looking for this in the right place. The subject, however, would lead us too far for the present occasion.

Having said so much of what the work before us does contain, we cannot conclude without drawing the author's attention to one thing which it should have contained and does not. He has met and overthrown many of the fallacies by which the delivering over of the powers of government to partial interests is wont to be defended; but he has nowhere directly faced the master fallacy of all, the theory of *class-representation*, though it is one which attacks the very foundation of his doctrines. The theory in question maintains, that a good popular representation should represent, not the people, but all the various *classes* or *interests* among the people. The landed interest, it is said, should be represented; the mercantile interest should be represented; the monied, manufacturing, shipping interests, the lawyers, the clergy—each of these bodies should command the election of a certain number of members of the legislature; and the bulk of the people, it is commonly added,

*[J. S. Mill, in] Bulwer's *England and the English*, App. [B] to Vol. II [pp. 342–3. Reprinted, "Remarks on Bentham's Philosophy," in *Collected Works*, Vol. X, p. 17].

considered what was best adapted to their own times, but only what had existed in former times, even in times that had long gone by. It is not very many years since such were the principal grounds on which parliamentary reform itself was defended. Mr. Bentham has done much service in discrediting, as he has done completely, this school of politicians, and exposing the absurd sacrifice of present ends to antiquated means; but he has, I think, himself fallen into a contrary error.

*n*33   for

should also have the nomination of a certain small number of representatives. The essence of this system is, that it proposes to place a small fraction only of the ruling body under any inducements from their position to consult the general interest of the community; while it renders all the remainder the mere attorneys of certain small knots and confederacies of men, each of which, the theory itself admits, has a private interest of its own, which sinister interest, if it possessed the undivided control of the legislature, it would ruthlessly pursue, to the complete sacrifice of the general interest. The expectation then is, that because the ruling power is divided among several of these knots, instead of being wholly bestowed upon one of them, they, instead of combining, as they have the strongest motives to do, and sharing the benefits of misrule among them, will, with an incapacity of pursuing their obvious interest, unknown to any tribe of savages, employ their whole exertions in protecting the community against one another. Whether this be likely to be the fact let English history speak; for England has been ruled by a class-representation ever since the revolution. We subjoin an apologue, from a speech delivered in 1826, which shadows forth very faithfully what has been the course of history in this particular.*

*"Once upon a time there happened an insurrection among the beasts. The little beasts grew tired of being eaten by the great ones. The goatish, sheepish, and swinish multitude grew weary of the sway of the 'intellectual and virtuous.' They demanded to be governed by equal laws, and, as a security for those laws, to have the protection of a representative government. The Lion, finding himself hard pressed, called together the aristocracy of the forest, and they jointly offered a rich reward to whoever could devise a scheme for extricating them from their embarrassment. The Fox offered himself, and his offer being accepted, went forth to the assembled multitude, and addressed them thus: 'You demand a representative government: nothing can be more reasonable—absolute monarchy is my abhorrence. But you must be just in your turn. It is not numbers that ought to be represented, but *interests*. The tigerish interest should be represented, the wolfish interest should be represented, all the other great interests of the country should be represented, and the great body of the beasts should be represented. Would you, because you are the majority, allow no class to be represented except yourselves? My royal master has an objection to anarchy, but he is no enemy to a rational and well-regulated freedom; if you forthwith submit, he grants you his gracious pardon and a class representation.' The people, delighted to have got the name of a representation, quietly dispersed, and writs were issued to the different interests to elect their representatives. The tigers chose six tigers, the panthers six panthers, the crocodiles six crocodiles, and the wolves six wolves. The remaining beasts, who were only allowed to choose six, chose by common consent six dogs. The Parliament was opened by a speech from the Lion, recommending unanimity. When this was concluded, the Jackal, who was Chancellor of the Exchequer, introduced the subject of the Civil List; and, after a panegyric on the royal virtues, proposed a grant, for the support of those virtues, of a million of sheep a-year. The proposition was received with acclamations from the ministerial benches. The Tiger, who was at that time in opposition, made an

The ready answer to the doctrine of representation of interests is, that representation of separate and sinister interests we do not want. The only interest which we wish to be consulted is the general interest, and that, therefore, is the only one which we desire to see represented. How this, in the actual circumstances of a country, can best be accomplished, is the only question; and it must be decided by the considerations already adduced.

What, in contradistinction to a representation of classes, every rational person does wish to see exemplified in Parliament, is not the interests, but the peculiar position, and opportunities of knowledge, of all the classes whom the theory enumerates, and many more; not in order that partial interests may, but in order that they may not, be consulted. The first desideratum is, to place every member of the legislature under the most complete responsibility to the community at large, which the state of civilization of the community renders consistent with other necessary ends. The second is, to compose the legislature, in as large a proportion as possible, of persons so highly cultivated, intellectually and morally, as to be free from narrow or partial views, and from any peculiar bias. But as such persons are rarely to be found in sufficient numbers, it is doubtless desirable that the remainder of the body should be of as miscellaneous a composition as possible (consistently with accountability to the people), in order that the twist of one person may be neutralized by the contrary twist of another; and if the individuals must be biassed, the evil be at least avoided of having them all biassed one way. An indistinct perception of this truth, is what gives all its plausibility to the doctrine of class-representation. But the principle thus stated, needs

---

eloquent speech, in which he enlarged upon the necessity of economy, inveighed against the profusion of ministers, and moved that his Majesty be humbly requested to content himself with half a million. The Dogs declared, that as kings must eat, they had no objection to his Majesty's devouring as many dead sheep as he pleased; but vehemently protested against his consuming any of their constituents alive. This remonstrance was received with a general howl. The first impulse of the representatives of the aristocracy was to fall tooth and nail upon the representatives of the people. The Lion, however, representing that such conduct would be dishonourable, and the Fox that it might provoke a renewal of the insurrection, they abandoned the intention of worrying these demagogues, and contented themselves with always outvoting them. The sequel may be guessed. The Lion got his million of sheep; the Fox his pension of a thousand geese a-year: the Panthers, Wolves, and the other members of the aristocracy, got as many kids and lambs, in a quiet way, as they could devour. Even the Dogs, finding resistance useless, solicited a share of the spoil; and when they were last heard of, they were gnawing the bones which the Lion had thrown to them from the relics of his royal table." [J. S. Mill, "On the British Constitution," speech in the London Debating Society, 19 May, 1826. Printed in H. J. Laski, ed., J. S. Mill, *Autobiography* (London: Oxford University Press, 1924), pp. 282-3.]

no especial provision to be made for it in a scheme of representation. The diversity of local circumstances, and the varying spirit of local constituencies, provide for it sufficiently.

Recommending this important subject to the consideration of our author in his next edition, we take leave of him; cordially wishing that his country may be enriched with many similar productions from his pen, and regretting that he has not yet obtained the opportunity he sought, of proclaiming in the House of Commons the great principles which this work will contribute so largely to diffuse. That he failed to obtain that opportunity is anything but creditable, all circumstances considered, to the electors of the great and important town for which he offered himself as a candidate. We trust that, ere long, some liberal constituency will claim for itself the honour which his own townsmen knew not how to appreciate.

DE TOCQUEVILLE ON DEMOCRACY IN AMERICA [I]

1835

EDITOR'S NOTE

London Review, I (Oct., 1835), 85–129 (equivalent to *Westminster Review*, XXX). Headed: "Art. IV. / De Tocqueville on Democracy in America. / 1. *De la Démocratie en Amérique*. Par Alexis de Tocqueville, / Avocat à la Cour Royal de Paris; l'un des auteurs du livre / intitulé *Du Systême Pénitentiaire aux Etats-Unis*. Orné / d'une Carte d'Amérique. [Paris: Gosselin,] 1835. 8vo. 2 vols. 2nd edition. / 2. *Democracy in America*. By Alexis de Tocqueville, Avocat / à la Cour Royale de Paris, &c. &c. Translated by Henry / Reeve, Esq. In 2 vols. Vol. I. [London:] Saunders and Otley. 1835." Signed "A." Running title: "De Tocqueville on Democracy in America." Republished in part as second portion of "Appendix," *Dissertations and Discussions*, I, 470–4, and in part in "De Tocqueville on Democracy in America [II]," *ibid.*, II, 34–5 (see 650–3 and 174–5 below). Identified in JSM's bibliography as "A review of De Tocqueville's 'Democracy in America' in the third number of the London Review (October 1835.)" (MacMinn, 45.) The copy of the article in the Somerville College Library has no corrections or emendations. Also in Somerville, without corrections or emendations. is a sewn, uncut offprint, paged 1–45, signed "A."

For a discussion of the composition of this article, and JSM's relations with Tocqueville, see the Textual Introduction, lxxii–lxxiv above.

The republication of part of the review (71–74n) as the concluding portion of "Appendix," *D&D*, I, 470–4, led to some rewriting, as did the incorporation of parts of the review (see 78–9) in the final version of "De Tocqueville on Democracy in America [II]" in *D&D*, II. In the variant notes, "59" indicates *D&D*, I, 1st ed., 1859; "67" indicates *D&D*, 2nd ed., 1867.

References to both the original and to the Reeve translation are given for quotations from Vol. I of Tocqueville; for those from Vol. II, there are references only to the original, as evidently the second volume of Reeve was not available to JSM at the time.

De Tocqueville on Democracy in America [I]

"AMONGST THE NOVEL OBJECTS," says M. de Tocqueville* in the opening of his work,

that attracted my attention during my stay in the United States, nothing struck me more forcibly than the general equality of conditions. I readily discovered the prodigious influence which this primary fact exercises on the whole course of society: it gives a certain direction to public opinion, and a certain character to the laws; it imparts new maxims to the governing powers, and peculiar habits to the governed. I speedily perceived that the influence of this fact extends far beyond the political character and the laws of the country, and that it has no less empire over private society than over the government: it creates opinions, engenders sentiments, suggests the ordinary practices of life, and modifies whatever it does not produce.

The more I advanced in the study of American society, the more I perceived that the equality of conditions was the fundamental fact from which all others seemed to be derived, and the central point at which all my observations constantly terminated. I then turned my thoughts to our own hemisphere, and imagined that I discerned there also something analogous to the spectacle which the New World presented to me. I observed that the equality of conditions, though it has not yet reached, as in the United States, its extreme limits, is daily progressing towards them; and that the democracy which governs the American communities appears to be rapidly rising into power in Europe. From that moment I conceived the idea of the book which is now before the reader.[*]

To depict accurately, and to estimate justly, the institutions of the United States, have been therefore but secondary aims with the original and profound author of these volumes—secondary, we mean, in themselves, but indispensable to his main object. This object was, to inquire, what light is thrown, by the example of America, upon the question of democracy; which he considers as the great and paramount question of our age.

In turning to America for materials with which to discuss that question, M. de Tocqueville, it needs hardly be remarked, is not singular. All who write

*In our extracts we follow, as far as possible, Mr. Reeve's translation. We have used, however, very freely, the privilege of alteration, when, even at the expense of elegance, we deemed it possible to render the meaning more intelligible, or to keep closer than Mr. Reeve has done to the spirit of the original.

[*Reeve, Vol. I, pp. xiii–xiv; Tocqueville, I, pp. 3–4.]

or speak on either side of the dispute, are prompt enough in pressing America into their service: but it is for purposes, in general, quite different from that of M. de Tocqueville.

America is usually cited by the two great parties which divide Europe, as an argument for or against democracy. Democrats have sought to prove by it that we ought to be democrats; aristocrats, that we should cleave to aristocracy, and withstand the democratic spirit.

It is not towards deciding this question, that M. de Tocqueville has sought to contribute, by laying before the European world the results of his study of America. He considers it as already irrevocably decided.

The crowd of English politicians, whether public men or public writers, who live in a truly insular ignorance of the great movement of European ideas, will be astonished to find, that a conclusion which but few among them, in their most far-reaching speculations, have yet arrived at, is the point from which the foremost continental thinkers *begin* theirs; and that a philosopher, whose impartiality as between aristocracy and democracy is unparalleled in our time, considers it an established truth, on the proof of which it is no longer necessary to insist, that the progress of democracy neither can nor ought to be stopped. Not to determine whether democracy shall come, but how to make the best of it when it does come, is the scope of M. de Tocqueville's speculations.

That comprehensive survey of the series of changes composing the history of our race, which is now familiar to every continental writer with any pretensions to philosophy, has taught to M. de Tocqueville, that the movement towards democracy dates from the dawn of modern civilization, and has continued steadily advancing from that time. Eight centuries ago, society was divided into barons and serfs: the barons being everything, the serfs nothing. At every succeeding epoch this inequality of condition is found to have somewhat abated; every century has done something considerable towards lowering the powerful and raising the low. Every step in civilization —every victory of intellect—every advancement in wealth—has multiplied the resources of the many; while the same causes, by their indirect agency, have frittered away the strength and relaxed the energy of the few. We now find ourselves in a condition of society which, compared with that whence we have emerged, might be termed equality; yet not only are the same levelling influences still at work, but their force is vastly augmented by new elements which the world never before saw. For the first time, the power and the habit of reading begins to permeate the hitherto inert mass. Reading is power: not only because it is knowledge, but still more because it is a means of communication—because, by the aid of it, not only do opinions and feelings spread to the multitude, but every individual who holds them knows that they are held by the multitude; which of itself suffices, if they continue to be held, to ensure their speedy predominance. The many, for the first time, have now learned the lesson, which, once learned, is never forgotten—that their strength, when they choose to exert it, is invincible. And, for the first time, they have learned to unite for their own objects, without waiting for any section of the aristocracy to place itself at their head. The capacity of co-operation for a common purpose, heretofore a monopolized instrument of power in the hands of the higher classes, is now a most formidable one in those of the lowest. Under these influences it is not surprising that society makes greater strides in ten years, towards the levelling of inequalities, than lately in a century, or formerly in three or four.

M. de Tocqueville is unable to imagine that a progress, which has continued with uninterrupted steadiness for so many centuries, can be stayed now. He assumes that it will continue, until all artificial inequalities shall have disappeared from among mankind; those inequalities only remaining which are the natural and inevitable effects of the protection of property. This appears to him a tremendous fact, pregnant with every conceivable possibility of evil, but also with immense possibilities of good: leaving, in fact, only the alternative of democracy or despotism; and unless the one be practicable, the other, he is deliberately convinced, will be our lot.

The contemplation of the entirely new position into which mankind are entering, and of their supine insensibility to the new exigencies of that new position, fills our author with solemn and anxious emotions. We invite the attention of English readers to a long and deeply interesting passage from his introductory chapter, as a specimen of a mode of thinking concerning the great changes now in progress, which will be new to many of them:

The Christian nations of our age seem to me to present a fearful spectacle; the impulse which is bearing them forward is so strong that it cannot be stopped, but it is not yet so rapid that it cannot be guided: their fate is in their own hands; yet a little while, and it may be so no longer.

The first duty which is at this time imposed upon those who direct our affairs is to educate the democracy; to reanimate its faith, if that be possible; to purify its morals; to regulate its energies; to substitute for its inexperience a knowledge of business, and for its blind instincts an acquaintance with its true interests; to adapt its government to time and place, and to modify it in compliance with circumstances and characters.

A new science of politics is indispensable to a world which has become new. This, however, is what we think of least; launched in the middle of a rapid stream, we obstinately fix our eyes on the ruins which may still be descried upon the shore we have left, whilst the current sweeps us along, and drives us toward an unseen abyss.

In no country in Europe has the great social revolution which I have been describing made such rapid progress as in France; but it has always been borne on by chance. The heads of the State have never thought of making any preparation for it, and its victories have been obtained in spite of their resistance, or without their knowledge. The most powerful, the most intelligent, and the most moral classes of the nation have never attempted to connect themselves with it in order to guide it. Democracy has consequently been abandoned to its untutored instincts, and it has grown up like those outcasts who receive their education in the public streets, and who are unacquainted with aught of society but its vices and its miseries. The existence of a democracy was seemingly unknown, when on a sudden it took possession of the supreme power. Everything then servilely submitted to its smallest wish; it was worshipped as the idol of strength; until, when it was enfeebled by its own excesses, the legislator conceived the rash project of annihilating it, instead of instructing it and correcting its bad tendencies. No attempt was made to fit it to govern; the sole thought was of excluding it from the government.

The consequence of this has been, that the democratic revolution has been effected only in the *material* parts of society, without that concomitant change in laws, ideas, habits, and manners which was necessary to render such a revolution beneficial. We have gotten a democracy, severed from whatever would lessen its vices and render its natural advantages more prominent; and although we already perceive the evils it brings, we are yet ignorant of the benefits it might confer. (Reeve, Vol. I, pp. xxii–xxiv; Tocqueville, Vol. I, pp. 10–12.)

M. de Tocqueville then rises into the following powerful delineation of the state of society which has passed never to return, and of the happier, though, in his opinion, less brilliant state, to which we ought now to aspire: of the good which democracy takes away, and of that which, if its natural capabilities are improved, it may bring.

While the power of the Crown, supported by the aristocracy, peaceably governed the nations of Europe, society possessed, in the midst of its wretchedness, several advantages which cannot easily be appreciated or conceived in our times.

The power of a part of his subjects set insurmountable barriers to the tyranny of the prince; and the monarch, who felt the almost divine character which he enjoyed in the eyes of the multitude, derived from the respect which he inspired. a motive for the just use of his power.

Although lifted so high above the people, the nobles, nevertheless, took that calm and kindly interest in its fate which the shepherd feels towards his flock; and without acknowledging the poor man as their equal, they watched over his destiny as a trust which Providence had confided to their care.

The people, never having conceived the idea of a state of society different from their own, and entertaining no expectation of ever becoming the rivals of their chiefs, accepted their benefits without discussing their rights. They felt attached to them when they were clement and just, and submitted without resistance or servility to their oppressions, as to inevitable visitations of the arm of God. Usages and manners had, moreover, created a species of law in the midst of violence, and established certain limits to oppression.

As the noble never suspected that any one would attempt to deprive him of privileges which he believed to be legitimate, and as the serf looked upon his own inferiority as a consequence of the immutable order of nature, it is easy to imagine that a sort of mutual good-will might arise between two classes so differently favoured by fate. Inequality and wretchedness were then to be found in society; but the souls of neither rank of men were degraded.

It is not by the exercise of power or by the habit of obedience that men are debased; it is by the exercise of a power which they believe to be illegitimate, and by obedience to a rule which they consider to be usurped and unjust.

On one side were wealth, strength, and leisure, accompanied by the refinements of luxury, the elegances of taste, the pleasures of intellect, and the culture of art. On the other were labour, rudeness, and ignorance; but in the midst of this coarse and ignorant multitude, it was not uncommon to meet with energetic passions, generous sentiments, profound religious convictions, and wild virtues. Society thus organized might possess stability, power, and, above all, glory.

But the scene is now changed, and gradually the two ranks mingle; the barriers which once severed mankind are lowered; properties are broken down, power is subdivided, the light of intelligence spreads, and the capacities of all classes are more equally cultivated; the state of society becomes democratic, and the empire of democracy is slowly and peaceably introduced into institutions and manners.

I can now conceive a society in which all, regarding the law as emanating from themselves, would give it their attachment and their ready submission; in which the authority of the State would be respected as necessary, though not as divine; and the loyalty of the subject to the chief magistrate would not be a passion, but a quiet and rational persuasion. Every individual being in the possession of rights, and feeling secure of retaining them, a kind of manly reliance and reciprocal courtesy would arise between all classes, alike removed from pride and meanness.

The people, well acquainted with their true interests, would allow, that, in order to profit by the advantages of society, it is necessary to submit to its burthens. In this state of things, the voluntary association of the citizens might supply the place of the individual power of the nobles, and the community would be alike protected from anarchy and from oppression.

I admit that, in a democratic state thus constituted, society will not be stationary; but the impulses of the social body may be duly regulated, and directed towards improvement. If there be less splendour than in the halls of an aristocracy, the contrast of misery will be less frequent also; enjoyments may be less intense, but comfort will be more general; the sciences may be less highly cultivated, but ignorance will be less common; the impetuosity of the feelings will be repressed, and the habits of the nation softened; there will be more vices, and fewer crimes.

In the absence of enthusiasm and of an ardent faith, great sacrifices may be obtained from the members of such a commonwealth by an appeal to their understandings and their experience. Each individual, being equally weak, will feel an equal necessity for uniting with his fellow-citizens; and as he knows that he can obtain their good offices only by giving his, he will readily perceive that his personal interest is identified with the interest of the community.

The nation, taken as a whole, will be less brilliant, less glorious, and perhaps less powerful; but the majority of the citizens will enjoy a greater degree of prosperity: and the people will remain quiet, not because they despair of being better, but because they know that they are well.

If all the consequences of this state of things were not good or useful, society would at least have appropriated all such of them as were so; and having once and for ever renounced the social advantages of aristocracy, mankind would enter into possession of all the benefits which democracy can afford. (Reeve, Vol. I, pp. xxiv–xxviii; Tocqueville, Vol. I, pp. 12–15.)

In the picture which follows, the author has had chiefly in view the state of France; and much of it would be grossly exaggerated as a description of

England: but we may receive it as a warning of what we may in time expect, if our influential classes continue to forego the exercise of the faculty which distinguishes rational creatures from brutes, and either blindly resist the course of events, or allow them to rush on wildly without any aid from human foresight:

But we—what have we adopted in the place of those institutions, those ideas, and those customs of our forefathers which we have abandoned? The spell of royalty is broken, but it has not been succeeded by the majesty of the laws; the people have learned to despise all authority, but fear now extorts a larger tribute of obedience than that which was formerly paid by reverence and by love.

I perceive that we have destroyed those independent existences which were able to cope with tyranny single-handed: but the government has alone inherited the privileges of which families, corporations, and individuals have been deprived: to the strength, sometimes oppressive, but often conservative, of a few, has succeeded the weakness of all.

The division of property has lessened the distance which separated the rich from the poor; but the nearer they draw to each other, the greater seems their mutual hatred, and the more vehement the envy and the dread with which they resist each other's claims to power; the notion of right is alike a stranger to both classes, and force is, in the eyes of both, the only argument for the present, and the only resource for the future.

The poor man retains the prejudices of his forefathers without their faith, and their ignorance without their virtues; he has adopted the doctrine of self-interest as the rule of his actions, without having acquired the knowledge which enlightens it, and his selfishness is no less blind than his devotedness was formerly.

If society is tranquil, it is not because it is conscious of its strength and of its well-being, but, on the contrary, because it believes itself weak and infirm, and fears that a single effort may cost it its life. Everybody feels the evil, but no one has courage or energy enough to seek the cure; the desires, the regrets, the sorrows, and the joys of the time produce no visible or permanent fruits.

We have, then, abandoned whatever advantages the old state of things afforded, without receiving the compensations naturally belonging to our present condition; we have destroyed an aristocratic society, and we seem inclined to survey its ruins with complacency, and to fix our abode in the midst of them. (Reeve, Vol. I, pp. xxviii–xxx; Tocqueville, Vol. I, pp. 15–17.)

In quoting so much of this striking passage, we would not be understood as adopting the whole and every part of it, as the expression of our own sentiments. The good which mankind have lost, is coloured, we think, rather too highly, and the evils of the present state of transition too darkly; and we think, also, that more than our author seems to believe, of what was good in the influences of aristocracy, is compatible, if we really wish to find it so, with a well-regulated democracy. But though we would soften the colours of the picture, we would not alter them; M. de Tocqueville's is, in our eyes, the true view of the position in which mankind now stand: and on the timely recognition of it as such, by the influential classes of our own and other countries, we believe the most important interests of our race to be greatly dependent.

It is under the influence of such views that M. de Tocqueville has examined the state of society in America.

There is a country, says he, where the great change, progressively taking place throughout the civilized world, is consummated. In the United States, democracy reigns with undisputed empire; and equality of condition among mankind has reached what seems its ultimate limit.* The place in which to

*In quoting the assertions that the democratic principle is carried out in America to its utmost length, and that equality of condition among mankind has there reached its ultimate limit, we cannot refrain from observing (though the remark is foreign to the specific purpose of the present Article) that both these propositions, though true in our author's sense, and so far as is necessary for his purpose, must, in another sense, be received with considerable limitations. We do not allude merely to the exclusion of paupers and menial servants, or to the existence, in many States, of a property qualification for electors, because the qualification probably in no case exceeds the means of a large majority of the free citizens. We allude, in the first place, to the slaves; and not only to them, but to all free persons having the slightest admixture of negro blood, who are ruthlessly excluded, in some States by law, and in the remainder by actual bodily fear, from the exercise of any the smallest political right. As for social equality, it may be judged how far they are in possession of it, when no white person will sit at the same table with them, or on the same bench in a public room, and when there is scarcely any lucrative occupation open to them except that of domestic servants, which in that country the white race do not relish. It is scarcely necessary to add, that in America as elsewhere, one entire half of the human race is wholly excluded from the political equality so much boasted of, and that in point of social equality their position is still more dependent than in Europe. In the American democracy, the aristocracy of skin, and the aristocracy of sex, retain their privileges.

While we are on the subject of the aristocracy of sex, we will take the opportunity of correcting an error of expression in a recent article (Review of the *Rationale of Representation*, p. 353, note [see 29n above]), which having conveyed to an otherwise friendly critic (the editor of the *Monthly Repository*) an erroneous notion of our meaning, has drawn upon us from him a reproof, which we should have deserved if we had really meant what we unguardedly said. [See [William Johnson Fox,] "*The London Review*. No. II," *Monthly Repository*, n.s. IX (Sept., 1835), 627–8.] After expressing our concurrence with the author of the *Rationale*, in the opinion that there was no ground for the exclusion of women, any more than of men, from a voice in the election of those on whose fiat the whole destinies of both may depend, we declined entering further into the subject at that time, as not being one "which, in the present state of the public mind, could be made a topic of popular discussion with any prospect of practical advantage." Now, all we meant to say was (although we did not express it correctly), that we saw no practical advantage in discussing the mere *political* question apart from the social question, and discussing it *as* a political question, in the heart of a dissertation devoted wholly to politics: whereby the claim made in behalf of women would be left apparently resting upon a bare abstract principle, and would be divested of all the advantages which it derives from being considered as part of a far more comprehensive question—that of the whole position of women in modern society. That position appears to us, both in idea and in practice, to be radically and essentially wrong; nor can we conceive any

study democracy, must be that where its natural tendencies have the freest scope; where all its peculiarities are most fully developed and most visible. In America, therefore, if anywhere, we may expect to learn—first, what portion of human well-being is compatible with democracy in any form; and, next, what are the good and what the bad properties of democracy, and by what means the former may be strengthened, the latter controlled. We have it not in our power to choose between democracy and aristocracy; necessity and Providence have decided that for us. But the choice we are still called upon to make is between a well and an ill-regulated democracy; and on that depends the future well-being of the human race.

When M. de Tocqueville says, that he studied America, not in order to disparage or to vindicate democracy, but in order to understand it, he makes no false claim to impartiality. Not a trace of a prejudice, or so much as a previous leaning either to the side of democracy or aristocracy, shows itself in his work. He is indeed anything but indifferent to the ends, to which all forms of government profess to be means. He manifests the deepest and steadiest concern for all the great interests, material and spiritual, of the human race. But between aristocracy and democracy he holds the balance straight, with all the impassibility of a mere scientific observer. He was indeed most favourably placed for looking upon both sides of that great contest with an unbiassed judgment; for the impressions of his early education were royalist, while among the influences of society and the age liberalism is predominant. He has renounced the impressions of his youth, but he looks back to them with no aversion. It is indifferent to him what value we set upon the good or evil of aristocracy, since that in his view is past and gone. The good and evil of democracy, be they what they may, are what we must now look to; and for us the questions are, how to make the best of democracy, and what that best amounts to.

We have stated the purposes of M. de Tocqueville's examination of America. We have now to add its result.

The conclusion at which he has arrived is, that this irresistible current, which cannot be stemmed, may be guided, and guided to a happy termination.

---

greater abuse of social arrangements than that of regularly educating an entire half of the species for a position of systematic dependence and compulsory inferiority. But we never could have meant that the faulty social position and consequent bad education of women, cannot be usefully discussed in the present state of the public mind; on the contrary, we know of no question of equal importance which the time is more completely come for thoroughly discussing.

Among many indications which we could give of an improved tone of feeling and thinking on this subject, we would point to a late pamphlet, evidently by a man's hand, entitled, *Thoughts on the Ladies of the Aristocracy, by Lydia Tomkins* [London: Hodgsons, 1835].

The bad tendencies of democracy, in his opinion, admit of being mitigated; its good tendencies of being so strengthened as to be more than a compensation for the bad. It is his belief that a government, substantially a democracy, but constructed with the necessary precautions, may subsist in Europe, may be stable and durable, and may secure to the aggregate of the human beings living under it, a greater sum of happiness than has ever yet been enjoyed by any people. The universal aim, therefore, should be, so to prepare the way for democracy, that when it comes, it may come in this beneficial shape; not only for the sake of the good we have to expect from it, but because it is literally our only refuge from a despotism resembling not the tempered and regulated absolutism of modern times, but the tyranny of the Cæsars. For when the equality of conditions shall have reached the point which in America it has already attained, and there shall be no power intermediate between the monarch and the multitude; when there remains no individual and no class capable of separately offering any serious obstacle to the will of the government; then, unless the people are fit to rule, the monarch will be as perfectly autocratic as amidst the equality of an Asiatic despotism. Where all are equal, all must be alike free, or alike slaves.

The book, of which we have now described the plan and purpose, has been executed in a manner worthy of so noble a scheme. It has at once taken its rank among the most remarkable productions of our time; and is a book with which, both for its facts and its speculations, all who would understand, or who are called upon to exercise influence over their age, are bound to be familiar. It will contribute to give to the political speculations of our time a new character. Hitherto, aristocracy and democracy have been looked at chiefly in the mass, and applauded as good, or censured as bad, on the whole. But the time is now come for a narrower inspection, and a more discriminating judgment. M. de Tocqueville, among the first, has set the example of analysing democracy; of distinguishing one of its features, one of its tendencies, from another; of showing which of these tendencies is good, and which bad, in itself; how far each is necessarily connected with the rest, and to what extent any of them may be counteracted or modified, either by accident or foresight. He does this, with so noble a field as a great nation to demonstrate upon; which field he has commenced by minutely examining; selecting, with a discernment of which we have had no previous example, the material facts, and surveying these by the light of principles, drawn from no ordinary knowledge of human nature. We do not think his conclusions always just, but we think them always entitled to the most respectful attention, and never destitute of at least a large foundation of truth. The author's mind, except that it is of a soberer character, seems to us to resemble Montesquieu most among the great French writers. The book is such as Montesquieu might have written, if to his genius he had superadded good sense, and the lights which mankind have since gained from the experiences of a period in which they may be said to have lived centuries in fifty years.

We feel how impossible it is, in the space of an article, to exemplify all the features of a work, every page of which has nearly as great a claim to citation as any other. For M. de Tocqueville's ideas do not float thinly upon a sea of words; none of his propositions are unmeaning, none of his meanings superfluous; not a paragraph could have been omitted without diminishing the value of the work. We must endeavour to make a selection.

The first volume, the only one of which a translation has yet appeared, describes chiefly the institutions of the United States: the second, the state of society, which he represents to be the fruit of those institutions. We should have been glad to assume that the reader possessed a general acquaintance with the subject of the former volume, and to refer him, for details, to the work itself. But it so happens that in no one point has M. de Tocqueville rendered a greater service to the European public, than by actually giving them their first information of the very existence of some of the most important parts of the American constitution. We allude particularly to the municipal institutions; which, as our author shows, and as might have been expected, are the very fountain-head of American democracy, and one principal cause of all that is valuable in its influences; but of which English travellers, a race who have eyes and see not, ears and hear not,[*] have not so much as perceived the existence.

In the New England States, the part of the Union in which the municipal system which generally prevails through the whole, has been brought to the greatest perfection, the following are its leading principles. The country is parcelled out into districts called townships, containing, on an average, from two to three thousand inhabitants. Each township manages its local concerns within itself; judicial business excepted, which, more wisely than their English brethren, the Americans appear to keep separate from all other functions. The remaining part—that is, the administrative part of the local business—is not only under the complete control of the people—but the people themselves, convened in general assembly, vote all local taxes, and decide on all new and important undertakings. While the deliberative part of the administration is thus conducted directly by the people, the executive part is in the hands of a variety of officers, annually elected by the people, and mostly paid. The following details will be read with interest:

In New England the majority acts by representatives in the conduct of the public business of the state; but if such an arrangement be necessary in general affairs—in the townships, where the legislative and administrative action of the

[*Cf. Psalms, 135:16–17.]

government is in more immediate contact with the governed, the system of representation is not adopted. There is no town-council; the body of electors, after having appointed its magistrates, directs them in everything that exceeds the mere execution of the laws.

This state of things is so contrary to our ideas, and so opposed to our habits, that it is necessary for me to adduce some examples to explain it thoroughly.

The public functions in the township are extremely numerous, and minutely divided, as we shall see further on; but the larger portion of the business of administration is vested in the hands of a small number of individuals, called the selectmen.

The general laws of the state impose a certain number of obligations on the selectmen, which they may fulfil without the authorization of the body they represent, and which if they neglect they are personally responsible. The law of the state obliges them, for instance, to draw up the list of electors in their townships; and if they omit this part of their functions, they are guilty of a misdemeanor. In all the affairs, however, which are left to be determined by the local authorities, the selectmen are the organs of the popular mandate, as in France the Maire executes the decree of the municipal council. They usually act upon their own responsibility, and merely put in practice principles which have been previously recognised by the majority. But if any change is to be introduced in the existing state of things, or if they wish to undertake any new enterprise, they are obliged to refer to the source of their power. If, for instance, a school is to be established, the selectmen convoke the whole body of electors on a certain day at an appointed place; they state the exigency of the case; they give their opinion on the means of satisfying it, on the probable expense, and the site which seems to be most favourable. The meeting is consulted on these several points; it adopts the principle, determines the site, votes the rate, and leaves the execution of its resolution to the selectmen.

The selectmen have alone the right of summoning a town-meeting; but they may be called upon to do so: if ten landed proprietors are desirous of submitting a new project to the assent of the township, they may demand a general convocation of the inhabitants; the selectmen are obliged to comply, and retain only the right of presiding at the meeting.

The selectmen are elected every year, in the month of April or of May. The town-meeting chooses at the same time a number of other municipal officers, who are intrusted with important administrative functions. The assessors rate the township; the collectors receive the rate. A constable is appointed to keep the peace, to watch the streets, and to lend his personal aid to the execution of the laws; the town-clerk records the proceedings of the town-meetings, and keeps the register of births, deaths, and marriages; the treasurer keeps the funds; the overseer of the poor performs the difficult task of superintending the administration of the poor-laws; committee-men are appointed for the superintendence of the schools and public instruction; and the inspectors of roads, who take care of the greater and lesser thoroughfares of the township, complete the list of the principal functionaries. There are, however, still further subdivisions: amongst the municipal officers are to be found parish commissioners, who audit the expenses of public worship; different classes of inspectors, some of whom are to direct the efforts of the citizens in case of fire; tithing-men, listers, haywards, chimney-viewers, fence-viewers to maintain the bounds of property, timber-measurers, and inspectors of weights and measures.

There are nineteen principal offices in a township. Every inhabitant is constrained, under a pecuniary penalty, to undertake these different functions; which, however, are almost all paid, in order that the poorer citizens may be able to give up their time without loss. In general the American system is not to grant a fixed salary to public functionaries. Every service has its price, and they are remunerated in proportion to what they have done. (Reeve, Vol. I, pp. 75–8; Tocqueville, Vol. I, pp. 99–103.)

In this system of municipal self-government, coeval with the first settlement of the American colonies—a system which the herd of English travellers either have not observed, or have not thought worth mentioning, classing it doubtless in point of importance with their own parish affairs at home—our author beholds the principal instrument of that political education of the people, which alone enables a popular government to maintain itself, or renders it desirable that it should. It is a fundamental principle in his political philosophy, as it has long been in ours, that only by the habit of superintending their local interests can that diffusion of intelligence and mental activity, as applied to their joint concerns, take place among the mass of a people, which can qualify them to superintend with steadiness or consistency the proceedings of their government, or to exercise any power in national affairs except by fits, and as tools in the hands of others.

"The commune," says M. de Tocqueville (we borrow the French word, because there is no English word which expresses the unit of the body politic, whether that unit be a town or a village)—

The commune is the only association which has so completely its foundation in nature, that wherever a number of human beings are collected, a commune arises of itself.

The commune, therefore, must necessarily exist in all nations, whatever may be their laws and customs: monarchies and republics are creations of man, the commune seems to issue directly from the hands of God. But although the existence of the commune is coeval with that of man, communal freedom is rare, and difficult to be maintained. A nation is always able to establish great political assemblies, because it is sure to contain a certain number of persons whose intellectual cultivation stands them to a certain extent instead of practical experience. But the commune is composed of rude materials, which are often not to be fashioned by the legislator. The difficulty of introducing municipal freedom is apt to increase, instead of diminishing, with the increased enlightenment of the people. A highly civilized community can ill brook the first rude attempts of village independence; is disgusted at the multitude of blunders; and is apt to despair of success before the experiment is completed.

Again, no immunities are so ill protected against the encroachments of the supreme power, as those of municipal bodies. Left to themselves, these local liberties are ill able to maintain themselves against a strong or an enterprising government: to resist successfully, they must have attained their fullest development, and have become identified with the habits and ways of thinking of the people. Thus, until municipal freedom is amalgamated with the manners of a people, it is easily destroyed, and only after a long existence in the laws can it be thus amalgamated.

Municipal freedom, therefore, is not, if I may so express myself, the fruit of human device. Accordingly it is rarely created, but is, as it were, of spontaneous growth, developed almost in secret, in the midst of a semi-barbarous state of society. The long-continued action of laws and of manners, favourable circumstances, and, above all, time, can alone consolidate it. Of all the nations of the continent of Europe, we may affirm that there is not one which has any knowledge of it.

Nevertheless, it is in the commune that the strength of a free people resides. Municipal institutions are to liberty what primary schools are to knowledge; they bring it within the reach of the people, give them a taste for its peaceable exercise, and practice in its use. Without municipal institutions, a nation may give itself a free government, but it has not the spirit of freedom. Transient passions, momentary interests, or the chance of circumstances, may give it the outward forms of independence; but the despotic principle, which has been driven back into the interior of the body politic, will sooner or later re-appear at the surface.*

Nor is the salutary influence of this invaluable part of the American constitution seen only in *creating*, but at least equally so in *regulating*, the spirit of interference in public affairs. This effect, together with the influence of the same cause in generating patriotism and public spirit, are instructively delineated in the following passage:

The township of New England possesses two advantages which infallibly secure the attentive interest of mankind, namely, independence and power. Its sphere is indeed small and limited, but within that sphere its action is unrestrained; and its independence gives to it a real importance which its extent and population would not always insure.

It is to be remembered that the affections of men seldom attach themselves but where there is power. Patriotism is not durable in a conquered nation. The New Englander is attached to his township, not so much because he was born in it, as because it constitutes a free and powerful corporation, of which he is a member, and of which to influence the government is an object worth exerting himself for.

In Europe the absence of local public spirit is a frequent subject of regret even to governments themselves; for every one agrees that there is no surer guarantee of order and tranquillity, but nobody knows how to create it. They fear that if the localities were made powerful and independent, the authorities of the nation might be disunited, and the state exposed to anarchy. Yet, deprive the locality of power and independence, it may contain subjects, but it will have no citizens.

Another important fact is, that the township of New England is so constituted as to excite the warmest of human affections, without arousing strongly the ambitious passions of the heart of man. The officers of the county are not elective,

*Vol. I, pp. 95–7, of the original. [Cf. Reeve, Vol. I, pp. 71–3.]

and their authority is very limited. Even the state is only a second-rate community, whose tranquil and obscure administration offers no inducement to most men, sufficient to draw them away from the centre of their private interests into the turmoil of public affairs. The federal government confers power and honour on the men who conduct it; but these can never be very numerous. The high station of the Presidency can only be reached at an advanced period of life; and the other federal offices of a high order are generally attained, as it were accidentally, by persons who have already distinguished themselves in some other career. Their attainment cannot be the permanent aim of an ambitious life. In the township, therefore, in the centre of the ordinary relations of life, become concentrated the desire of public esteem, the thirst for the exercise of influence, and the taste for authority and popularity; and the passions which commonly embroil society, change their character when they find a vent so near the domestic hearth and the family circle.

In the American States power has been disseminated with admirable skill, for the purpose of interesting the greatest possible number of persons in the common weal. Independently of the electors, who are from time to time called to take a direct share in the government, there are innumerable functionaries who all, in their several spheres, represent the same powerful whole in whose name they act. The local administration thus affords an unfailing source of profit and interest to a vast number of individuals.

The American system, while it divides the local authority among so many citizens, does not scruple to multiply the obligations imposed by the township upon its members. For in the United States it is believed, and with truth, that patriotism is a kind of devotion which is strengthened by ritual observance.

In this manner, every person is continually reminded that he belongs to the community; his connexion with it is daily manifested in the fulfilment of a duty, or the exercise of a right; and a constant though gentle motion is thus kept up in society, which animates without disturbing it.

The American attaches himself to the state for the same reason which makes the mountaineer cling to his hills; because he finds in his country more marked features, a more decided physiognomy than elsewhere.

The existence of the townships of New England is in general a happy one. Their government is suited to their tastes, and chosen by themselves. In the midst of the profound peace and general comfort which reign in America, the commotions of municipal discord are unfrequent. The conduct of local business is easy. Besides, the political education of the people has long been complete; say rather that it was complete when the people first set foot upon the soil. In New England the distinction of ranks does not exist even in memory; no portion of the community, therefore, is tempted to oppress the remainder; and acts of injustice which injure isolated individuals, are forgotten in the general contentment which prevails. If the government is defective, (and it would no doubt be easy to point out its deficiencies,) yet so long as it contrives to go on, the fact that it really emanates from those it governs, casts the protecting spell of a parental pride over its faults. Besides, they have nothing to compare it with. England formerly ruled over the aggregation of the colonies, but the people always managed their own local affairs. The sovereignty of the people is, in the commune, not only an ancient but a primitive state.

The native of New England is attached to his township, because it is independent and powerful: he feels interested in it, because he takes part in its management: the prosperity he enjoys in it makes it an object of his attention: he centres in it his ambition and his hopes. He takes a part in every occurrence in the place; he practises the art of government in the small sphere within his reach; he accustoms himself to those forms, without which liberty can only take the shape of revolution; he imbibes their spirit; he acquires a taste for order, comprehends the mutual play of concurrent authorities, and collects clear practical notions on the nature of his duties and the extent of his rights. (Reeve, Vol. I, pp. 82–6; Tocqueville, Vol. I, pp. 107–11.)

These considerations are of the highest importance. It is not without reason that M. de Tocqueville considers local democracy to be the school as well as the safety-valve of democracy in the state,—the means of training the people to the good use of that power, which, whether prepared for it or not, they will assuredly in a short time be in the full exercise of. There has been much said of late—and truly not a word too much—on the necessity, now that the people are acquiring power, of giving them education, meaning school instruction, to qualify them for its exercise. The importance of school instruction is doubtless great; but it should also be recollected, that what really constitutes education is the formation of habits; and as we do not learn to read or write, to ride or swim, by being merely told how to do it, but by doing it, so it is only by practising popular government on a limited scale, that the people will ever learn how to exercise it on a larger.

M. de Tocqueville does not pretend, nor do we, that local self-government should be introduced into Europe in the exact shape in which it exists in New England. An assembly of the rateable inhabitants of a district, to discuss and vote a rate, would usually be attended only by those who had some private interest to serve, and would in general, as is proved by the experience of open vestries, only throw the cloak of democratic forms over a jobbing oligarchy. In a country like America, of high wages and high profits, every citizen can afford to attend to public affairs, as if they were his own; but in England it would be useless calling upon the people themselves to bestow habitually any larger share of attention on municipal management than is implied in the periodical election of a representative body. This privilege has recently been conferred, though in an imperfect shape, upon the inhabitants of all our considerable towns; but the rural districts, where the people are so much more backward, and the system of training so forcibly described by M. de Tocqueville is proportionally more needed,—the rural districts are not yet empowered to elect officers for keeping their own jails and highways in repair: that is still left where the feudal system left it, in the hands of the great proprietors; the tenants at will, so dear to aristocracy, being thought qualified to take a share in no elections save those of the great council of the nation. But some of the greatest political benefits ever acquired by mankind have been the accidental result of arrangements devised for quite different ends; and thus, in the unions of parishes formed under the new poor law,[*] and the boards of guardians chosen by popular election to superintend the management of those unions, we see the commencement of an application of the principle of popular representation, for municipal purposes, to extensive rural districts, and the creation of a machinery which, if found to work well, may easily be extended to all other business for which local representative bodies are requisite.

M. de Tocqueville, though he is not sparing in pointing out the faults of the institutions of the United States, regards those institutions on the whole with no inconsiderable admiration. The federal constitution, in particular, (as distinguished from the various state constitutions,) he considers as a remarkable monument of foresight and sagacity. The great men by whom, during two years' deliberation, that constitution was constructed, discerned, according to him, with great wisdom, the vulnerable points both of democracy and of federal government, and did nearly everything which could have been done, in their circumstances, to strengthen the weak side of both.

Our space will not allow us to follow our author through the details of the American institutions; but we cannot pass without particular notice his remarks on one general principle which pervades them.

Two modes, says M. de Tocqueville, present themselves for keeping a government under restraint: one is to diminish its power; the other, to give power liberally, but to subdivide it among many hands.

There are two methods of diminishing the force of the government in any country:—

The first is, to weaken the supreme power in its very principle, by forbidding or preventing society from acting in its own defence under certain circumstances. To weaken authority in this manner, is what is generally termed in Europe to establish political freedom.

The second manner of diminishing the influence of the government does not consist in stripping society of any of its rights, nor in paralysing its efforts, but in distributing the exercise of its privileges among various hands, and in multiplying functionaries, to each of whom all the power is intrusted which is necessary for the performance of the task specially imposed upon him. There may be nations whom this distribution of social powers might lead to anarchy; but in itself it is not anarchical. The power of government, thus divided, is indeed rendered less irresistible and less perilous, but it is not destroyed.

The revolution of the United States was the result of a calm and considerate love of freedom, and not of a vague and indefinite craving for independence. It contracted no alliance with the turbulent passions of anarchy; its course was marked, on the contrary, by an attachment to order and legality.

It was never assumed in the United States, that the citizen of a free country has a right to do whatever he pleases; on the contrary, social obligations were there imposed upon him, more various than anywhere else. No idea was entertained of calling in question or limiting the rights or powers of society; but the

[*4 & 5 William IV, c. 76 (1834).]

exercise of those powers was divided among many hands, to the end that the office might be powerful and the officer insignificant, and that the community should be at once regulated and free. (Reeve, Vol. I, pp. 89–90; Tocqueville, Vol. I, pp. 115–16.)

The principle of sharing the powers of government among a great variety of functionaries, and keeping these independent of one another, is the mainspring of the American institutions. The various municipal officers are independent of each other, and of the general government of the state. The state governments, within their lawful sphere, are wholly independent of the federal government, and the federal government of them.* Each of the state governments consists of two chambers and a governor; and the federal government consists of the House of Representatives, the Senate, and the President of the United States. Of each of these tripartite bodies the three branches are mutually independent, and may, and frequently do, place themselves in direct opposition to one another.

In what manner is harmony maintained among these jarring elements? How is so minute a division of the governing power rendered compatible with the existence of government? Since the concurrence of so many wills is necessary to the working of the machine, by what means is that concurrence obtained? The town-officers, for instance, are often the sole agency provided for executing the laws made or orders issued by the federal or by the state government; but those authorities can neither dismiss them if they disobey, nor promote them to a higher post in their department, for zealous service. How, then, is their obedience secured?

The securities are of two kinds. First, all those functionaries who are made independent of each other within their respective spheres, depend upon, for they are periodically elected by, a common superior—the People. No one, therefore, likes to venture upon a collision with any co-ordinate authority, unless he believes that, at the expiration of his office, his conduct will be approved by his constituents.

This check, however, cannot suffice for all cases; for, in the first place, the authorities may be accountable to different constituencies. In a dispute, for instance, between the officers of a township and the state government, or between the federal government and a state, the constituents of each party may support their representatives in the quarrel. Moreover, the check often operates too slowly, and is not of a sufficiently energetic character for the graver delinquencies.

The remedy provided for all such cases is the interference of the courts of justice.

*We must except the influence reserved to the state governments in the composition of the federal government, through the choice of the members of the Senate by the state legislatures.

The share of the tribunals in the government of the United States is of a most extensive and important kind. The tribunals are the supreme arbiters between each member of the sovereignty and every other. Not only are all executive officers amenable to them for acts done in their public capacity, but the legislatures themselves are so. They cannot, indeed, punish a legislature for having overstepped its authority, but they can set aside its acts. They are avowedly empowered to refuse to enforce any law, whether enacted by the federal or by the state legislatures, which they consider unconstitutional.

Two questions will naturally be asked: First—does not this remarkable provision render the constitution of the United States, what the French constitution affects to be, unalterable? And, secondly, are not the judges, who thus wield without responsibility the highest power in the state, an impediment to good government, analogous and almost equal to our House of Lords?

We answer both questions in the negative.

The constitution, though it cannot be altered by the ordinary legislature, may be solemnly revised by an assembly summoned for the purpose, in the forms prescribed by the constitution itself. Before such an authority, the tribunals would of course be powerless. Their control, in the mean time, prevents the letter and spirit of the constitution from being infringed upon, indirectly and by stealth, by authorities not lawfully empowered to alter it.

The other danger, that of the irresponsible power conferred upon the judges by making them in some sort the legislators in the last resort, is chimerical. We agree with M. de Tocqueville in thinking that the founders of the American constitution have nowhere manifested, more than in this provision, the practical sagacity which distinguished them. They saw that where both the laws and the habits of the people are thoroughly impregnated with the democratic principle, powers may safely be intrusted to the judges, which it would be most dangerous to confide to them in any other circumstances. A judge is one of the most deadly instruments in the hands of a tyranny of which others are at the head; but, while he can only exercise political influence through the indirect medium of judicial decisions, he acts within too confined a sphere for it to be possible for him to establish a despotism in his own favour. The Americans saw that courts of justice, without a monarchy or an aristocracy to back them, could never oppose any permanent obstacle to the will of the people; and knowing that aversion to change was not likely to be the fault of their government, they did not deem it any serious objection to an institution, that it rendered organic changes rather more difficult. In short, as in every government there must be some supreme arbiter, to keep the peace among the various authorities, and as, consistently with the spirit of the American institutions, that supreme arbiter could not be the federal government, the founders of the constitution deemed that this moderating power, which must exist somewhere, was nowhere so safe as in the hands of the courts of justice.

The Americans have retained, [says our author,] all the ordinary characteristics of judicial authority, and have carefully restricted its action to the ordinary circle of its functions.

The first characteristic of judicial power in all nations is, that its function is that of an arbitrator. To warrant the interference of a tribunal, there must be a dispute: before there can be a judgment, somebody must bring an action. As long, therefore, as an enactment gives rise to no lawsuit, the judicial authority is not called upon to discuss it, and it may exist without being perceived. When a judge, in a given case, attacks a law relating to that case, he extends the circle of his customary duties, without however stepping beyond it; since he is in some measure obliged to decide upon the law, in order to decide the case. But if he pronounces upon a law without resting upon a case, he clearly steps beyond his sphere, and invades that of the legislative authority.

The second characteristic of judicial power is, that it pronounces upon special cases, and not upon general principles. If a judge in deciding a particular case destroys a general principle, by showing that every other consequence of the principle will be annulled in a similar manner, he remains within the ordinary limits of his functions. But if he directly attacks a general principle, and sets it aside, without having a particular case in view, he quits the circle in which all nations have agreed to confine his authority; he assumes a more important, and perhaps a more useful part than that of the magistrate, but he ceases to be a representative of the judicial power.

The third characteristic of the judicial power is its inability to act until it is appealed to—until a case is brought before it. This characteristic is less universal than the other two; but notwithstanding the exceptions, I think it may be regarded as essential. The judicial power is in its own nature devoid of action; it cannot act without an impulse from without. When a criminal is brought before it to be tried, it will convict and punish him; when called upon to redress a wrong, it is ready to redress it; when an act requires interpretation, it is prepared to interpret it; but it does not pursue criminals, hunt out wrongs, or inquire into facts, of its own accord. A judicial functionary who should take the initiative, and erect himself into a censor of the laws, would in some measure do violence to this passive nature of his authority.

The Americans have retained these three distinguishing characteristics of the judicial power. An American judge can only pronounce a decision when litigation has arisen; he can only pronounce upon an individual case, and he cannot act until the cause has been duly brought before the court. (Reeve, Vol. I, pp. 136–8; Tocqueville, Vol. I, pp. 164–6.)

The political power which the Americans have intrusted to their courts of justice is therefore immense; but the dangers of this power are considerably diminished by debarring them from the use of any except strictly judicial means. If the judge had been empowered to contest the laws in a sweeping and general way; if he had been enabled to take the initiative, and to pass a censure on the legislator, he would have played a prominent part in the political sphere; and as the champion or the antagonist of a party, he would have arrayed the hostile passions of the nation in the conflict. But when a judge contests a law, in an obscure proceeding, and in some particular application, the importance of his attack is partly concealed from the public gaze; his decision is aimed directly only at the interest of an individual, and if the law is wounded, it is only as it were by accident. Moreover, although it be censured it is not abolished; its moral force may be diminished, but its cogency is by no means suspended; and its final destruction can only be accomplished by the reiterated attacks of the tribunals. It will, moreover, be readily understood that by leaving it to private interests to call the *veto* of the tribunals into action, and by closely uniting the attack upon the law with a suit against an individual, the laws are protected from wanton assailants, and from the daily aggressions of party-spirit. The errors of the legislator are exposed only in obedience to an exigency which is actually felt; it is always a positive and appreciable fact which serves as the basis of a prosecution.

I am inclined to believe this practice of the American courts to be the most favourable to liberty as well as to public order.

If the judge could only attack the legislator openly and directly, he would sometimes be afraid to oppose any resistance to his will; and at other moments party spirit might encourage him to brave it at every turn. The laws would consequently be attacked when the power from which they emanate is weak, and obeyed when it is strong. That is to say, when it would be useful to respect them, they would be contested; and when it would be easy to convert them into an instrument of oppression, they would be respected. But the American judge is brought into the political arena independently of his own will. He only judges the law because he is obliged to judge a case. The political question which he is called upon to resolve is connected with the interest of the parties, and he cannot refuse to decide it without being guilty of a denial of justice. He performs his functions as a citizen by fulfilling the precise duties which belong to his profession as a magistrate. It is true that upon this system the judicial censorship which is exercised by the courts of justice over the acts of the legislature cannot extend to all laws indefinitely, inasmuch as some of them can never give rise to that formal species of contestation which is termed a lawsuit; and even when such a contestation is possible, it may happen that no one is inclined to carry it into a court of justice.

The Americans have often felt this disadvantage, but they have left the remedy incomplete, lest they should give it an efficacy which might in some cases prove dangerous.

Even within these limits, the power vested in the American courts of justice of pronouncing a statute to be unconstitutional, forms one of the most powerful barriers which has ever been devised against the tyranny of political assemblies. (Reeve, Vol. I, pp. 142–4; Tocqueville, Vol. I, pp. 170–2.)

Having concluded his description of the institutions of the United States, M. de Tocqueville, in the second volume, proceeds to an examination of the practical working of those institutions: the character actually exhibited by democratic government in the American republic, and the inferences to be thence drawn as to the tendencies of democracy in general. The following is his statement of the question between democracy and aristocracy:

We ought carefully to distinguish between the end which the laws have in view, and the manner in which they pursue it; between their absolute goodness, and their goodness considered only as means to an end.

Suppose that the purpose of the legislator is to favour the interest of the few at the expense of the many; and that his measures are so taken as to attain the result he aims at, in the shortest time, and with the least effort possible. The law will be well made, but its purpose will be evil; and it will be dangerous in the direct ratio of its efficiency.

The laws of a democracy tend in general to the good of the greatest number: for they emanate from the majority of the entire people, which may be mistaken, but which cannot have an interest contrary to its own interest.

The laws of an aristocracy tend, on the contrary, to monopolize wealth and power in the hands of the small number; because an aristocracy is, in its very nature, a minority.

We may therefore lay it down as a maxim, that the intentions of a democracy, in its legislation, are more beneficial to mankind than those of an aristocracy.

There, however, its advantages terminate.

Aristocracy is infinitely more skilful in the art of legislation than democracy can be. She is not subject to passing *entrainements*: she forms distant projects, and matures them until the favourable opportunity arrives. Aristocracy proceeds scientifically: she understands the art of making the aggregate force of all her laws converge at the same time to one and the same point.

It is otherwise with democracy; her laws are almost always defective or ill-timed.

The means, therefore, employed by democracy are more imperfect than those of aristocracy: often, without intending it, she labours to defeat herself; but her ends are more useful.

Conceive a society which nature, or its own constitution, has so organized, that it can sustain the temporary agency of bad laws, and is able, without perishing, to await the result of the *general tendency* of the laws, and you will perceive that democratic government, in spite of its defects, is the fittest government to make that society prosperous.

This is precisely the case of the United States. As I have elsewhere observed, it is the great privilege of the Americans that they can commit reparable mistakes.

Something of the same sort may be said as to the appointment of public functionaries.

It is easy to see that the American democracy is often mistaken in choosing the men to whom it confides public trusts; but it is not so easy to say why the state prospers in their hands.

Observe, in the first place, that in a democratic state, if the governors are less honest or less able, the governed are more enlightened and more vigilant.

The people, in a democracy, being incessantly occupied with their affairs, and jealous of their rights, restrain their representatives from wandering out of a certain general direction, which the interest of the people points out.

Observe, moreover, that if the magistrate in a democracy uses his power worse than in another government, he generally possesses it a shorter time.

But there is a more general, and a more satisfactory, reason than this.

It is, no doubt, of importance to a nation that its rulers should have virtues or talents; but what is perhaps of still greater importance to them is, that the rulers shall not have interests contrary to those of the great mass of the governed. For, in that case, their virtues might become almost useless, and their talents fatal. . . .

Those who, in the United States, are appointed to the direction of public affairs, are often inferior in capacity and in morality to those whom aristocracy would raise to power. But their interest is blended and identified with that of the majority of their fellow-citizens. They may therefore commit frequent breaches of trust, and serious errors; but they will never systematically adopt a tendency hostile to the majority; and it can never happen to them to give an exclusive or a dangerous character to their measures of government.

Besides, the bad administration of a magistrate in a democracy is an insulated fact, which has influence only during his brief continuance in office. Corruption and incapacity are not common interests, capable of producing a permanent alliance among men. A corrupt or incapable functionary will not unite his efforts with another functionary, for no reason but because he too is incapable and corrupt, and for the purpose of making corruption and incapacity flourish in future generations. On the contrary, the ambition and the manœuvres of the one will serve to unmask the other. The vices of the magistrate in democracies are in general wholly personal to himself.

But under an aristocratic government, public men have a class interest, which, if sometimes in harmony with that of the multitude, is often distinct from it. That interest forms among them a permanent tie: it prompts them to ally themselves together, and combine their efforts, for a purpose which is not always the happiness of the many: and it not only binds the rulers to one another, it unites them also with a considerable portion of the governed; for many citizens, without holding any employment, form a part of the aristocracy. The aristocratic magistrate, therefore, meets with a constant support in society itself, as well as in the government.

This common object, which in aristocracies allies the magistrates with the interests of a portion of their cotemporaries, also identifies them with that of future generations. They labour for futurity as well as for the present. The aristocratic functionary is, therefore, pushed in one and the same direction by the passions of the governed, by his own, and I might almost say, by the passions of his posterity.

What wonder, if he does not withstand them? Accordingly, in aristocracies, we often see the class spirit governing even those whom it does not corrupt, and making them unconsciously strive to accommodate society to their use, and to leave it as a patrimony to their descendants. . . .

In the United States, where public functionaries have no class interest to give predominance to—the general and permanent working of the government is beneficial, although the governors are often unskilful, and sometimes despicable.

There is, therefore, in democratic institutions, a hidden tendency, which often makes men instrumental to the general prosperity in spite of their vices or their blunders; while in aristocratic institutions there is sometimes discovered a secret leaning, which, in spite of talents and virtues, draws them to contribute to the misery of their fellow-creatures. It is thus that in aristocracies public men sometimes do ill without meaning it; and in democracies they produce good without having any thought of it. (Tocqueville, Vol. II, pp. 108–11.)

These ideas are considerably expanded, and some others added to them, in other parts of the volume.

In a general way, the following may be given as a summary of M. de Tocqueville's opinion on the good and bad tendencies of democracy.

On the favourable side, he holds, that alone among all governments its systematic and perpetual end is the good of the immense majority. Were this its only merit, it is one, the absence of which could ill be compensated by all other merits put together. Secondly, no other government can reckon upon so willing an obedience, and so warm an attachment to it, on the part of the people at large. And, lastly, as it works not only *for* the people, but, much more extensively than any other government, *by means* of the people, it has a tendency which no other government has in the same degree, to call forth and sharpen the intelligence of the mass.

The disadvantages which our author ascribes to democracy are chiefly two:—First, that its policy is much more hasty and short-sighted than that of aristocracy. In compensation, however, he adds, that it is more ready to correct its errors, when experience has made them apparent. The second is, that the interest of the majority is not always identical with the interest of all; and hence the sovereignty of the majority creates a tendency on their part to abuse their power over all minorities.

To commence with the unfavourable side: we may remark, that the evils which M. de Tocqueville represents as incident to democracy, can only exist in so far as the people entertain an erroneous idea of what democracy ought to be. If the people entertained the right idea of democracy, the mischief of hasty and unskilful legislation would not exist; and the omnipotence of the majority would not be attended with any evils.

The difference between the true and the false idea of a representative democracy, is a subject to which we have drawn attention in a recent Article,* and it cannot be too often recurred to. All the dangers of democracy, and all that gives any advantage to its enemies, turn upon confounding this distinction.

*a*The idea of a rational democracy is, not that the people themselves govern, but that they have *b*security*b* for good government. This security they cannot have, by any other means than by retaining in their own hands the ultimate control. If they renounce this, they give themselves up to tyranny. A governing class not accountable to the people are sure, in the main, to sacrifice the people to the pursuit of separate interests and inclinations of their own. Even their feelings of morality, even their ideas of excellence, have reference, not to the good of the people, but to their own good; their very virtues are class virtues—their noblest acts of patriotism and self-devotion are but the sacrifice of their private interests to the interests of their class. The heroic public virtue of a Leonidas was quite compatible with the exis-

*Review of *The Rationale of Political Representation*, *London Review*, No. 2. [I.e., that appearing on pp. 15–46 above.]

a–*a*74n [*republished as second part of* "Appendix," *Dissertations and Discussions*, I, 470–4; see below, 650–3]
b–*b*59, 67   security

tence of Helots. In no government will the interests of the people be the object, except where the people are able to dismiss their rulers as soon as the devotion of those rulers to the interests of the people becomes questionable. But this is the only *c*purpose for which it is good to intrust power to the people*c*. Provided good intentions can be secured, the best government, (need it be said?) must be the government of the wisest, and these must always be a few. The people ought to be the masters, but they are masters who must employ servants more skilful than themselves: like a ministry when they employ a military commander, or the military commander when he employs an army-surgeon. When the minister ceases to confide in the commander, he dismisses him, and appoints another; but he does not *d* send him instructions when and where to fight. He holds him responsible only for *e* results. The people must do the same. This does not render the control of the people nugatory. The control of a government over the commander of *f*its*f* army is not nugatory. A man's control over his physician is not nugatory, *g*although*g* he does not direct his physician what medicine to administer. *h*He either obeys the prescription of his physician, or, if dissatisfied with him, takes another. In that consists his security. In that consists also the people's security; and with that it is their wisdom to be satisfied.*h*

But in government, as in everything else, the danger is, lest those who can do whatever they will, may will to do more than is for their ultimate interest. The interest of the people is, to choose for their rulers the most instructed and the ablest persons who can be found, and having done so, to allow them to exercise their knowledge and ability for the good of the people *i*freely, or with the least possible control*i*—as long as it *is* the good of the people, and not some private end, that they are aiming at. A democracy thus administered, would unite all the good qualities ever possessed by any government. Not only would its ends be good, but its means would be as well chosen as the wisdom of the age would allow; and the omnipotence of the majority would be exercised through the agency and *j*at the discretion*j* of an enlightened minority, accountable to the majority in the last resort.

But it is not possible that the constitution of the democracy itself should provide adequate security for its being understood and administered in this spirit *k*, and not according to the erroneous notion of democracy*k*. This rests

*c-c*59, 67   fit use to be made of popular power
*d*67   , if he is wise,
*e*59, 67   intentions and for
*f-f*59, 67   an
*g-g*59, 67   though
h-h—59, 67
*i-i*59, 67   , under the check of the freest discussion and the most unreserved censure, but with the least possible direct interference of their constituents
*j-j*59, 67   according to the judgment
k-k—59, 67

with the good sense of the people themselves. If the people can remove their rulers for one thing, they can for another. That ultimate control, without which they cannot have security for good government, may, if they please, be made the means of themselves interfering in the government, and making their legislators mere delegates for carrying into execution the preconceived judgment of the majority. If the people do this, they mistake their interest; and such a government, though better than most aristocracies, is not the kind of democracy which wise men desire.*

[l]*Some persons, and persons, too, whose desire for enlightened government cannot be [m]doubted[m], do not take so serious a view of this perversion of the true idea of [n]democracy as we do[n]. They say, it is well that the many should evoke all political questions to their own tribunal, and decide them according to their own judgment, because then philosophers will be compelled to enlighten the multitude, and render them capable of appreciating their more profound views.

[o] No one can attach greater value than we do to this consequence of popular government, [p]in[p] so far as we believe it capable of being realized; and the argument would be irresistible if, in order to instruct the people, all that is requisite were to will it; if it were only the *discovery* of political truths which required study and wisdom, and the [q]evidence[q] of them when discovered, could be made apparent at once to any person of common sense, as well educated as every individual in the community might and ought to be. But the fact is not so. Many of the truths of politics (in political economy for instance) are the result of a concatenation of propositions, the very first steps of which no one who has not gone through a course of study is prepared to concede; there are others, to have a complete perception of which requires much meditation, and experience of human nature. How will philosophers bring these home to the perceptions of the multitude? Can they enable common sense to judge of science, or inexperience of experience? Every one who has even crossed the threshold of political philosophy knows, that on many of its questions the false view is greatly the most plausible; and a large portion of its truths are, and must always remain, to all but those who have specially studied them, paradoxes; as contrary, in appearance, to common sense, as the proposition that the earth moves round the sun. The multitude will never believe [r]these[r] truths, until tendered to them from an authority in which they have as unlimited confidence as they have in the unanimous voice of astronomers on a question of astronomy.

[s] That they should have no such confidence at present is no discredit to them; for [t]show us the men who are entitled to it![t] But we are well satisfied that it will be given, as soon as knowledge shall have made sufficient progress among the instructed classes themselves, to produce something like a general agreement

[l]59, 67   [*continued, not as footnote, but as part of text*]
[m-m]59, 67   questioned
[n-n]59, 67   an enlightened democracy
[o]59, 67   [*no paragraph*]
[p-p]—59, 67
[q-q]59, 67   evidences
[r-r]59, 67   those
[s]59, 67   [*no paragraph*]
[t-t]59, 67   where are the persons who . . . it?

The substitution of delegation for representation is therefore the one and only danger of democracy. What is the amount of this danger?

In America, according to M. de Tocqueville, it is not only a great but a growing danger. "A custom," says he, "is spreading more and more in the United States, which tends ultimately to nullify the securities of representative government. It happens very frequently that the electors, in naming a representative, lay down a plan of conduct for him, and impose on him a certain number of positive injunctions, from which he is by no means to deviate. Tumult excepted, it is exactly as if the majority itself were to deliberate in general meeting."*

The experience of America is, in our author's opinion, equally unfavourable to the expectation that the people in a democracy are likely to select as their rulers the ablest men:

Many people in Europe believe without asserting, or assert without believing, that one of the great advantages of universal suffrage consists in calling to the direction of public affairs men worthy of public confidence. The people, it is affirmed, cannot themselves govern, but they always sincerely desire the public good; and they have an instinct which seldom fails to point out to them those who are actuated by a similar desire, and who are the best qualified for the possession of power.

For myself, I am obliged to say, what I have seen in America does not warrant me in believing this to be the case. On my arrival in America I was struck with surprise in discovering to what a degree merit is common among the governed, and how rare it is among the governors. It is an unquestionable fact that in our day, in the United States, the most distinguished men are seldom called to public functions, and one is forced to acknowledge that this has been more and more the case as democracy has more and more overstepped her ancient limits. It is manifest that the race of American statesmen has decidedly *dwarfed* within the last half-century.

Several causes may be indicated for this phenomenon. It is impossible, do what we will, to raise the instruction of the people beyond a certain level. In vain

---

in their opinions *u* . Even now, on those points on which the instructed classes are agreed, the uninstructed have generally adopted their opinions.*a* The doctrine of free trade, for example, is now, in this country, almost universal, except among those who expect to be personal sufferers by it. When there shall exist as near an approach to unanimity among the instructed, on all the great points of moral and political knowledge, we have no fear but that the many will not only defer to their authority, but cheerfully acknowledge them as their superiors in wisdom, and the fittest to rule.

Mankind are seldom reluctant to allow the superiority of those who have worked harder than themselves. That is but a trifling humiliation to their *amour propre*. They readily admit the claims of superior application, whatever may be the case with those of superior genius.

*Tocqueville, Vol. II, pp. 135–6.

*u*59, 67 on the leading points of moral and political doctrine

do you facilitate the access to knowledge, improve the methods of teaching, and render science cheap, you will never enable persons to instruct themselves, and to develope their intelligence, without devoting time to it.

The greater or less facility which the people enjoy of living without labour, constitutes therefore the necessary limit of their intellectual advancement. That limit is placed higher in some countries, lower in others; but, for it not to exist, the people must no longer be under the necessity of occupying themselves with physical labour—that is, they must cease to be the people. It would be as difficult, therefore, to imagine a society in which all mankind were highly enlightened, as one in which they were all rich. I will readily admit that the mass of the people very sincerely desire the good of the country; I will go farther, and say that the inferior classes appear to me generally to mix with that desire fewer schemes of personal interest than the higher ranks; but what is always more or less wanting to them, is the art of judging of the means, even while sincerely aiming at the end. How long a study, what a variety of ideas, are necessary for forming an accurate conception of the character of a single person! The greatest geniuses commit mistakes in the attempt: can it be expected that the multitude should succeed? The people never have the time or the means to go through this labour. They are obliged always to judge in haste, and to fasten on the most salient points. Hence it is that charlatans of all sorts know so well the secret of pleasing them, while their real friends most frequently fail.

Besides, what prevents the democracy from choosing persons of merit is not always want of the capacity, but want of the desire and the inclination.

It cannot be dissembled that democratic institutions develope, to a very high degree, the feeling of envy in the human breast. This is not so much because those institutions offer to every one the means of rising to the level of others, but because those means are perpetually tried and found wanting. Democratic institutions call forth and flatter the passion for equality, without ever being able to give it complete satisfaction.

Many persons imagine that the secret instinct which, with us, leads the inferior classes to exclude the superior as much as they can from the direction of their affairs, is seen only in France. This is an error. The instinct is not a French, but a democratic instinct. Our political circumstances may have given it a peculiar character of bitterness, but they are not the cause of it.

In the United States the people have no hatred for the higher classes of society, but they feel little good-will towards those classes, and exclude them carefully from the government. They are not afraid of great talents, but they have little relish for them. In general it may be remarked, that whatever raises itself without the people's assistance, finds little favour in their eyes. . . .

I am satisfied that those who consider universal suffrage as a security for a good choice, are under a complete illusion. Universal suffrage has other advantages, but it has not that. (Tocqueville, Vol. II, pp. 43–7.)

Considered as matter of evidence—as the testimony of a highly-qualified observer—these statements deserve the utmost attention. It is for that reason that we quote them. For ourselves, we see much to be said in qualification of them; and this, too, our author's own pages in part supply. A little farther on, after remarking that in America, from the frequent changes in the persons raised to office by the elective principle, a public function cannot, as in

Europe, be considered a provision for life, he adds, as a consequence of this fact—

Hence it follows that in quiet times public functions offer little allurement to ambition. In the United States it is those who are moderate in their desires that engage in public business. The men of great talents and great passions usually abandon the pursuit of power, and engage in that of riches; and it often happens that the person who undertakes to direct the concerns of the public, is he who feels himself little capable of successfully conducting his own.

It is to these causes, as much as to the bad choice of the people, that we must ascribe the great number of inferior men who occupy public situations. I know not whether the people of the United States would choose superior men if they sought to be chosen, but it is certain that they do not seek it. (Tocqueville, Vol. II, pp. 58–9.)

The fact that the ablest men seldom offer themselves to the people's suffrages, is still more strongly stated by our author in another place, and is a point on which there is a striking concurrence of testimony. It may be said that they do not present themselves because they know that they would not be chosen; but a reason less discreditable to the American people was given to our author's fellow-traveller, M. de Beaumont,* by an American: "Comment voulez-vous qu'un médecin se montre habile, si vous mettez entre ses mains un homme bien portant?" The truth is that great talents are not needed for carrying on, in ordinary times, the government of an already well-ordered society. In a country like America little government is required: the people are prosperous, and the machinery of the state works so smoothly, by the agency of the people themselves, that there is next to nothing for the government to do. When no great public end is to be compassed; when no great abuse calls for remedy, no national danger for resistance, the mere every-day business of politics is an occupation little worthy of any mind of first-rate powers, and very little alluring to it. In a settled state of things, the commanding intellects will always prefer to govern mankind from their closets, by means of literature and science, leaving the mechanical details of government to mechanical minds.

In national emergencies, which call out the men of first-rate talents, such men always step into their proper place. M. de Tocqueville admits, that during the struggle for independence, and the scarcely less difficult struggle which succeeded it, to keep the confederacy together, the choice of the people fell almost invariably upon the first men in the country. Such a body of men as composed the assembly which framed the federal constitution, never were

*See a note (Vol. I, pp. 313–14) to M. [Gustave] de Beaumont's interesting and instructive story, *Marie; ou, l'Esclavage aux Etats Unis* [2 vols. 2nd. ed. (Paris: Gosselin, 1835)]. We shall probably say something of this valuable work in a future Number. [See J.S. Mill, "State of Society in America," pp. 91–115 below.]

brought together at any period of history. No wonder that, when compared with them, the present generation of public men appear like dwarfs. But are they such when compared with the present race of English statesmen? Which of these could have drawn such a state paper as President Jackson's address to the people of South Carolina, or framed Mr. Livingston's Draught of a Penal Code?[*]

M. de Tocqueville also states that the tendency, which he deems inherent in democracy, to be satisfied with a bad choice, manifests itself in a very mitigated degree in the older and more civilized states:

In New England, where education and liberty are the outgrowth of morality and religion—where society, already old and long-established, has been able to form habits and maxims—the people, while quite independent of all the superiorities which were ever created among mankind by riches or birth, have accustomed themselves to respect intellectual and moral superiorities, and to submit to them without reluctance. Accordingly we see that in New England the democracy makes a far better choice of public functionaries than any where else.

In proportion as we descend towards the south, and reach the states in which the bonds of society are less ancient and less strong—where instruction is less diffused—and where the principles of morality, of religion, and of liberty, are less happily combined, we may perceive that talents and virtues become more and more rare among public men.

When we penetrate at length to the new states in the south-west, where the social union is but of yesterday, and presents as yet only an agglomeration of adventurers or speculators, one is confounded at the sight of the hands in which the powers of government are placed; and one asks oneself by what force, independent of legislation and of the ruling power, the state is able to advance and the people to prosper. (Tocqueville, Vol. II, pp. 49–50.)

In these important statements, our author bears testimony to the effects not merely of national education, but of mere lapse of time, and the growth of population and wealth, in correcting more and more the liability of the people to make a mistaken choice of representatives.

But put these evils at their worst: let them be as great as it is possible they should be in a tolerably educated nation: suppose that the people do not choose the fittest men, and that whenever they have an opinion of their own, they compel their representatives, without the exercise of any discretion, merely to give execution to that opinion—thus adopting the false idea of democracy propagated by its enemies, and by some of its injudicious friends—the consequence would no doubt be abundance of unskilful legislation. But would the abundance, after all, be so much greater than in most aristocracies? In the English aristocracy there has surely been, at all periods,

[*Andrew Jackson, *Proclamation by the President of the United States* (10 Dec., 1832). (London: Miller, 1833); Edward Livingston, *A System of Penal Law for the United States of America* (Washington: Gales & Seaton, 1828).]

[v][w]crude and ill-considered legislation enough. This[w] is the character of all governments whose laws are made, and acts of administration performed, *impromptu*, not in pursuance of a general design, but from the pressure of some present occasion: of all governments, in which the ruling power is to any great extent exercised by persons not trained to government as a business.[v]

In attributing, as general characteristics, prudence and steadiness to aristocratic governments, our author has, we think, generalized on an insufficient examination of the facts on which his conclusion is founded. The only steadiness which aristocracy *never* fails to manifest, is tenacity in clinging to its own privileges. Democracy is equally tenacious of the fundamental maxims of its own government. In all other matters, [x][y]the[y] opinion of a [z] ruling class is as fluctuating, as liable to be wholly given up to immediate impulses, as the opinion of the people. Witness the whole course of English history. All our laws have been made upon temporary impulses. In [a]what country has the course of legislation been less directed to any steady and consistent purpose?[a][x]—except, indeed, that of perpetually adding to the power and privileges of the rich; and that, not because of the deep-laid schemes, but because of the passions, of the ruling class. And as for the talents and virtues of those whom aristocracy chooses for its leaders, read Horace Walpole or Bubb Doddington, that you may know what to think of them.

M. de Tocqueville has, we think, affirmed of aristocracy in general, what should have been predicated only of some particular aristocracies. [b]It is true that the governments which have been celebrated for their profound policy have generally been aristocracies. But they have been very narrow aristocracies: consisting of so few members, that every member could personally participate in the business of administration. These are the governments which have a natural tendency to be administered steadily—that is, according to fixed principles. Every member of the governing body being trained to government as a profession, like other professions, they respect precedent, transmit their experience from generation to generation, acquire and preserve a set of traditions, and, all being competent judges of each other's

---

[v][v] [*incorporated in* "De Tocqueville on Democracy in America [II]"; *see* 174[u][u] *below*]

[w][w]59, 67   Crude and ill-considered legislation

[x][x] [*incorporated in* "De Tocqueville on Democracy in America [II]"; *see* 175[c][c] *below*]

[y][y]59, 67   The

[z]59, 67   numerous

[a][a]59, 67   no country . . . purpose.

[b][b] [*incorporated in* "De Tocqueville on Democracy in America [II]"; *see* 174[w][w] *below*]

merits, the ablest easily rises to his proper level. The governments *c*(so unlike in other respects)*c* of ancient Rome, and modern Venice, were of this character; and, as all know, for ages conducted the affairs of those states with admirable constancy and skill, upon fixed principles, often unworthy enough, but always eminently adapted to the ends of *d*these*d* governments.*b*

These aristocracies, however, which manifest the most skill in adapting their means to their ends, are distinguished even beyond other aristocracies in the badness of their ends. So narrow an aristocracy is cut off, even more completely than a more numerous one, from fellow-feeling with the people; and any other aristocracy, we conceive, has not the advantages ascribed to that government by M. de Tocqueville.

*e*When the governing body, whether it *f*consist*f* of the many or of a privileged class, is so numerous, that the large majority of it do not and cannot make the practice of government the main occupation of their lives, it is *g*utterly*g* impossible that there should be wisdom, foresight, and caution in the governing body itself. These qualities must be found, if found at all, not in the body, but in those whom the body trust.*e* If the people in America, or the higher classes in England or France, make a practice of themselves dictating and prescribing the measures of government, it is impossible that those countries should be otherwise than ill administered. There has been ample proof of this in the government of England, where we have had, at all times, the clumsiness of an ill-regulated democracy, with a very small portion indeed of her good intentions.

In a numerous aristocracy, as well as in a democracy, the sole chance for considerate and wise government lies not in the wisdom of the democracy or of the aristocracy themselves, but in their willingness to place themselves under the guidance of the wisest among them. And it would be difficult for democracy to exhibit less of this willingness than has been shown by the English aristocracy in all periods of their history, or less than is shown by them at this moment.

But, while we do not share all the apprehensions of M. de Tocqueville from the unwillingness of the people to be guided by superior wisdom, and while this source of evil tells for very little with us in the comparison between democracy and aristocracy, we consider our author entitled to applause and gratitude for having probed this subject so unsparingly, and given us so striking a picture of his own impressions; and we are clearly of opinion that his fears, whether excessive or not, are in the right place. If democracy should

c-c—59, 67
*d-d*59, 67   those [*printer's error in 35?*]
e-e [*incorporated in* "De Tocqueville on Democracy in America [II]"; *see* 175*z-z below*]
*f-f*59, 67   consists
g-g—59, 67

disappoint any of the expectations of its more enlightened partisans, it will be from the substitution of delegation for representation; of the crude and necessarily superficial judgment of the people themselves, for the judgment of those whom the people, having confidence in their honesty, have selected as the wisest guardians whose services they could command. All the chances unfavourable to democracy lie here; and whether the danger be much or little, all who see it ought to unite their efforts to reduce it to the *minimum*.

We have no space to follow M. de Tocqueville into the consideration of any of the palliatives which may be found for this evil tendency. We pass to that which he regards as the most serious of the inconveniences of democracy, and that to which, if the American republic should perish, it will owe its fall. This is, the omnipotence of the majority.

M. de Tocqueville's fears from this source are not of the kind which haunt the imaginations of English alarmists. He finds, under the American democracy, no tendency on the part of the poor to oppress the rich—to molest them in their persons or in their property. That the security of person and property are the first social interests not only of the rich but of the poor, is obvious to common sense. And the degree of education which a well-constituted democracy ensures to all its citizens, renders common sense the general characteristic. Truths which are obvious, it may always be expected that the American democracy will see. It is true, no one need expect that, in a democracy, to keep up a class of rich people living in splendour and affluence will be treated as a national object, which legislation should be directed to promote, and which the rest of the community should be taxed for. But there has never been any complaint that property in general is not protected in America, or that large properties do not meet with every protection which is given to small ones. Not even in the mode of laying on taxes have we seen any complaint that favour is shown to the poor at the expense of the rich.

But when we put inequalities of property out of the question, it is not easy to see what sort of minority it can be, over which the majority can have any interest in tyrannizing. The only standing and organized minority which exists in any community, constituted as communities usually are, is the rich. All other minorities are fluctuating, and he who is in the majority to-day is in the minority to-morrow: each in his turn is liable to this kind of oppression; all, therefore, are interested in preventing it from having existence.

The only cases which we can think of, as forming possible exceptions to this rule, are cases of antipathy on the part of one portion of the people towards another: the antipathies of religion, for example, or of race. Where these exist, iniquity will be committed, under any form of government, aristocratic or democratic, unless in a higher state of moral and intellectual improvement than any community has hitherto attained.

M. de Tocqueville's fears, however, are not so much for the security and the ordinary worldly interests of individuals, as for the moral dignity and progressiveness of the race. It is a tyranny exercised over opinions, more than over persons, which he is apprehensive of. He dreads lest all individuality of character, and independence of thought and sentiment, should be prostrated under the despotic yoke of public opinion.

When we come to examine in what condition, in the United States, is the exercise of thought, it is then that we see clearly how far the power of the majority surpasses any power which we know in Europe.

Thought is an invisible and almost unconfinable force, which laughs at all tyrannies. In our time, the most absolute princes of Europe cannot prevent certain ideas, hostile to their authority, from circulating underhand in their dominions, and even in the midst of their courts. It is otherwise in America: as long as the majority is in doubt, there is discussion; but as soon as it has irrevocably decided, all hold their peace; and friends and enemies seem equally to yoke themselves to its car. The reason is simple. No monarch, however absolute, can concentrate in his own hands all the influences of society, and vanquish all resistance, as a majority, invested with the power of making and executing the laws, can do.

A king, besides, wields only a physical power, which controls the actions but cannot influence the inclinations; but the majority is possessed of a power at once physical and moral, which acts upon the will as much as upon the conduct, and restrains at once the act and the desire to perform it.

I am acquainted with no country in which there reigns, in general, less independence of mind, and real freedom of discussion, than in America.

There is no theory, religious or political, which cannot be freely promulgated in the constitutional states of Europe, or which does not penetrate into the others; for there is no country in Europe so completely subjected to one power, that he who wishes to speak the truth may not find a support sufficient to protect him against the consequences of his independence. If he has the misfortune to live under an absolute monarchy, he often has the people with him; if he inhabits a free country, he can, in case of need, shelter himself under the royal authority. The aristocratic fraction of society sustains him in the democratic countries, and the democracy in the others. But in a democracy organized like that of the United States, there exists only one power, one single source of influence and success, and nothing beyond its limits.

In America, the majority traces a formidable circle around the province of thought. Within that boundary the writer is free, but woe to him if he dare to overstep it. He needs not indeed fear an *auto-da-fé*; but he is a mark for every-day persecutions, and subject to an infinity of chagrins. To him the career of politics is closed; he has offended the sole power which could admit him into it. All is refused to him, even glory. Before he published his opinions, he fancied that he had partisans; now, when he has discovered himself to all, he seems to have them no longer; for those who disapprove blame him openly, and those who think with him, without having his courage, are silent and keep aloof. He yields, he bends at last under the burden of daily efforts, and is again silent, as if he felt remorse for having spoken the truth. . . .

In the proudest nations of the old world, books have been published destined to depict faithfully the vices and the *ridicules* of the age. La Bruyère lived in the palace of Louis XIV when he composed his chapter *sur les grands*;[*] and Molière satirized the court in pieces written to be represented before the courtiers. But the power which is predominant in the United States will not be thus trifled with. The slightest reproach offends it; the smallest trait of *piquant* truth excites its anger; everything must be lauded, from the turn of its phraseology to its most solid virtues. No writer, whatever his renown, is exempted from this obligation of offering incense to his countrymen. The majority, therefore, lives in a perpetual adoration of itself. Foreigners only, or experience, can make certain truths reach the ears of the Americans.

If America has not yet had great writers, we need not look farther for the reason. There is no literary genius but where there is freedom of thought, and there is no freedom of thought in America. (Tocqueville, Vol. II, pp. 149–53.)

M. de Tocqueville complains that the courtier-spirit, which in other governments is confined to those who immediately surround the persons of the powerful, is universal in America, because there every one has access to the sovereign's ear.

In free countries, where every one is called upon, more or less, to give his opinion on affairs of state; in democratic republics, where public and private life are intimately blended, where the sovereign is everywhere accessible, and to reach his ear one has only to raise one's voice, many more persons are tempted to speculate upon the sovereign's weaknesses, and live at the expense of his passions, than in absolute monarchies. It is not that men are naturally worse there than elsewhere; but the temptation is stronger, and offers itself to more persons at once. There results a much more general degradation of soul.

Democratic republics bring the courtier-spirit within the reach of almost everybody, and make it penetrate into all classes at once. This is one of their greatest inconveniences.

This is more particularly true in democratic states constituted like the American republics, where the majority possesses an empire so absolute and so irresistible, that whoever quits the path it has traced out must in a manner renounce the rights of citizenship, and almost those of humanity.

Among the immense multitude who, in the United States, crowd into the career of politics, I have seen very few who evinced that manly candour, that vigorous independence of thought, which has often distinguished the Americans of former times, and which, wherever it is found, is as it were the salient feature of a great character. At first sight one would say that in America all intellects have been cast in the same mould, so exactly do they all follow the same paths. A foreigner, indeed, occasionally encounters Americans who emancipate themselves from the yoke of the prescribed opinions: these sometimes deplore the defects of the laws, the versatility of the democracy, and its want of enlightened wisdom; they even go so far as to remark the faults of the national character, and point out the means which might be taken to correct them; but nobody, except yourself, is within hearing, and you, to whom they confide these secret thoughts, are but a foreigner, and about to depart. They willingly make you a present of truths which are to you of no use, and when they address the public they hold quite a different language.

[*Jean de La Bruyère, "Des grands," Chap. xi of his *Les Caractères ou les mœurs de ce siècle* (1688).]

If these lines ever reach America, I feel assured of two things: the one, that all my readers will raise their voices in condemnation of me; the other, that many of them will acquit me in the secrecy of their conscience.

I have heard Americans talk of the love of their country. I have met with real patriotism in the mass of the people; I have often looked for it in vain in those by whom the people are led. This is intelligible by analogy. Despotism is much more depraving to those who submit to it than to those who impose it. In an absolute monarchy, the king often has great virtues, but the courtiers are always vile.

It is true that the courtiers in America do not say, *Sire*, and *Your Majesty*—a grand and capital distinction! But they talk incessantly of the natural judgment of their master: they do not propose, as a prize-question, to determine which of the prince's virtues merits the greatest admiration; for they declare that he possesses all virtues, without having learned them, and almost independently of his own will: they do not offer to him their wives and daughters, that he may deign to raise them to the rank of his mistresses; but in sacrificing their opinions to him, they prostitute *themselves*.

Moralists and philosophers are not obliged, in America, to wrap up their opinions in the cloak of an allegory; but, before risking a disagreeable truth, they say, "We know that we are addressing a people too superior to human weaknesses not to remain always master of itself. We should not hold such a language were we not speaking to men whom their virtues and their instruction render alone, among all nations, worthy to remain free."

What could the flatterers of Louis XIV do more? (Tocqueville, Vol. II, pp. 155–8.)

This picture, whether overcharged or not, exhibits evils, the liability to which is inherent in human nature itself. Whatever be the ruling power, whether the One, the Few, or the Many, to that power all who have private interests to serve, or who seek to rise by mean arts, will habitually address themselves. In a democracy, the natural resource of all such persons will be to flatter the inclination towards substituting delegation for representation. All who have a bad cause will be anxious to carry it before the least discerning tribunal which can be found. All individuals and all classes who are aiming at anything, which, in a government where the most instructed had the ascendancy, they would not be allowed to have, will of course in a democracy, as they do in the English aristocracy, endeavour to bring superior instruction into disrepute; and to persuade the many, that their own common sense is quite sufficient, and that the pretenders to superior wisdom are either dreamers or charlatans.

From this tendency it cannot be expected that, in any government, great evils should not arise. Mankind must be much improved before we obtain a democracy not characterised by the absence of enlarged and commanding views. But, without pretending ourselves competent to judge whether our author overstates the evils as they exist in America, we can see reasons for thinking that they would exist in a far inferior degree in Europe.

America is not only destitute of the very equivocal advantage so strongly dwelt upon by our author, the existence of classes having a private interest in protecting opinions contrary to those of the majority; she labours, also, under a much more serious deficiency. In America there is no highly instructed class; no numerous body raised sufficiently above the common level, in education, knowledge, or refinement, to inspire the rest with any reverence for distinguished mental superiority, or any salutary sense of the insufficiency of their own wisdom. Our author himself was struck with the general equality of intelligence and mental cultivation in America. He has, moreover, fully accounted for the fact.

The equality which exists in America is not confined to fortune; it extends, in a certain degree, to intellects themselves.

I do not believe, that in any country in the world there are found, in proportion to the population, so few uninstructed persons, or fewer persons who are highly instructed.

Elementary instruction is within the reach of everybody: superior instruction is hardly attainable by any.

This is easily intelligible; it is the almost necessary result of the facts already stated.

Almost all Americans are in easy circumstances; they can therefore easily procure the first elements of human knowledge.

In America, few persons are rich; almost all the Americans are therefore obliged to engage in a profession. But all professions require an apprenticeship. The Americans, therefore, can only give their earliest years to the general cultivation of their intellects. At fifteen they enter into the business of life; and their education usually ends where ours may be said to begin. If it continues farther, it is directed only to some special and money-getting end. They study a science as they learn a trade, and attend to none of its applications but those which tend to an immediate practical object.

In America, most rich people were originally poor; nearly all the people of leisure were in their youth people of business. The consequence is, that when they might have a taste for study they have not time for it; and when they have acquired the leisure, they have ceased to have the inclination.

There exists, therefore, in America, no class, in which the relish for intellectual pleasures is transmitted along with hereditary affluence and leisure, and which holds in honour the labours of the intellect.

Accordingly, both the will and the power to undertake those labours are wanting in America.

There has established itself in America, in respect to knowledge, a certain level of mediocrity. All intellects have approximated themselves to this level; some have risen up to it; others have come down to it.

There are therefore found an immense multitude of individuals possessing very nearly the same number of ideas in religion, in history, in the sciences, in political economy, in legislation, and in government.*

*Vol. I, pp. 84–5 (of the original).

When all are in nearly the same pecuniary circumstances, all educated nearly alike, and all employed nearly alike, it is no wonder if all think nearly alike; and where this is the case, it is but natural, that when here and there a solitary individual thinks differently, nobody minds him. These are exactly the circumstances in which public opinion is generally so unanimous, that it has most chance to be in reality, and is sure to be in appearance, intolerant of the few who happen to dissent from it.

M. de Tocqueville has himself told us, that there is no indisposition in the Many of the United States to pay deference to the opinions of an instructed class, where such a class exists, and where there are obvious signs by which it may be recognized. He tells us this, by what he says of the extraordinary influence of the lawyers—in his opinion one of the great causes which tend to restrain the abuse of the power of the majority. We recommend especial attention to the section devoted to this topic. (Tocqueville, Vol. II, p. 165.)

The faults incident to the character of a lawyer, in our author's opinion, happily counterbalance those to which democracy is liable. The lawyer is naturally a lover of precedent; his respect for established rules and established formalities is apt to be unreasonable; the spirit of his profession is everywhere a stationary spirit. He usually has in excess the qualities in which democracy is apt to be deficient. His influence, therefore, is naturally exerted to correct that deficiency.

If the minds of lawyers were not, both in England and America, almost universally perverted by the barbarous system of technicalities—the opprobrium of human reason—which their youth is passed in committing to memory, and their manhood in administering,—we think with our author that they are the class in whom superiority of instruction, produced by superior study, would most easily obtain the stamp of general recognition; and that they would be the natural leaders of a people destitute of a leisured class.

But in countries which, if in some respects worse, are in the other respects far more happily situated than America; in countries where there exist endowed institutions for education, and a numerous class possessed of hereditary leisure, there is a security, far greater than has ever existed in America, against the tyranny of public opinion over the individual mind. Even if the profession of opinions different from those of the mass were an exclusion from public employment—to a leisured class offices moderately paid, and without a particle of irresponsible authority, hold out little allurement, and the diminution of their chance of obtaining them would not be severely felt. A leisured class would always possess a power sufficient not only to protect in themselves, but to encourage in others, the enjoyment of individuality of thought; and would keep before the eyes of the many, what is of so much importance to them, the spectacle of a standard of mental cultivation superior to their own. Such a class, too, would be able, by means of combination, to force upon the rest of the public attention to their opinions. In America, all large minorities exercise this power; even, as in the case of the tariff, to the extent of electing a convention, composed of representatives from all parts of the country, which deliberates in public, and issues manifestoes in the name of its party. A class composed of all the most cultivated intellects in the country; of those who, from their powers and their virtues, would command the respect of the people, even in combating their prejudices—such a class would be almost irresistible in its action on public opinion. In the existence of a leisured class, we see the great and salutary corrective of all the inconveniences to which democracy is liable. We cannot, under any modification of the laws of England, look forward to a period when this grand security for the progressiveness of the human species will not exist.

While, therefore, we see in democracy, as in every other state of society or form of government, possibilities of evil, which it would ill serve the cause of democracy itself to dissemble or overlook; while we think that the world owes a deep debt to M. de Tocqueville for having warned it of these, for having studied the failings and weaknesses of democracy with the anxious attention with which a parent watches the faults of a child, or a careful seaman those of the vessel in which he embarks his property and his life; we see nothing in any of these tendencies, from which any serious evil need be apprehended, if the superior spirits would but join with each other in considering the instruction of the democracy, and not the patching of the old worn-out machinery of aristocracy, the proper object henceforth of all rational exertion. No doubt, the government which will be achieved will long be extremely imperfect, for mankind are as yet in a very early stage of improvement. But if half the exertions were made to prepare the minds of the majority for the place they are about to take in their own government, which are made for the chimerical purpose of preventing them from assuming that place, mankind would purchase at a cheap price safety from incalculable evils, and the benefit of a government indefinitely improveable; the only possible government which, to ensure the greatest good of the community subject to it, has only to take an enlightened view of its own.

We shall conclude this article with some striking passages from M. de Tocqueville, illustrative of the collateral benefits of democracy, even in the imperfect form in which he states it to exist in America; where the people, not content with security for good government, are to a great degree the government itself.

After mankind have outgrown the child-like, unreflecting, and almost instinctive love of country, which distinguishes a rude age, patriotism and public spirit, as a sentiment diffused through the community, can only exist under a democracy:

There is a love of country which takes its rise principally in the unreflecting, disinterested, and undefinable sentiment which attaches the heart of man to the place of his birth. This instinctive affection is blended with the taste for old customs, with the respect for ancestors, and with historical recollections; those who experience it cherish their country with a feeling resembling the love of our paternal home. They love the tranquillity which they enjoy in it; they relish the peaceful habits which they have contracted in it; they are attached to the recollections it affords them, and even find some pleasure in passing in it a life of obedience. This love of country often acquires a still more energetic character from religious zeal; and then it performs wonders. It is itself a kind of religion; it does not reason, it believes, feels, and acts. Nations have been known to personify their country (if we may so speak) in the person of their prince. They have then transferred to him a part of the sentiments of which patriotism is composed; they have been proud of his power, and elated by his triumph. There was a time, under the old monarchy, when Frenchmen felt a kind of joy in feeling themselves irredeemably subject to the arbitrary power of the monarch; they said with pride, "We live under the most powerful monarch in the world."

Like all unreflecting passions, this love of country excites to great temporary efforts rather than to continuous exertion. After saving the country in a time of emergency, it often allows it to perish by inches in the midst of peace.

While mankind are as yet simple in their manners, and firm in their belief— while society rests quietly upon old-established social arrangements, of which the legitimacy is not contested—this instinctive love of country is in its vigour.

There is another kind of patriotism, more reasoning than the former; less generous, less ardent, perhaps, but more fruitful and more durable. This feeling is the result of instruction; it unfolds itself by aid of the laws; it grows with the exercise of political rights, and ends by becoming, in a manner, identified with personal interest. The individual comprehends the influence which the good of the country has over his own good; he knows that the law permits him to bear his part in producing that good; and he takes interest in the prosperity of his country, first, as a thing useful to himself, and next, as in part the result of his own efforts.

But there sometimes comes a time in the history of nations, when old customs are changed, old habits destroyed, old convictions shaken; when the *prestige* of the past disappears, and when, nevertheless, instruction is still incomplete, and political rights ill secured or restricted. Mankind then see their country through a dim and uncertain medium: they no longer place it in the mere soil, which to them has become inanimate earth; nor in the usages of their ancestors, which they have been taught to consider as a yoke; nor in their religion, of which they have begun to doubt; nor in the laws, which are not of their own making; nor in the legislator, whom they dread and despise. They see it, therefore, nowhere; neither where it is, nor where it is not; and they retire within a narrow and unenlightened self-interest. Men in this state of things throw off prejudices, without recognizing the empire of reason; they have neither the instinctive patriotism of monarchy, nor the reflecting patriotism of a republic; they have stopped short betwixt the two, in confusion and wretchedness.

What is then to be done? To go back? But a people can no more return to the feelings of their youth, than a man to the innocent pleasures of his infantine years; they may regret, but cannot revive them. There is nothing for us but to go forward, and hasten to identify in the minds of the people individual interest with the public interest: the disinterested love of country is gone, not to return.

I am assuredly far from pretending, that to arrive at this result political rights should be suddenly extended to all mankind. But I say that the most potent, and perhaps the only means which remain, of interesting the whole people in the fate of their country, is to make them participate in its government. In our times, the feelings of a citizen seem to me to be inseparable from the exercise of political rights; and I think that henceforth we shall see in Europe the number of good citizens increase or diminish, in proportion to the extension of those rights.

Whence comes it, that in the United States, where the inhabitants have arrived but yesterday on the soil which they occupy; where they have brought with them neither usages nor recollections; where they meet each other for the first time without knowing each other; where, to say all in one word, the instinct of country can hardly exist; whence comes it that every one is as interested in the affairs of his township, of his district, and of the state itself, as he is in his private concerns? It is because every one, in his sphere, takes an active part in the government of society.

The man of the lowest class, in the United States, has taken into his mind the influence which the general prosperity has on his own happiness; a notion so simple, and yet so little known to the people. More than this,—he is accustomed to regard that prosperity as partly his own work. He sees, therefore, in the fortunes of the public his own fortunes, and he co-operates for the good of the state, not merely from pride, or from a sense of duty, but I might almost say from cupidity. (Tocqueville, Vol. II, pp. 114–17.)

In a democracy only can there ever again be, on the part of the community generally, a willing and conscientious obedience to the laws:

It is not always expedient to call the entire people, either directly or indirectly, to contribute to the framing of the law; but it cannot be denied, that, when this is practicable, the law acquires thereby a great authority. That popular origin, which is often injurious to the goodness and wisdom of legislation, augments in a remarkable degree its power.

There is in the expression of the will of a whole people a prodigious force; and when this force displays itself in open day, the imaginations even of those who would willingly resist it are, as it were, overwhelmed by it.

The truth of this is well known to political parties. Accordingly, we find them contesting the majority, wherever it is contestable. When they have it not among those who have voted, they insist that they would have had it among those who have abstained from voting; and when it escapes them even there, they claim it again among those who had not the right of voting.

In the United States, excepting slaves, menial servants, and the paupers maintained by the townships, there is no man who is not an elector, and who in that capacity has not an indirect influence in making the law. Those, therefore, who wish to attack the laws are reduced to do ostensibly one of two things—they must either change the opinion of the nation, or be able to trample upon its will.

To this first reason is to be added another, more direct and more powerful. In the United States every one has a kind of personal interest in a universal obedience to the law; for he who to-day is not in the majority, will perhaps form part of it to-morrow; and the respect he now professes for the will of the legislator, he may soon have occasion to exact for his own. The inhabitant of the United States submits, therefore, to the law, (however disagreeable to him,) not only as the work of the majority, but also as his own; he looks at it in the light of a contract, to which he is a party.

We do not, therefore, see in the United States a numerous and always turbulent crowd, who, regarding the law as their natural enemy, view it with no eyes but those of fear and suspicion. It is impossible, on the contrary, not to see that the mass of the people evince a great confidence in the legislation which governs the country, and feel for it a sort of paternal affection. (Vol. II, pp. 123–5.)

Of the general activity, and the diffusion of intelligence, which are the fruits of democracy,

It is incontestable, that the people often direct public affairs very ill; but the people cannot meddle in public affairs without the circle of their ideas being extended, and their minds emancipated from their ordinary routine. The man of the lower class, who exercises a part in the government of society, conceives a certain esteem for himself. As he is then a power in the state, intellects of a high order of instruction devote themselves to the service of his intellect. He sees on all sides of him people address themselves to him, courting his support; and in seeking to deceive him in a thousand different ways, they enlighten him. In politics he takes part in undertakings which have not originated with himself, but which give him a general taste for enterprises. Every day there are suggested to him new improvements to be made in the common property, and he feels his desire sharpened to ameliorate that which is his own. He is neither more virtuous nor happier, perhaps, but he is more enlightened and more active than his predecessors. I am satisfied that democratic institutions, combined with the physical character of the country, are the cause—not, as so many people say, the direct, but the indirect cause—of the prodigious industrial prosperity observable in the United States. The laws do not generate it, but the people learn to produce it in making the laws.

When the enemies of democracy affirm that a single person does better what he undertakes, than the government of All, they seem to me to be in the right. The government of One, if we suppose on both sides equality of instruction, has more *suite* in its undertakings than the multitude; it shows more perseverance, a more comprehensive plan, more perfection in the details, a juster discernment in the selection of individuals. Those who deny these things have never seen a democratic republic, or have judged of it from a small number of examples. Democracy, even where local circumstances and the state of the people's minds permit it to subsist, does not present a spectacle of administrative regularity and methodical order in the government—that is true. Democratic freedom does not execute each of its enterprises with the same perfection as an intelligent despotism. It often abandons them without having reaped their fruit, or undertakes such as are perilous. But in the long run it produces greater results; it does less well each particular thing, but it does a greater number of things. Under its empire, what is truly great is, not what the public administration does, but what is done without it, and independently of its aid. Democracy does not give to the people the most skilful government, but it does what the most skilful government is often unable to do,—it diffuses through all society a restless activity, a superabundance of force, an energy, which never exist where democracy is not, and which, wherever circumstances are at all favourable, may give birth to prodigies. Therein consist its true advantages. (Tocqueville, Vol. II, pp. 130–2.)

We must here pause. We have left many interesting parts of the book altogether unnoticed; and among the rest two most instructive chapters— "On the Causes which maintain Democracy in America," (among the foremost of these he places the religious spirit, and among the chief causes which maintain that spirit, the removal of religion from the field of politics by the entire separation of church and state,) and "On the Condition and Prospects of the three Races," black, white, and red. We have preferred giving the reader a full idea of part of M. de Tocqueville's work, rather than a mere abstract of the whole. But we earnestly recommend the study of the entire work, both to the philosophical statesman and to the general reader; and to facilitate its reaching the latter, we greatly rejoice at its appearance in an English dress.

STATE OF SOCIETY IN AMERICA

1836

EDITOR'S NOTE

London Review, II (Jan., 1836), 365–89 (equivalent to *Westminster Review*, XXXI). Headed: "Art V. / State of Society in America. / 1. *Marie; ou l'Esclavage aux Etats Unis, Tableau de Mœurs / Américaines*; par Gustave de Beaumont, l'un des Auteurs de / l'Ouvrage [*sic*] intitulé: Du Système Pénitentiaire aux Etats / Unis. Seconde Edition, revue et corrigée [Paris: Gosselin], 1835. 2 vols. / 2. *Journal of a Residence and Tour in the United States of North America, from April*, 1833, *to October*, 1834. By E. / S. Abdy, Fellow of Jesus College, Cambridge. 1835. 3 vols. [London:] Murray. / 3. *The Rambler in North America*: 1832–1833. By Charles / Joseph Latrobe, author of the 'Alpenstock,' &c. 1835. / 2 vols. [London:] Seeley and Burnside. / 4. *The Stranger in America*: comprising Sketches of the Manners, Society, and National Peculiarities of the United / States: in a Series of Letters to a Friend in Europe. By / Francis Lieber, Editor of the Encyclopædia Americana. / 1835. 2 vols. [London:] Bentley. / 5. [Alexander Hill Everett,] *A Review of Men and Manners in America*. By [Thomas Hamilton,] the author of 'Cyril Thornton.' Reprinted from the North American Review [XXXVIII]. 1834. [London:] Miller, Henrietta Street." Signed "A." Running title: "State of Society in America." Not republished. Identified in JSM's bibliography as "An article entitled 'State of Society in America,' being a review of works on the United States; in the fourth number of the London Review." (MacMinn, 46.) The copy of the article in the Somerville College Library has no corrections or emendations. There are no references to the writing of the article in the *Autobiography* or extant letters.

State of Society in America

TWO SOURCES OF INSTRUCTION, which, however highly appreciated in name, have remained, till near the present time, almost entirely useless in fact, are beginning at length to be turned to some account: we mean, history and travelling. Intelligent investigation into past ages, and intelligent study of foreign countries, have commenced: both processes being substantially the same—with only this difference, that for the latter we have more ample materials—it was natural that they should commence about the same time. Both are yet in their infancy. Neither historians nor travellers in any former age, and few even in the present, have had a glimmering of what it is to study a people.

We would not exaggerate the value of either of these sources of knowledge. They are useful *in aid* of a more searching and accurate experience, not *in lieu* of it. No one learns any thing very valuable either from history or from travelling, who does not come prepared with much that history and travelling can never teach. No one can know other people so well as he may know himself, nor other ages and countries so well as he may know his own age and country: and the wisdom acquired by the study of ourselves, and of the circumstances which surround us, can alone teach us to interpret the comparatively little which we know of other persons and other modes of existence; to make a faithful picture of them in our own minds, and to assign effects to their right causes. Even to the philosopher, the value both of history and of travelling is not so much positive as negative; they teach little, but they are a protection against much error. Nations, as well as individuals, until they have compared themselves with others, are apt to mistake their own idiosyncracies for laws of our common being, and the accidents of their position, for a part of the destiny of our race. The type of human nature and of human life with which they are familiar, is the only one which presents itself to their imagination; and their expectations and endeavours continually presupposes, as an immutable law, something which, perhaps, belongs only to the age and state of society through which they are rapidly passing.

The correction of narrowness is the main benefit derived from the study of various ages and nations: of narrowness, not only in our conceptions of what is, but in our standard of what ought to be. The individualities of nations are serviceable to the general improvement, in the same manner as the individualities of persons: since none is perfect, it is a beneficial arrangement that all are not imperfect in the same way. Each nation, and the same nation in every different age, exhibits a portion of mankind, under a set of influences, different from what have been in operation anywhere else: each, consequently, exemplifies a distinct phasis of humanity; in which the elements which meet and temper one another in a perfect human character are combined in a proportion more or less peculiar. If all nations resembled any one nation, improvement would be apt to take place only within the limits of the peculiar type of imperfection which that nation would be sure to exhibit. But when each nation beholds in some other a model of the excellencies corresponding to its own deficiencies; when all are admonished of what they want, by what others have (as well as made to feel the value of what they have by what others want), they no longer go on confirming themselves in their defects by the consciousness of their excellencies, but betake themselves, however tardily, to profiting by each other's example.

Omitting former ages, there are in the present age four great nations, England, France, Germany, and the United States. Each of these possesses, either in its social condition, in its national character, or in both, some points of indisputable and pre-eminent superiority over all the others. Each again has some deep-seated and grievous defects from which the others are comparatively exempt. The state of society in each, and the type of human nature which it exhibits, are subjects of most instructive study to the others: and whoever, in the present age, makes up his system of opinions from the contemplation of only one of them, is in imminent danger of falling into narrow and one-sided views.

The tendency, therefore, now manifesting itself on the continent of Europe, towards the philosophic study of past and of foreign civilizations, is one of the encouraging features of the present time. It is a tendency not wholly imperceptible even in this country, the most insular of all the provinces of the republic of letters. In France and Germany it has become a characteristic of the national intellect; and such works as M. Guizot's Lectures, reviewed in our present, and M. de Tocqueville's America, in our last Number, are among its results.[*]

The four nations which we have named, have all contributed their part towards the collection of works on America, the titles of which stand prefixed to the present article. They comprise the testimony of one Frenchman, two

[*François Pierre Guillaume Guizot, *Cours d'histoire moderne*. 6 vols. (Paris: Pichon and Didier, 1828–32); reviewed by Joseph Blanco White and J. S. Mill, "Guizot's Lectures on European Civilization," *London Review*, II (Jan., 1836), 306–36. Alexis de Tocqueville, *De la Démocratie en Amérique*; reviewed by J. S. Mill, "De Tocqueville on Democracy in America [I]" (see 47–90 above).]

Englishmen, and one German, respecting the United States, and the reply of an American to the hostile criticisms of another Englishman. All are interesting; and more than one, of distinguished merit.

The first on the list is the most attractive to the general reader. The author, M. Gustave de Beaumont, the friend and fellow-traveller of M. de Tocqueville, has thrown his impressions of America into a form which combines the authenticity of a book of travels with the attractions of a well-conceived and well-executed work of fiction. Out of a few incidents and characters, and those of the simplest description, he has constructed, without affectation or straining, one of the most pathetic stories of our time; which, as a mere novel, would have entitled the author to no small literary reputation, but which is also a highly impressive picture of American life; while the facts and remarks, which are partly interspersed through it, and partly appended in the form of notes and dissertations, superadd to its merits as a pictorial delineation, the value of a formal treatise.

M. de Beaumont is no aristocrat, but a warm friend to the American Government, and to popular institutions generally. Nevertheless, we have read no book which has represented American social life in such *sombre* colours, or which is more calculated to deter persons of highly-cultivated faculties and lofty aspirations, from making that country their abode. A part of this disagreeable impression is, no doubt, a consequence of the melancholy colouring given by that deplorable feature in American life on which the interest of the fictitious narrative chiefly turns—the inhuman antipathy against the negro race. The heroine of the story of *Marie* is a girl of colour—or at least is reputed such, for the brand of degradation attaches not to colour, but to pedigree. Undistinguishable by any outward mark from women of purely European descent—the daughter of a man of weight and consideration in the State to which he belongs—she grows up to womanhood in ignorance of the defect in her genealogy, and with the feelings of a highly-educated and sensitive girl. At this period, by the malice of an enemy, it is bruited abroad, that, two or three generations before, a drop of negro blood had mingled itself with that of one of her ancestors, and had been transmitted to her. The remainder of the story is occupied with the misery brought ￼ on this unfortunate girl, upon her brave and high-spirited brother, her father, and her lover, by the effects of that direful prejudice, so lamentable that we hardly know how to call it detestable.

Even independently of this dark spot in the character and destiny of the Americans, M. de Beaumont's representation of them is not flattering. There is, however, a caution to be observed by an English reader, lest he should draw from the terms in which M. de Beaumont expresses himself, inferences never intended by the author. M. de Beaumont's is a picture of American life as it appears to a Frenchman. But to a Frenchman, English life would, as to many of its features, appear in a light very similar, and not much less unfavourable. In many things which strike M. de Beaumont with the force of novelty, and of which he speaks with strong, and possibly well-grounded, dislike, an Englishman would see merely the peculiarities of his own country and people a little heightened; but being probably unaware of the degree in which things so familiar to him may appear strange and repulsive to foreigners, he will be in danger of measuring the divergence of America from the English standard, by the strong terms in which M. de Beaumont expresses her distance from the French. The picture thus mentally heightened would become a ridiculous caricature. Even a work of a far higher order of philosophy than M. de Beaumont's, the *Democracy in America* of M. de Tocqueville, will be apt, if read without this necessary caution, to convey a conception of America, in many respects very wide of the truth.

In Mr. Abdy's, still more than in M. de Beaumont's book, the main topic is the condition and treatment of the negro and mixed races; of whose cause Mr. Abdy is an enthusiastic advocate, and of whose wrongs even M. de Beaumont's fiction scarcely gives so appalling a conception as Mr. Abdy's accumulation of facts. But into this painful subject, which is almost wholly unconnected with any of the other features of society in America, we shall at this time refrain from entering; and the more willingly, as, in the present state of our knowledge, we are quite unable either to suggest a remedy, or even to hazard a conjecture as to the solution which fate has in reserve for that terrible problem.

Mr. Abdy, in respect of his political opinions, is an enlightened Radical; and in respect of understanding and acquirements, appears a very competent observer and witness, as to the state of things in America. Few books of travels in that country, which have fallen under our notice, have a greater number of useful and interesting facts and observations scattered through them. The real and great interest, however, in Mr. Abdy's mind, is the condition of the coloured population; and his sympathy with them gives him, in spite of his radicalism, a decided bias against the Americans. The contrary is the case with Mr. Latrobe. This gentleman seems, with respect to his native country, England, to be a Tory, or at least a decided anti-reformer. But we are acquainted with no traveller whose sentiments as to home politics have less influenced his judgment or feelings respecting foreign countries. Being, as he evidently is, of an amiable and highly sociable disposition; meeting, like all other travellers, not merely with hospitality, but with the most remarkable kindness and sociability throughout the United States, and deriving the keenest enjoyment from the sublime natural objects which he witnessed, and of which he has furnished some of the most attractive descriptions we ever read; Mr. Latrobe has seen all objects illuminated by his own feelings of pleasure: and the impression which he communicates of America and the Americans is highly favourable. In this work, as in the others, we have found some judicious and valuable remarks; but its greatest merit lies in its pictures of scenery, in which department it ranks among the first productions of our day, and may probably engage some further share of our attention in another article.

Dr. Lieber's work is the least valuable of the set. The author is a German, permanently settled in the United States, where he has acquired, we believe, a respectable position as a man of letters, and is the same who has recently published, in this country, his Reminiscences of Niebuhr the historian.[*] His book contains something about America, with which he is in the highest good humour, and something about every other subject whatsoever, especially about the author himself, of whose adventures in the campaign of Waterloo we have a long, and it must be admitted, interesting narrative, *à propos* of nothing at all. It is a book of lively and rather clever gossip, which adds something, though not much, to our knowledge of America; and has, for that reason, been deemed worthy of a place at the head of this article.

Our list is closed by a paper reprinted in this country from the *North American Review*, in which one of the most smooth-tongued of the detractors of America, the author of *Cyril Thornton*, is gently, but most effectually demolished.[†] The exposure of the incompetency and presumption of the travelling Tory is complete. As to the subject itself, the reviewer endeavours to make out, in behalf of his country, more points than, judging from other authorities, we incline to think he can succeed in; but he is well entitled to a hearing, and we eagerly expect the judgment of the same writer on M. de Tocqueville, and on the various authors reviewed in our present article.

For ourselves, we are less desirous of transferring to our pages (for which, indeed, we have not room) a selection of the most interesting passages from these various works, than of stating the opinion which, from these and from all other sources of information, we have formed as to the manner in which America has usually been judged.

Scarcely any one has looked at the United States with any other apparent purpose than to find arguments for and against popular government. America has been discussed, as if she were nothing but a democracy: a society, differing from other human societies in no essential point, except the popular character of her institutions. The friends or enemies of parliamentary reform have been more or less in the habit of ascribing to democracy whatever of

[*Francis Lieber, *Reminiscences of an intercourse with George Berthold Niebuhr* (London: Bentley, 1835).]

[†The review, by Alexander Hill Everett, is of Thomas Hamilton, *Men and Manners in America*, 2 vols. (Edinburgh: Blackwood, 1833); the other work referred to is Hamilton's *The Youth and Manhood of Cyril Thornton*, 3 vols. (Edinburgh: Blackwood, 1827).]

good or evil they have found or dreamed of in the United States. One class of writers, indeed, the political economists, have taken notice of a second circumstance, namely, that population in America does not press upon the means of subsistence—and have traced the consequences of this as far as high wages, but seldom further; while the rest of the world, if their partialities happened to lie that way, have gone on ascribing even high wages to the government; which we are informed is the prevalent opinion among the Americans themselves, of all ranks and parties. But the Government is only one of a dozen causes which have made America what she is. The Americans are a democratic people: granted; but they are also a people without poor; without rich; with a "far west" behind them; so situated as to be in no danger of aggressions from without; sprung mostly from the Puritans; speaking the language of a foreign country; with no established church; with no endowments for the support of a learned class; with boundless facilities to all classes for "raising themselves in the world;" and where a large family is a fortune.

Without analysing minutely the effects of all these causes, let us glance at some few of the numerous considerations which they suggest.

America, then, is a country in which there are no poor. This is not the effect of the government. There are, indeed, governments in the world which would make any people poor; but to such governments, a people as civilized as the Americans never would submit. Where there is sufficient protection of property, and sufficient freedom from arbitrary exaction, to enable capital to accumulate with rapidity, and where population does not increase still more rapidly, no one who is willing to work can possibly be poor. Where there is no poverty, there will be a remarkable freedom from the vices and crimes which are the consequences of it. It is remarkable how much of those national characteristics which are supposed to be peculiarly the result of democracy, flow directly from the superior condition of the people—and would exist under any government, provided the competition of employers for labourers were greater than that of labourers for employment. The personal independence, for example, of the labouring classes; their distaste for menial occupations, and resolute taking of their own way in the manner of performing them, contrasted with that absolute and blind obedience to which European employers are accustomed: what are these but the result of a state of the labour-market, in which to consent to serve another is doing a sort of favour to him, and servants know that they, and not the masters, can dictate the conditions of the contract?* The unpleasant peculiarities which are complained of by travellers, in the manners of the most numerous class in America, along with the substantial kindness to which every traveller bears testimony, would be manifested by the English peasantry if they were in the same circumstances—satisfied with their condition, and therefore

*Mr. Abdy has some sensible observations on this point, Vol. I, p. 88.

evincing the degree of social feeling and mutual good will which a prosperous people always exhibit; but freed from the necessity of servility for bread, and, consequently, at liberty to treat their superiors exactly as they treat one another.

If we add to this, that the original founders of the colonies, from whom the present race of Americans are descended, were of the middle class, were people who could read, and who valued reading as the means of being instructed in their religion, we shall not wonder that this well-paid people are also a reading people; and that this well-paid and reading people are a democratic people. High wages and universal reading are the two elements of democracy; where they co-exist, all government, except the government of public opinion, is impossible. While the thirteen states were dependent colonies of Great Britain, they were, as to internal government, nearly as complete democracies as they now are; and we know what was the consequence of attempting to impose burdens upon them without their own consent.

But, secondly, there are not only no poor, there are scarcely any rich—and no hereditary rich. Here again is a fact over which the government has some indirect influence, but of which it cannot be considered the cause. There are no laws to keep large fortunes together; but neither are there laws, as in France, to divide them. If the rich chose to leave all their property to their eldest sons, there is nothing in the institutions of any of the states of America to prevent them; it is only in case of intestacy that the law interferes, and in most of the states effects an equal distribution. Public opinion seems to enjoin, in most cases, equality of division; but it enforces its mandates only by a moral sanction.*

Here, then, is a circumstance of immense influence on the civilization of any country; an influence on which in our article on M. de Tocqueville's America we have enlarged, and which is further dwelt upon in the first article of our present Number.[*] That important portion of a people, who are its natural leaders in the higher paths of social improvement—a leisured class, a class educated for leisure—is wanting in America. It is not necessary, it is not even desirable, that this class should possess enormous incomes. The

---

*The beneficial effects of the absence of a law and custom of primogeniture, in producing union in families—a fact so strongly felt in France, as to be matter of general remark and acknowledgment among French politicians and writers—appear to be almost equally conspicuous in America. (See Abdy, Vol. I, p. 2, also p. 70.)

The state of law and manners in America on the subject of inheritance is described with great distinctness and minuteness in pp. 112–14 of the first volume of Mr. Abdy's work.

[*Mill, "De Tocqueville [I]," pp. 47–90 above, and James Mill, "Aristocracy," *London Review*, II (Jan., 1836), 283–306.]

class exists largely in France and Germany, where the standard of incomes is very low. But in America there is no class exempted from the necessity of bestowing the best years of life on the acquisition of a subsistence. To say nothing of the refinements and elegancies of social life—all distinguished eminence in philosophy, and in the nobler kinds of literature, is in a manner denied to America by this single circumstance. There may, indeed, be writers by profession, and these may drive a thriving trade; but, in no state of society ever known, could the writings which were addressed to the highest order of minds, and which were in advance of their age, have afforded a subsistence to their authors. These have been produced by persons who had at least the means of supporting life, independently of their literary labours; and even the few works of a high order, which have been written in the intervals of a life devoted to other business, have commonly been addressed to a leisured class.*

We do not remember to have seen it noticed by any writer except the author of *England and America*;[*] but it is a most significant fact, that a large majority of all the Americans who are known out of their own country, and five of her seven presidents, including Washington, Jefferson, and Madison, were from the slave states. The reason is manifest: there, and there alone, was there a leisured class.

To the absence of such a class must be added another circumstance, to which due weight has scarcely yet been assigned—this is, that, to all intents except government, the people of America are *provincials*. Politically, the United States are a great and independent nation; but in all matters social or literary, they are a province of the British empire. This peculiarity of position, to which even their descent contributes, is indissolubly fixed by the identity of language.

The characteristic of provincialism, in society and literature, is imitation: provincials dare not be themselves; they dare do nothing for which they have not, or think they have not, a warrant from the metropolis. In regard to society, this remark is too hacknied to need illustration. It is equally true in respect to literature. In the one, as in the other, the provinces take their tone from the capital. It rarely happens that a book has any success in the provinces, unless a reputation acquired in the capital has preceded its arrival. But, in regard to literature, Boston and New York are as much provincial cities as Norwich or Liverpool, and much more so than Edinburgh (which

*An interesting description of American authorship is given by M. de Beaumont, Chap. xii. [Vol. I, pp. 262-3.] He describes it as a mere trade; a means of earning a livelihood; a profession—a branch of industry, and one of the lower, not the higher, branches.

[*Edward Gibbon Wakefield, *England and America*, 2 vols. (London: Bentley, 1833).]

indeed is a kind of literary and social metropolis in itself, and partakes but partially of the provincial character). There *has* been a Franklin, and there has been a Burns: there will always be persons of extraordinary genius, or extraordinary energy, capable of making their way against one kind of obstacle as against another. But, of the illustrious men of letters in France and England, though a majority have been provincials by birth, nearly all have spent their best years in the capital, and their works have been written in and for London and Paris. The courage which has made them dare trust to their own inspirations, either in thought or in language, as well as the modesty which has saved them from (what stops the progress of most aspirants in a very early stage) the misfortune of being too easily pleased with their own performances—have been learned in the literary metropolis of the nation, and in contact with the direct influence of its leading minds.

Subtract from the British empire London and Edinburgh, and all or nearly all who are born to independence; leave at the summit of this *frustum* of the social pyramid the merchants of Liverpool, the manufacturers of Manchester, the bar of London spread over the whole of England, and the physicians, attorneys, and dissenting clergy; then raise the working classes to the enjoyment of ample wages—give them universally the habit of reading, and an active interest in public affairs; and you will have a society constituted almost identically with that of the United States, and the only standard with which this last can either be likened or contrasted.* The present government of France has been called *la monarchie des épiciers*; America is a republic peopled with a provincial middle class.

The virtues of a middle class are those which conduce to getting rich—integrity, economy, and enterprise—along with family affections, inoffensive conduct between man and man, and a disposition to assist one another, whenever no commercial rivalry intervenes. Of all these virtues the Americans appear to possess a large share.† And the qualities of a more questionable description, which there seems to be most ground for ascribing to them, are the same which are seen to be characteristic of a middle class in other countries: a general indifference to those kinds of knowledge and mental culture which cannot be immediately converted into pounds, shillings, and pence; very little perception or enjoyment of the beautiful, either in nature or in the productions of genius, along with great occasional affectation of it; the predominant passion that of money—the passion of those who have

*"I find," says Dr. Lieber, "that people often compare America with Europe, when they mean London, Paris, or Rome." (Vol. I, p. 16.)

†All the works before us bear the strongest testimony to the degree in which these qualities are diffused through the whole people of America. We would instance particularly M. de Beaumont's note on the "Sociability of the Americans" (Vol. I, p. 301); meaning by sociability, their disposition to aid and oblige all who come in their way.

no other; indifference to refinements and elegancies for their own sake, but a vehement desire to possess what are accounted such by others.

Another circumstance which has important consequences, both as to society and national character, is the unrivalled *industrial* prosperity of the United States. This circumstance enables the country to do with less government than any other country in existence. It is easy to keep the peace among a people all of whom are not only well off, but have unlimited means of making themselves still better off without injury to any one. The facilities of acquiring riches are such, that according to M. de Tocqueville, that is the career which engrosses all the ambitious spirits.[*] But this same industrial prosperity has some undesirable effects. Both wages and profits being higher than in any other part of the world, the temptation is strong to all classes (but especially to those who, as managers of their own capital, can unite both sources of emolument) to *enter into life*, as it is called, in other words, to plunge into money-getting, at the earliest possible age. It is affirmed that hardly any American remains at a place of general education beyond the age of fifteen. Here again we recognise the habits and ways of thinking of a middle class; the very causes which are accountable for the comparative failure of the London University. Further, the chances of rapid gain, combined with the facility of recovering after a fall, offer a temptation to hazardous speculations greater than in any other country. In Europe, a person who loses his all, falls into beggary; in America, only into a condition from whence, in a few years, he may emerge restored to affluence. A most adventurous spirit may, therefore, be expected to prevail in the conduct of business. Not only does this appear to be the fact, but the sympathy of the public generally with that adventurous spirit, seems to produce extraordinary indulgence even to its ill success. It is a remarkable circumstance, that although the power is expressly reserved to Congress, of framing a general law of bankruptcy for the United States, public opinion has never permitted any such law to be enacted. The laws of some of the states are lenient to excess towards even fraudulent bankruptcy;* and failures inflict no discredit in the opinion of society. One cause of this indulgence towards bankruptcies may be their extreme frequency. "A short time," says M. de Beaumont (Vol. I, pp. 284–6),

after my arrival in America, as I entered a *salon*, which contained the *élite* of the society of one of the principal cities of the Union, a Frenchman, long settled in the country, said to me, "Be sure to say nothing disparaging of bankrupts." I took his advice, very fortunately as it happened; for, among all the rich personages to whom I was presented, there was not one who had not failed once, or more

[*See *De la Démocratie en Amérique*, Vol. II, p. 58.]
*See Abdy, Vol. III, pp. 69–70, as to the state of the law on this subject, in the highly prosperous and industrious state of Ohio.

than once, before making his fortune. All Americans being in business, and all having failed once or oftener, it follows that to have been a bankrupt in the United States is nothing at all. The indulgence towards bankruptcy comes, in the first place, from its being the common case; but principally from the extreme facility with which the insolvent can re-establish his fortunes. If he were ruined for ever, he would perhaps be left to his fate; but mankind are more indulgent to one who is in misfortune, when they know that he will not always be so.

M. de Beaumont adds, with discriminating candour, "Because the Americans are tolerant of bankruptcy, it does not follow that they approve of it. Self-interest, observes Chateaubriand, is the greatest vice of the Mussulmans,[*] and yet liberality is the virtue they hold in highest esteem. In like manner, these traders, who continually violate their engagements, applaud and honour good faith."

It is, in fact, evident that in such bankruptcies the creditor has nothing to complain of; as he loses by others, so others are in constant danger of losing by him; and losses by bankruptcy are counted among the ordinary risks of trade. The proof is, that notwithstanding the frequency of failures, in no country is credit given more profusely and readily. "The system of trading upon credit," says Mr. Abdy (Vol. II, p. 130), "has been carried to a ruinous extent. The facility with which bills are indorsed, and mutual accommodation procured, has exposed commerce to reverses and expedients unknown in the old world; and the tendency to erect mercantile enterprise on the basis of borrowing, is such as to present the spectacle of a nation, composed in a great degree of individuals who have mortgaged their bones and muscles to the exigencies and speculations of the moment."*

Another circumstance in American society has been noticed by almost all travellers; and M. de Beaumont, Mr. Latrobe and Dr. Lieber bear strong

[*François René de Chateaubriand, *Itinéraire de Paris à Jerusalem et de Jerusalem à Paris*, 3 vols. (Paris: Le Normant, 1811), Vol. II, p. 44.]

*The following observation by Dr. Lieber (Vol. II, p. 184) is "germane to the matter" [see *Hamlet*, V, ii, 152–4]: "General Moreau, when residing in this country (so said a French gentleman, an acquaintance of mine), believed that no soldier would be equal to an American if well and thoroughly disciplined (to be sure the present militia would require some 'rubbings'); because, said he, 'an American doubts of nothing.' It was true what Moreau observed, that an American doubts of nothing; sometimes owing to enterprising boldness; sometimes to want of knowledge or to self-confidence; always, in a measure, to the fact, that want of success in an enterprise is not followed in the United States by obloquy or ridicule, even though the undertaking may have been injudicious."

M. de Beaumont was much struck, as it was natural that a Frenchman should be, with the fact, that the Americans, never much elated by success, are never disheartened by failure, but bear the severest losses with an external stoicism which is also eminently English, or Scotch, but which is more natural in America than elsewhere, from the comparative ease with which all such misfortunes can be repaired.

testimony to it:—the uninfluential position of married women, their seclusion from society, and the housemaid-like drudgery which appears to fill up their lives. There have not been wanting persons who have seen, even in this, one of the "degrading influences of democracy." It is, however, an obvious consequence of that state of the labour-market, which renders early marriages and numerous families universal. Such a state of society naturally produces what, by rather a pedantic use of the term, is called regularity of morals; but when the boundlessness of the field of employment, compared with the numbers to be employed, renders a large family a fortune instead of a burden, women are likely, in their present relation to men (and while in such matters they have as little of a will of their own as everywhere, except in France, they seem to have), to be little else than machines for bringing forth and nursing multitudes of children. And it is evident, that where such is their destiny as wives, and where they become wives almost before they are women, they are likely to be sufficiently inferior in mental endowments, fully to justify, in the eyes of men, the inferiority of their social position.*

*Yet even these disadvantages are, in the opinion of M. de Beaumont, more than compensated, so far as respects the intelligence of the American women, by the single fact, that their education continues to the day of their marriage, which, early though it be, is not *so* early as the period at which the boys of America enter into the pursuits of money-getting. The women of America are, in his opinion, superior in mental culture to the men.

"The American, from his earliest years, is absorbed in business. He can scarcely read and write before he becomes *commercial*: the first sound which strikes his ears is *money*; the first voice which he hears is that of interest; he breathes an atmosphere of trade from his very birth; and all his earliest impressions tend to fix in his mind, that a life of business is the only life suitable to man. The fate of a young girl is different; her moral education lasts to the day of her marriage: she acquires some knowledge of literature, of history—she usually learns a foreign language (most commonly the French),—she knows a little music. Her pursuits and feelings are of an intellectual cast. This young man and this young woman, so unlike each other, are united in marriage. The former, according to his habits, passes his time at the banking-house or the warehouse; the latter, who becomes solitary as soon as she has taken a husband, compares the lot which has fallen to her in real life, with the existence she had dreamed of. As nothing in the new world into which she has entered satisfies her affections, she feeds on chimeras, and reads novels. Having but little happiness, she is extremely religious, and reads sermons. When she has children, she lives among them, tends them, and caresses them. Thus she passes her life. In the evening the American returns home, anxious, unquiet, oppressed with fatigue. He brings to his wife the earnings of his labour, and broods already over the next day's speculation. He calls for his dinner, and utters not another word; his wife knows nothing of the business which engrosses his thoughts; she is an insulated being even in the presence of her husband. The sight of his wife and children does not withdraw the American from his *practical* world; and it so rarely happens to him to give them marks of affection and tenderness, that the families in which the husband, after an absence, kisses his wife

On looking back to the foregoing observations, some readers will perhaps be surprised to find, that nearly all which has ever been complained of as bad in America, and a great part of what is good, are accounted for independently of democracy. This would have been still more obvious, if, instead of confining our attention, as we have hitherto done, to the northern and eastern states, we had extended it to the whole Union. So far as the slave-states are concerned, it is a mere perversion of terms to call the government a democracy. The entire white population of these states are an aristocracy; and from all credible accounts, appear to have a large share of all the personal qualities which belong everywhere to those who rule by force, and are supported by the labour of others.* Little could probably be traced among them of the influences either of democracy or of any other of the general features of American society, were it not for that incessant and rapid communication, which brings into daily contact the inhabitants of all parts of the Union, and has helped to produce throughout its whole extent a similarity of personal character, not, indeed, so complete as is often supposed, but greater than could have been produced by any other circumstance among so diversified a population.

We have equally left out of our consideration the back-woods, and have not thought it necessary to justify democracy from being in any way accessary to "Lynch-law." We have not forgotten Sir Robert Peel's Tamworth speech;[*] but (we must say) we think that speech chiefly remarkable as a specimen of what the conservative baronet thought would *go down* with his Tamworth auditory; or, we may perhaps add, with his party. There are Tories enough, probably, who are ignorant of the difference between the state of Mississippi and the state of New York; but we much doubt his being one of them. Sir Robert Peel is not so ignorant as to suppose,

---

and children, are called, by way of nickname, *the kissing families*. In the eyes of the American, his wife is not a companion, but a partner, who assists him in laying out, for his well-being and comfort, the money he gains by his business. The sedentary and retired lives of the women in the United States, and the rigour of the climate, explain the general feebleness of their constitution: they rarely go from home, take no exercise, live on light food; they almost all have a great number of children; it is no wonder that they grow old so fast, and die so young.— Such is this life of contrast, agitated, adventurous, almost febrile for men; dull and monotonous for women. It passes in this uniform manner, till the day when the husband informs the wife that he is a bankrupt; then they must remove, and begin again elsewhere the same sort of existence." (Vol. I, pp. 268–9.)

We leave it to the English reader to discriminate how much of this picture is properly American, and how much is English.

*See M. de Beaumont, Vol. I, p. 303n, for an instructive sketch of the difference in manners and social life between the southern, or slave-states, and the northern. The parallel throws much light upon many important questions.

[*See *The Times*, 5 Sept., 1835, p. 4, cols. 1–3.]

that *any* government could establish good order and obedience to law, in countries which count nearly as many square miles as inhabitants. He must have read Mr. Crawford's report;[*] from which he might have learnt that in the back settlements not more than one crime in a hundred either is, or possibly can be, made the subject of legal redress; and each person consequently retains the right of self-defence which belongs to man in a state of nature.* Least of all can Sir Robert Peel be sincere in laying the blame upon democracy, of lawless proceedings which are exclusively confined to the south-western states, where all the bad passions arising from slavery, are blended with the vices natural to a country colonized almost exclusively, as M. de Tocqueville says, by adventurers and speculators.[†] Even Lynch-law, which, though it occasionally sanctions its mandates by death, limits them in the first instance to removal from the neighbourhood, is probably a real improvement upon the state of society previously existing, in which every man's rifle was his own protector and avenger.

Nothing is farther from our intention than to say that the experience of America throws no light upon principles of government, or that America is not a proper theatre in which to study the tendencies of democracy. Whoever has read our review of M. de Tocqueville's book,[‡] knows that we think the contrary. Democracy may be studied in America—but *studied* it must be; its effects are not apparent on the mere surface of the facts; a greater power of discriminating essentials from non-essentials than travellers or politicians usually possess, is required for deducing from the phenomena of American society inferences of any kind with respect to democracy. The facts themselves must first be sifted, more carefully than they ever are by any but a most highly-qualified observer. Next, we have to strike off all such of the facts as, from the laws of human nature, democracy can have nothing to do with, and all those which are sufficiently accounted for by other causes.

[*"Report of *William Crawford*, Esq., on the Penitentiaries of the *United States*, addressed to His Majesty's Principal Secretary of State for the Home Department," *Parliamentary Papers*, 1834, XLVI, 349–669.]

*"You may see in the farthest west, beyond the boundaries of organized society, the incipient stages of political relations, of law and justice laid bare, as if prepared for the student of history, and of the gradual development of man as a member of political society. Perhaps all this would become clearer to you, should I write you about the 'regulators,' and the manner in which communities, beyond the limits of established law, meet the imperious necessity of dealing out justice. Of this kind was one of the most interesting cases that ever came to my knowledge, when, lately, the assembled men of a district arrested, tried, and executed a murderer. By what right? By the right to punish crime, natural, indispensable, and inalienable to every society, and growing out of the necessity, both physical and moral, of punishment." (Lieber, Vol. I, pp. 16–17.)

[†See *De la Démocratie en Amérique*, Vol. II, p. 50.]

[‡See pp. 47–90 above.]

The residuum alone can, by even a plausible conjecture, be traced home to democracy.

One truth, at least, we think, sufficiently manifest. The Tory writers have said, and said truly, that tranquillity and prosperity, in a country placed in the peculiar physical circumstances of America, proves little for the safety of democratic institutions among the crowded population, the innumerable complications and causes of dissatisfaction, which exist in older countries. Had they stopped there, every rational person would have been of their opinion. But when they proceed to argue as if the experiment of democracy had been tried in America under circumstances wholly favourable, they are totally mistaken. America is, in many important points, nearly the most unfavourable field in which democracy could have been tried. With regard, indeed, to the vulgar apprehensions which haunt vulgar minds, of agrarian laws, and schemes of sweeping confiscation, the circumstances of the experiment are undoubtedly as favourable as could be desired. But these are the fears only of those to whom *omne ignotum* is terrible. In everything which concerns the influences of democracy on intellect and social life, its virtues could nowhere be put upon a harder trial than in America; for no civilized country is placed in circumstances tending more to produce mediocrity in the one, or dullness and inelegance in the other. Everything in the position of America tends to foster the spirit of trade, the passion of money-getting, and that almost alone.

We should not wonder if it were found that, in point of fact, the Americans exhibit, not more, but less, of these undesirable characteristics, than is the natural result of circumstances independent of their government; and that, instead of evidence *against* democracy, there is a balance to be set down in its favour, as an actual counteractive of many of the unfavourable influences to which some other circumstances in the position of America tend to subject her.

If so, unquestionably the condition of America must be regarded as highly promising and hopeful: for, of all the circumstances in her position which have appeared to us calculated to produce unfavourable effects upon her national character, there is not one which has not a tendency to disappear. Her greatest deficiency—the absence of a leisured class—the mere progress of accumulation must be gradually supplying. If indeed the deleterious influence in America were democracy, her case would be hopeless; for that is an influence which must be strengthened, and not weakened, by the natural course of events. But of every other element of evil she will in time get rid. Accordingly there is valuable testimony to the existence of a tendency to improvement in those very points in which it seems to be most needed. The *North American Review*, January, 1833, p. 47, a work attached to the federalist, not the democratic party, says, "We rejoice to have it in our power to assure the friends of liberty in England, that they have nothing to fear for the charities and ornaments of life in the progress of reform. Improvement was never in any country or age more active, more visibly diffusing itself, than in the United States at this time. Schools of all kinds are multiplying, sound learning in all its branches is more and more cultivated, the polite arts are in a state of creditable progress, and all these good influences are producing their natural good effects."[*]

The same *Review*, in the article on Colonel Hamilton's *Men and Manners in America*, contains the following passages, which it is but justice in us to insert, having so recently extracted from M. de Tocqueville the expression of opinions directly contrary on the points alluded to. Future observers must decide which statement is nearest to the truth.

The devotion to literary—or to speak more generally—intellectual power, that prevails in this country, is, in fact, one of the remarkable traits in the national character, and is much more deep and fervent,—whatever our author may think of it,—than that which is paid to wealth. Mere wealth commands in this country, —as it must, and when tolerably well administered, ought to command every where,—consideration and respect; but creates no feeling of interest in its owner. Intellectual eminence, especially when accompanied by high moral qualities, seems to operate like a charm upon the hearts of the whole community. This effect is much more perceptible here than in Europe, where the intellectual men are overshadowed by an hereditary privileged class, who regard them every where as inferior, and in some countries refuse to associate with them at all. The highest professional or literary distinction gives no admission to most of the courts of Europe, and only on a very unequal footing to the fashionable circles. A lawyer or a clergyman of talent is occasionally allowed a seat at the foot of a nobleman's table, but to aspire to the hand of his daughter would be the height of presumption. At the close of a long life of labour he takes his seat, too late to receive any great satisfaction from his new position, in the House of Lords, as Chancellor, Chief-Justice, or Bishop. Through the whole active period of his life he has moved, as a matter of course, in a secondary sphere. With us, on the contrary, great wealth, the only accidental circumstance that confers distinction, is commonly the result of a life of labour. The intellectual men assume at once, and maintain through life, a commanding position among their contemporaries,—give the tone in the first social circles,—and, at the maturity of their powers and influence, receive from their fellow-citizens demonstrations of attachment and respect, which have rarely, if ever, been shown before to the eminent men of any other country. The Presidentships and the Governorships, the places in the cabinet, and on the bench of justice, in Congress and in the State Legislatures,—the commissions in the Army and Navy,—the foreign embassies,—elsewhere the monopoly of a few privileged families,—are here the rewards of intellectual preeminence. Lord Brougham, though certainly in every way one of the most illustrious and truly deserving public characters that have appeared in England in modern times, has never received from his countrymen any proof of approbation half so flattering,

[*Edward Everett, "Prince Pückler Muscau and Mrs. Trollope," *North American Review*, XXXVI (Jan., 1833), p. 47.]

as the sort of civic triumph with which Mr. Clay and Mr. Webster were lately welcomed on their respective visits to the East and the West. Mr. Irving, since his late return from Europe, has been the object of more attention of a public kind, than was shown through the whole course of his life to Sir Walter Scott, undoubtedly the most popular British writer of the last century.

This respect for intellectual power, which forms so remarkable a feature in the national character, ought not to have escaped the attention of a traveller, whose pretensions to notice are founded entirely upon that basis, and who had experienced the operation of it so favourably in his own person. It has often been evinced, in a very pleasing way, in the testimonials of regard shown to the memory of distinguished literary men, even of foreign countries. At the late lamented decease of the illustrious British poet just alluded to, the public feeling of regret was evidently quite as strong in this country as in England. Subscriptions were raised at New York, to aid in the purchase of Abbotsford for his family; and a monument to his memory is now in preparation at Albany. We regret to learn that the object, in which the New York subscriptions were intended to aid, is not likely to be effected. The marble tablet that covers the remains of Henry Kirke White, in the churchyard of Nottingham in England, was placed there by a gentleman of this city, no otherwise interested in his memory, than by the pleasure he had taken in reading his poems.[*]

This view of the matter receives confirmation from the hostile testimony of Colonel Hamilton himself. If the Americans are so vain of their distinguished intellectual characters, as that gentleman affirms, most assuredly they must be anything but indifferent to the value of intellect itself.

On the capacity and disposition of the people to make a good selection of persons to fill the highest offices, the American reviewer, though attached to what is esteemed the aristocratic party, is so far from agreeing with M. de Tocqueville, that he considers the experience of his country to be not only favourable, but decisively so.

So far as the office of President of the United States is concerned, which our author appears to have had particularly in view, we had supposed it to be generally acknowledged, not that the experiment had failed, but that it had succeeded a good deal better than perhaps could reasonably have been expected. Of the seven Presidents who have been elected under it, the six first, viz. Washington, the two Adamses, Jefferson, Madison, and Monroe,—though certainly far from being on a level in point of qualifications for the office,—were all, by general acknowledgment, among the most eminent and best qualified persons in the country. Mr. Monroe, the least conspicuous of the number, is yet spoken of by our author, deservedly, in very handsome terms, and was as much superior to the hereditary rulers of the ordinary European standard, as Washington was to him. As to the qualifications of the present incumbent, which are still the subject of party controversy, there would no doubt be a difference of opinion. A large and respectable portion of the citizens who opposed his election would probably say, that in his case, the system has in fact failed. But were this even admitted, it might

[*Alexander Hill Everett. "Men and Manners in America," *North American Review*, XXXVIII (Jan., 1834), 241–3. Mill gives the reference to the reprint, pp. 33–4. The "gentleman of this city" was Francis Boott.]

still be pertinently asked, whether any system can be expected to produce the best possible results oftener than six times out of seven. On the other hand, the large majority of the citizens who elected General Jackson look upon him as the very Phœnix of Presidents, and from the tone of our author's remarks upon the subject, we should have supposed that he inclined to this opinion. He certainly, if his account may be believed, "retired from the interview he had with General Jackson, with sentiments of very sincere respect for the intellectual and moral qualities of the American President." We doubt whether he could have said as much as this of a majority of the hereditary rulers of Europe. Add to this, that in the innumerable instances in which the same system has been applied in the several States, it has brought out, almost uniformly, men of great respectability, —often the very first men in the country, such as Jefferson, Dewitt Clinton, and Jay,—and in no one case, as far as we are informed, any person notoriously incapable. We cannot but think, that instead of having grossly failed, it must be regarded, on the whole, as having in a remarkable manner succeeded. In fact, the capacity of the people at large to elect the principal political functionaries, is considered, by competent judges, as one of the least questionable points in the theory of government. Montesquieu, at least as high an authority on a political question as the author of *Cyril Thornton*, tells us that "the people are admirably well qualified to elect those who are to be intrusted with any portion of their power. If there were a doubt of this, we need only to recollect the continual succession of astonishing elections that were made by the Athenians and the Romans, which certainly cannot be attributed to chance."[*] The history of the United States, so far as we have proceeded, will be regarded by future political philosophers, as furnishing another example, not less striking than those of Athens and Rome.[†]

There are two or three obvious mistakes in this reasoning. Athens and Rome were not democracies, but altogether, and exclusively, governments by a leisured class: their experience, therefore, though it throws light upon many of the effects of free institutions in general, cannot be quoted as evidence on the subject of democracy. The Presidents of America, too, should have been contrasted, not with the hereditary kings of the various countries of Europe, who generally have little to do in the government of those countries, but with the prime ministers. That comparison, however, is anything but unfavourable to America; and the reviewer is warranted in his triumphant appeal to the distinguished merit of the seven Presidents who have been elected by the people of the United States.

A question to which we should be more anxious to have the reviewer's answer, would be, why the Washingtons and Jeffersons have left no successors? Why, in an age so far superior in intellectual facilities and resources to that in which those eminent men were educated, the man whom common opinion even now apparently places at the head of the public men of the

[*Charles de Secondat, Baron de Montesquieu, *De l'Esprit des loix*, 2 vols. (Geneva: Barillot, 1748), Vol. I, pp. 14–15.]

[†A. H. Everett, "Men and Manners in America," pp. 262–4. Mill's reference is to the reprint, pp. 54–5.]

United States, is the survivor of President Jefferson's cabinet, Mr. Albert Gallatin?*

We are the more desirous to have this question answered by the reviewer, as we can ourselves suggest an answer for his consideration. The great men alluded to were sprung from a leisured class. The families which gave birth to Washington and Jefferson, and, we believe, to Madison and Monroe, belonged to a class of proprietors maintained by the labour of slaves, and enjoying hereditary landed possessions in the then flourishing and opulent state of Virginia. From causes not satisfactorily explained in any of the works before us, but which are apparently connected with vicissitudes of cultivation and markets, the prosperity of that state has greatly declined, and nearly the whole of these families are bankrupt.† We are much mistaken if this be not part of the solution of the mystery. The stream has ceased to flow, because its fountain is dried up. Why a corresponding number of examples of like excellence have not been produced in the other slave states we cannot pretend to say. Were we perfectly versed in the history and local circumstances of those states, the fact might admit of explanation. We do not affirm that wherever there is a leisured class there will be high mental culture. But we contend that the existence of such a class is a necessary condition of it.‡

As to the general standard of mental cultivation and acquirements in the United States, the testimony of all travellers confirms the assertion of M. de Tocqueville, that a certain "*niveau mitoyen*" has established itself, which few either fall below or soar above.[*] "It is probable," says Mr. Abdy, (Vol. I, p. 13,) "that the average of literary accomplishments is higher among our brethren in the new world, than among ourselves, while the extremes at either end are less distant from the middle point of the scale." "The instruction given to children," says M. de Beaumont,

is purely practical: it does not aim at the cultivation of the higher moral and intellectual faculties, but seeks only to form men fitted for the business of social life: all are able to speak and write, but without talent, though not without pretension. ... That purely intellectual existence which withdraws from the trivialities of outward life, and feeds upon ideas—for which meditation is a want, science a duty,

*The federalist reviewer might possibly deny our fact, and claim the palm of superiority for Mr. Webster; but, viewing that gentleman as one of the leaders of the absurd Tariff party, we scruple to allow the claim.

†Mr. Abdy ascribes the ruin of a large proportion of the planters in the older slave states to the spirit of reckless speculation fostered by slavery. For the fact itself, see pp. 227 and 247 of the second volume of his work.

‡It is a fact strikingly illustrative of the difference between the spirit of the slave-owning aristocracies of the south, and the middle-class democracies of the north, that the northern states encourage schools and neglect colleges, the southern encourage colleges and neglect elementary schools. Some striking details on this interesting subject are given by Mr. Abdy, Vol. II, pp. 252–6.

[*De la Démocratie en Amérique, Vol. I, p. 85; cf. p. 84 above.]

and literary creation a delightful enjoyment—is unknown in America. That country is ignorant of the very existence of the modest man of science, who keeping
aloof from political life and the struggle *to rise*, devotes himself to study, loving it
for its own sake, and enjoys, in silence, its honourable leisure.... Europeans, who
admire Cooper, fancy that the Americans must adore him; but the fact is not so.
The Walter Scott of America finds in his own country neither fortune nor renown.
He earns less by his writings than a dealer in stuffs; the latter therefore is a greater
man than the dealer in ideas. This reasoning is unanswerable. (Vol. I, pp. 252–3,
261–3.)

There is one topic on which we desire to say a few words, particularly as
it is one on which the testimony of travellers is not uniform—the inordinate
national vanity of which the Americans are accused, and their imputed excess of sensitiveness to criticism. On these points the testimony of M. de
Tocqueville, M. de Beaumont, and Mr. Abdy, is extremely unfavourable.
They all agree in representing the mass of Americans as not only offended by
any disparagement of their country, even in the most unessential particular,
but dissatisfied with any moderate praise; and as nourishing the most extravagant ideas of the superiority of their country over all others. All these
authors agree also in ascribing this national weakness to the fulsome flattery
heaped on the nation *en masse* by nearly all their politicians and writers:
flattery, of which Mr. Abdy (who excels almost any traveller we remember
in the abundance of specific facts with which he usually substantiates his
general observations) produces a number of very ludicrous instances.

Mr. Latrobe does not appear to have seen these peculiarities (except, indeed, the sensitiveness) in quite so strong a light. The *North American Review* altogether denies them. "We aver upon our consciences," says the reviewer of Mrs. Trollope,[*]

that we do not remember an occasion on which a good-natured joke, from any
quarter, on any part of America, has been taken amiss. By whom has Mr. Irving's
Knickerbocker,[†] two entire volumes of satire on the Dutch of New York, been
more keenly relished than by his countrymen; and where is Mr. Hacket more
warmly greeted than at Boston? But we go farther than this. Not only has no offence, that we know of, been taken at well-meant pleasantry; but that which was
not well-meant, the ribaldry, the exaggerations, the falsehoods of the score of
tourists in this country, who have published their journals, seasoned to the taste
for detraction prevailing in England, [among the English aristocracy, he should
have said,] and in order to find reimbursement in the sale for the expense of the
tour; we say the abuse of this race of travellers has never, that we recollect, in
itself, moved the ire of the public press in this country. Not one of these travellers
has been noticed, till his libels had been endorsed by the *Quarterly*, and, we are

[*Frances Trollope, *Domestic Manners of the Americans*, 2 vols. (London:
Whittaker, Treacher and Co., 1832).]

[†Washington Irving, *History of New York from the beginning of the world
to the end of the Dutch Dynasty*, by Diedrich Knickerbocker (London: Sharpe,
1821).]

grieved to add, sometimes by the *Edinburgh Review*, or by some other responsible authority. Then, when the leading journals in Europe had done their best to authenticate the slander, we have thought it sometimes deserving refutation. ([Edward Everett, "Prince Pückler Muscau and Mrs. Trollope,"] *North American Review* for January, 1833, p. 42.)

Dr. Lieber is of the same opinion.

You may little expect to hear an assertion of this kind, after having read so many charges to the contrary; yet I must be permitted to state, that I consider the Americans eminently good-natured, and disposed to allow any one to speak with perfect freedom of America and her institutions. Of such a thing as taking amiss, as it is termed, they hardly know. That those of them who have seen little of the world are often conceited in regard to their country is natural; every villager, all over the world, thinks his steeple the highest, and assures you that the bottom of his pond has never been found yet. But even such as these among the Americans will allow you freely to make your remarks upon their country, laugh heartily with you, and never get angry on account of your free remarks. I have found this so constantly, and in so striking instances, that I do not hesitate to state it as a fact. If a man in the west asks you, "How do you like our country?" or a Bostonian, "Don't you think, after all, our climate very fine?" you must not forget that, perhaps, the remark is made from a kind disposition, and that, in this, as in all similar cases, it is but one that bothers you, while a hundred others remain silent, and you remember only the one who may have troubled you, if you are so sensitive as to call this troubling. It is certainly a fact worth notice, that the severest books against the United States sell rapidly, and often run through several editions; and when I once conversed with one of the first publishers as to a work on the United States, he said, "Any one who writes on this country ought to know, that the severer he is, the better his book will sell. I am convinced of this fact by repeated experience."* Which is no encouraging prospect for all those who wish to say what they think and know, that eagles soar high, and geese cackle loud all over the world.

That this good-natured equanimity of the Americans may be somewhat disturbed when a gentleman travels *tout le temps en maître d'école*, all the time pronouncing his opinion *ex cathedrâ*, finding fault and ridiculing, might be supposed; though I have, even then, seen the Americans, almost without exception, pertinaciously good-natured. (Vol. II, pp. 77–9.)

This is the testimony of a trustworthy witness, who, during a far longer residence in the country than that of Mr. Abdy, or MM. de Tocqueville and de Beaumont, has enjoyed ample opportunities of observation. The discrepancy may be easily reconciled. It is but natural to suppose that the Americans, like all other people, will bear more from one person than from another; and that so warm an admirer as Dr. Lieber may have met with a more good-

---

*Mr. Shirreff, the intelligent author of a recent agricultural tour through Canada and the United States, mentions that even a work so obviously malignant as that of Mrs. Trollope has had a salutary influence in correcting many of the minor absurdities which it holds up to ridicule. [Patrick Shirreff, *A Tour through North America* (Edinburgh: Oliver and Boyd, 1835),] pp. 9–10. [JSM's footnote.]

humoured reception for his small criticisms, than is given to the strictures of men who, like the other three gentlemen, have opinions which place them at direct variance with some of the strongest prejudices and most prominent characteristics of the American people.

As for their inordinate conceit of the superiority of their country, all the nations of Europe had the like, until they began to know one another; and the cure for it, in America as elsewhere, is greater intercourse with foreigners. Nor must it be forgotten that, to a stranger, both the conceit and the sensitiveness to criticism are likely to appear greater than they are. He sees the Americans in their awkwardest aspect—when they are attempting to do the honours of their country to a foreigner. They are not at their ease with him. They have the feelings as a nation, which we usually see in an individual whose position in society is not fixed. Their place in the estimation of the civilized world is not yet settled. They have but recently come to their importance, and they cannot yet afford to despise affronts. On this subject the liberal remarks of Mr. Latrobe deserve attention. He says, (Vol. I, p. 68,)—

The English have not, as a nation, whatever may be supposed by those who gather their estimate of national feeling from the Reviews, much sympathy with this kind of sensitiveness. We have arrived at that happy pitch of national self-esteem, and our national pride is so little disturbed by unwelcome surmises or suspicions that in this or that particular we are really emulated or surpassed by our neighbours, that we calmly set down any one who comes amongst us, and tells us that, in certain matters, John Bull is surpassed by other nations, or an object of ridicule to them, as an ignorant or spiteful twaddler at once, and do not suffer the national temper to be ruffled. *Having now, for so many years, been accustomed to have justice done to us by our neighbours on all main points*, however unwillingly, we can even afford to be satirized, or, as we would say, caricatured in some minor particulars, and can magnanimously laugh at the same. But not so with America. She feels, and with reason, that justice has not always been done her in essentials, and by Britain in particular. She knows that there has been a spirit abroad having a tendency to keep the truth and her real praise away from the eye of the world, shrouded behind a vein of coarse ribaldry, and detail of vulgarities which, if not positively untrue, were at least so invidiously chosen, and so confirmatory of prejudice, and so far caricature, when applied to the people as a mass, as almost to bear the stigma of untruth. She has felt that the progress made in a very limited period of time, and amidst many disadvantages, in reclaiming an immense continent from the wilderness, in covering it with innumerable flourishing settlements; her success in the mechanic arts; her noble institutions in aid of charitable purposes; the public spirit of her citizens; their gigantic undertakings to facilitate interior communication; their growing commerce in every quarter of the globe; the indomitable perseverance of her sons; the general attention to education, and the reverence for religion, wherever the population has become permanently fixed; and the generally mild and successful operation of their government, have been overlooked, or only casually mentioned: while the failings, rawness of character, and ill-harmonised state of society in many parts; the acts of lawless individuals, and the slang and language of the vulgar, have been held prominently forward to excite scorn, provoke satire, and strengthen prejudice. In short, she has felt that her true claims upon respect and admiration have been either unknown or undervalued in Europe; and that especially that nation with whom she had the greatest national affinity, was inclined to be the most perseveringly unjust.—Hence partly arises, it may be surmised, the querulous state of sensitiveness, to which allusion has been made, and also that disposition to swagger and exaggerate, which has been laid to the charge of many Americans, not without reason.

It must be said, to the honour of the *Quarterly Review*, that these and similar remarks of Mr. Latrobe have extorted from that journal (or perhaps only afforded it an opportunity for) an acknowledgment of error, accompanied with expressions of regret for the tone of former articles;[*] an example of candour which, though it does not cancel the turpitude of the previous offence, is highly laudable, and almost new in the morality of the periodical press.

[*Anon., "Tours in America, by Latrobe, Abdy, &c.," *Quarterly Review*, LIV (Sept., 1835), 408.]

CIVILIZATION

1836

EDITOR'S NOTE

Dissertations and Discussions, I (2nd ed., 1867), 160–205, where the title is footnoted, *"London and Westminster Review*, April 1836." Reprinted from *L&WR*, III & XXV (April, 1836), 1–28, where it is headed, "Art. I. / Civilization," and has right running title "Civilization" and left running title "Signs of the Times." Signed "A." Original article identified in JSM's bibliography as "An article entitled 'Civilization—Signs of the Times' in the London and Westminster Review for April, (No 5 and 48.)" (MacMinn, 47.) No corrections or emendations in the copy in the Somerville College Library.

For comment on the essay, see the Textual Introduction, lxxiv–lxxvi above.

The following text, taken from the 2nd ed. of *D&D* (the last in JSM's lifetime) is collated with that in *D&D*, 1st ed. (London: Parker, 1859), and that in *L&WR*. In the footnoted variants, "67" indicates *D&D*, 2nd ed.; "59" indicates *D&D*, 1st ed.; "36" indicates *L&WR*.

Civilization

THE WORD CIVILIZATION, like many other terms of the philosophy of human nature, is a word of double meaning. It sometimes stands for *human improvement* in general, and sometimes for *certain kinds* of improvement in particular.

We are accustomed to call a country more civilized if we think it more improved; more eminent in the best characteristics of Man and Society; *farther* advanced in the road to perfection; happier, nobler, wiser. This is one sense of the word civilization. But in another sense it stands for that kind of improvement only, which distinguishes a wealthy and *powerful* nation from savages or barbarians. It is in this sense that we may speak of the vices or the miseries of civilization; and that the question has been seriously propounded, whether civilization is on the whole a good or an evil? Assuredly, we entertain no doubt on this point; we hold that civilization is a good, that it is the cause of much good, and *e* not incompatible with any; but we think there is other good, much even of the highest good, which civilization in this sense does not provide for, and some which it has a tendency (though that tendency may be counteracted) to impede.

The inquiry into which these considerations would lead *f* , is calculated to throw light upon many of the characteristic features of our time. The present era is pre-eminently the era of civilization in the narrow sense; whether we consider what has already been achieved, or the rapid advances making towards still greater achievements. We do not regard the age as either equally advanced or equally progressive in many of the other kinds of improvement. In some it appears to us stationary, in some even retrograde. Moreover, *g* the irresistible consequences of a state of advancing civilization; the new position in which that advance has placed, and is every day more and more placing, mankind; the entire inapplicability of old rules to this new position, and the necessity, if we would either realize the benefits of the new state or preserve those of the old, that we should adopt many new rules, and new courses of

---

*a–a*36, 59 *human improvement*   *b–b*36, 59 *certain kinds*
*c–c*36 further   *d–d*36 populous
*e*36 is   *f*36 us
*g*36 the consequences,

action; are topics which seem to require a more comprehensive examination than they have usually received.

We shall [h]on the present occasion[h] use the word civilization [i]only in the restricted[i] sense: not that in which it is synonymous with improvement, but that in which it is the direct converse or contrary of rudeness or barbarism. Whatever be the characteristics of what we call savage life, the contrary of these, or [j] the qualities which society puts on as it throws off these, constitute civilization. Thus, a savage tribe consists of a handful of individuals, wandering or thinly scattered over a vast tract of country: a dense population, therefore, dwelling in fixed habitations, and largely collected together in towns and villages, we term civilized. In savage life there is no commerce, no manufactures, no agriculture, or next to none: a country rich in the fruits of agriculture, commerce, and manufactures, we call civilized. In savage communities each person shifts for himself; except in war (and even then very imperfectly), we seldom see any joint operations carried on by the union of many; nor do savages [k], in general,[k] find much pleasure in each other's society. Wherever, therefore, we find human beings acting together for common purposes in large bodies, and enjoying the pleasures of social intercourse, we term them civilized. In savage life there is little or no law, or administration of justice; no systematic employment of the collective strength of society, to protect individuals against injury from one another; every one trusts to his own strength or cunning, and where that fails, he is [l]generally[l] without resource. We accordingly call a people civilized, where the arrangements of society, for protecting the persons and property of its members, are sufficiently perfect to maintain peace among them; *i.e.* to induce the bulk of the community to rely for their security mainly upon [m] social arrangements, and renounce for the most part, and in ordinary circumstances, the vindication of their interests (whether in the way of aggression or of defence) by their individual strength or courage.

These ingredients of civilization are various, but consideration will satisfy us that they are not improperly classed together. History, and their own nature, alike show that they begin together, always co-exist, and accompany each other in their growth. Wherever there has [n]arisen[n] sufficient knowledge of the arts of life, and sufficient security of property and person, to render the progressive increase of wealth and population possible, the community becomes and continues progressive in all the elements which we have just enumerated. [o]These[o] elements exist in modern Europe, and especially in

[h-h]36   in the present article invariably   [i-i]36   in the narrow
[j]36   rather   [k-k]+59, 67
[l-l]+59, 67   [m]36   the
[n-n]36   introduced itself   [o-o]36   All these

Great Britain, in a more eminent degree, and in a state of more rapid progression, than at any other place or time. We [p]propose to consider[p] some of the consequences which that high and progressive state of civilization has already produced, and of the further ones which it is hastening to produce.

The most remarkable of those consequences of advancing civilization, which the state of the world is now forcing upon the attention of thinking minds, is this: that power passes more and more from individuals, and small knots of individuals, to masses: that the importance of the masses becomes constantly greater, that of individuals less.

The causes, evidences, and consequences of this law of human affairs, well deserve attention.

There are two elements of importance and influence among mankind: the one is, property; the other, powers and acquirements of mind. Both of these, in an early stage of civilization, are confined to a few persons. In the beginnings of society, the power of the masses does not exist; because property and intelligence have no existence beyond a very small portion of the community, and even if they had, those who possessed the smaller portions would be, from their incapacity of co-operation, unable to cope with those who possessed the larger.

[q] In the more backward countries of the present time, and in all Europe at no distant date, we see property entirely concentrated in a small number of hands; the remainder of the people being, with few exceptions, either the military retainers and dependents of the possessors of property, or serfs, stripped and tortured at pleasure by one master, and pillaged by a hundred. At no period could it be said that there was literally no middle class—but that class was extremely feeble, both in numbers and in power: while the labouring people, absorbed in manual toil, with difficulty earned, by the utmost excess of exertion, a more or less scanty and always precarious subsistence. The character of this state of society was the utmost excess of poverty and impotence in the masses; the most enormous importance and uncontrollable power of a small number of individuals, each of whom, within his own sphere, knew neither law nor superior.

We must leave to history to unfold the gradual rise of the trading and manufacturing classes, the gradual emancipation of the agricultural, the tumults and *bouleversements* which accompanied these changes in their course, and the extraordinary alterations in institutions, opinions, habits, and the whole of social life, which they brought in their train. We need only ask the reader to form a conception [r] of all that is implied in the words, growth of a middle class; and then [s]to[s] reflect on the immense increase of

[p-p]36 shall attempt to point out
[q]36 First, as to property:
[r]36 of the vastness
[s-s]36 bid him

the numbers and property of that class throughout Great Britain, France, Germany, and other countries, in every successive generation, and the novelty of a labouring class receiving such wages as are now commonly earned by nearly the whole of the manufacturing, that is, of the most numerous portion of the operative classes of this country—and ask himself whether, from causes so unheard-of, unheard-of effects ought not to be expected to flow. It must at least be evident, that if, as civilization advances, property and intelligence become thus widely diffused among the millions, it must also be an effect of civilization, that the portion of either of these which can belong to an individual must have a tendency to become less and less influential, and all results must more and more be decided by the movements of masses; provided that the power of combination among the masses keeps pace with the progress of their resources. And that it does so, who can doubt? There is not a more accurate test of the progress of civilization than the progress of the power of co-operation.

Consider the savage: he has bodily strength, he has courage, enterprise, and is often not without intelligence; what makes all savage communities poor and feeble? The same cause which prevented the lions and tigers from long ago extirpating the race of men—incapacity of co-operation. It is only civilized beings who can combine. All combination is compromise: it is the sacrifice of some portion of individual will, for a common purpose. The savage cannot bear to sacrifice, for any purpose, the satisfaction of his individual will. His *social cannot even temporarily prevail over his selfish feelings, nor his impulses* bend to his calculations. Look again at the slave: he is used indeed to make his will give way; but to the commands of a master, not to a superior purpose of his own. He is wanting in intelligence to form such a purpose; above all, he cannot frame to himself the conception of a fixed rule: nor if he could, has he the capacity to adhere to it; he is habituated to control, but not to self-control; when a driver is not standing over him with a *whip*, he is found more incapable of withstanding any temptation, or *restraining* any inclination, than the savage himself.

We have taken extreme cases, that the fact we seek to illustrate might stand out more conspicuously. But the remark itself applies universally. As any people approach to the condition of savages or of slaves, so are they incapable of acting in concert. *Consider even* war, the most serious business of a barbarous people; see what a figure rude nations, or semi-civilized and enslaved nations, have made against civilized ones, from Marathon downwards. Why? Because discipline is more powerful than numbers, and discipline, that is, perfect co-operation, is an attribute of civilization. To come to

*t–t*36	Look at	*u–u*36	impulses cannot
*v–v*36	cart-whip	*w–w*36	constraining
*x–x*36	Look even at		

our own times, [y]the whole history of the Peninsular War bears witness to the incapacity of an imperfectly civilized people for[y] co-operation. Amidst all the enthusiasm of the Spanish [z]nation[z] struggling against Napoleon, no one leader, military or political, could act in concert with another; no one would sacrifice one iota of his consequence, his authority, or his opinion, to the most obvious demands of the common cause; neither generals nor soldiers could observe the simplest rules of the military art. If there be an interest which one might expect to act forcibly upon the minds even of savages, it is the desire of simultaneously crushing a formidable neighbour whom none of them are strong enough to resist single-handed; yet none but civilized nations have ever been capable of forming an alliance. The native states of India have been conquered by the English one by one; Turkey made peace with Russia in the very moment of her invasion by France; the nations of the world never could form a confederacy against the Romans, but were swallowed up in succession, some of them being always ready to aid in the subjugation of the rest. Enterprises requiring the voluntary co-operation of many persons independent of one another, in the hands of all but highly civilized nations, have always failed.

It is not difficult to see why this incapacity of organized combination characterizes savages, and disappears with the growth of civilization. Co-operation, like other difficult things, can be learnt only by practice: and to be capable of it in great things, a people must be gradually trained to it in small. Now, the whole course of advancing civilization is a series of such training. The labourer in a rude state of society works singly, or if several are brought to work together by the will of a master, they work side by side, but not in concert; one man digs his piece of ground, another digs a similar piece of ground close by him. In the situation of an ignorant labourer, tilling even his own field with his own [a]hands[a], and [b]associating with[b] no one except his wife and his children, what is there that can teach him to co-operate? The division of employments—the accomplishment by the combined labour of several, of tasks which could not be achieved by any number of persons singly—is the great school of co-operation. What a lesson, for instance, is navigation, as soon as it passes out of its first simple stage; the safety of all, constantly depending upon the vigilant performance by each, of the part peculiarly allotted to him in the common task. Military operations, when not wholly undisciplined, are a similar school; so are all the operations of commerce and manufactures which require the employment of many hands upon

<hr>

[y-y]36   read Napier's *History of the Peninsular War* [William Napier, *History of the War in the Peninsula and in the South of France, from the year 1807 to the year 1814*, 6 vols. (London: Murray, 1828–40)]; see how incapable half-savages are of

[z-z]36   people

[a-a]36   hand [*printer's error?*]   [b-b]36   seeing

the same thing at the same time. By these operations, mankind learn the value of combination; they see how much and with what ease it accomplishes, which never could be accomplished without it; they learn a practical lesson of submitting themselves to guidance, and subduing themselves to act as interdependent parts of a complex whole. A people thus progressively trained to combination by the business of their lives, become capable of carrying the same habits into new things. For it holds universally, that the one only mode of learning to do anything, is actually doing something of the same kind under easier circumstances. Habits of discipline once acquired, qualify human beings to accomplish all other things for which discipline is needed. No longer either spurning control, or *c* incapable of seeing its advantages; whenever any object presents itself which can be attained by co-operation, and which they see or believe to be beneficial, they are ripe for attaining it.

The characters, then, of a state of high civilization being the diffusion of property and intelligence, and the power of co-operation; the next thing to observe is the *d*unexampled*d* development which all these elements have assumed of late years.

The rapidity with which property has accumulated and is accumulating in the principal countries of Europe, but especially in this island, is obvious to every one. The capital of the industrious classes overflows into foreign countries, and into all kinds of wild speculations. The amount of capital annually exported from Great Britain alone, surpasses probably the whole wealth of the most flourishing commercial republics of antiquity. But *e*this*e* capital, collectively so vast, is *f*mainly composed*f* of small portions; very generally so small that the owners cannot, without other means of livelihood, subsist on the profits of them. While such is the growth of property in the hands of the mass, the circumstances of the higher classes have undergone nothing like a corresponding improvement. Many large fortunes have, it is true, been accumulated, but many others have been wholly or partially dissipated; for the inheritors of immense fortunes, as a class, always live at least up to their incomes when at the highest, and the unavoidable vicissitudes of those incomes are always sinking them deeper and deeper into debt. *g*A large proportion of the*g* English landlords, as they themselves are constantly telling us, are *h*so overwhelmed with mortgages, that they have ceased to be the real owners of the bulk of their estates*h*. In other countries the large properties have very generally been broken down; in France, by revolution,

*c*36   being   *d-d*36   astonishing
*e-e*36 the   *f-f*36   composed almost entirely
*g-g*36 The
*h-h*36 a bankrupt body, and the real owners of the bulk of their estates are the mortgagees

and the revolutionary law of inheritance; in Prussia, by successive edicts of that substantially democratic, though *formally* absolute government.

With respect to knowledge and intelligence, it is the truism of the age, that the masses, both of the middle and even of the working classes, are treading upon the heels of their superiors.

If we now consider the progress made by those same masses in the capacity and habit of co-operation, we find it equally surprising. At what period were the operations of productive industry carried on upon anything like their present scale? Were so many hands ever before employed at the same time upon the same work, as now in all the principal departments of manufactures and commerce? To how enormous an extent is business now carried on by joint-stock companies—in other words, by many small capitals thrown together to form one great one. The country is covered with associations. There are societies for political, societies for religious, societies for philanthropic purposes. But the greatest novelty of all is the spirit of combination which has *grown up* among the working classes. The present age has seen the commencement of benefit societies; and they now, as well as the more questionable Trades Unions, overspread the whole country. A more powerful, though not so ostensible, instrument of combination than any of these, has but lately become universally accessible—the newspaper. The newspaper carries *home the voice of the many* to every individual among them; by the newspaper each learns that *l* others are feeling as he feels, and that if he is ready, he will find them also prepared to act upon what they feel. The newspaper is the telegraph which carries the signal throughout the country, and the flag round which it rallies. Hundreds of newspapers speaking in the same voice at once, and the rapidity of communication afforded by improved means of locomotion, were what enabled the whole country to combine in that simultaneous energetic demonstration of determined will which carried the Reform Act. Both these facilities are on the increase, every one may see how rapidly; and they will enable the people on all decisive occasions to form a collective will, and render that collective will irresistible.

To meet this wonderful development of physical and *mental* power on the part of the masses, can it be said that there has been any corresponding quantity of intellectual power or moral energy unfolded among those individuals or classes who have enjoyed superior advantages? No one, we think, will affirm it. There is a great increase of humanity, a decline of bigotry, *as well as of arrogance and the conceit of caste*, among our conspicuous classes;

---

*i-i*36   nominally   *j-j*36   gone forth
*k-k*36   the voice of the many home   *l*36   all
*m-m*36   intellectual
*n-n*36   and of many of the repulsive qualities of aristocracy

but there is, to say the least, no increase of shining ability, and a very marked decrease of vigour and energy. With all the advantages of this age, its facilities for mental cultivation, the incitements and *o* rewards which it holds out to exalted talents, there can scarcely be pointed out in the European annals any stirring times which have brought so little that is distinguished, either morally or intellectually, to the surface.

That this, too, is no more than was to be expected from the tendencies of civilization, when no attempt is made to correct them, we shall have occasion to show presently. But even if civilization did nothing to lower the eminences, it would produce an exactly similar effect by raising the plains. When the masses become powerful, an individual, or a small band of individuals, can *p*accomplish nothing considerable*p* except by influencing the masses; and to do this becomes daily more difficult, *q* from the constantly increasing number of those who are vying with one another to attract the public attention. Our position, therefore, is established, that by the natural growth of civilization, power passes from individuals to masses, and the weight and importance of an individual, as compared with the mass, sink into greater and greater insignificance.

The change which is thus in progress, and to a great extent consummated, is the greatest ever recorded in *r*social*r* affairs; the most complete, the most fruitful in consequences, and the most irrevocable. Whoever can meditate on it, and not see that so great a revolution vitiates all existing rules of government and policy, and renders all practice and all predictions grounded only on prior experience worthless, is wanting in the very first and most elementary principle of statesmanship in these times.

"Il faut," as M. de Tocqueville has said, "une science politique nouvelle à un monde tout nouveau."[*] The whole face of society is reversed—all the natural elements of power have definitively changed places, and there are people who talk *s* of standing up for ancient institutions, and the duty of sticking to the British Constitution settled in 1688! What is still more extraordinary, these are the people who accuse others of disregarding variety of circumstances, and imposing their abstract theories upon all states of society without discrimination.

We put it to those who call themselves Conservatives, whether, when the *t*chief*t* power in society is passing into the hands of the masses, they really think it possible to prevent the masses from making that power predominant as well in the government as elsewhere? The triumph of democracy, or, in

[*De la Démocratie en Amérique, Vol. I, p. 11; cf. p. 51 above.]

o36, 59   the
q36   and requires higher powers,
s36   to us

p–p36   be nothing
r–r36   human
t–t36   whole

other words, of the government of public opinion, does not depend upon the opinion of any individual or set of individuals that it ought to triumph, but upon the natural laws of the progress of wealth, upon the diffusion of reading, and the increase of the facilities of human intercourse. If Lord Kenyon or the Duke of Newcastle could stop these, they might accomplish something. There is no danger of the prevalence of democracy in Syria or Timbuctoo. But he must be a poor politician who does not know, that whatever is the growing power in society will force its way into the government, by fair means or foul. The distribution of constitutional power cannot long continue very different from that of real power, without a convulsion. Nor, if the institutions which impede the progress of democracy could be by any miracle preserved, could even they do more than render that progress a little slower. Were the Constitution of Great Britain to remain henceforth unaltered, we are not the less under the dominion, becoming every day more irresistible, of public opinion.

With regard to the advance of democracy, there are two different positions which it is possible for a rational person to take up, according as he thinks the masses prepared, or unprepared, to exercise the control which they are acquiring over their destiny, in a manner which would be an improvement upon what now exists. If he thinks them prepared, he will aid the democratic movement; or if he deem it to be proceeding fast enough without him, he will at all events refrain from resisting it. If, on the contrary, he thinks the masses unprepared for complete control over their government—seeing at the same time that, prepared or not, they cannot ^{u}long^u be prevented from acquiring it—he will exert his utmost efforts in contributing to prepare them; using all means, on the one hand, for making the masses themselves wiser and better; on the other, for so rousing the slumbering energy of the opulent and lettered classes, so storing the youth of those classes with the profoundest and most valuable knowledge, so calling forth whatever of individual greatness exists or can be raised up in the country, as to create a power which might partially rival the mere power of the masses, and might exercise the most salutary influence over them for their own good. When engaged earnestly in works like these, one can understand how a rational person might think that in order to give more time for the performance of them, it were well if the current of democracy, which can in no sort be stayed, could be prevailed upon for a time to flow less impetuously. With Conservatives of this sort, all ^{v}democrats^v of corresponding enlargement of ^{w}aims^w could fraternize as frankly and cordially as with ^{x}most^x of their own friends: and we speak from an extensive knowledge of the wisest and most high-minded of that body, when we take upon ourselves to answer for them, that they

$^{u-u}$+59, 67 $^{v-v}$36   Radicals
$^{w-w}$36   view, $^{x-x}$36   many

would never push forward their own political projects in a spirit or with a violence which could tend to frustrate any rational endeavours towards the object nearest their hearts, the instruction of the understandings and the elevation of the characters of all classes of their countrymen.

But who is there among the political party calling themselves Conservatives, that professes to have any such object in view? *y*Do they seek*y* to employ the interval of respite which *z*they*z* might hope to gain by withstanding democracy, in qualifying the people to wield the democracy more wisely when it comes? *a*Would they*a* not far rather resist any such endeavour, on the principle that knowledge is power, and that its further diffusion would make the dreaded evil come sooner? *b*Do the leading Conservatives in either house of parliament feel*b* that the character of the higher classes needs renovating, to qualify them for a more arduous task and a keener strife than has yet fallen to their lot? Is not the character of a Tory lord or country gentleman, or a Church of England parson, perfectly satisfactory to them? Is not the existing constitution of the two Universities—those bodies whose especial duty it was to counteract the debilitating influence of the circumstances of the age upon individual character, and to send forth into society a succession of minds, not the creatures of their age, but capable of being its improvers and regenerators—the Universities, by whom this their especial duty has been basely neglected, until, as is usual with *c* neglected duties, the very consciousness of it as a duty has faded from their remembrance,—is not, we say, the existing constitution and the whole existing system of these Universities, down to the smallest of their abuses, the exclusion of Dissenters, a thing for which every Tory, though he may not, as he pretends, die in the last ditch, will at least vote in the last division? The Church, professedly the other great instrument of national culture, long since perverted (we speak of rules, not exceptions) into *d*a grand instrument for discouraging all culture inconsistent with blind*d* obedience to established maxims and constituted authorities— what Tory has a scheme in view for any changes in this body, but such as may pacify assailants, and make the institution wear a less disgusting appearance to the eye? What political Tory will not resist to the very last moment any alteration in that Church, which *e*would*e* prevent its livings from being the provision for a family, its dignities the reward of political or of private services? The Tories, those at least connected with parliament or office, do not aim at having good institutions, or even at preserving the present ones: their object is to profit by them while they exist.

*y-y*36   Is there one who seeks   *z-z*36   he
*a-a*36   Is there one who would
*b-b*36   Again, is there a Conservative in either house of parliament who feels
*c*36, 59   all
*d-d*36   the great instrument of preventing all culture, except the inculcation of
*e-e*36   will

We scruple not to express our belief that a truer spirit of *conservation*,
as to everything good in the principles and professed objects of our old institutions, lives in many who are determined enemies of those institutions in
their present state, than in most of those who call themselves Conservatives.
But there are many well-meaning people who always confound attachment
to an end, with *pertinacious* adherence to any set of means by which it
either is, or is pretended to be, already pursued; and have yet to learn, that
bodies of men who live in honour and importance upon the pretence of fulfilling ends which they never honestly seek, are the great hindrance to the
attainment of those ends; and *that* whoever has the attainment really at
heart, must *expect a war of extermination with all such confederacies*.

Thus far as to the political effects of Civilization. Its moral effects, which
as yet we have only glanced at, demand further elucidation. They may be
considered under two heads: the direct influence of Civilization itself upon
individual character, and the moral effects produced by the insignificance
into which the individual falls in comparison with the masses.

One of the effects of a high state of civilization upon character, is a relaxation of individual energy: or rather, the concentration of it within the
narrow sphere of the individual's money-getting pursuits. As civilization
advances, every person becomes dependent, for more and more of what
most nearly concerns him, not upon his own exertions, but upon the general
arrangements of society. In a rude state, each man's personal security, the
protection of his family, his property, his liberty itself, *depend* greatly upon
his bodily strength and his mental energy or cunning: in a civilized state, all
this is secured to him by causes extrinsic to himself. The growing mildness
of manners is a protection to him against much that he was before exposed
to, while for the remainder he may rely with constantly increasing assurance
upon the soldier, the policeman, and the judge; and (where the efficiency
or purity of those instruments, as is usually the case, lags behind the general
march of civilization) upon the advancing strength of public opinion. There
remain, as inducements to call forth energy of character, the desire of wealth
or of personal aggrandizement, the passion of philanthropy, and the love of
active virtue. But the objects to which these various feelings point are matters
of choice, not of necessity, nor do the feelings act with anything like equal
force upon all minds. The only one of them which can be considered as anything like universal, is the desire of wealth; and wealth being, in the case of
the majority, the most accessible means of gratifying all their other desires,

*f–f*36 Conservation
*g–g*36 blind
h–h+59, 67
*i–i*36 begin by sweeping them from his path
*j–j*36 depends

nearly the whole of the energy of character which exists in highly civilized societies concentrates itself on the pursuit of that object. In the case, however, of the most influential classes—those whose energies, if they had them, might be exercised on the greatest scale and with the most considerable result —the desire of wealth is already sufficiently satisfied, to render them averse to suffer pain or incur *k*much*k* voluntary labour for the sake of any further increase. The same classes also enjoy, from their station alone, a high degree of personal consideration. Except the high offices of the *l*State*l*, there is hardly anything to tempt the ambition of men in their circumstances. Those offices, when a great nobleman could have them for asking for, and keep them with less trouble than he could manage his private estate, were, no doubt, desirable enough possessions for such persons; but when they become posts of labour, vexation, and anxiety, and besides cannot be had without paying the price of some previous toil, experience shows that among men unaccustomed to sacrifice their amusements and their ease, the number upon whom these high offices operate as incentives to activity, or in whom they call forth any vigour of character, is extremely limited. Thus it happens that in highly civilized countries, and particularly among ourselves, the energies of the middle classes are almost confined to money-getting, and those of the higher classes are nearly extinct.

There is another circumstance to which we may trace much both of the good and of the bad qualities which distinguish our civilization from the rudeness of former times. One of the effects of civilization (not to say one of the ingredients in it) is, that the spectacle, and even the very idea, of pain, is kept more and more out of the sight of those classes who enjoy in their fulness the benefits of civilization. The state of perpetual personal conflict, rendered necessary by the circumstances of *m* former times, and from which it was hardly possible for any person, in whatever rank of society, to be exempt, necessarily habituated every one to the spectacle of harshness, rudeness, and violence, to the struggle of one indomitable will against another, and to the alternate suffering and infliction of pain. These things, consequently, were not as revolting even to the best and most actively benevolent men of former days, as they are to our own; and we find the recorded conduct of those men frequently such as would be universally considered very unfeeling in a person of our own day. They, however, thought less of the infliction of pain, because they thought less of pain altogether. When we read of actions of the Greeks and Romans, or *n*of*n* our own ancestors, denoting callousness to human suffering, we must not think that those who committed these actions were as cruel as we must become before we could do the like. The pain which they inflicted, they were in the habit of voluntarily un-

k-k+59, 67   *l-l*36   state
*m*36   all   *n-n*+59, 67

dergoing from slight causes; it did not appear to them as great an evil, as it appears, and as it really is, to us, nor did it in any way degrade their minds. In our own time the necessity of personal collision between one person and another is, comparatively speaking, almost at an end. All those necessary portions of the business of society which oblige any person to be the immediate agent or ocular witness of the infliction of pain, are delegated by common consent to peculiar and narrow classes: to the judge, the soldier, the surgeon, the butcher, and the executioner. To most people in easy circumstances, any pain, except that inflicted upon the body by accident or disease, and ^oupon the mind by the inevitable sorrows of life^o, is rather a thing known of than actually experienced. This is much more emphatically true in the more refined classes, and as refinement advances: for it is in ^pavoiding the presence not only of actual pain, but of whatever suggests offensive or disagreeable ideas, that a great part of^p refinement consists. We may remark too, that this is possible only by a perfection of mechanical arrangements impracticable in any but a high state of civilization. Now, most kinds of pain and annoyance appear much more unendurable to those who have little experience of them, than to those who have much. The consequence is that, compared with former times, there is in the ^qmore opulent^q classes of modern civilized communities much more of the amiable and humane, and much less of the heroic. The heroic essentially consists in being ready, for a worthy object, to do and to suffer, but especially to do, what is painful or disagreeable: and whoever does not early learn ^rto be capable of^r this, will never be a great character. There has crept over the refined classes, over the whole class of gentlemen in England, a moral effeminacy, an inaptitude for every kind of struggle. They shrink from all effort, from everything which is troublesome and disagreeable. ^sThe same causes which render them sluggish and unenterprising, make them, it is true, for the most part, stoical under inevitable evils.^s But heroism is an active, not a passive quality; and when it is necessary not to bear pain but to seek it, little needs be expected from the men of the present day. They cannot undergo labour, they cannot ^tbrook ridicule, they cannot brave^t evil tongues: they have not hardihood to say an unpleasant thing to any one whom they are in the habit of seeing, or to face, even with a nation at their back, the coldness of some little ^ucoterie^u which

^{o–o}36   the more delicate and refined griefs of the imagination and the affections

^{p–p}36   keeping as far as possible out of sight, not only actual pain, but all that can be offensive or disagreeable to the most sensitive person, that

^{q–q}36   refined

^{r–r}+59, 67

^{s–s}36   When an evil *comes to* them, they can sometimes bear it with tolerable patience, (though nobody is less patient when they can entertain the slightest hope that by raising an outcry they may compel somebody else to make an effort to relieve them).

^{t–t}36   brave ridicule, they cannot stand

^{u–u}36   *coterie*

surrounds them. This torpidity and cowardice, as a general characteristic, is new in the world: but (modified by the different temperaments of different nations) it is a natural consequence of the progress of civilization, and will continue until met by a system of cultivation adapted to counteract it.

If the source of great virtues thus dries up, great vices are placed, no doubt, under considerable restraint. The *régime* of public opinion is adverse to at least the indecorous vices: and as that restraining power gains strength, and certain classes or individuals cease to possess a virtual exemption from it, the change is highly favourable to the outward decencies of life. Nor can it be denied that the diffusion of even such knowledge as civilization naturally brings, has no slight tendency to rectify, though it be but partially, the standard of public opinion; to undermine many of those prejudices and superstitions which ᵛmadeᵛ mankind hate each other for things not really odious; to make them take a juster measure of the tendencies of actions, and weigh more correctly the evidence on which they condemn or applaud their fellow-creatures; to make, in short, their approbation direct itself more correctly to good actions, and their disapprobation to bad. What are the limits to this natural improvement in public opinion, when there is no other sort of cultivation going on than that which is the accompaniment of civilization, we need not at present inquire. It is enough that within those limits there is an extensive range; that as much ʷ improvement in the general understanding, softening of the feelings, and decay of pernicious errors, as naturally attends the progress of wealth and the spread of reading, suffices to render the judgment of the public upon actions and persons, so far as evidence is before them, much more discriminating and correct.

But here presents itself another ramification of the effects of civilization, which it has often surprised us to find so little attended to. The individual becomes so lost in the crowd, that though he depends more and more upon opinion, he is apt to depend less and less upon well-grounded opinion; upon the opinion of those who know him. An established character becomes at once more difficult to gain, and more easily to be dispensed with.

It is in a small society, where everybody knows everybody, that public opinion, ˣso far asˣ well directed, exercises its most salutary influence. Take the case of a tradesman in a small country town: to every one of his customers he is long and ʸaccuratelyʸ known; their opinion of him has been formed after repeated trials; if he could deceive them once, he cannot hope to go on deceiving them in the quality of his goods; he has no other customers to look ᶻforᶻ if he loses these, while, if his goods are really what they ᵃprofessᵃ to be, he may hope, among so few competitors, that this also will be known

---

ᵛ⁻ᵛ36   make   ʷ36   of
ˣ⁻ˣ36   when   ʸ⁻ʸ36   intimately
ᶻ⁻ᶻ36   to
ᵃ⁻ᵃ36   pretend

and recognised, and that he will acquire the character, [b]individually and professionally[b], which his conduct entitles him to. Far different is the case of a man setting up in business in the crowded streets of a great city. If he trust solely to the quality of his goods, to the honesty and faithfulness with which he performs what he undertakes, he may remain ten years without a customer: be he ever so honest, he is driven to cry out on the housetops that his wares are the best of wares, past, present, and to come; while, if he proclaim this, [c]however[c] false, with sufficient loudness to excite the curiosity of passers by, and can give his commodities [d]"a gloss, a saleable look,"[d] not easily to be seen through at a superficial glance, he may drive a thriving trade though no customer ever enter his shop twice. There has been much complaint of late years, of the growth, both in the world of trade and in that of intellect, of quackery, and especially of puffing: but nobody seems to have remarked, that these are the inevitable [e]fruits[e] of immense competition; of a state of society where any voice, not pitched in an exaggerated key, is lost in the hubbub. Success, in so crowded a field, depends not upon what a person is, but upon what he seems: mere marketable qualities become the object instead of substantial ones, and a man's labour and capital are expended less in [f]doing[f] anything, than in persuading other people that he has done it. Our own age has seen this evil brought to its consummation. Quackery there always was, but it once was a test of the absence of sterling qualities: there was a proverb that good wine needed no bush. It is our own age which has seen the honest dealer driven to quackery, by hard necessity, and the certainty of being undersold by the dishonest. For the first time, arts for attracting public attention form a necessary part of the qualifications even of the deserving: and skill in these goes farther than any other quality towards ensuring success. The same intensity of competition drives the trading public more and more to play high for success, to throw for all or nothing; and this, together with the difficulty of sure calculations in a field of commerce so widely extended, renders bankruptcy no longer disgraceful, because no longer [g]an almost certain presumption of either[g] dishonesty or imprudence: the discredit which it still incurs belongs to it, alas! mainly as an indication of poverty. Thus public opinion loses another of those simple criteria of desert, which, and which alone, it is capable of correctly applying; and the very cause which has rendered it omnipotent in the gross, weakens the precision and force with which its judgment is brought home to individuals.

It is not solely on the private virtues, that this growing insignificance of the individual in the mass is productive of mischief. It corrupts the very fountain of the improvement of public opinion itself; it corrupts public

b–b36   as a man and a tradesman   c–c36   true or
d–d36   [no quotation marks]   e–e36   outgrowth
f–f36   doing
g–g36   a presumption either of]   59   an almost certain presumption either of

teaching; it weakens the influence of the more cultivated few over the many. Literature has suffered more than any other human production by the common disease. When there were few books, and when few read at all save those who had been accustomed to read the best authors, books were written with the well-grounded expectation that they would be read carefully, and if they deserved it, would be read often. A book of sterling merit, when it came out, was sure to be heard of, and might hope to be read, by the whole reading class; it might succeed by its real [h]excellences, though[h] not got up to strike at once; and even if so got up, unless it had the support of genuine merit, it fell into oblivion. The rewards were then for him who wrote *well*, not *much*; for the laborious and learned, not the crude and ill-informed writer. But now the case is reversed.

[i] This is a reading age; and precisely because it is so reading an age, any book which is the result of profound meditation is, perhaps, less likely to be duly and profitably read than at a former period. The world reads too much and too quickly to read well. When books were few, to get through one was a work of time and labour: what was written with thought was read with thought, and with a desire to extract from it as much of the materials of knowledge as possible. But when almost every person who can spell, can and will write, what is to be done? It is difficult to know what to read, except by reading everything; and so much of the world's business is now transacted through the press, that it is necessary to know what is printed, if we desire to know what is going on. Opinion weighs with so vast a weight in the balance of events, that ideas of no value in themselves are of importance from the mere circumstance that they *are* ideas, and have a *bonâ fide* existence as such anywhere out of Bedlam. The world, in consequence, gorges itself with intellectual food, and in order to swallow the more, *bolts* it. Nothing is now read slowly, or twice over. Books are run through with no less rapidity, and scarcely leave a more durable impression, than a newspaper article. It is for this, among other causes, that so few books are produced of any value. The lioness in the fable boasted that though she produced only one at a birth, that one was a lion. But if each lion only counted for one, and each leveret for one, the advantage would all be on the side of the hare. When every unit is individually weak, it is only multitude that tells. What wonder[j] that the newspapers should carry all before them? A book produces [k]hardly a[k] greater effect than an article, and there can be 365 of these in one year. He, therefore, who should and would write a book, and write it in the proper manner of writing a book, now dashes down his first hasty thoughts, or what he mistakes for thoughts, in a periodical. And the public is in the predicament of an indolent man, who cannot bring himself to apply his mind vigorously to his own affairs, and over whom, therefore, not he who speaks most wisely, but he who speaks most frequently, obtains the influence.*

*[l]From a paper by the author, not included in the present collection.[l]

[h-h]36 excellencies, although]   59 excellencies, though
[i]36 [*paragraph*]
[j-j]Source, 36 Who wonders   [k-k]Source, 36 no
[l-l]36 Review of "Austin's Lectures on Jurisprudence," in *Tait's* [*Edinburgh*] *Magazine* for December, 1832 [Vol. IX, p. 343].

Hence we see that literature is becoming more and more ephemeral: books, of any solidity, are *almost* gone by; even reviews are not now considered sufficiently light; the attention cannot sustain itself on any serious subject, even for the space of a review-article. In the more attractive kinds of literature, *novels and magazines, though* the demand has so greatly increased, the supply has so outstripped it, that even a novel is seldom a lucrative speculation. It is only under circumstances of rare attraction that a bookseller will now give anything to an author for copyright. As the difficulties of success thus progressively increase, all other ends are more and more sacrificed for the attainment of it; literature becomes more and more a mere reflection of the current sentiments, and has almost entirely abandoned its mission as an enlightener and improver of them.

There are now in this country, we may say, but two modes left in which an individual mind can hope to produce much direct effect upon the minds and destinies of his countrymen generally; as a member of parliament, or an editor of a London newspaper. In both these capacities much may still be done by an individual, because, while the power of the collective body is very great, the number of participants in it does not admit of much increase. One of these monopolies will be opened to competition when the newspaper stamp is taken off;[*] whereby the importance of the newspaper press in the aggregate, considered as the voice of public opinion, will be *o* increased, and the influence of any one writer in helping to form that opinion *necessarily* diminished. This we might regret, did we not remember to what ends that influence is now used, and is sure to be so while newspapers are a mere investment of capital for the sake of mercantile profit.

Is there, then, no remedy? Are the decay of individual energy, the weakening of the influence of superior minds over the multitude, the growth of *charlatanerie*, and the diminished efficacy of public opinion as a restraining power,—are these the price we necessarily pay for the benefits of civilization; and can they only be avoided by checking the diffusion of knowledge, discouraging the spirit of combination, prohibiting improvements in the arts of life, and repressing the further increase of wealth and of production? Assuredly not. Those advantages which civilization cannot give—which in its uncorrected influence it has even a tendency to destroy—may yet coexist with civilization; and it is only when joined to civilization that they can pro-

[*See 6 & 7 William IV, c. 76 (1836).]

*m–m*36 actually
*n–n*36 the novel and the magazine, although
*o*36 much
*p–p*36 greatly
*q–q*36 *charlatanerie*

duce their fairest fruits. All that we are in danger of losing we may preserve, all that we have lost we may regain, and bring to a perfection hitherto unknown; but not by slumbering, and leaving things to themselves, no more than by ridiculously trying our strength against their irresistible tendencies: only by establishing counter-tendencies, which may combine with those tendencies, and modify them.

The evils are, that the individual is lost and becomes impotent in the crowd, and that individual character itself becomes relaxed and enervated. For the first evil, the remedy is, greater and more perfect combination among individuals; for the second, national institutions of education, and forms of polity, calculated to invigorate the individual character.

The former of these ʳdesiderataʳ, as its attainment depends upon a change in the habits of society itself, can only be realized by degrees, as the necessity becomes felt; but circumstances are even now to a certain extent forcing it on. In Great Britain especially (which so far surpasses the rest of the ˢoldˢ world in the extent and rapidity of the accumulation of wealth) the fall of profits, consequent upon the vast increase of population and capital, is rapidly extinguishing the class of small dealers and small producers, from the impossibility of living on their diminished profits, and is throwing business of all kinds more and more into the hands of large capitalists—whether these be rich individuals, or joint-stock companies formed by the aggrega-ion of many small capitals. We are not among those who believe that this progress is tending to the complete extinction of ᵗ competition, or that the entire productive resources of the country will within any assignable number of ages, if ever, be administered by, and for the benefit of, a general associa-tion of the whole community. But we believe that the multiplication of com-petitors in all branches of business and in all professions—which renders it more and more difficult to obtain success by merit alone, more and more easy to obtain it by plausible pretence—will find a limiting principle in the progress of the spirit of co-operation; that in every overcrowded department there will arise a tendency among individuals so to unite their ᵘlabour or their capitalᵘ, that the purchaser or employer will have to choose, not among innumerable individuals, but among a few groups. Competition will be as active as ever, but the number of competitors will be brought within man-ageable bounds.

Such a spirit of co-operation is most of all wanted among the intellectual classes and professions. The amount of human labour, and labour of the most precious kind, now wasted, and wasted too in the cruelest manner, for want of combination, is incalculable. What a spectacle, for instance, does the medical profession present! One successful practitioner burthened with

ʳ⁻ʳ36 *desiderata*   ˢ⁻ˢ+59, 67
ᵗ36 individual   ᵘ⁻ᵘ36 labours or their capitals

more work than mortal man can perform, and which he performs so summarily that it were often better let alone;—in the surrounding streets twenty unhappy men, each of whom has been as laboriously and expensively trained as he has to do the very same thing, and is possibly as well qualified, wasting their capabilities and starving for want of work. Under better arrangements these twenty would form a corps of subalterns marshalled under their more successful leader; who (granting him to be really the ablest physician of the set, and not merely the most successful imposter) is wasting time in physicking people for headaches and heartburns, which he might with better economy of mankind's resources turn over to his subordinates, while he employed his maturer powers and greater experience in studying and treating those more obscure and difficult cases upon which science has not yet thrown sufficient light, and to which ordinary knowledge and abilities would not be adequate. By such means every person's capacities would be turned to account, and the highest minds being kept for the highest things, these would make progress, while ordinary occasions would be no losers.

But it is in literature, above all, that a change of this sort is of most pressing urgency. There the system of individual competition has fairly worked itself out, and things ^vcan hardly^v continue much longer as they are. Literature is a province of exertion upon which more, of the first value to human nature, depends, than upon any other; a province in which the highest and most valuable order of works, those which most contribute to form the opinions and shape the characters of subsequent ages, are, more than in any other class of productions, placed beyond the possibility of appreciation by those who form the bulk of the purchasers in the book-market; insomuch that, even in ages when these were a far less numerous and more select class than now, it was an admitted point that the only success which writers of the first order could look to was the verdict of posterity. That verdict could, in those times, be confidently expected by whoever was worthy of it; for the good judges, though few in number, were sure to read every work of merit which appeared; and as the recollection of one book was not in those days immediately obliterated by a hundred others, they remembered it, and kept alive the knowledge of it to subsequent ages. But in our day, from the immense multitude of writers (which is now not less remarkable than the multitude of readers), and from the manner in which the people of this age are obliged to read, it is difficult for what does not strike during its novelty, to strike at all: a book either misses fire altogether, or is so read as to make no permanent impression; and the ^wgood equally with the worthless^w are forgotten by the next day.

For this there is no remedy, while the public have no guidance beyond

^{v–v}36   cannot
^{w–w}36   best equally with the worst

booksellers' advertisements, and the *ill-considered and hasty criticisms* of newspapers and small periodicals, to direct them in distinguishing what is not worth reading from what is. The resource must in time be, some organized co-operation among the leading intellects of the age, whereby works of first-rate merit, of whatever class, and of whatever tendency in point of opinion, might come forth with the stamp on them, from the first, of the approval of those whose *names* would carry authority. There are many causes why we must wait long for such a combination; but (with enormous defects, both in plan and in execution) the Society for the Diffusion of Useful Knowledge was as considerable a step towards it, as could be expected in the present state of men's minds, and in a first attempt. Literature has had in this country two ages; it must now have a third. The age of patronage, as Johnson a century ago proclaimed, is gone. The age of booksellers, it has been proclaimed *by Mr. Carlyle, has* well nigh died out.[*] In the first there was nothing intrinsically base, nor in the second anything inherently independent and liberal. Each has done great things; both have had their day. The time is *perhaps* coming when authors, as a collective guild, *will* be their own patrons and their own booksellers.

These things must bide their time. But the other of the two great *desiderata*, the regeneration of individual character among our lettered and opulent classes, by the adaptation to that purpose of our institutions, and, above all, of our educational institutions, is an object of more urgency, and for which more might be immediately accomplished, if the will and the understanding were not alike wanting.

This, unfortunately, is a subject on which, for the inculcation of rational views, everything is yet to be done; for, all that we would inculcate, all that we deem of vital importance, all upon which we conceive the salvation of the next and all future ages to rest, has the misfortune to be almost equally opposed to the most popular doctrines of our own time, and to the prejudices of those who cherish the empty husk of what has descended from ancient times. We are at issue equally with the admirers of Oxford and Cambridge, Eton and Westminster, and with the generality of their professed reformers. We regard the system of those institutions, as *administered for two centuries*

[*Thomas Carlyle, "Boswell's Life of Johnson," *Fraser's Magazine*, V (May, 1832), 397. On pp. 396–7, without specific reference to Johnson, Carlyle says that the age of booksellers had succeeded to the age of patronage.]

*x–x*36   venal paragraphs
*y–y*36   name [*printer's error?*]
*z–z*36   in our own time, has now
a–a+59, 67
*c–c*36   *desiderata*

*b–b*36   must
*d–d*36   actually administered

past^d, with sentiments little short of utter abhorrence. But we do not conceive that their vices would be cured by bringing their studies into a closer connexion with what it is the fashion to term "the business of the world;" by dismissing the logic and classics which are still ^{e}professedly^e taught, to substitute modern languages and experimental physics. We would have classics and logic taught far more really and deeply than at present, and we would add to them other studies more alien than any which yet exist to the "business of the world," but more germane to the great business of every rational being—the strengthening and enlarging of his own intellect and character. The empirical knowledge which the world demands, which is the stock in trade of money-getting-life, we would leave the world to provide for itself; content with infusing into the youth of our country a spirit, and training them to habits, which would ensure their acquiring such knowledge easily, and using it well. These, we know, are not the sentiments of the vulgar; but we believe them to be those of the best and wisest of all parties: and we are glad to corroborate our opinion by a quotation from a work written by a friend to the Universities, and by one whose tendencies are rather Conservative than Liberal; a book which, though really, and not in form merely, one of fiction, contains much subtle and ingenious thought, and the results of much psychological experience, combined, we are compelled to say, with much caricature, and very provoking (though we are convinced unintentional) distortion and misinterpretation of the opinions of some of those with whose philosophy that of the author does not agree.

"You believe" (a clergyman *loquitur*) "that the University is to prepare youths for a successful career in society: I believe the sole object is to give them that manly character which will enable them to resist the influences of society. I do not care to prove that I am right, and that any university which does not stand upon this basis will be rickety in its childhood, and useless or mischievous in its manhood; I care only to assert that this was the notion of those who founded Oxford and Cambridge. I fear that their successors are gradually losing sight of this principle—are gradually beginning to think that it is their business to turn out clever lawyers and serviceable Treasury clerks—are pleased when the world compliments them upon the goodness of the article with which they have furnished it—and that this low vanity is absorbing all their will and their power to create great men, whom the age will scorn, and who will save it from the scorn of the times to come."

"One or two such men," said the Liberal, "in a generation, may be very useful; but the University gives us two or three thousand youths every year. I suppose you are content that a portion shall do week-day services."

"I wish to have a far more hard-working and active race than we have at present," said the clergyman; "men more persevering in toil, and less impatient of reward; but all experience, a thing which the schools are not privileged to despise, though the world is—all experience is against the notion, that the means to procure a supply of good ordinary men is to attempt nothing higher. I know

$^{e-e}$36 nominally

that nine-tenths of those whom the University sends out must be hewers of wood and drawers of water; but, if I train the ten-tenths to be so, depend upon it the wood will be badly cut, the water will be spilt. Aim at something noble; make your system such that a great man may be formed by it, and there will be a manhood in your little men of which you do not dream. But when some skilful rhetorician, or lucky rat, stands at the top of the ladder—when the University, instead of disclaiming the creature, instead of pleading, as an excuse for themselves, that the healthiest mother may, by accident, produce a shapeless abortion, stands shouting, that the world may know what great things they can do, 'we taught the boy!'—when the hatred which worldly men will bear to religion always, and to learning whenever it teaches us to soar and not to grovel, is met, not with a frank defiance, but rather with a deceitful argument to show that trade is the better for them; is it wonderful that a puny beggarly feeling should pervade the mass of our young men? that they should scorn all noble achievements, should have no higher standard of action than the world's opinion, and should conceive of no higher reward than to sit down amidst loud cheering, which continues for several moments?"*

Nothing can be more just or more forcible than the description here given of the objects which University education should aim at: we are at issue with the writer, only on the proposition that these objects ever were attained, or ever could be so, consistently with the principle which has always been the foundation of the English Universities; a principle, unfortunately, by no means confined to them. The difficulty ᵍ which continues to oppose either such reform of our old academical institutions, or the establishment of such new ones, as shall give us an education capable of forming great minds, is, that in order to do so it is necessary to begin by eradicating the idea which nearly all the upholders and nearly all the impugners of the Universities rootedly entertain, as to the objects not merely of academical education, but of education itself. What is this idea? That the object of education is, not to qualify the pupil for judging what is true or what is right, but to provide that he shall think true what we think true, and right what we think right— that ʰto teach, means to inculcate our own opinions, and that our business is not to make thinkers or inquirers, but disciplesʰ. This is the deep-seated error, the inveterate prejudice, which the real reformer of English education has to struggle against. Is it astonishing that great minds are not produced, in a country where the test of a great mind is, agreeing in the opinions of the small minds? where every institution for spiritual culture which the country has—the Church, the Universities, and almost every dissenting community

*From ⱼthe novel of *Eustace Conway*, attributed to Mr. Mauriceⱼ. [John Frederick Denison Maurice, *Eustace Conway: or, The Brother and Sister*, 3 vols. (London: Bentley, 1834), Vol. II, pp. 79–81.]

ⱼ-ⱼ36   a novel called *Eustace Conway*, Vol. II, Chap. vi
ᵍ36   , the all but insuperable difficulty,
ʰ-ʰ36   not the spirit in which the person's opinions are arrived at and held, but the opinions themselves, are the main point

—are constituted on the following as their avowed principle: that the object is, *not* that the individual should go forth determined and qualified to seek truth ardently, vigorously, and disinterestedly; *not* that he be furnished at setting out with the needful aids and facilities, the needful materials and instruments for that search, and then left to the unshackled use of them; *not* that, by a free communion with the thoughts and deeds of the great minds which preceded him, he be inspired at once with the courage to dare all which truth and *i* conscience require, and the modesty to weigh well the grounds of what others think, before adopting contrary opinions of his own: *not* this—no; but that the triumph of the system, the merit, the excellence in the sight of God which it possesses, or which it can impart to its pupil, is, that his speculations shall terminate in the adoption, in words, of a particular set of opinions. That provided he adhere to these opinions, it matters little whether he receive them from authority or from examination; and worse, that it matters little by what temptations of interest or vanity, by what voluntary or involuntary sophistication with his intellect, and deadening of his noblest feelings, that result is arrived at; that it even matters comparatively little whether to his mind the words are mere words, or the representatives of realities—in what sense he receives the favoured set of propositions, or whether he attaches to them any sense at all. Were ever great minds thus formed? *i*Never.*j* The few great minds which this country has produced have been formed in spite of nearly everything which could be done to stifle their growth. And all thinkers, much above the common order, who have grown up in the Church of England, or in any other Church, have been produced in latitudinarian epochs, or while the impulse of intellectual emancipation which gave existence to the Church had not quite spent itself. The flood of burning metal which issued from the furnace, flowed on a few paces before it congealed.

That the English Universities have, throughout, proceeded on the principle, that the intellectual association of mankind must be founded upon articles, *i.e.* upon a promise of belief in certain opinions; that the scope of all they do is to prevail upon their pupils, by fair means or foul, to acquiesce in the opinions which are set down for them; that the abuse of the human faculties so forcibly denounced by Locke under the name of "principling" their pupils,[*] is their sole method in religion, politics, morality, or philosophy—is vicious indeed, but the vice is equally prevalent without and within their pale, and is no farther disgraceful to them than inasmuch as a better doctrine has been taught for a century past by the superior spirits,

[*See, e.g., John Locke, *Some Thoughts Concerning Education,* in *Works,* Vol. IX, pp. 29, 148.]

*i*36   his
*i-i*36   Never!

with whom in point of intelligence it was their duty to maintain themselves
on a level. But, that when this object was attained they cared for no other;
that if they could make churchmen, they cared not to make religious men;
that if they could make Tories, whether they made patriots was indifferent
to them; that if they could prevent heresy, they cared not if the price paid
were stupidity—this constitutes the peculiar baseness of those bodies. Look
at them. While their sectarian character, while the exclusion of all who will
not sign away their freedom of thought, is contended for as if life depended
upon it, there is *k*hardly*k* a trace in the system of the Universities that any
other object whatever is seriously cared for. Nearly all the professorships
have degenerated into sinecures. Few of the professors ever deliver a lecture.
One of the few great scholars who have issued from either University for a
century (and he was such before he went thither), the Rev. Connop Thirlwall, has published to the world that in his University at least, even *l*theology
—even Church of England theology*l*—is not taught;[*] and his dismissal, for
this piece of honesty, from the tutorship of his college, is one among the
daily proofs how much safer it is for twenty men to neglect their duty, than
for one man to impeach them of the neglect. The only studies really encouraged are classics and mathematics; *m*both of them highly valuable studies*m*,
though the last, as an *n*exclusive*n* instrument for fashioning the mental
powers, greatly overrated; but Mr. Whewell, a high authority against his own
University, has *o* published a pamphlet,[†] chiefly to prove that the kind of
mathematical attainment by which Cambridge honours are gained, expert-
ness in the use of the calculus, is not that kind which has any tendency to
produce superiority of intellect.* The mere shell and husk of the syllogistic

[*See Connop Thirlwall, *A Letter to Thomas Turton on the Admission of Dissenters to Academical Degrees* (Cambridge: Deighton, 1834), pp. 6 ff.]

[†*Thoughts on the Study of Mathematics, as a Part of a Liberal Education*
(Cambridge, 1835).]

*The erudite and able writer in the *Edinburgh Review* *p*[Sir William Hamil-
ton]*p*, who has expended an almost superfluous weight of argument and authority
in *q*combating*q* the position incidentally maintained in Mr. Whewell's pamphlet,
of the great value of mathematics as an exercise of the mind, was, we think, bound
to have noticed the fact that the far more direct object of the pamphlet was one
which partially coincided with that of its reviewer. [See "Study of Mathematics—
University of Cambridge," *Edinburgh Review*, LXII (Jan., 1836), 409–55.] We
do not think that Mr. Whewell has done well what he undertook: he is vague, and
is always attempting to be a profounder metaphysician than he can be; but the
main proposition of his pamphlet is true and important, and he is entitled to no
little credit for having discerned that important truth, and expressed it so strongly.

*k-k*36   not
*l-l*36   religion—even what the Church of England terms religion
*m-m*36, 59   neither of them a useless study
n-n+59, 67   *o*36   just
p-p+59, 67   [*JSM's square brackets*]   *q-q*36   refuting

logic at the one University, the wretchedest smattering of Locke and Paley at the other, are all of moral or psychological science that is taught at either.* As a means of educating the many, the Universities are absolutely null. The youth of England are not educated. The attainments ʳof any kindʳ required for taking all the degrees ˢ conferred by these bodies are, at Cambridge, utterly contemptible; at Oxford, we believe, of late years, somewhat higher, but still very low. Honours, indeed, are not gained but by a severe struggle; ᵗand if even the candidates for honours were mentally benefited, the systemᵗ would not be worthless. But what have the senior wranglers done, even in mathematics? Has Cambridge produced ᵘ, since Newton, one great mathematical geniusᵘ? ᵛWe do not say an Euler, a Laplace, or a Lagrange, but such as France has produced a score of during the same period.ᵛ How many books which have thrown light upon the history, antiquities, philosophy, art, or literature of the ancients, have the two Universities sent forth since the Reformation? Compare them not merely with Germany, but even with Italy or France. When a man is pronounced by them to have excelled in their studies, what do the Universities do? They give him an income, not for continuing to learn, but for having learnt; not for doing anything, but for what he has already done: on condition solely of living like a monk, and putting on the livery of the Church at the end of seven years. They bribe men by high rewards to get their arms ready, but do not require them to fight.†

Are these the places ˣof educationˣ which are to send forth minds capable of maintaining a victorious struggle with the debilitating influences of the age, and strengthening the ʸweakerʸ side of Civilization by the support of a higher Cultivation? This, however, is what we require from these institutions; or, in their default, from others which ᶻshouldᶻ take their place. And

*We should except, at Oxford, the Ethics, Politics, and Rhetoric of Aristotle. These are part of the course of classical instruction, and are so far an exception to the rule, otherwise pretty faithfully observed at both Universities, of cultivating only the least useful parts of ancient literature.

†[59] Much of what is here said of the Universities, has, in a great measure, ceased to be true. The legislature has at last asserted its right of interference [see 17 & 18 Victoria, c. 81 (1854), and 19 & 20 Victoria, c. 88 (1856)]; and even before it did so, ʷthoseʷ bodies had already entered into a course of as decided improvement as any other English institutions. But I leave these pages unaltered, as matter of historical record, and as an illustration of tendencies. [1859.]

ʳ⁻ʳ36   *of any kind*   ˢ36   (except professional ones) ever
   ᵗ⁻ᵗ36   but the candidates for honours are the few, not the many. Still, if even the few were mentally benefited, the places
   ᵘ⁻ᵘ36   one great mathematician since Newton
   ᵛ⁻ᵛ+59, 67   ʷ⁻ʷ59   the
   ˣ⁻ˣ+59, 67   ʸ⁻ʸ36, 59   weak
   ᶻ⁻ᶻ36   must

the very first step towards their reform *should* be to unsectarianize them wholly—not by the paltry measure of allowing Dissenters to come and be taught orthodox sectarianism, but by putting an end to sectarian teaching altogether. The principle itself of dogmatic religion, dogmatic morality, dogmatic philosophy, is what requires to be rooted out; not any particular manifestation of that principle.

The very corner-stone of an education intended to form great minds, must be the recognition of the principle, that the object is to call forth the greatest possible quantity of intellectual *power*, and to inspire the intensest *love of truth*: and this without a particle of regard to the results to which the exercise of that power may lead, even though it should conduct the pupil to opinions diametrically opposite to those of his teachers. We say this, not because we think opinions unimportant, but *b* because of the immense importance which we attach to them; for in proportion to the degree of intellectual power and love of truth which we succeed in creating, is the certainty that (whatever may happen in any one particular instance) in the aggregate of instances true opinions will be the result; and intellectual power and practical love of truth are alike impossible where the reasoner is shown his conclusions, and informed beforehand that he is expected to arrive at them.

We are not so absurd as to propose that the teacher should not *set forth* his own opinions as the true ones, and exert his utmost powers to exhibit their truth in the strongest light. To abstain from this would be to nourish the worst intellectual habit of all, that of not finding, and not looking for, certainty in anything. But the teacher himself should not be held to any creed; nor should the question be whether *his own opinions* are the true ones, but whether he *is well instructed in those of other people*, and, in enforcing his own, states the arguments for all conflicting opinions fairly. In this spirit it is that all the great subjects are taught from the chairs of the German and French Universities. *As a general rule, the* most distinguished teacher is selected, whatever be his particular views, and he consequently teaches in the spirit of free inquiry, not of dogmatic imposition. *g*

Such is the principle of all academical instruction which aims at forming great minds. The details *cannot be too various and comprehensive.* Ancient

---

a-a36   , must   b36   precisely
c-c36   inculcate   d-d36   the opinions he inculcates
e-e36   knows all creeds   f-f36   The

g36   Were such the practice here, we believe that the results would greatly eclipse France and Germany, because we believe that when the restraints on free speculation and free teaching were taken off, there would be found in many individual minds among us, a vein of solid and accurate thought, as much superior in variety and sterling value to any which has yet manifested itself in those countries (except in one or two distinguished instances) as the present tone of our national mind is in many important points inferior.

h-h36   we have not much space for the discussion of. We may, however, just indicate a part of what we have not room to enter into more fully.

literature would fill a large place in such a course of instruction; because it *brings* before us the thoughts and actions of many great minds, minds of many various orders of greatness, and these related and exhibited in a manner tenfold more impressive, tenfold more calculated to call forth *high* aspirations, than in any modern literature. Imperfectly as these impressions are made by the current modes of classical teaching, it is incalculable what we owe to this, the sole ennobling feature in the slavish, mechanical thing which the moderns call education. Nor is it to be forgotten among the benefits of familiarity with the monuments of antiquity, and especially those of Greece, that we are taught by it to appreciate and to admire intrinsic greatness, amidst opinions, habits, and institutions most remote from ours; and are thus trained to that large and catholic toleration, which is founded on understanding, not on indifference—and to a habit of free, open sympathy with powers of mind and nobleness of character, howsoever exemplified. Were but the languages and literature of antiquity so taught that the glorious images they present might stand before the student's eyes as living and glowing realities—that, instead of lying a *caput mortuum* at the bottom of his mind, like some foreign substance in no way influencing the current of his thoughts or the tone of his feelings, they might circulate through it, and become assimilated, and be part and parcel of himself!—then should we see how little these studies have yet done for us, compared with what they have yet to do.

An important place in the system of education which we contemplate would be occupied by history: *k* because it is the record of all *l* great things which have been achieved by mankind, and *m* because when philosophically studied it gives a certain largeness of conception to the student, and familiarizes him with the action of great causes. In no other way can he so completely realize in his own mind (howsoever he may be satisfied with the proof of them as abstract propositions) the great principles by which the progress of man and the condition of society are governed. Nowhere else will the infinite varieties of human nature be so vividly brought home to him, and anything cramped or one-sided in his own standard of it so effectually corrected; and nowhere else will he behold so strongly exemplified the astonishing pliability of our nature,[*] and the vast effects which may under good guidance be produced upon it by honest endeavour. The literature of our own and other modern nations should be studied along with the history, or rather as *n* part of the history.

[*See J. S. Mill, *Autobiography*, ed. Jack Stillinger (Boston: Houghton Mifflin, 1969), p. 107, where the phrase "extraordinary pliability of human nature" is attributed to John Austin.]

*i-i*36   places   *j-j*36   the highest
*k*36   not under the puerile notion that political wisdom can be founded upon it; but partly
*l*36   the   *m*36   partly
*n*36   a

In the department of pure intellect, the highest place will belong to logic and the philosophy of mind: the one, the instrument for the cultivation of all sciences; the other, the root from which they all grow. It scarcely needs be said that the former *ought not to* be taught as a mere system of technical rules, nor the latter as a set of concatenated abstract propositions. The tendency, so strong everywhere, is strongest of all here, to receive opinions into the mind without any real understanding of them, merely because they seem to follow from certain admitted premises, and to let them lie there as forms of words, lifeless and void of meaning. The pupil must be led to interrogate his own consciousness, to observe and experiment upon himself: of the mind, by any other process, little will he ever know.

With these should be joined all those sciences, in which great and certain results are arrived at by mental processes of some length or nicety: not that all persons should study all these sciences, but that some should study all, and all some. These may be divided into sciences of mere ratiocination, as mathematics; and sciences partly of ratiocination, and partly of what is far more difficult, comprehensive observation and analysis. Such are, in their *rationale*, even the sciences to which *mathematical processes are applicable:* and such are all those which relate to human nature. The philosophy of morals, of government, of law, of political economy, of poetry and art, should form subjects of systematic instruction, under the most eminent professors who could be found; these being chosen, not for the particular doctrines they might happen to profess, but as being those who were most likely to send forth pupils qualified in point of disposition and attainments to choose doctrines for themselves. And why should not religion be taught in the same manner? Not *until then will one step be made towards the healing of religious differences: not until* then will the spirit of English religion become catholic instead of sectarian, favourable instead of hostile to freedom of thought and the progress of the human mind.

With regard to the changes, in forms of polity and social arrangements, which in addition to reforms in education, we conceive to be required for regenerating the character of the higher classes; to express them even summarily would require a long discourse. But the general idea from which they all emanate, may be stated briefly. Civilization has brought about a degree of security and fixity in the possession of all advantages once acquired, which

---

*o–o*36   will not
*p–p*36   mathematics are subservient;
*q–q*36   till then . . . not till
*r–r*36   We have dwelt so long on the reforms in education necessary for regenerating the character of the higher classes, that we have not space remaining to state what changes in forms of polity and social arrangements we conceive to be required for the same purpose. We can only just indicate the leading idea.

has rendered it *s* possible for a rich man to lead the life of a Sybarite, and nevertheless enjoy throughout life a degree of power and consideration which could formerly be earned or retained only by personal activity. We cannot undo what civilization has done, and again stimulate the energy of the higher classes by insecurity of property, or danger of life or limb. The only adventitious motive it is in the power of society to hold out, is reputation and consequence; and of this as much use as possible should be made for the encouragement of desert. The main thing which social changes can do for the improvement of the higher classes—and it is what the progress of democracy is insensibly but certainly accomplishing—is gradually to put an end to every kind of unearned distinction, and let the only road open to honour and ascendancy be that of personal qualities.

*s*36   , for the first time in Europe,

ESSAYS ON GOVERNMENT

1840

EDITOR'S NOTE

London and Westminster Review, XXXIV (Sept., 1840), 518–19, in "Philosophy and Legislation" section, headed "ESSAYS ON GOVERNMENT, 1839. [London:] Effingham Wilson." Signed "A." Not republished. Identified in JSM's bibliography as "A short notice of a book entitled 'Essays on Government' in the same number of the same review." (I.e., in the same number as his review of Milnes's *Poetry for the People*, the previous item in the bibliography.) (MacMinn, 52.) No copy in the Somerville College Library. There are no references to this brief review in JSM's *Autobiography* or letters.

Essays on Government

THIS LITTLE VOLUME is unquestionably the production of a thinker, though of one who has not yet thought with much originality or depth. It is, however, interesting, as indicative of the ideas which thinkers of a numerous and increasing class are now becoming possessed of, and eagerly turning to use.

For instance, the author's first fundamental principle is, that the successive changes which take place in human affairs are no more left to chance "in the moral than in the physical world, but that the progress of society, social, moral, and political, together with the whole train of events which compose the history of the human race, are as much the effect of certain fixed laws as the motions of the planets or the rotation of the seasons." [P. 2.] His second principle is, that the changes in political institutions are the effects of previous changes in the condition of society and of the human mind. It may truly be said, that whoever knows these two principles, possesses more of the science of politics than was known even to eminent thinkers fifty years ago.

Setting out from this starting point, our author ends his inquiries in the common conclusions of radicalism; but shows less acquaintance than might be wished with the real difficulties of the subject, and with the point which the discussion has now reached among political philosophers. He lays it down as a maxim that there is everywhere a natural aristocracy, that is, a class who are looked up to by the community generally; that, in a rude age, nobles, or priests, or persons of large property, form this class; in an enlightened period, it consists of the persons most distinguished for wisdom and virtue. In every age, unless the natural aristocracy be the power which governs, there will be growing disaffection to the government, and at length either a peaceable or a violent change. Having established that the natural aristocracy in a highly civilised society is the aristocracy of personal qualities, he affirms, and has little difficulty in showing, that neither an aristocracy of birth nor one of wealth affords any guarantee for the existence of these qualities. He therefore recommends, wherever the community is sufficiently advanced to admit of it, a republican government by universal suffrage and ballot, as a means of selecting and installing the natural aristocracy. But this part of his doctrine, which is the part most likely to be assailed with objections, is unfortunately that which he has taken least pains to fortify against them. That the people in a democracy would know where to find the natural aristocracy, or would wish to be governed by them, is the point to be proved, not assumed. We cannot find that anything is said to prove it by our author. He thinks, indeed, that the people cannot themselves govern, but can only choose their governors, and will prefer, as they must choose somebody, to choose those to whom they already look up. "Democracy may cause its feelings and opinions to be attended to and respected, but it can never govern." [P. 169.] We think that democracy *can* govern: it can make its legislators its mere delegates, to carry into effect *its* preconceived opinions. We do not say that it *will* do so. Whether it will, appears to us the great question which futurity has to resolve; and on the solution of which it depends whether democracy will be that social regeneration which its partisans expect, or merely a new form of bad government, perhaps somewhat better, perhaps somewhat worse, than those which preceded it.

There seems to be something wavering and undecided in our author's conception of what constitutes the test of good government. He continually enumerates among the requisites of government that it should be conformable to the *opinions* of the governed. He insists, as often, upon another requisite, that the governors shall be the wisest and best persons in the community. But the wisest and best members of the community very often would not consent to govern in conformity with the opinions of the less wise portion: our author must elect, therefore, which of the two requisites he will in that case dispense with. Perhaps he will say that, by a government in conformity to the opinions of the people, he does not mean one which implicitly obeys public opinion, but one which pays that degree of regard to it as an existing fact, which the best and wisest government must pay, and which would be paid to any other fact of equal importance. If so, the test is unexceptionable; but then, he is on the other horn of the dilemma: is this that kind and degree of deference to their opinions which a democratic people, electing their rulers by universal suffrage, will be likely to be content with?

After all, our author's practical conclusions fall short of what his speculative principles would seem to warrant, since he is for constituting the legislative body of two elective chambers, the one representative of numbers, the other of property. We believe that this would be theoretically the best form of government for a state of society like that of modern Europe; subject to the two conditions, that it were possible to introduce it, and that, if introduced, it would *work* without a civil war between the two houses. Perhaps when the two great classes, the propertied and non-propertied, shall have tried their strength and found their inability to conquer one another, this, as a possible mode of peaceable compromise, may in time suggest itself to the wiser leaders of both.

DE TOCQUEVILLE ON DEMOCRACY IN AMERICA [II]

1840

EDITOR'S NOTE

Dissertations and Discussions, II (2nd ed.), 1–83, where it is headed "M. de Tocqueville on Democracy in America," the title footnoted: "*Edinburgh Review*, October 1840." Reprinted from *ER*, LXXII (Oct., 1840), 1–47, where it is unsigned, and headed: "Art. I.—1. *De la Démocratie en Amérique*. Par ALEXIS DE TOCQUEVILLE, Membre de l'Institut. 4 vols. 8vo. Paris: / [Gosselin,] 1835–40. / 2. *Democracy in America*. By ALEXIS DE TOCQUEVILLE, Member of the Institute of France. *Translated by* HENRY / REEVE, Esq., Barrister-at-Law. 4 vols. 8vo. London: [Saunders and Otley,] 1835–40." Running title: "Democracy in America." Identified in JSM's bibliography as "A review of Tocqueville's 'Democracy in America' in the Edinburgh Review for October 1840 (No. 145.)" (MacMinn, 52.) In the copy of the *Edinburgh* article in the Somerville College Library JSM has indicated three changes: two of them (see 163^{t-t} and 192^{x-x}, the latter being a correction of a typographical error) were adopted in the revised text; the third (164^{w-w}) was further rewritten.

For comment on the composition of this article and JSM's relations with Tocqueville, see the Textual Introduction, lxxvi–lxxviii above.

The following text, taken from *D&D*, II, 2nd ed., is collated with that in *D&D*, 1st ed., and that in the *Edinburgh*. In two places (174–5 and 200–4) JSM adapts parts of his "De Tocqueville on Democracy in America [I]" and "Duveyrier's Political Views of French Affairs" (1846); these passages have been collated with their originals. In the footnoted variants, "67" indicates *D&D*, 2nd ed.; "59" indicates *D&D*, 1st ed.; "40" indicates *Edinburgh Review*; "Source" indicates Reeve's translation of Tocqueville; "35" indicates "De Tocqueville on Democracy in America [I]"; and "46" indicates "Duveyrier's Political Views."

In the references to *De la Démocratie en Amérique*, both Reeve's translation and the original (identified as Tocqueville) are cited.

De Tocqueville on Democracy in America [II]

IT HAS BEEN the rare fortune of M. de Tocqueville's book to have achieved an easy triumph, both over the indifference of our at once busy and indolent public to profound speculation, and over the particular obstacles which oppose the reception of speculations from a foreign, and above all from a French source. There is some ground for the remark often made upon us by foreigners, that the character of our national intellect is insular. The general movement of the European mind sweeps past us without our being drawn into it, or even looking sufficiently at it to discover in what direction it is tending; and if we had not a tolerably rapid original movement of our own, we should long since have been left in the distance. The French language is almost universally cultivated on this side of the Channel; a flood of human beings perpetually ebbs and flows between London and Paris; national prejudices and animosities are becoming numbered among the things that were; yet the revolution which has taken place in the tendencies of French thought, which has changed the character of the higher literature of France, and almost that of the French language, seems hitherto, as far as the English public are concerned, to have taken place in vain. At a time when the prevailing tone of French speculation is one of exaggerated reaction against the doctrines of the eighteenth century, French philosophy, with us, is still synonymous with Encyclopedism. The Englishmen may almost be numbered who are aware that France has produced any great names in prose literature since Voltaire and Rousseau; and while modern history has been receiving a new aspect from the labours of men who are not only among the profoundest thinkers, but the clearest and most popular writers of their age, even those of their works which are expressly dedicated to the history of our own country remain mostly untranslated, and in almost all cases unread.

To this general neglect M. de Tocqueville's book forms, however, as we have already said, a brilliant exception. Its reputation was as sudden, and is as extensive, in this country as in France, and in that large part of Europe which receives its opinions from France. The progress of political dissatisfaction, and the comparisons made between the fruits of a popular constitution on one side of the Atlantic, and of a mixed government with a preponderating aristocratic element on the other, had made the working of

American institutions a party question. For many years, every book of travels in America had been a party pamphlet, or had at least fallen among partisans, and been pressed into the service of one party or of the other. When, therefore, a new book, of a grave and imposing character, on Democracy in America, made its appearance even on the other side of the British Channel, it was not likely to be overlooked, or to escape an attempt to convert it to party purposes. If ever political writer had reason to believe that he had laboured successfully to render his book incapable of such a use, M. de Tocqueville was entitled to think so. But though his theories are of an impartiality without example, and his practical conclusions lean towards Radicalism, some of his phrases are susceptible of a Tory application. One of these is "the tyranny of the majority."[*] This phrase was forthwith adopted into the Conservative dialect, and trumpeted by Sir Robert Peel in his Tamworth oration, when, as booksellers' advertisements have since frequently reminded us, he "earnestly requested the perusal" of the book by all and each of his audience.[†] And we believe it has since been the opinion of the country gentlemen that M. de Tocqueville is one of the pillars of Conservatism, and his book a definitive demolition of America and of Democracy. The error has done more good than the truth would perhaps have done; since the result is, that the English public now know and read the first philosophical book ever written on Democracy, as it manifests itself in modern society; a book, the essential doctrines of which it is not likely that any future speculations will subvert, to whatever degree they may modify them; while its spirit, and the general mode in which it treats its subject, constitute it the beginning of a new era in the scientific study of politics.

The importance of M. de Tocqueville's speculations is not to be estimated by the opinions which he has adopted, be these true or false. The value of his work is less in the conclusions, than in the mode of arriving at them. He has applied to the greatest question in the art and science of government, those principles and methods of philosophizing to which mankind are indebted for all the advances made by modern times in the other branches of the study of nature. It is not risking too much to affirm of these volumes, that they contain the first analytical inquiry into the *a*influences of Democracy*a*. For the first time, that phenomenon is treated of as something which, being a reality in nature, and no mere mathematical or metaphysical abstraction, manifests itself by innumerable properties, not by some one only; and must be looked at in many aspects before it can be made the subject

[*Reeve, Vol. II, p. 151; Tocqueville, Vol. II, p. 142.]

[†See "Opinions of the Present Work," in the advertisement pages in Reeve, where Peel's speech of 12 Jan., 1837, at Glasgow (not Tamworth) is quoted. For Peel's speech, see *The Times*, 16 Jan., 1837, p. 4.]

*a-a*40   influence of democracy]   59   influence of Democracy

even of that modest and conjectural judgment, which is alone attainable respecting a fact at once so great and so new. Its consequences are by no means to be comprehended in one single description, nor in one summary verdict of approval or condemnation. So complicated and endless are their ramifications, that he who sees furthest into them will *b*, in general,*b* longest hesitate before finally pronouncing whether the good or the evil of its influence, on the whole, preponderates.

M. de Tocqueville has endeavoured to ascertain and discriminate the various properties and tendencies of Democracy; the separate relations in which it stands towards the different interests of society, and the different moral and social requisites of human nature. In the investigation he has *c*of necessity left much undone,*c* and much which will be better done by those who come after him, and build upon his foundations. But he has earned the double honour of being the first to make the attempt, and of having done more towards the success of it than probably will ever again be done by any one individual. His method is, as that of a philosopher on such a subject must be—a combination of deduction with induction: his evidences are, laws of human nature, on the one hand; the example of America, and France, and other modern nations, so far as applicable, on the other. His conclusions never rest on either species of evidence alone; whatever he classes as an effect of Democracy, he has both ascertained to exist in those countries in which the state of society is democratic, and has also succeeded in connecting with Democracy by deductions *à priori*, *d*tending to show*d* that such would naturally be its influences upon beings constituted as mankind are, and placed in a world such as we know ours to be. If this be not the true Baconian and Newtonian method applied to society and government; if any better, or even any other be possible, M. de Tocqueville would be the first to say, *candidus imperti*: if not, he is entitled to say to political theorists, whether calling themselves philosophers or practical men, *his utere mecum*.[*]

That part of *Democracy in America* which was first published, professes to treat of the political effects of Democracy: the second *e* is devoted to its influence on society in the widest sense; on the relations of private life, on intellect, morals, and the habits and modes of feeling which constitute national character. The last is both a newer and a more difficult subject of inquiry than the first; there are fewer who are competent, or who will even think themselves competent, to judge M. de Tocqueville's conclusions. But,

[*Horace, "Epistle I," in *Satires, Epistles and Ars Poetica*, p. 290 (vi, 68).]

b–b+67
*c–c*40   left much undone, as who could possibly avoid?
*d–d*40   showing
*e*40   (published only this year)

we believe, no one, in the least entitled to an opinion, will refuse to him the praise of having probed the subject to a depth which had never before been sounded; of having carried forward the controversy into a wider and a loftier region of thought; and pointed out many questions essential to the subject which had not been before attended to: questions which he may or may not have solved, but of which, in any case, he has greatly facilitated the solution.

The comprehensiveness of M. de Tocqueville's views, and the impartiality of his feelings, have not led him into the common infirmity of those who see too many sides to a question—that of thinking them all equally important. He is able to arrive at a decided opinion. Nor has the more extensive range of considerations embraced in his Second Part, affected practically the general conclusions which resulted from his First. They may be stated as follows:—That Democracy, in the modern world, is inevitable; and that it is on the whole desirable; but desirable only under certain conditions, and those conditions capable, by human care and foresight, of being realized, but capable also of being missed. The progress and ultimate ascendancy of the democratic principle has in his eyes the character of a law of nature. He thinks it an inevitable result of the tendencies of a progressive civilization; by which expressions he by no means intends to imply either praise or censure. No human effort, no accident even, unless one which should throw back civilization itself, can avail, in his opinion, to defeat, or even very considerably to retard, this progress. But though the fact itself appears to him removed from human control, its salutary or baneful consequences do not. Like other great powers of nature, the tendency, though it cannot be counteracted, may be guided to good. Man cannot turn back the rivers to their source;[*] but it rests with himself whether they shall fertilize or lay waste his fields. Left to its spontaneous course, with nothing done to prepare before it that set of circumstances under which it can exist with safety, and to fight against its worse by an apt employment of its better peculiarities, the probable effects of Democracy upon human well-being, and upon whatever is best and noblest in human character, appear to M. de Tocqueville extremely formidable. But with as much of wise effort devoted to the purpose as it is not irrational to hope for, most of what is mischievous in its tendencies may, in his opinion, be corrected, and its natural capacities of good so far strengthened and made use of, as to leave no cause for regret in the old state of society, and enable the new one to be contemplated with calm contentment, if without exultation.

It is necessary to observe that by Democracy M. de Tocqueville does not in general mean any particular form of government. He can conceive a Democracy under an absolute monarch. Nay, he entertains no small dread

[*Cf. *Considerations on Representative Government*, p. 380 below.]

lest in some countries it should actually appear in that form. By Democracy, M. de Tocqueville understands equality of conditions; the absence of all aristocracy, whether constituted by political privileges, or by superiority in individual importance and social power. It is towards Democracy in this sense, towards equality between man and man, that he conceives society to be irresistibly tending. ʲTowardsʲ Democracy in the other, and more common sense, it may or may not be travelling. Equality of conditions tends naturally to produce a popular government, but not necessarily. Equality may be equal freedom, or equal servitude. America is the type of the first; France, he thinks, is in danger of falling into the second. The latter country is in the condition which, of all that civilized societies are liable to, he regards with the greatest alarm—a democratic state of society without democratic institutions. For, in democratic institutions, M. de Tocqueville sees not an aggravation, but a corrective, of the most serious evils incident to a democratic state of society. No one is more opposed than he is to that species of democratic radicalism, which would admit at once to the highest of political franchises, untaught masses who have not yet been experimentally proved fit even for the lowest. But the ever-increasing intervention of the people, and of all classes of the people, in their own affairs, he regards as a cardinal maxim in the modern art of government: and he believes that the nations of civilized Europe, though not all equally advanced, are all advancing, towards a condition in which there will be no distinctions of political rights, no great or very permanent distinctions of hereditary wealth; when, as there will remain no classes nor individuals capable of making head against the government, unless all are, and are fit to be, alike citizens, all will ere long be equally slaves.

The opinion that there is this irresistible tendency to equality of conditions, is, perhaps, of all the leading doctrines of the book, that which most stands in need of confirmation to English readers. M. de Tocqueville devotes but little space to the elucidation of it. To French readers, the historical retrospect upon which it rests is familiar; and facts known to every one establish its truth, so far as relates to that country. But to the English public, who have less faith in irresistible tendencies, and who, while they require for every political theory an historical basis, are far less accustomed to link together the events of history in a connected chain, the proposition will hardly seem to be sufficiently made out. Our author's historical argument is, however, deserving of their attention.

Let us recollect the situation of France seven hundred years ago, when the territory was divided amongst a small number of families, who were the owners of the soil and the rulers of the inhabitants: the right of governing descended with the family inheritance from generation to generation; force was the only means by which man could act on man; and landed property was the sole source of power.

Soon, however, the political power of the clergy was founded, and began to extend itself: the clergy opened its ranks to all classes, to the poor and the rich, the villein and the lord; equality penetrated into the government through the church, and the being who as a serf must have vegetated in perpetual bondage, took his place as a priest in the midst of nobles, and not unfrequently above the heads of kings.

The different relations of men became more complicated and more numerous, as society gradually became more stable and more civilized. Thence the want of civil laws was felt; and the order of legal functionaries soon rose from the obscurity of ᵍtheirᵍ tribunals and their dusty chambers, to appear at the court of the monarch, by the side of the feudal barons in their ermine and their mail.

Whilst the kings were ruining themselves by their great enterprises, and the nobles exhausting their resources by private wars, the lower orders were enriching themselves by commerce. The influence of money began to be perceptible in state affairs. The transactions of business opened a new road to power, and the financier rose to a station of political influence, in which he was at once flattered and despised.

Gradually the spread of mental acquirements, and the increasing taste for literature and the arts, opened chances of success to talent; knowledge became a means of government, intelligence became a social power, and the man of letters took a part in the affairs of the state.

The value attached to the privileges of birth decreased, in the exact proportion in which new paths were struck out to advancement. In the eleventh century nobility was beyond all price; in the thirteenth it might be purchased: it was conferred for the first time in 1270; and equality was thus introduced into the government through aristocracy itself.

In the course of these seven hundred years, it sometimes happened that, in order to resist the authority of the crown, or to diminish the power of their rivals, the nobles granted a certain share of political rights to the people. Or, more frequently, the king permitted the inferior orders to enjoy a degree of power, with the intention of lowering the aristocracy.

As soon as land was held on any other than a feudal tenure, and personal property began in its turn to confer influence and power, every improvement which was introduced in commerce or manufactures was a fresh element of ʰ equality of conditions. Henceforward every new discovery, every new want which ⁱgrew upⁱ, and every new desire which craved satisfaction, was a step towards the universal level. The taste for luxury, the love of war, the sway of fashion, the most superficial as well as the deepest passions of the human heart, co-operated to enrich the poor and to impoverish the rich.

From the time when the exercise of the intellect became a source of ʲpowerʲ and of wealth, it is impossible not to consider every addition to science, every fresh truth, every new idea, as a germ of power placed within the reach of the people. Poetry, eloquence, and memory, the grace of wit, the glow of imagination, the depth of thought, and all the gifts which are bestowed by Providence without respect of persons, turned to the advantage of ᵏ democracy; and even

---

ᵍ⁻ᵍSource,40 the
ⁱ⁻ⁱ40 it engendered
ᵏSource,40 the

ʰ40,59 the
ʲ⁻ʲ40 strength

when they were in the possession of its adversaries, they still served its cause, by *bringing*[*l*] into relief the natural greatness of man; its conquests spread, therefore, with those of civilization and knowledge; and literature became an arsenal, where the poorest and the weakest could always find weapons to their hand.

In perusing the pages of our history, we shall scarcely meet with a single great event, in the lapse of seven hundred years, which has not turned to the advantage of equality.

The Crusades, and the wars with the English, decimated the nobles and divided their possessions; the erection of corporate towns introduced an element of democratic liberty into the bosom of feudal monarchy; the invention of fire-arms equalized the villein and the noble on the field of battle; printing opened the same resources to the minds of all classes; the post was established, so as to bring the same information to the door of the poor man's cottage and to the gate of the palace; and Protestantism proclaimed that all men are alike able to find the road to heaven. The discovery of America offered a thousand new paths to fortune, and placed riches and power within the reach of the adventurous and the obscure.

If we examine what *was happening*[*m*] in France at intervals of fifty years, beginning with the eleventh century, we shall invariably perceive that a twofold revolution has taken place in the state of society. The noble has gone down on the social ladder, and the *roturier* has gone up; the one descends as the other rises. Every half century brings them nearer to each other.

Nor is this phenomenon at all peculiar to France. Whithersoever we turn our eyes, we witness the same continual revolution throughout the whole of Christendom.

Everywhere the various occurrences of national existence have turned to the advantage of democracy; all men have aided it by their *exertions. Those*[*n*] who have intentionally laboured in its cause, and those who have served it unwittingly; those who have fought for it, and those who have declared themselves its opponents—have all been driven along in the same *track*[*o*], have all laboured to one end, some ignorantly and some unwillingly; all have been blind instruments in the hands of God.

The gradual development of the equality of conditions is therefore a providential fact, and possesses all the characteristics of a Divine decree: it is universal, it is durable, it constantly eludes all human interference, and all events as well as all men contribute to its progress.

Would it be wise to imagine that a social impulse which dates from so far back, can be checked by the efforts of a generation? Is it credible that the democracy which has annihilated the feudal system, and vanquished kings, will respect the *bourgeois*[*p*] and the capitalist? Will it stop now that it is grown so strong, and its adversaries so weak?

It is not necessary that God himself should speak, in order to disclose to us the unquestionable signs of his will. We can discern them in the habitual course of nature, and in the invariable tendency of events.

The Christian nations of our age seem to me to present a most alarming spectacle. The impulse which is bearing them along is so strong that it cannot be stopped, but it is not yet so rapid that it cannot be guided. Their fate is in their

*l–l*Source,40   throwing
*n–n*40   exertions: those
*p–p*Source,40   citizen

*m–m*Source,40   has happened
*o–o*40   tract [*printer's error?*]

hands; yet a little while, and it may be so no longer. (*Introduction to the First Part.*) [Reeve, Vol. I, pp. xv–xxii; Tocqueville, Vol. I, pp. 4–10.] *q*

That such has been the actual course of events in modern history, nobody can doubt, and as truly in England as in France. Of old, every proprietor of land was sovereign over its inhabitants, while the cultivators could not call even their bodily powers their own. It was by degrees only, and in a succession of ages, that their personal emancipation was effected, and their labour became theirs, to sell for whatever they could obtain for it. They became the rich men's equals in the eye of the law; but the rich had still the making of the law, and the administering of it; and the equality was at first little more than nominal. The poor, however, could now acquire property; the path was open to them to quit their own class for a higher; their rise even to a considerable station, gradually became a common occurrence; and to those who acquired a large fortune, the other powers and privileges of aristocracy were successively opened, until hereditary honours have become less a power in themselves, than a symbol and ornament of great riches. While individuals thus continually rose from the mass, the mass itself multiplied and strengthened; the towns obtained a voice in public affairs; the many, in the aggregate, became even in property more and more a match for the few; and the nation became a power, distinct from the small number of individuals who once disposed even of the crown, and determined all public affairs at their pleasure. The Reformation was the dawn of the government of public opinion. Even at that early period, opinion was not formed by the higher classes exclusively; and while the publicity of all ʳStateʳ transactions, the liberty of petition and public discussion, the press—and of late, above all, the periodical press—have rendered public opinion more and more the supreme power, the same causes have rendered the formation of it less and less dependent upon the initiative of the higher ranks. Even the direct participation of the people at large in the government had, in various ways, been greatly extended, before the political events of the last few years, when democracy has given so signal a proof of its progress in society, by the inroads it has been able to make into the political constitution. And in spite of the alarm which has been taken by the possessors of large property, who are far more generally opposed than they had been within the present generation to any additional strengthening of the popular element in the House of Commons, there is at this moment a much stronger party for a further parliamentary reform, than many good observers thought there was, twelve years ago, for that which has already taken place.

*q*40 [*footnote:*] In this, and our other extracts, we have followed generally, though not implicitly, Mr. Reeve's translation. Though not always unexceptionable, it is spirited, and sometimes felicitous.
ʳ–ʳ40 state

But there is a surer mode of deciding the point than any historical retrospect. Let us look at the powers which are even now at work in society itself.

To a superficial glance at the condition of our own country, nothing can seem more unlike any tendency to equality of condition. The inequalities of property are apparently greater than in any former period of history. Nearly all the land is parcelled out in great estates, among comparatively few families; and it is not the large, but the small properties, which are in process of extinction. A hereditary and titled nobility, more potent by their vast possessions than by their social precedency, are constitutionally and really one of the great powers in the state. To form part of their order is ˢthat whichˢ every ambitious man aspires ᵗtoᵗ, as the crowning glory of a successful career. The passion for equality of which M. de Tocqueville speaks almost as if it were the great moral lever of modern times, is hardly known in this country even by name. On the contrary, all ranks seem to have a passion for inequality. The hopes of every person are directed to rising in the world, not to pulling the world down to him. The greatest enemy of the political conduct of the House of Lords, submits to their superiority of rank as he would to the ordinances of nature; and often thinks any amount of toil and watching repaid by a nod of recognition from one of their number.

We have put the case as strongly as it could be put by an adversary, and have stated as facts some things which, if they have been facts, are giving visible signs that they will not always be so. If we look back even twenty years, we shall find that the popular respect for the higher classes is by no means the thing it was; and ᵘthoughᵘ all who are rising wish for the continuance of advantages which they themselves hope to share, there are among those who do not expect to rise, increasing indications that a levelling spirit is abroad, and political discontents, in whatever manner originating, show an increasing tendency to take that shape. But it is the less necessary to dwell upon these things, as we shall be satisfied with making out, in respect to the tendency to equality in England, much less than M. de Tocqueville contends for. We do not maintain that the time is drawing near when there will be no distinction of classes; but we do contend that the power of the higher classes, both in government and in society, is diminishing; while that of the middle and even the lower classes is increasing, and likely to increase.

The constituent elements of political importance are property, intelligence, and the power of combination. In every one of these elements, is it the higher classes, or the other ᵛportionsᵛ of society, that have lately made and are continuing to make the most rapid advances?

ˢ⁻ˢ40   what
ᵗ⁻ᵗ+59,67   [omitted through printer's error? added by JSM in Somerville College copy of 40]
ᵘ⁻ᵘ40   although
ᵛ⁻ᵛ40,59   portion

Even with regard to the element of property, there cannot be room for more than a momentary doubt. The class who are rich by inheritance, are so far from augmenting their fortunes, that it is much if they can be said to keep them up. A territorial aristocracy always live up to their means—generally beyond them. Our own is no exception to the rule; and as their control over the taxes becomes every day more restricted, and the liberal professions more overcrowded, they are condemned more and more to bear the burden of their own large families; which ᵂit is not easy to do, compatibly with leaving to the heir the means of keeping up, without becoming embarrassed, the old family establishments. It is matter of notoriety how severely the difficulty of providing for younger sons is felt even in the highest rank; and that, as a provision for daughters, alliances are now courted which would not have been endured a generation ago. The additions to the "money-power" of the higher ranks, consist of the riches of the *novi homines*[*] who are continually aggregated to that class from among the merchants and manufacturers, and occasionally from the professions. But many of these are merely successors to the impoverished owners of the land they buy; and the fortunes of others are taken, in the way of marriage, to pay off the mortgages of older families. Even with these allowances, no doubt the number of wealthy persons is steadily on the increase; but what is this to the accumulation of capitals and growth of incomes in the hands of the middle class? It is that class which furnishes all the accessions to the aristocracy of wealth; and for one who makes a large fortune, fifty acquire, without exceeding, a moderate competency, and leave their children to work, like themselves, at the labouring oar.

In point of intelligence, it can still less be affirmed that the higher classes maintain the same proportional ascendancy as of old. They have shared with the rest of the world in the diffusion of information. They have improved, like all other classes, in the decorous virtues. Their humane feelings and refined tastes form in general a striking contrast to the coarse habits of the same class a few generations ago. But it would be difficult to point out what new idea in speculation, what invention or discovery in the practical arts, what useful institution, or what permanently valuable book, Great Britain has owed for the last hundred years to her hereditary aristocracy, titled or untitled;*—what great public enterprise, what important national movement in religion or politics, those classes have originated, or ˣhave so much as

[*See Cicero, *The Letters to his Friends* (Latin and English), trans. W. Glynn Williams, 3 vols. (London: Heinemann; New York: Putnam's Sons, 1927–29), Vol. I, p. 403 (V.18.1).]

*[59] The chief exceptions since the accession of the House of Hanover, are the chemist Cavendish in the last century, and the Earl of Rosse in the present.

ᵂ⁻ᵂ40   is no easy burden; and at the same time to leave [*Somerville College copy of* 40 *altered by JSM to* it is not easy to do & at the same time to leave &c.]
ˣ⁻ˣ40   in which they have so much as taken

taken in it^x the principal share. Considered in respect to active energies and laborious habits, to the stirring qualities which fit men for playing a considerable part in the affairs of mankind, few will say that our aristocracy have not deteriorated. It is, on the other hand, one of the commonplaces of the age, that knowledge and intelligence are spreading, in a degree which was formerly thought impossible, to the lower, and down even to the lowest rank. And this is a fact, not accomplished, but in the mere dawn of its accomplishment, and which has shown hitherto but a slight promise of its future fruits. It is easy to scoff at the kind of intelligence which is thus diffusing itself; but it is intelligence still. The knowledge which is power, is not the highest description of knowledge only: any knowledge which gives the habit of forming an opinion, and the capacity of expressing that opinion, constitutes a political power; and if combined with the capacity and habit of acting in concert, a formidable one.

It is in this last element, the power of combined action, that the progress of the Democracy has been the most gigantic. What combination can do has been shown by an experiment, of now many years duration, among a people the most backward in civilization (thanks to English misgovernment) between the Vistula and the Pyrenees. Even on this side of the Irish Channel we have seen something of what could be done by Political Unions, Anti-Slavery Societies, and the like; to say nothing of the less advanced, but already powerful organization of the working classes, the progress of which has been suspended only by the temporary failure arising from the manifest impracticability of its present objects. And these various associations are not the machinery of democratic combination, but the occasional weapons which that spirit forges as it needs them. The real Political Unions of England are the Newspapers. It is these which tell every person what all other persons are feeling, and in what manner they are ready to act: it is by these that the people learn, it may truly be said, their own wishes, and through these that they declare them. The newspapers and the railroads are solving the problem of bringing the democracy of England to vote, like that of Athens, simultaneously in one *agora*; and the same agencies are rapidly effacing those local distinctions which rendered one part of our population strangers to another; and are making us more than ever (what is the first condition of a powerful public opinion) a homogeneous people. If America has been said to prove that in an extensive country a popular government may exist, England seems destined to afford the proof that after a certain stage in civilization it must; for as soon as the numerically stronger have the same advantages, in means of combination and celerity of movement, as the smaller number, they are the masters; and, except by their permission, no government can any longer exist.

It may be said, doubtless, that though the aristocratic class may be no longer in the ascendant, the power by which it is succeeded is not that of the numerical majority; that the middle class in this country is as little in danger of being outstripped by the democracy below, as of being kept down by the aristocracy above; and that there can be no difficulty for that class, aided as it would be by the rich, in making head by its property, intelligence, and power of combination, against any possible growth of those elements of importance in the inferior classes; and in excluding the mass of mere manual labourers from any share in political rights, unless such a restricted and subordinate one as may be found compatible with the complete ascendancy of property.

We are disposed partially to agree in this opinion. Universal suffrage is never likely to exist ^{y}and maintain itself^y where the majority are *prolétaires*; and we are not unwilling to believe that a labouring class in abject poverty, like ^{z}a great^z part of our rural population, or which expends its surplus earnings in gin or in waste, like so much of the better paid population of the towns, may be kept politically in subjection, and that the middle classes are safe from the permanent rule of such a body, though perhaps not from its Swing outrages, or Wat Tyler insurrections. But this admission leaves the fact of a tendency towards democracy practically untouched. There is a democracy short of pauper suffrage; the working classes themselves contain a middle as well as a lowest class. Not to meddle with the *vexata quæstio*, whether the lowest class is or is not improving in condition, it is certain that a larger and larger body of manual labourers are rising above that class, and acquiring at once decent wages and decent habits of conduct. A rapidly increasing multitude of our working people are becoming, in point of condition and habits, what ^{a} the American working people are. And if our boasted improvements are of any worth, there must be a growing tendency in society and government to make this condition of the labouring classes the general one. The nation must be most slenderly supplied with wisdom and virtue, if it cannot do something to improve its own physical condition, to say nothing of its moral. It is something gained, that well-meaning persons of all parties now at length profess to have this end in view. But in proportion as it is approached to—in proportion as the working class becomes, what all proclaim their desire that it should be—well paid, well taught, and well conducted; in the same proportion will the opinions of that class tell, according to its numbers, upon the affairs of the country. Whatever portion of the class succeeds in thus raising itself, becomes a part of the ruling body; and if the suffrage be necessary to make it so, it will not be long without the suffrage.

Meanwhile, we are satisfied if it be admitted, that the government of

y-y+59,67
z-z40   the greatest
a40   all

England is progressively changing from the government of a few, to the government, not indeed of *the* many, but of many;—from an aristocracy with a popular infusion, to the *régime* of the middle class. To most purposes, in the constitution of modern society, the government of a numerous middle class is democracy. Nay, it not merely *is* democracy, but the only democracy of which there is yet any example; what is called universal suffrage in America arising from the fact that America is *all* middle class; the whole people being in a condition, both as to education and pecuniary means, corresponding to the middle class here. The consequences which we would deduce from this fact will appear presently, when we examine M. de Tocqueville's view of the moral, social, and intellectual influences of democracy. This cannot be done until we have briefly stated his opinions on the purely political branch of the question. To this part of our task we shall now proceed; with as much conciseness as is permitted by the number and importance of the ideas which, holding an essential place among the grounds of his general conclusions, have a claim not to be omitted even from the most rapid summary.

We have already intimated that M. de Tocqueville recognises such a thing as a democratic state of society without a democratic government; a state in which the people are all equal, and subjected to one common master, who selects indiscriminately from all of them the instruments of his government. In this sense, as he remarks, the government of the Pasha of Egypt is a specimen of democracy; and to this type (with allowance for difference of civilization and manners) he thinks that all nations are in danger of approximating, in which the equalization of conditions has made greater progress than the spirit of liberty.[*] Now, this he holds to be the condition of France. The kings of France have always been the greatest of levellers; Louis XI, Richelieu, Louis XIV, alike laboured to break the power of the noblesse, and reduce all intermediate classes and bodies to the general level. After them came the Revolution, bringing with it the abolition of hereditary privileges, the emigration and dispossession of half the great landed proprietors, and the subdivision of large fortunes by the revolutionary law of inheritance. While the equalization of conditions was thus rapidly reaching its extreme limits, no corresponding progress of public spirit was taking place in the people at large. No institutions capable of fostering an interest in the details of public affairs were created by the Revolution: it swept away even those which despotism had spared; and if it admitted a portion of the population to a voice in the government, gave it them only on the greatest but rarest occasion —the election of the great council of the state. A political act, to be done only once in a few years, and for which nothing in the daily habits of the citizen has prepared him, leaves his intellect and moral dispositions very

[*See Reeve, Vol. II, p. 174; Tocqueville, Vol. II, p. 164.]

much as it found them; and the citizens not being encouraged to take upon themselves collectively that portion of the business of society which had been performed by the privileged classes, the central government easily drew to itself not only the whole local administration, but much of what, in countries like ours, is performed by associations of individuals. Whether the government was revolutionary or counter-revolutionary made no difference; under the one and the other, everything was done *for* the people, and nothing *by* the people. In France, consequently, the arbitrary power of the magistrate in detail is almost without limit. And when of late some attempts have been made to associate a portion of the citizens in the management of local affairs, comparatively few have been found, even among those in good circumstances, (anywhere but in the large towns,) who could be induced willingly to take any part in that management; who, when they had no personal object to gain, felt the public interest sufficiently their own interest, not to grudge every moment which they withdrew from their occupations or pleasures to bestow upon it. With all the eagerness and violence of party contests in France, a nation more passive in the hands of any one who is uppermost does not exist. M. de Tocqueville has no faith in the virtues, nor even in the prolonged existence, of a superficial love of freedom, in the face of a practical habit of slavery; and the question whether the French are to be a free people, depends, in his opinion, upon the possibility of creating a spirit and a habit of local self-government.

M. de Tocqueville sees the principal source and security of American freedom, not so much in the election of *b*the*b* President and Congress by popular suffrage, as in the administration of nearly all the business of society by the people themselves. This it is which, according to him, keeps up the habit of attending to the public interest, not in the gross merely, or on a few momentous occasions, but in its dry and troublesome details. This, too, it is which enlightens the people; which teaches them by experience how public affairs must be carried on. The dissemination of public business as widely as possible among the people, is, in his opinion, the only means by which they can be fitted for the exercise of any share of power over the legislature; and generally also the only means by which they can be led to desire it.

For the particulars of this education of the American people by means of political institutions, we must refer to the work itself; of which it is one of the minor recommendations, that it has never been equalled even as a mere statement and explanation of the institutions of the United States. The general principle to which M. de Tocqueville has given the sanction of his authority, merits more consideration than it has yet received from the professed labourers in the cause of national education. It has often been said, and requires to be repeated still oftener, that books and discourses alone are

b–b+59,67

not education; that life is a problem, not a theorem; that action can only be learnt in action. A child learns to write its name only by a succession of trials; and is a man to be taught to use his mind and guide his conduct by mere precept? What can be learnt in schools is important, but not all-important. The main branch of the education of human beings is their habitual employment; which must be either their individual vocation, or some matter of general concern, in which they are called to take a part. The private money-getting occupation of almost every one is more or less a mechanical routine; it brings but few of his faculties into action, while its exclusive pursuit tends to fasten his attention and interest exclusively upon himself, and upon his family as an appendage of himself; making him indifferent to the public, to the more generous objects and the nobler interests, and, in his inordinate regard for his personal comforts, selfish and cowardly. Balance these tendencies by contrary ones; give him something to do for the public, whether as a vestryman, a juryman, or an elector; and, in that degree, his ideas and feelings are taken out of this narrow circle. He becomes acquainted with more varied business, and a larger range of considerations. He is made to feel that besides the interests which separate him from his fellow-citizens, he has interests which connect him with them; that not only the common weal is his weal, but that it partly depends upon his exertions. Whatever might be the case in some other constitutions of society, the spirit of a commercial people will be, we are persuaded, essentially mean and slavish, wherever public spirit is not cultivated by an extensive participation of the people in the business of government in detail; nor will the desideratum of a general diffusion of intelligence among either the middle or lower classes be realized, but by a corresponding dissemination of public functions and a voice in public affairs.

Nor is this inconsistent with obtaining a considerable share of the benefits (and they are great) of what is called centralization. The principle of local self-government has been undeservedly discredited, by being associated with the agitation against the new poor-law.[*] The most active agency of a central authority in collecting and communicating information, giving advice to the local bodies, and even framing general rules for their observance, is no hindrance, but an aid, to making the local liberties an instrument of educating the people. The existence of such a central agency allows of intrusting to the people themselves, or to local bodies representative of them, many things of too great national importance to be committed unreservedly to the localities; and completes the efficacy of local self-government as a means of instruction, by accustoming the people not only to judge of particular facts, but to understand, and apply, and feel practically the value of, principles. The mode of administration provided for the English poor-laws by

[*4 & 5 William IV, c. 76 (1834).]

the late Act seems to us to be in its general conception almost theoretically perfect. And the extension of a similar mixture of central and local management to several other branches of administration, thereby combining the best fruits of popular intervention with much of the advantage of skilled supervision and traditional experience, would, we believe, be entitled to no mean rank in M. de Tocqueville's list of correctives to the inconveniences of ^{c}Democracy^c.

In estimating the effects of ^{d}democratic government^d as distinguished from a ^{e}democratic condition of society^e, M. de Tocqueville assumes the state of circumstances which exists in America—a popular government in the ^{f}State^f, combined with popular local institutions. In such a government he sees great advantages, balanced by no inconsiderable evils.

Among the advantages, one which figures in the foremost rank is that of which we have just spoken, the diffusion of intelligence; the remarkable impulse given by democratic institutions to the active faculties of that portion of the community who in other circumstances are the most ignorant, passive, and apathetic. These are characteristics of America which strike all travellers. Activity, enterprise, and a respectable amount of information, are not the qualities of a few among the American citizens, nor even of many, but of all. There is no class of persons who are the slaves of habit and routine. Every American will carry on his manufacture, or cultivate his farm, by the newest and best methods applicable to the circumstances of the case. The poorest American understands and can explain the most intricate parts of his country's institutions; can discuss her interests, internal and foreign. Much of this may justly be attributed to the universality of easy circumstances, and to the education and habits which the first settlers in America brought with them; but our author is certainly not wrong in ascribing a certain portion of it to the perpetual exercise of the faculties of every man among the people, through the universal practice of submitting all public questions to his judgment.

It is incontestable that the people frequently conduct public business very ill; but it is impossible that the people should take a part in public business without extending the circle of their ideas, and without quitting the ordinary routine of their mental ^{g}occupations^g. The humblest individual who is called upon to co-operate in the government of society, acquires a certain degree of self-respect; and, as he possesses power, minds more enlightened than his own offer him their services. He is canvassed by a multitude of claimants who need his support; and who, seeking to deceive him in a thousand different ways, instruct him ^{h}during the

$^{c-c}$40 democracy $^{d-d}$40 Democratic Government
$^{e-e}$40 Democratic State of Society $^{f-f}$40 state
$^{g-g}$Source,40 acquirements
$^{h-h}$Source by their deceit] 40 in their deceit

process[h]. He takes a part in political undertakings which did not originate in his own conception, but which give him a [i]general taste for such undertakings[i]. New ameliorations are daily suggested to him in the property which he holds in common with others, and this gives him the desire of improving that property which is peculiarly his own. He is, perhaps, neither happier nor better than those who came before him; but he is better informed and more active. I have no doubt that the democratic institutions of the United States, joined to the physical constitution of the country, are the cause (not the direct, as is so often asserted, but the indirect cause) of the prodigious commercial activity of the inhabitants. It is not engendered by the laws, but it proceeds from habits acquired through participation in making the laws.

When the opponents of Democracy assert that a single individual performs the functions which he undertakes, better than the government of the people at large, it appears to me that they are perfectly right. The government of an individual, supposing an equal degree of instruction on either side, has more constancy, more perseverance, than that of a multitude; more combination in its plans, and more perfection in its details; and is better qualified judiciously to discriminate the characters of the men it employs. If any deny this, they have never seen a democratic government, or have formed their opinion only upon a few instances. It must be conceded that even when local circumstances and the disposition of the people allow democratic institutions to subsist, they never display a regular and methodical system of government. Democratic liberty is far from accomplishing all the projects it undertakes with the skill of an [j]intelligent[j] despotism. It frequently abandons them before they have borne their fruits, or risks them when the consequences may prove dangerous; but in the end it produces greater results than any absolute government. It does fewer things well, but it does a greater number of things. Not what is done by a democratic government, but what is done under a democratic government by private agency, is really great. Democracy does not confer the most skilful kind of government upon the people, but it produces that which the most skilful governments are frequently unable to awaken, namely, an all-pervading and restless activity—a superabundant force—an energy which is never seen elsewhere, and which may, under favourable circumstances, beget the most amazing benefits. These are the true advantages of democracy. [k](Tocqueville, Vol. II, Chap. vi [pp. 130–2].)[k]

The other great political advantage which our author ascribes to Democracy, requires less illustration, because it is more obvious, and has been oftener treated of; that the course of legislation and administration tends always in the direction of the interest of the [l]greatest[l] number. Although M. de Tocqueville is far from considering this quality of Democracy as the [m]panacea[m] in politics which it has sometimes been supposed to be, he expresses his sense of its importance, if in measured, in no undecided terms. America does not exhibit to us what we see in the best mixed constitutions— the class interests of small minorities wielding the powers of legislation, in

[i-i]Source   taste for undertakings of the kind]   40   taste for other undertakings
[j-j]Source,40   adroit
[k-k]40   (Reeve, Vol. II, Chap. ii [pp. 138–40].) [Cf. 89–90 above.]
[l-l]40   greater
[m-m]40   *panacea*

opposition both to the general interest and to the general opinion of the community; still less does she exhibit what has been characteristic of most representative governments, and is only gradually ceasing to characterize our own—a standing league of class interests—a tacit compact among the various knots of men who profit by abuses, to stand by one another in resisting reform. Nothing can subsist in America that is not recommended by arguments which, in appearance at least, address themselves to the interest of the many. However frequently, therefore, that interest may be mistaken, the direction of legislation towards it is maintained in the midst of the mistakes; and if a community is so situated or so ordered that it can "support the transitory action of bad laws, and can await without destruction the result of the *general tendency* of the laws," that country, in the opinion of M. de Tocqueville, will prosper more under a democratic government than under any other.[*] But in aristocratic governments, the interest, or at best the honour and glory, of the ruling class, is considered as the public interest; and all that is most valuable to the individuals composing the subordinate classes, is apt to be immolated to that public interest with all the rigour of antique patriotism.

The men who are intrusted with the direction of public affairs in the United States are frequently inferior, both in point of capacity and of morality, to those whom aristocratic institutions would raise to power. But their interest is identified and confounded with that of the majority of *n*their*n* fellow-citizens. They may frequently be faithless and frequently mistaken, but they will never systematically adopt a line of conduct hostile to the majority; and it is impossible that they should give a dangerous or an exclusive character to the government.

The mal-administration of a democratic magistrate is, moreover, a mere isolated fact, the effects of which do not last beyond the short period for which he is elected. Corruption and incapacity do not act as common interests, which *o* connect men permanently with one another. A corrupt or an incapable magistrate will not concert his measures with another magistrate, simply because that individual is corrupt and incapable like himself; and these two men will never unite their endeavours to promote or screen the corruption or inaptitude of their remote posterity. The ambition and the manœuvres of the one will serve, on the contrary, to unmask the other. The vices of the magistrate in democratic states are usually those of his individual character.

But, under aristocratic governments, public men are swayed by the interest of their order, which, if it is sometimes blended with the interests of the majority, is frequently distinct from them. This interest is a common and lasting bond which unites them together. It induces them to coalesce, and combine their efforts towards attaining an end which is not always the happiness of the greatest number; and it not only connects the persons in authority with each other, but links them also to a considerable portion of the governed, since a numerous body of

[*Reeve, Vol. II, pp. 115–16; Tocqueville, Vol. II, p. 109.]

*n-n*40   those [*printer's error?*]
*o*Source,40   may

citizens belongs to the aristocracy, without being invested with official functions. The aristocratic magistrate, therefore, finds himself supported in his own natural tendencies by a portion of society itself, as well as by the government of which he is a member.

The common object which connects the interest of the magistrates in aristocracies with that of a portion of their *p*cotemporaries*p*, identifies it also with future generations of their order. They labour for ages to come as well as for their own time. The aristocratic magistrate is thus urged towards the same point by the passions of those who surround him, by his own, and, I might almost say, by those of his posterity. Is it wonderful that he should not resist? And hence it is that the class spirit often hurries along with it those whom it does not corrupt, and makes them unintentionally fashion society to their own particular ends, and *q*pre-fashion*q* it for their descendants. (Reeve, Vol. II, pp. 118–19; Tocqueville, Vol. II, pp. 111–13.)[*]

These, then, are the advantages ascribed by our author to a democratic government. We are now to speak of its disadvantages.

According to the opinion which is prevalent among the more cultivated advocates of democracy, one of its greatest recommendations is that by means of it the wisest and worthiest are brought to the head of affairs. The people, it is said, have the strongest interest in selecting the right men. It is presumed that they will be sensible of that interest; and, subject to more or less liability of error, will in the main succeed in placing a high, if not the highest, degree of worth and talent in the highest situations.

M. de Tocqueville is of another opinion. He was forcibly struck with the general want of merit in the members of the American legislatures, and other public functionaries. He accounts for this, not solely by the people's incapacity to discriminate merit, but partly also by their indifference to it. He thinks there is little preference for men of superior intellect, little desire to obtain their services for the public; occasionally even a jealousy of them, especially if they be also rich. They, on their part, have still less inclination to seek any such employment. Public offices are little lucrative, confer little power, and offer no guarantee of permanency: almost any other career holds out better pecuniary prospects to a man of ability and enterprise; nor will instructed men stoop to those mean arts, and those compromises of their private opinions, to which their less distinguished competitors willingly resort. The depositaries of power, after being chosen with little regard to merit, are, partly perhaps for that very reason, frequently changed. The rapid return of elections, and even a taste for variety, M. de Tocqueville thinks, on the part of electors (a taste not unnatural wherever little regard is paid to qualifications), produces a rapid succession of new men in the *r*legislature*r*, and

[*Cf. pp. 69–70 above.]

*p–p*40   contemporaries
*q–q*Source,40   prepare
*r–r*40   legislatures [*printer's error?*]

in all public posts. Hence, on the one hand, great instability in the laws—every new comer desiring to do something in the short time *he has before him*; while, on the other hand, there is no political *carrière*—statesmanship is not a profession. There is no body of persons educated for public business, pursuing it as their occupation, and who transmit from one to another the results of their experience. There are no traditions, no science or art of public affairs. A functionary knows little, and cares less, about the principles on which his predecessor has acted; and his successor thinks as little about his. Public transactions are therefore conducted with a reasonable share indeed of the common sense and common information which are general in a democratic community, but with little benefit from specific study and experience; without consistent system, long-sighted views, or persevering pursuit of distant objects.

This is likely enough to be a true picture of the American Government, but can scarcely be said to be peculiar to it: there are now few governments remaining, whether representative or absolute, of which something of the same sort might not be said. In no country where the real government resides in the minister, and where there are frequent changes of ministry, are far-sighted views of policy likely to be acted upon; whether the country be England or France, in the eighteenth century or in the nineteenth.* *ᵘᵛCrude and ill-considered legislationᵛ is the character of all governments whose laws are made and acts of administration performed *impromptu*, not in pursuance of a general design, but from the pressure of some present occasion; of all governments in which the ruling power is to any great extent exercised by persons not trained to government as a business.ᵘ ᵂIt is true that the governments which have been celebrated for their profound policy, have generally been aristocracies. But they have been very narrow aristocracies, consisting of so few members, that every member could personally participate in the business of administration. These are the governments which have a natural tendency to be administered steadily—that is, according to fixed principles. Every member of the governing body being trained to government as a profession, like other professions they respect precedent, transmit their experi-

---

*[59] A few sentences are here inserted from another paper by the author. ["De Tocqueville on Democracy in America [I]," pp. 78–9 above.]

ˢ⁻ˢ40 which he has

ᵗ⁻ᵗ+59,67 [*taken from* "De Tocqueville on Democracy in America [I]," *78–9 above; the passage is rearranged, and sentences from the original are omitted. The quoted parts, indicated by* ᵘ⁻ᵘ, ʷ⁻ʷ, ᶻ⁻ᶻ *and* ᶜ⁻ᶜ, *occur in the earlier essay in the order* ᵘ⁻ᵘ, ᶜ⁻ᶜ, ʷ⁻ʷ, ᶻ⁻ᶻ; *the other variant notes indicate, as usual, changes in wording. See 78–9 above for the omitted sentences.*]

ᵘ⁻ᵘ+59,67 [*see* ᵗ⁻ᵗ *above*]

ᵛ⁻ᵛ35 In the English aristocracy there has surely been, at all periods, crude and ill-considered legislation enough. This

ʷ⁻ʷ+59,67 [*see* ᵗ⁻ᵗ *above*]

ence from generation to generation, acquire and preserve a set of traditions, and all being competent judges of each other's merits, the ablest easily rises to his proper level. The governments ^{x} of ancient Rome and modern Venice were of this character; and as all know, for ages conducted the affairs of those states with admirable constancy and skill, on fixed principles, often unworthy enough, but always eminently adapted to the ends of ^{y}those^y governments.^{w} ^{z}When the governing body, whether it ^{a}consists^a of the many or of a privileged class, is so numerous, that the large majority of it do not and cannot make the practice of government the main occupation of their lives, it is ^{b} impossible that there should be wisdom, foresight, and caution in the governing body itself. These qualities must be found, if found at all, not in the body, but in those whom the body trust.^{z} ^{cd}The^d opinion of a ^{e}numerous^e ruling class is as fluctuating, as liable to be wholly given up to immediate impulses, as the opinion of the people. Witness the whole course of English history. All our laws have been made on temporary impulses. In ^{f}no country has the course of legislation been less directed to any steady and consistent purpose.^{fct}

^{g} In so far as it is true that there is a deficiency of remarkable merit in ^{h} American public men (and our author allows that there is a large number of exceptions), the fact may perhaps admit of a less discreditable explanation. America needs very little government. She has no wars, no neighbours, no complicated international relations; no old society with its thousand abuses to reform; no half-fed and untaught millions ^{i}in want of^i food and guidance. Society in America requires little but to be let alone. The current affairs which her ^{j}government^j has to transact can seldom demand much more than average capacity; and it may be in the Americans a wise economy, not to pay the price of great talents when common ones will serve their purpose. We make these remarks by way of caution, not of controversy. Like many other parts of our author's doctrines, that of which we are now speaking affords work for a succession of thinkers and of accurate observers, and must in the main depend on future experience to confirm or refute it.

We now come to that one among the dangers of Democracy, respecting which so much has been said, and which our author designates as "the despotism of the majority."

It is perhaps the greatest defect of M. de Tocqueville's book, that from the scarcity of examples, his propositions, even when derived from observa-

---

^{x}35   (so unalike in other respects)
$^{z-z}$+59,67   [see $^{t-t}$ above]
$^{a-a}$35   consist
$^{c-c}$+59,67   [see $^{t-t}$ above]
$^{e-e}$+59,67
^{g}40   [no paragraph]
$^{i-i}$40   crying for

$^{y-y}$35   these [printer's error?]
^{b}35   utterly
$^{d-d}$35   In all other matters, the
$^{f-f}$35   what country ... purpose?
^{h}40   the
$^{j-j}$40,59   Government

tion, have the air of mere abstract speculations. He speaks of the tyranny of the majority in general phrases, but gives hardly any instances of it, nor much information as to the mode in which it is practically exemplified. The omission was in the present instance the more excusable, as the despotism complained of was, at that time, politically at least, an evil in apprehension more than in sufferance; and he was uneasy rather at the total absence of security against the tyranny of the majority, than at the frequency of its actual exertion.

Events, however, which have occurred since the publication of the First Part of M. de Tocqueville's work, give indication of the shape which tyranny is most likely to assume when exercised by a majority.

It is not easy to surmise any inducements of interest, by which, in a country like America, the greater number could be led to oppress the smaller. When the majority and the minority are spoken of as conflicting interests, the rich and the poor are generally meant; but where the rich are content with being rich, and do not claim as such any political privileges, their interest and that of the poor are *generally* the same: complete protection to property, and freedom in the disposal of it, are alike important to both. When, indeed, the poor are so poor that they can scarcely be worse off, respect on their part for rights of property which they cannot hope to share, is never safely to be calculated upon. But where all have property, either in enjoyment or in reasonable hope, and an appreciable chance of acquiring a large fortune; and where every man's way of life proceeds on the confident assurance that, by superior exertion, he will obtain a superior reward; the importance of inviolability of property is not likely to be lost sight of. It is not affirmed of the Americans that they make laws against the rich, or unduly press upon them in the imposition of taxes. If a labouring class, less happily circumstanced, could prematurely force themselves into influence over our own legislature, there might then be danger, not so much of violations of property, as of undue interference with contracts; unenlightened legislation for the supposed interest of the many; laws founded on mistakes in political economy. A minimum of wages, or a tax on machinery, might be attempted: as silly and as inefficacious attempts might be made to keep up wages by law, as were so long made by the British legislature to keep them down by the same means. We have no wish to see the experiment tried, but we are fully convinced that experience would correct the one error as it has corrected the other, and in the same way; namely, by *complete* practical failure.

It is not from the separate interests, real or imaginary, of the majority, that minorities are in danger; but from its antipathies of religion, political

k–k+59,67
l–l40   the completest

party, or race; and experience in America seems to confirm what theory rendered probable, that the tyranny of the majority would not take the shape of tyrannical laws, but that of a dispensing power over all laws. The people of Massachusetts passed no law prohibiting Roman Catholic schools, or exempting Protestants from the penalties of incendiarism; they contented themselves with burning the Ursuline convent to the ground, aware that no jury would be found to redress the injury. In the same reliance the people of New York and Philadelphia sacked and destroyed the houses of the Abolitionists, and the schools and churches of their black fellow-citizens, while numbers who took no share in the outrage amused themselves with the sight. The laws of Maryland still prohibit murder and burglary; but in 1812, a Baltimore mob, after destroying the printing office of a newspaper which had opposed the war with England, broke into the prison to which the editors had been conveyed for safety, murdered one of them, left the others for dead; and the criminals were tried and acquitted. In the same city, in 1835, a riot which lasted four days, and the foolish history of which is related in M. Chevalier's *Letters*,[*] was occasioned by the fraudulent bankruptcy of the Maryland Bank. It is not so much the riots, in such instances, that are deplorable; these might have occurred in any country: it is the impossibility of obtaining aid from an executive dependent on the mob, or justice from juries which formed part of it: it is the apathetic cowardly truckling of disapproving lookers-on; almost a parallel to the passive imbecility of the people of Paris, when a handful of hired assassins perpetrated the massacres of September. For where the majority is the sole power, and a power issuing its mandates in the form of riots, it inspires a terror which the most arbitrary monarch often fails to excite. The silent sympathy of the majority may support on the scaffold the martyr of one man's tyranny; but if we would imagine the situation of a victim of the majority itself, we must look to the annals of religious persecution for a parallel.

Yet, neither ought we to forget that even this lawless violence is not so great, because not so lasting, an evil, as tyranny through the medium of the law. A tyrannical law remains; because, so long as it is submitted to, its existence does not weaken the general authority of the laws. But in America, tyranny will seldom use the instrument of law, because *m*there is in general*m* no permanent class to be tyrannized over. The subjects of oppression are casual objects of popular resentment, who cannot be reached by law, but only by occasional acts of lawless power; and to tolerate these, if they ever became frequent, would be consenting to live without law. Already, in the United States, the spirit of outrage has raised a spirit of resistance to outrage;

[*Michel Chevalier, *Lettres sur l'Amérique du Nord*, 2 vols. (Paris: Gosselin, 1836).]

m–*m*40   among the white population there is

of moral resistance first, as was to be wished and expected: if that fail, physical resistance will follow. The majority, like other despotic powers, will be taught by experience that it cannot enjoy both the advantages of civilized society, and the barbarian liberty of taking men's lives and property at its discretion. Let it once be generally understood that minorities will fight, and majorities will be shy of provoking them. The bad government of which there is any permanent danger under modern civilization, is in the form of bad laws and bad tribunals: government by the *sic volo* either of a king or a mob belongs to past ages, and can no more exist *n*, for long together,*n* out of the pale of Asiatic barbarism.

The despotism, therefore, of the majority within the limits of civil life, though a real evil, does not appear to us to be a formidable one. The tyranny which we fear, and which M. de Tocqueville principally dreads, is of another kind—a tyranny not over the body, but over the mind.

It is the complaint of M. de Tocqueville, as well as of other travellers in America, that in no country does there exist less independence of thought. In religion, indeed, the varieties of opinion which fortunately prevailed among those by whom the colonies were settled, *°have°* produced a toleration in law and in fact extending to the limits of Christianity. If by ill fortune there had happened to be a religion of the majority, the case would probably have been different. On every other subject, when the opinion of the majority is made up, hardly any one, it is affirmed, dares to be of any other opinion, or at least to profess it. The statements are not clear as to the nature or amount of the inconvenience that would be suffered by any one who presumed to question a received opinion. It seems certain, however, that scarcely any person has that courage; that when public opinion considers a question as settled, no further discussion of it takes place; and that not only nobody dares (what everybody may venture upon in Europe) to say anything disrespectful to the public, or derogatory to its opinions, but that its wisdom and virtue are perpetually celebrated with the most servile adulation and sycophancy.

These considerations, which were much dwelt on in the author's First Part, are intimately connected with the views promulgated in his Second, respecting the influence of Democracy on *ᵖintellectᵖ*.

The Americans, according to M. de Tocqueville, not only profess, but carry into practice, on all subjects except the fundamental doctrines of Christianity and Christian ethics, the habit of mind which has been so often inculcated as the one sufficient security against mental slavery—the rejection of authority, and the assertion of the right of private judgment. They regard

n-n+59,67
*o-o*40   has
*p-p*40   Intellect

the traditions of the past merely in the light of materials, and as "a useful study for doing otherwise and better."[*] They are not accustomed to look for guidance either to the wisdom of ancestors, or to eminent qcotemporaryq wisdom, but require that the grounds on which they act shall be made level to their own comprehension. And, as is natural to those who govern themselves by common-sense rather than by science, their cast of mind is altogether unpedantic and practical; they go straight to the end, without favour or prejudice towards any set of means, and aim at the substance of things, with something like a contempt for form.

From such habits and ways of thinking, the consequence which would be apprehended by some would be a most licentious abuse of individual independence of thought. The fact ris r the reverse. It is impossible, as our author truly remarks, that mankind in general should form all their opinions for themselves: an authority from which they mostly derive them may be rejected in theory, but it always exists in fact. That law above them, which older societies have found in the traditions of antiquity, or in the dogmas of priests or philosophers, the Americans find in the opinions of one another. All being nearly equal in circumstances, and all nearly alike in intelligence and knowledge, the only authority which commands an involuntary deference is that of numbers. The more perfectly each knows himself the equal of every single individual, the more insignificant and helpless he feels against the aggregate mass; and the more incredible it appears to him that the opinion of all the world can possibly be erroneous. "Faith in public opinion," says M. de Tocqueville, "becomes in such countries a species of religion, and the majority its prophet."[†] The idea that the things which the multitude believe are still disputable, is no longer kept alive by dissentient voices; the right of private judgment, by being extended to the incompetent, ceases to be exercised even by the competent; and speculation becomes possible only within the limits traced, not as of old by the infallibility of Aristotle, but by that of "our free and enlightened citizens," or "our free and enlightened age."

On the influence of Democracy upon the cultivation of science and art, the opinions of M. de Tocqueville are highly worthy of attention. There are many who, partly from theoretic considerations, and partly from the marked absence in America of original efforts in literature, philosophy, or the fine arts, incline to believe that modern democracy is fatal to them, and that wherever its spirit spreads they will take flight. M. de Tocqueville is not of this opinion. The example of America, as he observes, is not to the purpose, because America is, intellectually speaking, a province of England; a prov-

[*Reeve, Vol. III, p. 2; Tocqueville, Vol. III, p. 2.]
[†Reeve, Vol. III, p. 19; Tocqueville, Vol. III, p. 15.]

q–q40   contemporary
r–r40   proves

ince in which the great occupation of the inhabitants is making money, because for that they have peculiar facilities, and are therefore, like the people of Manchester or Birmingham, for the most part contented to receive the higher branches of knowledge ready-made from the capital. In a democratic nation, which is also free, and generally educated, our author is far from thinking that there will be no public to relish or remunerate the works of science and genius. Although there will be *s* great shifting of fortunes, and no hereditary body of wealthy persons sufficient to form a class, there will be, he thinks, from the general activity and the absence of artificial barriers, combined with the inequality of human intelligence, a far greater number of rich individuals (*infiniment plus nombreux*) than in an aristocratic society.[*] There will be, therefore, though not so complete a leisure, yet a leisure extending perhaps to more persons; while from the closer contact and greater mutual intercourse between classes, the love of intellectual pleasures and occupations will spread downward very widely among those who have not the same advantages of leisure. Moreover, *'talents'* and knowledge being in a democratic society the only means of rapid improvement in fortune, they will be, in the abstract at least, by no means undervalued; whatever measure of them any person is capable of appreciating, he will also be desirous of possessing. Instead, therefore, of any neglect of science and literature, the eager ambition which is universal in such a state of society takes that direction as well as others, and the number of those who cultivate these pursuits becomes "immense."[†]

It is from this fact—from the more active competition in the products of intellect, and the more numerous public to which they are addressed—that M. de Tocqueville deduces the defects with which the products themselves will be chargeable. In the multiplication of their quantity he sees the deterioration of their quality. Distracted by so great a multitude, the public can bestow but a moment's attention on each; they will be adapted, therefore, chiefly for striking at the moment. Deliberate approval, and a duration beyond the hour, become more and more difficult of attainment. What is written for the *"judgment"* of a highly instructed few, amidst the abundance of writings may very probably never reach them; and their suffrage, which never gave riches, does not now confer even glory. But the multitude of buyers affords the possibility of great pecuniary success and momentary notoriety, for the work which is made up to please at once, and to please the many. Literature thus becomes not only a trade, but is carried on by the

[*Reeve, Vol. III, p. 73; Tocqueville, Vol. III, pp. 57–8.]
[†Reeve, Vol. III, p. 75; Tocqueville, Vol. III, p. 59.]

*s*40   a
*t–t*40   talent
*u–u*40   judgments

maxims usually adopted by other trades which live by the number, rather than by the quality, of their customers; that much pains need not be bestowed on commodities intended for the general market, and that what is saved in the workmanship may be more profitably expended in self-advertisement. There will thus be an immense mass of third and fourth-rate productions, and very few first-rate. Even the turmoil and bustle of a society in which every one is striving to get on, is in itself, our author observes, not favourable to meditation. "Il règne dans le sein de ces nations un petit mouvement incommode, une sorte de roulement incessant des hommes les uns sur les autres, qui trouble et distrait l'esprit sans l'animer et l'élever."[*] Not to mention that the universal tendency to action, and to rapid action, directs the taste to applications rather than principles, and hasty approximations to truth rather than scientific accuracy in it.

Passing now from the province of intellect to that of ᵛsentiments and moralsᵛ, M. de Tocqueville is of opinion that the general softening of manners, and the remarkable growth, in modern times, of humanity and philanthropy, are in great part the effect of the gradual progress of social equality. Where the different classes of mankind are divided by impassable barriers, each may have intense sympathies with his own class, more intense than it is almost possible to have with mankind in general; but those who are far below him in condition are so unlike himself, that he hardly considers them as human beings; and if they are refractory and troublesome, will be unable to feel for them even that kindly interest which he experiences for his more unresisting domestic cattle. Our author cites a well-known passage of Madame de Sévigné's *Letters*, in exemplification of the want of feeling exhibited even by good sort of persons towards those with whom they have no *fellow*-feeling.[†] In America, except towards the slaves (an exception which proves the rule,) he finds the sentiments of philanthropy and compassion almost universal, accompanied by a general kindness of manner and obligingness of disposition, without much of ceremony and punctilio. As all feel that they are not above the possible need of the good-will and good offices of others, every one is ready to afford his own. The general equality penetrates also into the family relations: there is more intimacy, he thinks, than in Europe, between parents and children, but less, except in the earliest years, of paternal authority, and the filial respect which is founded on it. ʷThis, however, isʷ among the topics which we must omit; as well as the connexion which our author attempts to trace between equality of con-

[*Tocqueville, Vol. III, p. 64; cf. Reeve, Vol. III, p. 81.]

[†See Marie, Marquise de Sévigné, *Lettres*, ed. Gérard-Gailly, 3 vols. (Paris: Gallimard, 1953–57), Vol. I, pp. 894–6.]

ᵛ⁻ᵛ40   Sentiments and Morals
ʷ⁻ʷ40,59   These, however, are

ditions and strictness of domestic morals, and some other remarks on domestic society in America, which do not appear to us to be of any considerable value.

M. de Tocqueville is of opinion, that one of the tendencies of a democratic state of society is to make every one, in a manner, retire within himself, and concentrate his interests, wishes, and pursuits within his own business and household.

The members of a democratic community are like the sands of the seashore, each very minute, and no one adhering to any other. There are no permanent classes, and therefore no *esprit de corps*; few hereditary fortunes, and therefore few local attachments, or outward objects consecrated by family feeling. A man feels little connexion with his neighbours, little with his ancestors, little with his posterity. There are scarcely any ties to connect any two men together, except the common one of country. Now, the love of country is not, in large communities, a passion of spontaneous growth. When a man's country is his town, where his ancestors have lived for generations, of which he knows every inhabitant, and has recollections associated with every street and building—in which alone, of all places on the earth, he is not a stranger—which he is perpetually called upon to defend in the field, and in whose glory or shame he has an appreciable share, made sensible by the constant presence and rivalry of foreigners; in such a state of things patriotism is easy. It was easy in the ancient republics, or in modern Switzerland. But in great communities an intense interest in public affairs is scarcely natural, except to a member of an aristocracy, who alone has so conspicuous a position, and is so personally identified with the conduct of the government, that his credit and consequence are essentially connected with the glory and power of the nation he belongs to; its glory and power (observe,) not the well-being of the bulk of its inhabitants. It is difficult for an obscure person like the citizen of a *x*democracy*x*, who is in no way involved in the responsibility of public affairs, and cannot hope to exercise more than the minutest influence over them, to have the sentiment of patriotism as a living and earnest feeling. There being *y* no intermediate objects for his attachments to fix upon, they fasten themselves on his own private affairs; and, according to national character and circumstances, it becomes his ruling passion either to improve his condition in life, or to take his ease and pleasure by the means which it already affords him.

As, therefore, the state of society becomes more democratic, it is more and more necessary to nourish patriotism by artificial means; and of these none are so efficacious as free institutions—a large and frequent intervention of the citizens in the management of public business. Nor does the love of

*x-x*40   Democracy
*y*40   , then,

country alone require this encouragement, but every feeling which connects men either by interest or sympathy with their neighbours and fellow-citizens. Popular institutions are the great means of rendering general in a people, and especially among the richer classes, the desire of being useful in their generation; useful to the public, or to their neighbours without distinction of rank; as well as courteous and unassuming in their habitual intercourse.

When the public is supreme, there is no man who does not feel the value of public good-will, or who does not endeavour to court it by drawing to himself the esteem and affection of those amongst whom he is to live. Many of the passions which congeal and keep asunder human hearts, are then obliged to retire, and hide below the surface. Pride must be dissembled; disdain does not break out; selfishness is afraid of itself. Under a free government, as most public offices are elective, the men whose elevated minds or aspiring hopes are too closely circumscribed in private life, constantly feel that they cannot do without the population which surrounds them. Men learn at such times to think of their fellow-men from ambitious motives, and they frequently find it, in a manner, their interest, to be forgetful of self.

I may here be met by an objection, derived from electioneering intrigues, the meannesses of candidates, and the calumnies of their opponents. These are opportunities of animosity which occur ᶻ oftener, the more frequent elections become. Such evils are, doubtless, great, but they are transient; whereas the benefits which attend them remain. The desire of being elected may lead some men for a time to mutual hostility; but this same desire leads all men, in the long run, mutually to support each other; and if it happens that an election accidentally severs two friends, the electoral system brings a multitude of citizens permanently together who would always have remained unknown to each other. Freedom engenders private animosities, but despotism gives birth to general indifference. . . .

A brilliant achievement may win for you the favour of a people at one stroke; but to earn the love and respect of the population which surrounds you, requires a long succession of little services and obscure good offices, a constant habit of kindness, and an established reputation for disinterestedness. Local freedom, then, which leads a great number of citizens to value the affections of their neighbours, and of those with whom they are in contact, perpetually draws men back to one another, in spite of the propensities which sever them; and forces them to render each other mutual assistance.

In the United States, the more opulent citizens take great care not to stand aloof from the people: on the contrary, they constantly keep on easy terms with them; they listen to them; they speak to them every day. They know that the rich, in democracies, always stand in need of the poor; and that in democratic times a poor man's attachment depends more on manner than on benefits conferred. The very magnitude of such benefits, by setting the difference of conditions in a strong light, causes a secret irritation to those who reap advantage from them; but the charm of simplicity of manners is almost irresistible. . . . This truth does not penetrate at once into the minds of the rich. They generally resist it as long as the democratic revolution lasts, and they do not acknowledge it immediately after that revolution is accomplished. They are very ready to do good

ᶻSource, 40   the

to the people, but they still choose to keep them at arm's length; they think that is sufficient, but they are mistaken. They might spend fortunes thus, without warming the hearts of the population around them; that population does not ask them for the sacrifice of their money, but of their pride.

It would seem as if every imagination in the United States were on the stretch to invent means of increasing the wealth and satisfying the wants of the public. The best informed inhabitants of each district are incessantly using their information to discover new means of augmenting the general prosperity; and, when they have made any such discoveries, they eagerly surrender them to the mass of the people. . . .

I have often seen Americans make great and real sacrifices to the public welfare; and I have a hundred times remarked that, in case of need, they hardly ever fail to lend faithful support to each other. The free institutions which the inhabitants of the United States possess, and the political rights of which they make so much use, remind every citizen, and in a thousand ways, that he *a*is a member of*a* society. They *b*at*b* every instant impress upon his mind the notion that it is the duty as well as the interest of men to make themselves useful to their fellow-creatures; and as he sees no particular reason for disliking them, since he is never either their master or their slave, his heart readily leans to the side of kindness. Men attend to the interests of the public, first by necessity, afterwards by choice; what was calculation becomes an instinct; and, by dint of working for the good of one's fellow-citizens, the habit and the taste for serving them is at length acquired.

Many people in France consider equality of conditions as one evil, and political freedom as a second. When they are obliged to yield to the former, they strive at least to escape from the latter. But I contend that, in order to combat the evils which equality may produce, there is only one effectual remedy— *c* political freedom. *d*(Tocqueville, Vol. III, Part 2, Chap. iv [pp. 165–70].)*d*

With regard to the tone of moral sentiment characteristic of democracy, M. de Tocqueville holds an opinion which we think deserves the attention of moralists. Among a class composed of persons who have been born into a distinguished position, the habitual springs of action will be very different from those of a democratic community. Speaking generally, (and making abstraction both of individual peculiarities, and of the influence of moral culture,) it may be said of the first, that their feelings and actions will be mainly under the influence of pride; of the latter, under that of interest. Now, as in an aristocratic society the elevated class, though small in number, sets the fashion in opinion and feeling, even virtue will, in that state of society, seem to be most strongly recommended by arguments addressing themselves to pride; in a democracy, by those which address themselves to self-interest. In the one, we hear chiefly of the beauty and dignity of virtue,

*a–a*Source,40   lives in
b–b+59,67 [*not in* Source]
*c*40,59   namely,
*d–d*40   (Reeve, Vol. III, Chap. iv [pp. 212–18].)

the grandeur of self-sacrifice; in the other, of honesty the best policy, the value of character, and the common interest of every individual in the good of the whole.

Neither the one nor the other of these modes of feeling, our author is well aware, constitutes moral excellence; which must have a deeper foundation than either the calculations of self-interest, or the emotions of self-flattery. But as an auxiliary to that higher principle, and as far as possible a substitute for it when it is absent, the latter of the two, in his opinion, though the least sentimental, will stand the most wear.

The principle of enlightened self-interest is not a lofty one, but it is clear and sure. It does not aim at mighty objects, but it attains, without impracticable efforts, all those at which it aims. As it lies within the reach of all capacities, every one can without difficulty apprehend and retain it. By its adaptation to human weaknesses, it easily obtains great dominion; nor is its dominion precarious, since it employs self-interest itself to correct self-interest, and uses, to direct the passions, the very instrument which excites them.

The doctrine of enlightened self-interest produces no great acts of self-sacrifice, but it suggests daily small acts of self-denial. By itself it cannot suffice to make a virtuous man, but it disciplines a multitude of citizens in habits of regularity, temperance, moderation, foresight, self-command: and if it does not at once lead men to virtue by their will, it draws them gradually in that direction by their habits. If the principle of "interest rightly understood" were to sway the whole moral world, extraordinary virtues would doubtless be more rare; but I think that gross depravity would then also be less common. That principle, perhaps, prevents some men from rising far above the level of mankind; but a great number of others, who were falling below that level, are caught and upheld by it. Observe some few individuals, they are lowered by it; survey mankind, it is raised.

I am not afraid to say, that the principle of enlightened self-interest appears to me the best suited of all philosophical theories to the wants of the men of our time; and that I regard it as their chief remaining security against themselves. Towards it, therefore, the minds of the moralists of our age should turn; even should they judge it incomplete, it must nevertheless be adopted as necessary.

No power upon earth can prevent the increasing equality of conditions from impelling the human mind to seek out what is useful, or from inclining every member of the community to concentrate his affections on himself. It must therefore be expected that personal interest will become more than ever the principal, if not the sole, spring of men's actions; but it remains to be seen how each man will understand his personal interest.

I do not think that the doctrine of self-interest, as it is professed in America, is self-evident in all its parts; but it contains a great number of truths so evident, that men, if they are but instructed, cannot fail to see them. Instruct them, then, at all hazards; for the age of implicit self-sacrifice and instinctive virtues is already flying far away from us, and the time is fast approaching when freedom, public peace, and social order itself, will not be able to exist without instruction. *e*(Tocqueville, Vol. III, Part 2, Chap. viii [pp. 197–9].)*e*

e–e40   (Reeve, Vol. III, Chap. viii [pp. 253–6].)

M. de Tocqueville considers a democratic state of society as eminently tending to give the strongest impulse to the *f*desire of*f* physical well-being. He ascribes this, not so much to the equality of conditions as to their mobility. In a country like America every one may acquire riches; no one, at least, is artificially impeded in acquiring them; and hardly any one is born to them. Now, these are the conditions under which the passions which attach themselves to wealth, and to what wealth can purchase, are the strongest. Those who are born in the midst of affluence are generally more or less *g*blasés*g* to its enjoyments. They take the comfort or luxury to which they have always been accustomed, as they do the air they *h*breathe. It*h* is not *le but de la vie*, but *une manière de vivre*. An aristocracy, when put to the proof, has in general shown *i* wonderful facility in enduring the loss of riches and of physical comforts. The very pride, nourished by the elevation which they owed to wealth, supports them under the privation of it. But to those who have chased riches laboriously for half their lives, to lose it is the loss of all; *une vie manquée*; a disappointment greater than can be endured. In a democracy, again, there is no contented poverty. No one being forced to remain poor; many who were poor daily becoming rich, and the comforts of life being apparently within the reach of all, the desire to appropriate them descends to the very lowest rank. Thus,

The desire of acquiring the comforts of the world haunts the imagination of the poor, and the dread of losing them that of the rich. Many scanty fortunes spring up; those who possess them have a sufficient share of physical gratifications to conceive a taste for those pleasures—not enough to satisfy it. They never procure them without exertion, and they never indulge in them without apprehension. They are therefore always straining to pursue or to retain gratifications so precious, so incomplete, and so fugitive.

If I inquire what passion is most natural to men who are at once stimulated and circumscribed by the obscurity of their birth or the mediocrity of their fortune, I can discover none more peculiarly appropriate to them than this love of physical prosperity. The passion for physical comforts is essentially a passion of the middle classes; with those classes it grows and spreads, and along with them it becomes preponderant. From them it mounts into the higher orders of society, and descends into the mass of the people.

I never met in America with any citizen so poor as not to cast a glance of hope and longing towards the enjoyments of the rich, or whose imagination did not indulge itself by anticipation in those good things which fate still obstinately withheld from him.

On the other hand, I never perceived, amongst the wealthier inhabitants of the United States, that proud contempt of the indulgences of riches, which is sometimes to be met with even in the most opulent and dissolute aristocracies. Most of these wealthy persons were once poor; they have felt the stimulus of privation, they have long struggled with adverse fortune; and now that the victory is won,

---

*f-f*40   taste for   *g-g*40   *blasé* as [*printer's error?*]
*h-h*40   breathe; it   *i*40   a

the passions which accompanied the contest have survived it; their minds are, as it were, intoxicated by the petty enjoyments which they have pursued for forty years.

Not but that in the United States, as elsewhere, there are a certain number of wealthy persons, who, having come into their property by inheritance, possess, without exertion, an opulence they have not earned. But even these are not less devotedly attached to the pleasures of material life. The love of physical comfort *j*has*j* become the predominant taste of the nation; the great current of man's passions runs in that channel, and sweeps everything along in its course. *k*(Tocqueville, Vol. III, Part 2, Chap. x [pp. 206–7].)*k*

A regulated sensuality thus *l*established*l* itself—the parent of effeminacy rather than of debauchery; paying respect to the social rights of other people and to the opinion of the world; not "leading men away in search of forbidden enjoyments, but absorbing them in the pursuit of permitted ones. This spirit is frequently combined with a species of religious morality; men wish to be as well off as they can in this world, without foregoing their chance of another."[*]

From the preternatural stimulus given to the desire of acquiring and of enjoying wealth, by the intense competition which necessarily exists where an entire population are the competitors, arises the restlessness so characteristic of American life.

It is strange to see with what feverish ardour the Americans pursue their own welfare; and to watch the vague dread that constantly torments them lest they should not have chosen the shortest path which may lead to it. A native of the United States clings to this world's goods as if he were certain never to die, and is so hasty in grasping at all within his reach, that one would suppose he was constantly afraid of not living long enough to enjoy them. He clutches everything, he holds nothing fast, but soon loosens his grasp to pursue fresh gratifications. . . .

At first sight there is something surprising in this strange unrest of so many happy men, uneasy in the midst of abundance. The spectacle is, however, as old as the world; the novelty is to see a whole people furnish an example of it. . . .

When all the privileges of birth and fortune are abolished, when all professions are accessible to all, and a man's own energies may place him at the top of any one of them, an easy and unbounded career seems open to his ambition, and he will readily persuade himself that he is born to no vulgar destinies. But this is an erroneous notion, which is corrected by daily experience. The same equality which allows every citizen to conceive these lofty hopes, renders all he citizens individually feeble. It circumscribes their powers on every side, while it gives freer scope to their desires. Not only are they restrained by their own weakness, but they are met at every step by immense obstacles which they did not at first perceive. They have swept away the privileges of some of their fellow-creatures

[*Reeve, Vol. III, pp. 272, 271–2; Tocqueville, Vol. III, p. 211, 210–11.]

j–*j*Source,40,59   is
k–*k*40   (Reeve, Vol. III, Bk. 2, Chap. x [pp. 265–7].)
l–*l*40,59   establishes

which stood in their way; *m*but they have now*m* to encounter the competition of all. The barrier has changed its shape rather than its place. When men are nearly alike, and all follow the same track, it is very difficult for any one individual to get on fast, and cleave a way through the homogeneous throng which surrounds and presses upon him. This constant strife between the wishes springing from the equality of conditions and the means it supplies to satisfy them, harasses and wearies the mind. *n*(Tocqueville, Vol. III, Part 2, Chap. xiii [pp. 216–19].)*n*

And hence, according to M. de Tocqueville, *o* while every one is devoured by ambition, hardly any one is ambitious on a large scale. Among so many competitors for but a few great prizes, none of the candidates starting from the vantage ground of an elevated social position, very few can hope to gain those prizes, and they not until late in life. Men in general, therefore, do not look so high. A vast energy of passion in a whole community is developed and squandered in the petty pursuit of petty advancements in fortune, and the hurried snatching of petty pleasures.

To sum up our author's opinion of the dangers to which mankind are liable as they advance towards equality of condition; his fear, both in government and in intellect and morals, is not of too great liberty, but of too ready submission; not of anarchy, but of servility; not of too rapid change, but of Chinese stationariness. As democracy advances, the opinions of mankind on most subjects of general interest will become, he believes, as compared with any former period, more rooted and more difficult to change; and mankind are more and more in danger of losing the moral courage and pride of independence, which make them deviate from the beaten path, either in speculation or in conduct. Even in politics, it is to be apprehended *p*lest*p*, feeling their personal insignificance, and conceiving a proportionally vast idea of the importance of society at large; being jealous, moreover, of one another, but not jealous of the central power which derives its origin from the majority, or which at least is the faithful representative of its desire to annihilate every intermediate power—they should allow that central government to assume more and more control, engross more and more of the business of society; and, on condition of making itself the organ of the general mode of feeling and thinking, should suffer it to relieve mankind from the care of their own interests, and keep them under a kind of tutelage; trampling meanwhile with considerable recklessness, as often as convenient, upon the rights of individuals, in the name of society and the public good.

Against these political evils the corrective to which our author looks is popular education, and, above all, the spirit of liberty, fostered by the extension and dissemination of political rights. Democratic institutions, therefore,

---

*m-m*Source   they have now]   40   they have
*n-n*40   (Reeve, Vol. III, Bk. 2, Chap. xiii [pp. 278–82].)
*o*40   it is,
*p-p*40   that

are his remedy for the worst mischiefs to which a democratic state of society is exposed. As for those to which democratic institutions are themselves liable, these, he holds, society must struggle with, and bear with so much of them as it cannot find the means of conquering. For M. de Tocqueville is no believer in the reality of mixed governments. There is, he says, always and everywhere, a strongest power: in every government either the king, the aristocracy, or the people, have an effective predominance, and can carry any point on which they set their heart. "When a community really comes to have a mixed government, that is, to be equally divided between two adverse principles, it is either falling into a revolutionary state or into dissolution."[*] M. de Tocqueville believes that the preponderant power, which must exist everywhere, is most rightly placed in the body of the people. But he thinks it most pernicious that this power, whether residing in the people or else-. where, should be "checked by no obstacles which may retard its course, and force it to moderate its own vehemence."[†] The difference, in his eyes, is great between one sort of democratic institutions and another. That form of democracy should be sought out and devised, and in every way endeavoured to be carried into practice, which, on the one hand, most exercises and cultivates the intelligence and mental activity of the majority; and, on the other, breaks the headlong impulses of popular opinion, by delay, rigour of forms, and adverse discussion. "The organization and the establishment of democracy" on these principles "is the great political problem of our time."[‡]

And when this problem is solved, there remains an equally serious one; to make head against the tendency of democracy towards bearing down individuality, and circumscribing the exercise of the human faculties within narrow limits. To sustain the higher pursuits of philosophy and art; to vindicate and protect the unfettered exercise of reason, and the moral freedom of the individual—these are purposes to which, under a democracy, the superior spirits, and the government so far as it is permitted, should devote their utmost energies.

I shall conclude by one general idea, which comprises not only all the particular ideas which have been expressed in the present chapter, but also most of those which it is the object of this book to treat of.

In the ages of aristocracy which preceded our own, there were private persons of great power, and a social authority of extreme weakness. The principal efforts of the men of those times were required, to strengthen, aggrandize, and secure the supreme power; and, on the other hand, to circumscribe individual independence within narrower limits, and to subject private interests to *q* public. Other perils and other cares await the men of our age. Amongst the greater part of

[*Reeve, Vol. II, pp. 153–4; Tocqueville, Vol. II, pp. 144–5.]
[†Reeve, Vol. II, p. 154; Tocqueville, Vol. II, p. 145.]
[‡Reeve, Vol. II, p. 267; Tocqueville, Vol. II, p. 254.]

*q*Source   the interests of the]   40   the

modern nations, the government, whatever may be its origin, its constitution, or its name, has become almost omnipotent, and private persons are falling, more and more, into the lowest stage of weakness and dependence.

The general character of ʳoldʳ society was diversity; unity and uniformity were nowhere to be met with. In modern society, all things threaten to become so much alike, that the peculiar characteristics of each individual will be entirely lost in the uniformity of the general aspect. Our forefathers were ever prone to make an improper use of the notion, that private rights ought to be respected; and we are naturally prone, on the other hand, to exaggerate the idea, that the interest of an individual ought to bend to the interest of the many.

The political world is metamorphosed; new remedies must henceforth be sought for new disorders. To lay down extensive, but distinct and immovable limits to the action of the ruling power; to confer certain rights on private persons, and secure to them the undisputed enjoyment of their rights; to enable individual man to maintain whatever independence, strength, and originality he still possesses; to raise him by the side of society at large, and uphold him in that position;—these appear to me the main objects for the legislator in the age upon which we are now entering.

It would seem as if the rulers of our time sought only to use men in order to effect great things: I wish that they would try a little more to make great men; that they would set less value upon the work, and more upon the workman; that they would never forget that a nation cannot long remain strong when every man belonging to it is individually weak; and that no form or combination of social polity has yet been devised to make an energetic people, out of a community of citizens personally feeble and pusillanimous. ˢ(Tocqueville, Vol. IV, Part 4, Chap. vii [pp. 271–2].)ˢ

If we were here to close this article, and leave these noble speculations to produce their effect without further comment, the reader probably would not blame us. Our recommendation is not needed in their behalf. That nothing on the whole comparable in profundity to them ᵗhasᵗ yet been written on ᵘDemocracyᵘ, will scarcely be disputed by any one who has read even our hasty abridgment of them. We must guard, at the same time, against attaching to these conclusions, or to any others that can result from such inquiries, a character of scientific certainty that can never belong to them. Democracy is too recent a phenomenon, and of too great magnitude, for any one who now lives to comprehend its consequences. A few of its more immediate tendencies may be perceived or surmised; what other tendencies, destined to overrule or to combine with these, lie behind, there are not grounds even to conjecture. If we revert to any similar fact in past history, any change in human affairs approaching in greatness to what is passing before our eyes, we shall find that no prediction which could have been made at the time, or for many generations afterwards, would have borne

ʳ⁻ʳSource,40   olden
ˢ⁻ˢ40   (Reeve, Vol. IV, Chap. iii [pp. 341–4].)
ᵗ⁻ᵗ40,59   had
ᵘ⁻ᵘ40   democracy

any resemblance to what has actually been the course of events. When the Greek commonwealths were crushed, and liberty in the civilized world apparently extinguished by the Macedonian invaders; when a rude unlettered people of Italy stretched their conquests and their dominion from one end to the other of the known world; when that people in turn lost its freedom and its old institutions, and fell under the military despotism of one of its own citizens;—what similarity is there between the effects we now know to have been produced by these causes, and anything which the wisest person could then have anticipated from them? When the Roman empire, containing all the art, science, literature, and industry of the world, was overrun, ravaged, and dismembered by hordes of barbarians, everybody lamented the destruction of civilization, in an event which is now admitted to have been the necessary condition of its renovation. When the Christian religion had existed but for two centuries—when the Pope was only beginning to assert his ascendancy—what philosopher or statesman could have foreseen the destinies of Christianity, or the part which has been acted in history by the Catholic Church? It is thus with all other really great historical facts—the invention of gunpowder for instance, or of the printing-press; even when their direct operation is as exactly measurable, because as strictly mechanical, as these were, the mere scale on which they operate gives birth to endless consequences, of a kind which would have appeared visionary to the most far-seeing ᵛcotemporaryᵛ wisdom.

It is not, therefore, without a deep sense of the uncertainty attaching to such predictions, that the wise would hazard an opinion as to the fate of mankind under the new democratic dispensation. But without pretending to judge confidently of remote tendencies, those immediate ones which are already developing themselves require to be dealt with as we treat any of the other circumstances in which we are placed;—by encouraging those which are salutary, and working out the means by which such as are hurtful may be counteracted. To exhort men to this, and to aid them in doing it, is the end for which M. de Tocqueville has written: and in the same spirit we will now venture to make one criticism upon him;—to point out one correction, of which we think his views stand in need; and for want of which they have occasionally an air of over-subtlety and false refinement, exciting the distrust of common readers, and making the opinions themselves appear less true, and less practically important, than, it seems to us, they really are.

M. de Tocqueville, then, has, at least apparently, confounded the effects of Democracy with the effects of Civilization. He has bound up in one abstract idea the whole of the tendencies of modern commercial society, and given them one name—Democracy; thereby letting it be supposed that he ascribes to equality of conditions, several of the effects naturally arising

ᵛ⁻ᵛ40   contemporary

from the mere progress of national prosperity, in the form in which that progress manifests itself in modern times.

It is no doubt true, that among the tendencies of commercial civilization, a tendency to the equalization of conditions is one, and not the least conspicuous. When a nation is advancing in prosperity—when its industry is expanding, and its capital rapidly augmenting—the number also of those who possess capital increases in at least as great a proportion; and though the distance between the two extremes of society may not be much diminished, there is a rapid multiplication of those who occupy the intermediate positions. There may be princes at one end of the scale and paupers at the other; but between them there will be a respectable and well-paid class of artisans, and a middle class who combine property and industry. This may be called, and is, a tendency to equalization. But this growing equality is only one of the features of progressive civilization; one of the incidental effects of the progress of industry and wealth: a most important effect, and one which, as our author shows, re-acts in a hundred ways upon the other effects, but not therefore to be confounded with the cause.

So far is it, indeed, from being admissible, that *mere* equality of conditions is the mainspring of those moral and social phenomena which M. de Tocqueville has characterized, that when some unusual chance exhibits to us equality of conditions by itself, severed from that commercial state of society and that progress of industry of which it is the natural concomitant, it produces few or none of the moral effects ascribed to it. Consider, for instance, the French of Lower Canada. Equality of conditions is more universal there than in the United States; for the whole people, without exception, are in easy circumstances, and there are not even that considerable number of rich individuals who are to be found in all the great towns of the American Republic. Yet do we find in Canada that "go-ahead spirit"—that restless, impatient eagerness ˣforˣ improvement in circumstances—that mobility, that shifting and fluctuating, now up now down, now here now there—that absence of classes and class-spirit—that jealousy of superior attainments—that want of deference for authority and leadership—that habit of bringing things to the rule and square of each man's own understanding—which M. de Tocqueville imputes to the same cause in the United States? In all these respects the very contrary qualities prevail. We by no means deny that where the other circumstances which determine these effects exist, equality of conditions has a very perceptible effect in corroborating them. We think M. de Tocqueville has shown that it has. But that it is the exclusive, or even the principal cause, we think the example of Canada goes far to disprove.

ʷ–ʷ40   *go-ahead spirit*
ˣ–ˣ40   or   [*printer's error in 40; corrected in ink by JSM in Somerville College copy*]

For the reverse of this experiment, we have only to look at home. Of all countries in a state of progressive commercial civilization, Great Britain is that in which the equalization of conditions has made least progress. The extremes of wealth and poverty are wider apart, and there is a more numerous body of persons at each extreme, than in any other commercial community. From the habits of the population in regard to marriage, the poor have remained poor; from the laws which tend to keep large masses of property together, the rich have remained rich; and often, when they have lost the substance of riches, have retained its social advantages and outward trappings. Great fortunes are continually accumulated, and seldom redistributed. In this respect, therefore, England is the most complete contrast to the United States. But in commercial prosperity, in the rapid growth of industry and wealth, she is the next after America, and not very much inferior to her. Accordingly we appeal to all competent observers, whether, in nearly all the moral and intellectual features of American society, as represented by M. de Tocqueville, this country does not stand next to America? whether, with the single difference of our remaining respect for aristocracy, the American people, both in their good qualities and in their defects, resemble anything so much as an exaggeration of our own middle class? whether the spirit, which is gaining more and more the ascendant with us, is not in a very great degree American? and whether all the moral elements of an American state of society are not most rapidly growing up?

For example, that entire unfixedness in the social position of individuals —that treading upon the heels of one another—that habitual dissatisfaction of each with the position he occupies, and eager desire to push himself into the next above it—has not this become, and is it not becoming more and more, an English characteristic? In England, as well as in America, it appears to foreigners, and even to Englishmen recently returned from a foreign country, as if everybody had but one wish—to improve his condition, never to enjoy it; as if no Englishman cared to cultivate either the pleasures or the virtues corresponding to his station in society, but solely to get out of it as quickly as possible; or if that cannot be done, and until it is done, to *seem* to have got out of it. "The hypocrisy of luxury," as M. de Tocqueville calls the maintaining an appearance beyond one's real expenditure, he considers as a democratic peculiarity.[*] It is surely an English one. The highest class of all, indeed, is, as might be expected, comparatively exempt from these bad peculiarities. But the very existence of such a class, whose immunities and political privileges are attainable by wealth, tends to aggravate the struggle of the other classes for the possession of that passport to all other impor-

[*Reeve, Vol. III, p. 100; Tocqueville, Vol. III, p. 78.]

*y–y*40   *seem*

tance; and it perhaps required the example of America to prove that the "sabbathless pursuit of wealth"[*] could be as intensely prevalent, where there were no aristocratic distinctions to tempt to it.

Again, the mobility and fluctuating nature of individual relations—the absence of permanent ties, local or personal; how often has this been commented on as one of the organic changes by which the ancient structure of English society is becoming dissolved? Without reverting to the days of clanship, or to those in which the gentry led a patriarchal life among their tenantry and neighbours, the memory of man extends to a time when the same tenants remained attached to the same landlords, the same servants to the same zhousehold. Butz this, with other old customs, after progressively retiring to the remote corners of our island, has nearly taken flight altogether; and it may now be said that in all the relations of life, except those to which law and religion have given apermanencea, change has become the general rule, and constancy the exception.

The remainder of the tendencies which M. de Tocqueville has delineated, may mostly be brought under one general agency as their immediate cause; the growing insignificance of individuals in comparison with the mass. Now, it would be difficult to show any country in which this insignificance is more marked and conspicuous than in England, or any incompatibility between that tendency and aristocratic institutions. It is not because the individuals composing the mass are all equal, but because the mass itself has grown to so immense a size, that individuals are powerless in the face of it; and because the mass, having, by mechanical improvements, become capable of acting simultaneously, can compel not merely any individual, but any number of individuals, to bend before it. The House of Lords is the richest and most powerful collection of persons in Europe, yet they not only could not prevent, but were themselves compelled to pass, the Reform Bill. The daily actions of every peer and peeress are falling more and more under the yoke of *bourgeois* opinion; they feel every day a stronger necessity of showing an immaculate front to the world. When they do venture to disregard common opinion, it is in a body, and when supported by one another; whereas formerly every nobleman acted on his own notions, and dared be as eccentric as he pleased. No rank in society is now exempt from the fear of being peculiar, the unwillingness to be, or to be thought, in any respect original. Hardly anything now depends upon individuals, but all upon classes, and among classes mainly upon the middle class. That class is now the power in society, the arbiter of fortune and success. Ten times more money is made

[*See Francis Bacon, *Of the Dignity and Advancement of Learning*, in *Works*, ed. James Spedding, Robert Ellis, and Douglas Heath, 14 vols. (London: Longman, 1857–74), Vol. V, p. 77.]

z–z40   household; but
a–a40   perpetuity

by supplying the wants, even the superfluous wants, of the middle, nay of the lower classes, than those of the higher. It is the middle class that now rewards even literature and art; the books by which most money is made are the cheap books; the greatest part of the profit of a picture is the profit of the engraving from it. Accordingly, all the intellectual effects which M. de Tocqueville ascribes to Democracy, are taking place under the *b*democracy*b* of the middle class. There is a greatly augmented number of moderate successes, fewer great literary and scientific reputations. Elementary and popular treatises are immensely multiplied, superficial information far more widely diffused; but there are fewer who devote themselves to thought for its own sake, and pursue in retirement those profounder researches, the *c*results*c* of which can only be appreciated by a few. Literary productions are seldom highly finished—they are got up to be read by many, and to be read but once. If the work sells for a day, the author's time and pains will be better laid out in writing a second, than in improving the first. And this is not because books are no longer written for the aristocracy: they never were so. The aristocracy (saving individual exceptions) never were a reading class. It is because books are now written for a numerous, and therefore an unlearned public; no longer principally for scholars and men of science, who have knowledge of their own, and are not imposed upon by half-knowledge —who have studied the great works of genius, and can make comparisons.*

As for the decay of authority, and diminution of respect for traditional opinions, this could not well be so far advanced among an ancient people— all whose political notions rest on an historical basis, and whose institutions themselves are built on prescription, and not on ideas of expediency—as in America, where the whole edifice of government was constructed within

---

*On this account, among others, we think M. de Tocqueville right in the great importance he attaches to the study of Greek and Roman literature; not as being without faults, but as having the contrary faults to those of our own day. Not only do those literatures furnish *d*examples*d* of high finish and perfection in workmanship, to correct the slovenly habits of modern hasty writing, but they exhibit, in the military and agricultural commonwealths of antiquity, precisely that order of virtues in which a commercial society is apt to be deficient; and they altogether show human nature on a grander scale: with less benevolence but more patriotism, less sentiment but more self-control; if a lower average of virtue, more striking individual examples of it; fewer small goodnesses, but more *e* greatness, and appreciation of greatness; more which tends to exalt the imagination, and inspire high conceptions of the capabilities of human nature. If, as every one *f*may*f* see, the want of affinity of these studies to the modern mind is gradually lowering them in popular estimation, this is but a confirmation of the need of them, and renders it more incumbent upon those who have the power, to do their utmost towards preventing their decline. [See Reeve, Vol. III, pp. 124–8; Tocqueville, Vol. III, pp. 97–100.]

*b–b*40   Democracy   *c–c*40   result   [*printer's error?*]
*d–d*40   models   *e*40   of
*f–f*40   must

the memory of man upon abstract principles. But surely this change also is taking place as fast as could be expected under the circumstances. And even this effect, though it has a more direct connexion with Democracy, has not an exclusive one. Respect for old opinions must diminish wherever science and knowledge are rapidly progressive. As the people in general become aware of the recent date of the most important physical discoveries, they are liable to form a rather contemptuous opinion of their ancestors. The mere visible fruits of scientific progress in a wealthy society, the mechanical improvements, the steam-engines, the railroads, carry the feeling of admiration for modern and disrespect for ancient times down even to the wholly uneducated classes. For that other mental characteristic which M. de Tocqueville finds in America—a positive, matter-of-fact spirit—a demand that all things shall be made clear to each man's understanding—an indifference to the subtler proofs which address themselves to more cultivated and systematically exercised intellects; for what may be called, in short, the dogmatism of common sense—we need not look beyond our own country. There needs no Democracy to account for this; there needs only the habit of energetic action, without a proportional development of the taste for speculation. Bonaparte was one of the most remarkable examples of it; and the diffusion of half-instruction, without any sufficient provision made by society for sustaining the higher cultivation, tends greatly to encourage its excess.

Nearly all those moral and social influences, therefore, which are the subject of M. de Tocqueville's second part, are shown to be in full operation in aristocratic England. What connexion they have with equality is with the growth of the middle class, not with the annihilation of the extremes. They are quite compatible with the existence of peers and *prolétaires*; nay, with the most abundant provision of both those varieties of human nature. If we were sure of ᵍretainingᵍ for ever our aristocratic institutions, society would no less have to struggle against all these tendencies; and perhaps even the loss of those institutions would not have so much effect as is supposed in accelerating their ʰ triumph.

The evil is not in the preponderance of a democratic class, but of any class. The defects which M. de Tocqueville points out in the American, and which we see in the modern English mind, are the ordinary ones of a commercial class. The portion of society which is predominant in America, and that which is attaining predominance here, the American Many, and our middle class, agree in being commercial classes. The one country is affording a complete, and the other a progressive exemplification, that whenever any variety of human nature becomes preponderant in a community, it imposes upon all the rest of society its own type; forcing all, either to submit to it or to imitate it.

ᵍ⁻ᵍ40   preserving   ʰ40   ultimate

It is not in China only that a homogeneous community is naturally a stationary community. The unlikeness of one *person* to another is not only a principle of improvement, but would seem almost to be the only principle. It is profoundly remarked by M. Guizot, that the short duration or stunted growth of the earlier civilizations arose from this, that in each of them some one element of human improvement existed exclusively, or so preponderatingly as to overpower all the others; whereby the community, after accomplishing rapidly all which that one element could do, either perished for want of what it could not do, or came to a halt, and became immoveable.[*] It would be an error to suppose that such could not possibly be our fate. In the generalization which pronounces the "law of progress" to be an inherent attribute of human nature, it is forgotten that, among the inhabitants of our earth, the European family of nations is the only one which has ever *yet* shown any capability of spontaneous improvement, beyond a certain low level. Let us beware of supposing that we owe this peculiarity to any *superiority* of nature, and not rather to combinations of circumstances, which have existed nowhere else, and may not exist for ever among ourselves. The spirit of commerce and industry is one of the greatest instruments not only of civilization in the narrowest, but of improvement and culture in the widest sense: to it, or to its consequences, we owe nearly all that advantageously distinguishes the present period from the middle ages. So long as other coordinate elements of improvement existed beside it, doing what it left undone, and keeping its exclusive tendencies in equipoise by an opposite order of sentiments, principles of action, and modes of thought—so long the benefits which it conferred on humanity were unqualified. But example and theory alike justify the expectation, that with its complete preponderance would commence an era either of stationariness or of decline.

If to avert this consummation it were necessary that the class which wields the strongest power in society should be prevented from exercising its strength, or that those who are powerful enough to overthrow the government should not claim a paramount control over it, the case of civilized nations would be almost hopeless. But human affairs are not entirely governed by mechanical laws, nor men's characters wholly and irrevocably formed by their situation in life. Economical and social changes, though among the greatest, are not the only forces which shape the course of our species; ideas are not always the mere signs and effects of social circum-

[*See François Guizot, *Cours d'histoire moderne: Histoire générale de la civilisation en Europe, depuis, la chute de l'empire romain jusqu'à la révolution française* (Paris: Pichon and Didier, 1828), 2e leçon, pp. 3ff.]

*i-i*40   man
j-j+59,67
*k-k*40   necessity

stances, they are themselves a power in history. Let the idea take hold of the more generous and cultivated minds, that the most serious danger to the future prospects of mankind is in the unbalanced influence of the commercial spirit—let the wiser and better-hearted politicians and public teachers look upon it as their most pressing duty, to protect and strengthen whatever, in the heart of man or in his outward life, can form a salutary check to the exclusive tendencies of that spirit—and we should not only have individual testimonies against it, in all the forms of genius, from those who have the privilege of speaking not to their own age merely, but to all time; there would also gradually shape itself forth a national education, which, without overlooking any other of the requisites of human well-being, would be adapted to this purpose in particular.

What is requisite in politics for the same end, is not that public opinion should not be, what it is and must be, the ruling power; but that, in order to the formation of the best public opinion, there should exist somewhere a great social support for opinions and sentiments different from those of the mass. The shape which that support may best assume is a question of time, place, and circumstance; but (in a commercial country, and an age when, happily for mankind, the military spirit is gone by) there can be no doubt about the elements which must compose it: they are, an agricultural class, a leisured class, and a learned class.

The natural tendencies of an agricultural class are in many respects the reverse of those of a manufacturing and commercial. In the first place, from their more scattered position, and less exercised activity of mind, they have usually a greater willingness to look up to, and accept of, guidance. In the next place, they are the class who have local attachments; and it is astonishing how much of character depends upon this one circumstance. If the agricultural spirit is not felt in America as a counterpoise to the commercial, it is because American agriculturists have no local attachments; they range from place to place, and are to all intents and purposes a commercial class. But in an old country, where the same family has long occupied the same land, the case will naturally be different. From attachment to places, follows attachment to persons who are associated with those places. Though no longer the permanent tie which it once was, the connexion between tenants and landlords is one not *lightly* broken off;—one which both parties, when they enter into it, desire and hope *will* be permanent. Again, with attachment to the place comes generally attachment to the occupation: a farmer seldom becomes anything but a farmer. The rage of money-getting can scarcely, in agricultural occupations, reach any dangerous height: except where bad laws have aggravated the natural fluctuations of price, there is

*l-l*40   slightly [*printer's error?*]
*m-m*40   to

little room for gambling; the rewards of industry and skill are *sure* but moderate; an agriculturist can rarely make a large fortune. A manufacturer or merchant, unless he can outstrip others, knows that others will outstrip him, and ruin him; while, in the irksome drudgery to which he subjects himself as a means, there is nothing agreeable to dwell on except the ultimate end. But agriculture is in itself an interesting occupation, which few wish to retire from, and which men of property and education often pursue merely for their amusement. Men so occupied are satisfied with less gain, and are less impatient to realize it. Our town population, it has long been remarked, is becoming almost as mobile and *o* uneasy as the American. It ought not to be so with our agriculturists; they ought to be the counterbalancing element in our national character; they should represent the type opposite to the commercial,—that of moderate wishes, tranquil tastes, cultivation of the excitements and enjoyments near at hand, and compatible with their existing position.

To attain this object, how much alteration may be requisite in the system of rack-renting and tenancy at will, we cannot undertake to show in this place. It is sufficiently obvious also that the corn-laws[*] must disappear; there must be no feud raging between the commercial class and that by whose influence and example its excesses are to be tempered: men are not prone to adopt the characteristics of their enemies. Nor is this all. In order that the agricultural population should count for anything in politics, or contribute its part to the formation of the national character, it is absolutely necessary that it should be educated. And let it be remembered that, in an agricultural people, the diffusion of information and intelligence must necessarily be artificial;—the work of government, or of the superior classes. In populous towns, the mere collision of man with man, the keenness of competition, the habits of society and discussion, the easy access to reading—even the dulness of the ordinary occupations, which drives men to other excitements—produce of themselves a certain development of intelligence. The least favoured class of a town population are seldom actually stupid, and have often in some directions a morbid keenness and acuteness. It is otherwise with the peasantry. Whatever it is desired that they should know, they must be taught; whatever intelligence is expected to grow up among them, must first be implanted, and sedulously nursed.

It is not needful to go into a similar analysis of the tendencies of the other two classes—a leisured, and a learned class. The capabilities which they possess for controlling the excess of the commercial spirit by a contrary spirit, are at once apparent. We regard it as one of the greatest advantages

[*See 9 George IV, c. 60 (1828).]
*n-n*40   here [*printer's error?*]
*o*40   almost as

of this country over America, that it possesses both these classes; and we believe that the interests of the time to come are greatly dependent upon preserving them; and upon their being rendered, as they much require to be, better and better qualified for their important functions.

If we believed that the national character of England, instead of reacting upon the American character and raising it, was gradually assimilating itself to those points of it which the best and wisest Americans see with most uneasiness, it would be no consolation to us to think that we might possibly avoid *p*the institutions of America*p*; for we should have all the effects of her institutions, except those which are beneficial. The American Many are not essentially a different class from our ten-pound householders; and if the middle class are left to the mere habits and instincts of a commercial community, we shall have a "tyranny of the majority," not the less irksome because most of the tyrants may not be manual labourers. For it is a chimerical hope to overbear or outnumber the middle class; whatever modes of voting, whatever redistribution of the constituencies, are really necessary for placing the government in their hands, those, whether we like it or not, they will assuredly obtain.

The ascendancy of the commercial class in modern society and politics is inevitable, and, under due limitations, ought not to be regarded as an evil. That class is the most powerful; but it needs not therefore be all-powerful. Now, as ever, the great problem in government is to prevent the strongest from becoming the only power; and repress the natural tendency of the instincts and passions of the ruling body, to sweep away all barriers which are capable of resisting, even for a moment, their own tendencies. Any counterbalancing power can henceforth exist only by the sufferance of the commercial class; but that it should tolerate some such limitation, we deem as important as that it should not itself be held in vassalage.

* * * * *

*q*As a specimen of the contrivances for "organizing democracy," which, without sacrificing any of its beneficial tendencies, are adapted to counterbalance and correct its characteristic infirmities, an extract is subjoined from another paper by the author, published in 1846, being a review of the *Lettres Politiques*[*] of M. Charles Duveyrier;[†] a book which among many

[*2 vols, Paris: Beck, 1843.]

[†J. S. Mill, "Duveyrier's Political Views of French Affairs," *Edinburgh Review*, LXXXIII (Apr., 1846), 453–74. The quoted passage, which runs to the end of this article, is from pp. 462–6.]

*p-p*40   American institutions
*q-q*204+59,67

other valuable suggestions, anticipated Sir Charles Trevelyan in the proposal to make admission into the service of government in all cases the prize of success in a public and competitive examination.[*]

Every people ʳ, [says M. Duveyrier,]ʳ comprises, and probably will always comprise, two societies, an *administration* and a *public*; the one, of which the general interest is the supreme law, where positions are not hereditary, but the principle is that of classing its members according to their merit, and rewarding them according to their works; and where the moderation of salaries is compensated by their fixity, and especially by honour and consideration. The other, composed of landed proprietors, of capitalists, of masters and workmen, among whom the supreme law is that of inheritance, the principal rule of conduct is personal interest, competition and struggle the favourite elements.

These two societies serve mutually as a counterpoise; they continually act and react upon one another. The public tends to introduce into the administration the stimulus naturally wanting to it, the principle of emulation. The administration, conformably to its appointed purpose, tends to introduce more and more into the mass of the public, elements of order and forethought. In this twofold direction, the administration and the public have rendered and do render daily to each other, reciprocal services.[†]

The Chamber of Deputies (he proceeds to say) represents the public and its tendencies. The Chamber of Peers represents, or from its constitution is fitted to represent, those who are or have been public functionaries: whose appointed duty and occupation it has been to look at questions from the point of view not of any mere local or sectional, but of the general interest; and who have the judgment and knowledge resulting from labour and experience. To a body like this, it naturally belongs to take the initiative in all legislation, not of a constitutional or organic character. If, in the natural course of things, well-considered views of policy are anywhere to be looked for, it must be among such a body. To no other acceptance can such views, when originating elsewhere, be so appropriately submitted—through no other organ so fitly introduced into the laws.

We shall not enter into the considerations by which the author attempts to impress upon the Peers this elevated view of their function in the commonwealth. On a new body, starting fresh as a senate, those considerations might have influence. But the senate of France is not a new body. It set out on the discredited foundation of the old hereditary chamber; and its change of character only takes place gradually, as the members die off. To redeem a lost position is more difficult than to create a new one. The new members,

[*See "Report on the Organisation of the Permanent Civil Service," *Parliamentary Papers*, 1854, XXVII, 1–31.]

[†Translated from Charles Duveyrier, *La Pairie dans ses rapports avec la situation politique* (Paris: Guyot, 1842), p. 12.]

joining a body of no weight, become accustomed to political insignificance; they have mostly passed the age of enterprise; and the Peerage is considered little else than an honourable retirement for the invalids of the public service. M. Duveyrier's suggestion has made some impression upon the public; it has gained him the public ear, and launched his doctrines into discussion; but we do not find that the conduct of the Peers has been at all affected by it. Energy is precisely that quality which, if men have it not of themselves, cannot be breathed into them by other people's advice and exhortations. There are involved, however, in this speculation, some ideas of a more general character; not unworthy of the attention of those who concern themselves about the social changes which the future must produce.

There are, we believe, few real thinkers, of whatever party, who have not reflected with some anxiety upon the views which have become current of late, respecting the irresistible tendency of modern society towards democracy. The sure, and now no longer slow, advance, by which the classes hitherto in the ascendant are merging into the common mass, and all other forces ˢareˢ giving way before the power of mere numbers, is well calculated to inspire uneasiness, even in those to whom democracy *per se* presents nothing alarming. It is not the uncontrolled ascendancy of popular power, but of any power, which is formidable. There is no one power in society, or capable of being constituted in it, of which the influences do not become mischievous as soon as it reigns uncontrolled—as soon as it becomes exempted from any necessity of being in the right, by being able to make its mere will prevail, without the condition of a previous struggle. To render its ascendancy safe, it must be fitted with correctives and counteractives, possessing the qualities opposite to its characteristic defects. Now, the defects to which the government of numbers, whether in the pure American or in the mixed English form, is most liable, are precisely those of a public, as compared with an administration. Want of appreciation of distant objects and remote consequences; where an object is desired, want both of an adequate sense of practical difficulties, and of the sagacity necessary for eluding them; disregard of traditions, and of maxims sanctioned by experience; an undervaluing of the importance of fixed rules, when immediate purposes require a departure from them—these are among the acknowledged dangers of popular government: and there is the still greater, though less recognised, danger, of being ruled by a spirit of suspicious and intolerant mediocrity. Taking these things into consideration, and also the progressive decline of the existing checks and counterpoises, and the little probability there is that the influence of mere wealth, still less of birth, will be sufficient hereafter to restrain the tendencies of the growing power by mere passive resistance; we do not think that a nation whose historical 'antecedents' give it any choice, could select a fitter basis upon which to ground the counterbalancing power in the State, than the principle of the French Upper House. The defects of "representative assemblies" are, in substance, those of unskilled politicians. The mode of raising a power most competent to their correction, would be an organization and combination of the skilled. History affords the example of a government carried on for centuries with the greatest consistency of purpose, and the highest skill and talent, ever realized in public affairs; and it was constituted on this very principle. The Roman Senate was a Senate for life, composed of all who had filled high offices in the State, and were not disqualified by a public note of disgrace. The faults of the Roman policy were in its ends; which, however, were those of all the "states" of the ancient world. Its choice of means was consummate. This government, and others distantly approaching to it, have given to aristocracy all the credit which it has obtained for constancy and wisdom. A Senate of some such description, composed of persons no longer young, and whose reputation is already gained, will necessarily lean to the Conservative side; but not with the blind, merely instinctive spirit of conservatism, generated by mere wealth or social importance unearned by previous labour. Such a body would secure a due hearing and a reasonable regard for precedent and established rule. It would disarm jealousy, by its freedom from any class interest; and while it never could become the really predominant power in the State, still, since its position would be the consequence of recognised merit and actual services to the public, it would have as much personal influence, and excite as little hostility, as is compatible with resisting in any degree the tendencies of the really strongest power.

There is another class of considerations connected with "representative governments", to which we shall also briefly advert. In proportion as it has been better understood what legislation is, and the unity of plan as well as maturity of deliberation which are essential to it, thinking persons have asked themselves the question—Whether a popular body of 658 or 459 members, not specially educated for the purpose, having served no apprenticeship, and undergone no examination, and who transact business in the forms and very much in the spirit of a debating society, can have as its peculiarly appropriate office to make laws? Whether that is not a work certain to be spoiled by putting such a superfluous number of hands upon it? Whether it is not essentially a business for one, or a very small number, of most carefully prepared

---

*t–t*46 antécédens
*u–u*46 Representative Assemblies
*v–v*46 States
*w–w*46 Representative Governments

and selected individuals? And whether the proper office of a Representative Body, (in addition to controlling the public expenditure, and deciding who shall hold office,) be not that of *discussing* all national interests; of giving expression to the wishes and feelings of the country; and granting or with-holding its consent to the laws which others make, rather than themselves framing, or even altering them? The law of this and most other nations is already such a chaos, that the quality of what is yearly added, does not materially affect the general mass; but in a country possessed of a real Code or Digest, and desirous of retaining that advantage, who could think without dismay of its being tampered with at the will of a body like the House of Commons, or the Chamber of Deputies? Imperfect as is the French Code, the inconveniences arising from this cause are already strongly felt; and they afford an additional inducement for associating with the popular body a skilled Senate, or Council of Legislation, which, whatever might be its special constitution, must be grounded upon some form of the principle which we have now considered.[q]

REFORM OF THE CIVIL SERVICE

1854

EDITOR'S NOTE

"Papers relating to the Re-organisation of the Civil Service," *Parliamentary Papers*, 1854–55, XX, 92–8. Originally headed: "Mr. John Stuart Mill. / May 22, 1854." Identified in JSM's bibliography as "A paper on the proposed Reform of the Civil Service, included among those printed in a Collection of papers thereupon, laid before Parliament in the Session of 1854/5." (MacMinn, 88.) In the Somerville College Library there is a copy of the pamphlet reprint of the paper (*Paper on the Re-organisation of the Civil Service. By Mr. John Stuart Mill.* London: Eyre and Spottiswoode, 1855; paged 1–9).

For comment on the circumstances surrounding Mill's writing of the paper, see the Textual Introduction, lxxviii above.

Reform of the Civil Service

THE PROPOSAL to select candidates for the Civil Service of Government by a competitive examination[*] appears to me to be one of those great public improvements the adoption of which would form an era in history. The effects which it is calculated to produce in raising the character both of the public administration and of the people can scarcely be over-estimated.

It has equal claims to support from the disinterested and impartial among conservatives and among reformers. For its adoption would be the best vindication which could be made of existing political institutions, by showing that the classes who under the present constitution have the greatest influence in the government, do not desire any greater share of the profits derivable from it than their merits entitle them to, but are willing to take the chances of competition with ability in all ranks: while the plan offers to liberals, so far as the plan extends, the realization of the principal object which any honest reformer desires to effect by political changes, namely, that the administration of public affairs should be in the most competent hands; which, as regards the permanent part of the administrative body, would be ensured by the proposed plan, so far as it is possible for any human contrivance to secure it.

When we add to this consideration the extraordinary stimulus which would be given to mental cultivation in its most important branches, not solely by the hope of prizes to be obtained by means of it, but by the effect of the national recognition of it as the exclusive title to participation in the conduct of so large and conspicuous a portion of the national affairs; and when we further think of the great and salutary moral revolution, descending to the minds of almost the lowest classes, which would follow the knowledge that Government (to people in general the most trusted exponent of the ways of the world) would henceforth bestow its gifts according to merit, and not to favour; it is difficult to express in any language which would not appear exaggerated, the benefits which, as it appears to me, would ultimately be the consequences of the successful execution of the scheme.

[*See "Report on the Organisation of the Permanent Civil Service, together with a letter from the Rev. B. Jowett," *Parliamentary Papers*, 1854, XXVII, 1–31. The "Report" is by Sir Stafford Northcote and Sir Charles Trevelyan.]

The objections usually heard, or seen in print, against this great improvement, are either grounded on imperfect apprehension, or, when examined, are found to bear involuntary testimony to the existing need of such a change.

For example, it has been called, in Parliament and elsewhere, a scheme for taking patronage from the Crown and its officers, and giving it to a body of examiners.[*] This objection ignores the whole essence of the plan. As at present conducted, the bestowal of appointments is patronage. But the conferring of certificates of eligibility by the Board of Examiners would not be patronage, but a judicial act. The examiners for honours at the universities of Oxford, Cambridge, or London, have not the patronage of honours; nor has the Lord Chancellor, when he decrees an estate to one person instead of another, the patronage of the estate. If it be meant that the examiners would not be capable and impartial, the objection is intelligible. But capable and impartial examiners are found for university purposes, and for the purposes of the educational department of the Privy Council; and they will be found for the present purpose, supposing that there is a sincere desire to find them. The idea that an examination test is likely to be merely nominal, is grounded on the experience of a different kind of examination from that proposed. It is derived from examinations without competition. When the only object is to ascertain whether the candidate possesses a certain minimum of acquirement, it is usually thought that this minimum should be placed low enough to give a chance to all; and however low it may be placed, good nature interferes to prevent it from being rigidly enforced against any but absolute dunces; whilst the other candidates are willing to encourage and applaud this relaxation of duty, and even to connive at frauds on the part of the incompetent. The feelings of all concerned are very different, when the question to be resolved is, who among the candidates that present themselves are the *most* qualified. Indulgence to one, is then injustice to others, and wears a very different aspect to the conscience from that, falsely thought more venial, laxity, by which the public alone is damaged. In this case, too, the interests and feelings of the other competitors are enlisted in favour of preventing and detecting fraud. With a honest choice of examiners, a competitive examination is as unlikely to fail, as a mere test is unlikely to succeed.

Another objection is, that if appointments are given to talent, the Public Offices will be filled with low people, without the breeding or the feelings of gentlemen. If, as this objection supposes, the sons of gentlemen cannot be expected to have as much ability and instruction as the sons of low people, it would make a strong case for social changes of a more extensive character. If the sons of gentlemen would not, even under the stimulus of competition, maintain themselves on an equality of intellect and attainments with youths

[*See the comment by Lord Monteagle in *Parliamentary Debates*, 3rd ser., Vol. 131, col. 650 (13 March, 1854).]

of a lower rank, how much more below the mark must they be with their present monopoly; and to how much greater an extent than the friends of the measure allege, must the efficiency of the Public Service be at present sacrificed to their incompetency. And more: if, with advantages and opportunities so vastly superior, the youth of the higher classes have not honour enough, or energy enough, or public spirit enough, to make themselves as well qualified as others for the station which they desire to maintain, they are not fit for that station, and cannot too soon step out of it and give place to better people. I have not this unfavourable opinion of them: I believe that they will fairly earn their full share of every kind of distinction, when they are no longer able to obtain it unearned.

Another objection is, that no examination can test more than a part of the qualities required in a Public Servant; that it is a test of book knowledge, but neither of moral qualities, nor of those which form the foundation of ability in the practical conduct of life. And it is added, that the proposed examination would have excluded Wellington, Nelson, and many more of those who have most distinguished themselves in public functions.

With regard to practical talents, it may be very true that Nelson or Wellington could not have passed a literary examination. But if such an examination had been required in their day for entering the army or navy, can any one suppose that young men of their energy and capacity would not have qualified themselves for it; or that even they would have derived no benefit from it? The assumption, besides, is gratuitous, that the examination would be solely literary. It is proposed that it should be also scientific; and this should include the practical applications of science: and there would be great propriety in allowing persons to offer themselves for a competitive examination in any kind of knowledge which can be useful in any department whatever of the Public Service, such number of marks being assigned to each of these special acquirements, compared with the more general ones, as in the judgment of the Examining Board might correspond to their value. Above all, however, it ought to be remembered, that the worth of the examination is as a test of powers and habits of mind, still more than of acquirements; for talent and application will be sure to acquire the positive knowledge found necessary for their profession, but acquirements may be little more than a dead weight if there is not ability to turn them to use.

With regard to moral qualities, undoubtedly no examination can directly test them; but indirectly it must do so in no inconsiderable degree; for it is idleness, and not application, which is "the mother of vice;" and a well cultivated intellect will seldom be found unaccompanied by prudence, temperance, and justice, and generally by the virtues which are of importance in our intercourse with others. Whatever means of judging of the moral character of the applicants may be adopted, I will venture to express a hope that they may be of a different kind from those suggested by Mr. Jowett;[*] who would demand from every candidate for examination a certificate of baptism [Jowett, p. 24; pp. 654–5 below], thus excluding even the Christian sects which do not practise that rite; and would require, among other references, one to a clergyman or a dissenting minister [Jowett, p. 25; p. 655 below]; which, as they would of course give their recommendations only to those whose religious character they approved of, would amount to the severest penalty for non-attendance on some church or minister of religion, and would be in fact a religious test, excluding many highly qualified candidates. If by requiring a statement of the "school or college" where the young man has been educated [Jowett, p. 24; p. 655 below], it be meant that he must have been educated at a school or college, this is another unjust and injudicious limitation (by which, among others, the writer of this letter would have been excluded, having never been at either school or college). Above all, I would point out the terrible principle brought in by the truly inquisitor-like proceeding recommended by Mr. Jowett, of "confidential" inquiries, and rejection "absolute and without reasons." [Jowett, p. 25; p. 655 below.] A youth who has passed all the previous years of his life in fitting himself for examination, is, according to Mr. Jowett's notions of justice, to find himself, in consequence of a *secret* accusation, rejected, he knows not why, and without the possibility of clearing his character from the unknown imputation! If any young man is rejected on moral grounds, it ought, I conceive, to be on a definite charge, which he has had a full opportunity of answering.[†] I would also suggest reconsideration of the (as it appears to me) very questionable principle of excluding youths otherwise qualified, by requiring a medical examination.[‡] It would be easy to find other means of preventing a public appointment from being made a means of obtaining a provision in the form of a pension without having rendered service sufficient to earn it.

In the preceding observations I have assumed, as requiring no proof, that the object proposed is in itself desirable; that it would be a public benefit if the Public Service, or all that part of it the duties of which are of an intellectual character, were composed of the most intelligent and instructed persons who could be attracted to it. If there be any who maintain a contrary doctrine, and say that the world is not made only for persons of ability, and that mediocrity also ought to have a share in it; I answer, certainly, but not in managing the affairs of the State. Mediocrity should betake itself to those things in which few besides itself will be imperilled by its deficiences,—to

---

[*See Jowett's letter in "Report on the Organisation of the Permanent Civil Service," pp. 24–31, reprinted below as Appendix C.]

[†For the editorial footnote that appeared at this point, see App. C below, pp. 655–6.]

[‡See Jowett's letter, p. 25; App. C, p. 655.]

mechanical labour, or the mechanical superintendence of labour, occupations as necessary as any others, and which no person of sense considers disparaging. There will be, assuredly, ample space for the mediocrities, in employments which require only mediocrity, when all who are beyond mediocrity have found the employment in which their talents can be of most use.

I do not overlook the fact that the great majority, numerically speaking, of public employments, can be adequately filled by a very moderate amount of ability and knowledge; and I assume, that a proper distinction is made between these and the others. It would be absurd to subject a tide-waiter, a letter-carrier, or a simple copyist, to the same test as the confidential adviser of a Secretary of State; nor would the former situation be an object to any one capable of competing for the latter. The competition for the inferior posts must be practically limited to acquirements which are attainable by the persons who seek such employments; but it is by no means a consequence that it should be confined to such things as have a direct connexion with their duties. The classes which supply these branches of the Public Service are among those on whom it is most important to inculcate the lesson, that mental cultivation is desirable on its own account, and not solely as a means of livelihood or worldly advancement; that whatever tends to enlarge or elevate their minds, adds to their worth as human beings, and that the Government considers the most valuable human being as the worthiest to be a Public Servant, and is guided by that consideration in its choice, even when it does not require his particular attainments or accomplishments for its own use. A man may not be a much better postman for being able to draw, or being acquainted with natural history; but he who in that rank possesses these acquirements, has given evidence of qualities which it is important for the general cultivation of the mass that the State should take every fair opportunity of stamping with its approbation.

ON LIBERTY

1859

EDITOR'S NOTE

4th ed. London: Longmans, Green, Reader and Dyer, 1869. Reprinted from 3rd ed. London: Longman, Green, Longman, Roberts & Green, 1864; 2nd ed. London: Parker, 1859; and 1st ed. London: Parker, 1859. Identified in JSM's bibliography as " 'On Liberty' a small volume post 8vo, published in February, 1859" (MacMinn, 92). For an account of the composition of *On Liberty* and related matters, see the Textual Introduction, lxxviii–lxxxiii above.

The text below, that of the 4th edition (the last in JSM's lifetime), has been collated with those of the 3rd, 2nd, 1st, and People's Editions. In the footnoted variants, the 3rd edition is indicated by "64", the 2nd by "59²", and the 1st by "59¹". Substantive variants between the People's Edition and the 4th edition are given in Appendix D.

"The grand, leading principle,
towards which every argument unfolded in these pages directly converges,
is the absolute and essential importance of human development
in its richest diversity."
Wilhelm von Humboldt, *Sphere and Duties of Government.*
[Trans. Joseph Coulthard (London: Chapman, 1854), p. 65.]

To the beloved and deplored memory of her who was the inspirer, and in part the author, of all that is best in my writings—the friend and wife whose exalted sense of truth and right was my strongest incitement, and whose approbation was my chief reward—I dedicate this volume. Like all that I have written for many years, it belongs as much to her as to me; but the work as it stands has had, in a very insufficient degree, the inestimable advantage of her revision; some of the most important portions having been reserved for a more careful re-examination, which they are now never destined to receive. Were I but capable of interpreting to the world one half the great thoughts and noble feelings which are buried in her grave, I should be the medium of a greater benefit to it, than is ever likely to arise from anything that I can write, unprompted and unassisted by her all but unrivalled wisdom.

CHAPTER I

Introductory

THE SUBJECT of this Essay is not the so-called Liberty of the Will, so unfortunately opposed to the misnamed doctrine of Philosophical Necessity;
but Civil, or Social Liberty: the nature and limits of the power which can
be legitimately exercised by society over the individual. A question seldom
stated, and hardly ever discussed, in general terms, but which profoundly
influences the practical controversies of the age by its latent presence, and
is likely soon to make itself recognised as the vital question of the future. It
is so far from being new, that, in a certain sense, it has divided mankind,
almost from the remotest ages; but in the stage of progress into which the
more civilized portions of the species have now entered, it presents itself
under new conditions, and requires a different and more fundamental treatment.

The struggle between Liberty and Authority is the most conspicuous
feature in the portions of history with which we are earliest familiar, particularly in that of Greece, Rome, and England. But in old times this contest
was between subjects, or some classes of subjects, and the *a*Government*a*.
By liberty, was meant protection against the tyranny of the political rulers.
The rulers were conceived (except in some of the popular governments of
Greece) as in a necessarily antagonistic position to the people whom they
ruled. They consisted of a governing One, or a governing tribe or caste, who
derived their authority from inheritance or conquest, who, àt all events,
did not hold it at the pleasure of the governed, and whose supremacy men
did not venture, perhaps did not desire, to contest, whatever precautions
might be taken against its oppressive exercise. Their power was regarded as
necessary, but also as highly dangerous; as a weapon which they would attempt to use against their subjects, no less than against external enemies. To
prevent the weaker members of the community from being preyed upon by
innumerable vultures, it was needful that there should be an animal of prey
stronger than the rest, commissioned to keep them down. But as the king of
the vultures would be no less bent upon preying on the flock than any of the
minor harpies, it was indispensable to be in a perpetual attitude of defence
against his beak and claws. The aim, therefore, of patriots was to set limits

*a-a*591,592 government

to the power which the ruler should be suffered to exercise over the community; and this limitation was what they meant by liberty. It was attempted in two ways. First, by obtaining a recognition of certain immunities, called political liberties or rights, which it was to be regarded as a breach of duty in the ruler to infringe, and which, if he did infringe, specific resistance, or general rebellion, was held to be justifiable. A second, and generally a later expedient, was the establishment of constitutional checks, by which the consent of the community, or of a body of some sort, supposed to represent its interests, was made a necessary condition to some of the more important acts of the governing power. To the first of these modes of limitation, the ruling power, in most European countries, was compelled, more or less, to submit. It was not so with the second; and, to attain this, or when already in some degree possessed, to attain it more completely, became everywhere the principal object of the lovers of liberty. And so long as mankind were content to combat one enemy by another, and to be ruled by a master, on condition of being guaranteed more or less efficaciously against his tyranny, they did not carry their aspirations beyond this point.

A time, however, came, in the progress of human affairs, when men ceased to think it a necessity of nature that their governors should be an independent power, opposed in interest to themselves. It appeared to them much better that the various magistrates of the State should be their tenants or delegates, revocable at their pleasure. In that way alone, it seemed, could they have complete security that the powers of government would never be abused to their disadvantage. By degrees this new demand for elective and temporary rulers became the prominent object of the exertions of the popular party, wherever any such party existed; and superseded, to a considerable extent, the previous efforts to limit the power of rulers. As the struggle proceeded for making the ruling power emanate from the periodical choice of the ruled, some persons began to think that too much importance had been attached to the limitation of the power itself. *That* (it might seem) was a resource against rulers whose interests were habitually opposed to those of the people. What was now wanted was, that the rulers should be identified with the people; that their interest and will should be the interest and will of the nation. The nation did not need to be protected against its own will. There was no fear of its tyrannizing over itself. Let the rulers be effectually responsible to it, promptly removable by it, and it could afford to trust them with power of which it could itself dictate the use to be made. Their power was but the nation's own power, concentrated, and in a form convenient for exercise. This mode of thought, or rather perhaps of feeling, was common among the last generation of European liberalism, in the Continental section of which it still apparently predominates. Those who admit any limit to what a government may do, except in the case of such governments as they think ought not to exist, stand out as brilliant exceptions among the political thinkers of the Continent. A similar tone of sentiment might by this time have been prevalent in our own country, if the circumstances which for a time encouraged it, had continued unaltered.

But, in political and philosophical theories, as well as in persons, success discloses faults and infirmities which failure might have concealed from observation. The notion, that the people have no need to limit their power over themselves, might seem axiomatic, when popular government was a thing only dreamed about, or read of as having existed at some distant period of the past. Neither was that notion necessarily disturbed by such temporary aberrations as those of the French Revolution, the worst of which were the work of an usurping few, and which, in any case, belonged, not to the permanent working of popular institutions, but to a sudden and convulsive outbreak against monarchical and aristocratic despotism. In time, however, a democratic republic came to occupy a large portion of the earth's surface, and made itself felt as one of the most powerful members of the community of nations; and elective and responsible government became subject to the observations and criticisms which wait upon a great existing fact. It was now perceived that such phrases as "self-government," and "the power of the people over themselves," do not express the true state of the case. The "people" who exercise the power are not always the same people with those over whom it is exercised; and the "self-government" spoken of is not the government of each by himself, but of each by all the rest. The will of the people, moreover, practically means the will of the most numerous or the most active *part* of the people; the majority, or those who succeed in making themselves accepted as the majority; the people, consequently, *may* desire to oppress a part of their number; and precautions are as much needed against this as against any other abuse of power. The limitation, therefore, of the power of government over individuals loses none of its importance when the holders of power are regularly accountable to the community, that is, to the strongest party therein. This view of things, recommending itself equally to the intelligence of thinkers and to the inclination of those important classes in European society to whose real or supposed interests democracy is adverse, has had no difficulty in establishing itself; and in political speculations "the tyranny of the majority"[*] is now generally included among the evils against which society requires to be on its guard.

Like other tyrannies, the tyranny of the majority was at first, and is still vulgarly, held in dread, chiefly as operating through the acts of the public authorities. But reflecting persons perceived that when society is itself the tyrant—society collectively, over the separate individuals who compose it— its means of tyrannizing are not restricted to the acts which it may do by the

[*See Tocqueville, *De la Démocratie en Amérique*, Vol. II, p. 142.]

hands of its political functionaries. Society can and does execute its own mandates: and if it issues wrong mandates instead of right, or any mandates at all in things with which it ought not to meddle, it practises a social tyranny more formidable than many kinds of political oppression, since, though not usually upheld by such extreme penalties, it leaves fewer means of escape, penetrating much more deeply into the details of life, and enslaving the soul itself. Protection, therefore, against the tyranny of the magistrate is not enough: there needs protection also against the tyranny of the prevailing opinion and feeling; against the tendency of society to impose, by other means than civil penalties, its own ideas and practices as rules of conduct on those who dissent from them; to fetter the development, and, if possible, prevent the formation, of any individuality not in harmony with its ways, and compel all characters to fashion themselves upon the model of its own. There is a limit to the legitimate interference of collective opinion with individual independence: and to find that limit, and maintain it against encroachment, is as indispensable to a good condition of human affairs, as protection against political despotism.

But though this proposition is not likely to be contested in general terms, the practical question, where to place the limit—how to make the fitting adjustment between individual independence and social control—is a subject on which nearly everything remains to be done. All that makes existence valuable to any one, depends on the enforcement of restraints upon the actions of other people. Some rules of conduct, therefore, must be imposed, by law in the first place, and by opinion on many things which are not fit subjects for the operation of law. What these rules should be, is the principal question in human affairs; but if we except a few of the most obvious cases, it is one of those which least progress has been made in resolving. No two ages, and scarcely any two countries, have decided it alike; and the decision of one age or country is a wonder to another. Yet the people of any given age and country no more suspect any difficulty in it, than if it were a subject on which mankind had always been agreed. The rules which obtain among themselves appear to them self-evident and self-justifying. This all but universal illusion is one of the examples of the magical influence of custom, which is not only, as the proverb says, a second nature, but is continually mistaken for the first. The effect of custom, in preventing any misgiving respecting the rules of conduct which mankind impose on one another, is all the more complete because the subject is one on which it is not generally considered necessary that reasons should be given, either by one person to others, or by each to himself. People are accustomed to believe, and have been encouraged in the belief by some who aspire to the character of philosophers, that their feelings, on subjects of this nature, are better than reasons, and render reasons unnecessary. The practical principle which guides them to their opinions on the regulation of human conduct, is the feeling in each person's mind that everybody should be required to act as he, and those with whom he sympathizes, would like them to act. No one, indeed, acknowledges to himself that his standard of judgment is his own liking; but an opinion on a point of conduct, not supported by reasons, can only count as one person's preference; and if the reasons, when given, are a mere appeal to a similar preference felt by other people, it is still only many people's liking instead of one. To an ordinary man, however, his own preference, thus supported, is not only a perfectly satisfactory reason, but the only one he generally has for any of his notions of morality, taste, or propriety, which are not expressly written in his religious creed; and his chief guide in the interpretation even of that. Men's opinions, accordingly, on what is laudable or blameable, are affected by all the multifarious causes which influence their wishes in regard to the conduct of others, and which are as numerous as those which determine their wishes on any other subject. Sometimes their reason—at other times their prejudices or superstitions: often their social affections, not seldom their antisocial ones, their envy or jealousy, their arrogance or contemptuousness: but most commonly, their desires or fears for themselves—their legitimate or illegitimate self-interest. Wherever there is an ascendant class, a large portion of the morality of the country emanates from its class interests, and its feelings of class superiority. The morality between Spartans and Helots, between planters and negroes, between princes and subjects, between nobles and roturiers, between men and women, has been for the most part the creation of these class interests and feelings: and the sentiments thus generated, react in turn upon the moral feelings of the members of the ascendant class, in their relations among themselves. Where, on the other hand, a class, formerly ascendant, has lost its ascendancy, or where its ascendancy is unpopular, the prevailing moral sentiments frequently bear the impress of an impatient dislike of superiority. Another grand determining principle of the rules of conduct, both in act and forbearance, which have been enforced by law or opinion, has been the servility of mankind towards the supposed preferences or aversions of their temporal masters, or of their gods. This servility, though essentially selfish, is not hypocrisy; it gives rise to perfectly genuine sentiments of abhorrence; it made men burn magicians and heretics. Among so many baser influences, the general and obvious interests of society have of course had a share, and a large one, in the direction of the moral sentiments: less, however, as a matter of reason, and on their own account, than as a consequence of the sympathies and antipathies which grew out of them: and sympathies and antipathies which had little or nothing to do with the interests of society, have made themselves felt in the establishment of moralities with quite as great force.

The likings and dislikings of society, or of some powerful portion of it, are thus the main thing which has practically determined the rules laid down for general observance, under the penalties of law or opinion. And in general, those who have been in advance of society in thought and feeling, have left this condition of things unassailed in principle, however they may have come into conflict with it in some of its details. They have occupied themselves rather in inquiring what things society ought to like or dislike, than in questioning whether its likings or dislikings should be a law to individuals. They preferred endeavouring to alter the feelings of mankind on the particular points on which they were themselves heretical, rather than make common cause in defence of freedom, with heretics generally. The only case in which the higher ground has been taken on principle and maintained with consistency, by any but an individual here and there, is that of religious belief: a case instructive in many ways, and not least so as forming a most striking instance of the fallibility of what is called the moral sense: for the *odium theologicum*, in a sincere bigot, is one of the most unequivocal cases of moral feeling. Those who first broke the yoke of what called itself the Universal Church, were in general as little willing to permit difference of religious opinion as that church itself. But when the heat of the conflict was over, without giving a complete victory to any party, and each church or sect was reduced to limit its hopes to retaining possession of the ground it already occupied; minorities, seeing that they had no chance of becoming majorities, were under the necessity of pleading to those whom they could not convert, for permission to differ. It is accordingly on this battle field, almost solely, that the rights of the individual against society have been asserted on broad grounds of principle, and the claim of society to exercise authority over dissentients, openly controverted. The great writers to whom the world owes what religious liberty it possesses, have mostly asserted freedom of conscience as an indefeasible right, and denied absolutely that a human being is accountable to others for his religious belief. Yet so natural to mankind is intolerance in whatever they really care about, that religious freedom has hardly anywhere been practically realized, except where religious indifference, which dislikes to have its peace disturbed by theological quarrels, has added its weight to the scale. In the minds of almost all religious persons, even in the most tolerant countries, the duty of toleration is admitted with tacit reserves. One person will bear with dissent in matters of church government, but not of dogma; another can tolerate everybody, short of a Papist or an Unitarian; another, every one who believes in revealed religion; a few extend their charity a little further, but stop at the belief in a God and in a future state. Wherever the sentiment of the majority is still genuine and intense, it is found to have abated little of its claim to be obeyed.

In England, from the peculiar circumstances of our political history, though the yoke of opinion is perhaps heavier, that of law is lighter, than in most other countries of Europe; and there is considerable jealousy of direct interference, by the legislative or the executive power, with private conduct; not so much from any just regard for the independence of the individual, as from the still subsisting habit of looking on the government as representing an opposite interest to the public. The majority have not yet learnt to feel the power of the government their power, or its opinions their opinions. When they do so, individual liberty will probably be as much exposed to invasion from the government, as it already is from public opinion. But, as yet, there is a considerable amount of feeling ready to be called forth against any attempt of the law to control individuals in things in which they have not hitherto been accustomed to be controlled by it; and this with very little discrimination as to whether the matter is, or is not, within the legitimate sphere of legal control; insomuch that the feeling, highly salutary on the whole, is perhaps quite as often misplaced as well grounded in the particular instances of its application. There is, in fact, no recognised principle by which the propriety or impropriety of government interference is customarily tested. People decide according to their personal preferences. Some, whenever they see any good to be done, or evil to be remedied, would willingly instigate the government to undertake the business; while others prefer to bear almost any amount of social evil, rather than add one to the departments of human interests amenable to governmental control. And men range themselves on one or the other side in any particular case, according to this general direction of their sentiments; or according to the degree of interest which they feel in the particular thing which it is proposed that the government should do, or according to the belief they entertain that the government would, or would not, do it in the manner they prefer; but very rarely on account of any opinion to which they consistently adhere, as to what things are fit to be done by a government. And it seems to me that in consequence of this absence of rule or principle, one side is at present as often wrong as the other; the interference of government is, with about equal frequency, improperly invoked and improperly condemned.

The object of this Essay is to assert one very simple principle, as entitled to govern absolutely the dealings of society with the individual in the way of compulsion and control, whether the means used be physical force in the form of legal penalties, or the moral coercion of public opinion. That principle is, that the sole end for which mankind are warranted, individually or collectively, in interfering with the liberty of action of any of their number, is self-protection. That the only purpose for which power can be rightfully exercised over any member of a civilized community, against his will, is to prevent harm to others. His own good, either physical or moral, is not a sufficient warrant. He cannot rightfully be compelled to do or forbear because it will be better for him to do so, because it will make him happier, because, in the opinions of others, to do so would be wise, or even right. These are good reasons for remonstrating with him, or reasoning with him, or persuading him, or entreating him, but not for compelling him, or visiting him with any evil in case he do otherwise. To justify that, the conduct from which it is desired to deter him, must be calculated to produce evil to some one else. The only part of the conduct of any one, for which he is amenable to society, is that which concerns others. In the part which merely concerns himself, his independence is, of right, absolute. Over himself, over his own body and mind, the individual is sovereign.

It is, perhaps, hardly necessary to say that this doctrine is meant to apply only to human beings in the maturity of their faculties. We are not speaking of children, or of young persons below the age which the law may fix as that of manhood or womanhood. Those who are still in a state to require being taken care of by others, must be protected against their own actions as well as against external injury. For the same reason, we may leave out of consideration those backward states of society in which the race itself may be considered as in its nonage. The early difficulties in the way of spontaneous progress are so great, that there is seldom any choice of means for overcoming them; and a ruler full of the spirit of improvement is warranted in the use of any expedients that will attain an end, perhaps otherwise unattainable. Despotism is a legitimate mode of government in dealing with barbarians, provided the end be their improvement, and the means justified by actually effecting that end. Liberty, as a principle, has no application to any state of things anterior to the time when mankind have become capable of being improved by free and equal discussion. Until then, there is nothing for them but implicit obedience to an Akbar or a Charlemagne, if they are so fortunate as to find one. But as soon as mankind have attained the capacity of being guided to their own improvement by conviction or persuasion (a period long since reached in all nations with whom we need here concern ourselves), compulsion, either in the direct form or in that of pains and penalties for non-compliance, is no longer admissible as a means to their own good, and justifiable only for the security of others.

It is proper to state that I forego any advantage which could be derived to my argument from the idea of abstract right, as a thing independent of utility. I regard utility as the ultimate appeal on all ethical questions; but it must be utility in the largest sense, grounded on the permanent interests of man as a progressive being. Those interests, I contend, authorize the subjection of individual spontaneity to external control, only in respect to those actions of each, which concern the interest of other people. If any one does an act hurtful to others, there is a *primâ facie* case for punishing him, by law, or, where legal penalties are not safely applicable, by general disapprobation. There are also many positive acts for the benefit of others, which he may rightfully be compelled to perform; such as, to give evidence in a court of justice; to bear his fair share in the common defence, or in any other joint work necessary to the interest of the society of which he enjoys the protection; and to perform certain acts of individual beneficence, such as saving a fellow-creature's life, or interposing to protect the defenceless against ill-usage, things which whenever it is obviously a man's duty to do, he may rightfully be made responsible to society for not doing. A person may cause evil to others not only by his actions but by his inaction, and in either case he is justly accountable to them for the injury. The latter case, it is true, requires a much more cautious exercise of compulsion than the former. To make any one answerable for doing evil to others, is the rule; to make him answerable for not preventing evil, is, comparatively speaking, the exception. Yet there are many cases clear enough and grave enough to justify that exception. In all things which regard the external relations of the individual, he is *de jure* amenable to those whose interests are concerned, and if need be, to society as their protector. There are often good reasons for not holding him to the responsibility; but these reasons must arise from the special expediencies of the case: either because it is a kind of case in which he is on the whole likely to act better, when left to his own discretion, than when controlled in any way in which society have it in their power to control him; or because the attempt to exercise control would produce other evils, greater than those which it would prevent. When such reasons as these preclude the enforcement of responsibility, the conscience of the agent himself should step into the vacant judgment seat, and protect those interests of others which have no external protection; judging himself all the more rigidly, because the case does not admit of his being made accountable to the judgment of his fellow-creatures.

But there is a sphere of action in which society, as distinguished from the individual, has, if any, only an indirect interest; comprehending all that portion of a person's life and conduct which affects only himself, or if it also affects others, only with their free, voluntary, and undeceived consent and participation. When I say only himself, I mean directly, and in the first instance: for whatever affects himself, may affect others *b*through*b* himself; and the objection which may be grounded on this contingency, will receive consideration in the sequel. This, then, is the appropriate region of human liberty. It comprises, first, the inward domain of consciousness; demanding liberty of conscience, in the most comprehensive sense; liberty of thought and feeling; absolute freedom of opinion and sentiment on all subjects, practical or speculative, scientific, moral, or theological. The liberty of expressing and publishing opinions may seem to fall under a different principle, since it belongs to that part of the conduct of an individual which

b-b591, 592 *through*

concerns other people; but, being almost of as much importance as the liberty of thought itself, and resting in great part on the same reasons, is practically inseparable from it. Secondly, the principle requires liberty of tastes and pursuits; of framing the plan of our life to suit our own character; of doing as we like, subject to such consequences as may follow: without impediment from our fellow-creatures, so long as what we do does not harm them, even though they should think our conduct foolish, perverse, or wrong. Thirdly, from this liberty of each individual, follows the liberty, within the same limits, of combination among individuals; freedom to unite, for any purpose not involving harm to others: the persons combining being supposed to be of full age, and not forced or deceived.

No society in which these liberties are not, on the whole, respected, is free, whatever may be its form of government; and none is completely free in which they do not exist absolute and unqualified. The only freedom which deserves the name, is that of pursuing our own good in our own way, so long as we do not attempt to deprive others of theirs, or impede their efforts to obtain it. Each is the proper guardian of his own health, whether bodily, or mental and spiritual. Mankind are greater gainers by suffering each other to live as seems good to themselves, than by compelling each to live as seems good to the rest.

Though this doctrine is anything but new, and, to some persons, may have the air of a truism, there is no doctrine which stands more directly opposed to the general tendency of existing opinion and practice. Society has expended fully as much effort in the attempt (according to its lights) to compel people to conform to its notions of personal, as of social excellence. The ancient commonwealths thought themselves entitled to practise, and the ancient philosophers countenanced, the regulation of every part of private conduct by public authority, on the ground that the State had a deep interest in the whole bodily and mental discipline of every one of its citizens; a mode of thinking which may have been admissible in small republics surrounded by powerful enemies, in constant peril of being subverted by foreign attack or internal commotion, and to which even a short interval of relaxed energy and self-command might so easily be fatal, that they could not afford to wait for the salutary permanent effects of freedom. In the modern world, the greater size of political communities, and above all, the separation between spiritual and temporal authority (which placed the direction of men's consciences in other hands than those which controlled their worldly affairs), prevented so great an interference by law in the details of private life; but the engines of moral repression have been wielded more strenuously against divergence from the reigning opinion in self-regarding, than even in social matters; religion, the most powerful of the elements which have entered into the formation of moral feeling, having almost always been governed either by the ambition of a hierarchy, seeking control over every department of human conduct, or by the spirit of Puritanism. And some of those modern reformers who have placed themselves in strongest opposition to the religions of the past, have been noway behind either churches or sects in their assertion of the right of spiritual domination: M. Comte, in particular, whose social system, as unfolded in his *cSystèmec de Politique Positive*,[*] aims at establishing (though by moral more than by legal appliances) a despotism of society over the individual, surpassing anything contemplated in the political ideal of the most rigid disciplinarian among the ancient philosophers.

Apart from the peculiar tenets of individual thinkers, there is also in the world at large an increasing inclination to stretch unduly the powers of society over the individual, both by the force of opinion and even by that of legislation: and as the tendency of all the changes taking place in the world is to strengthen society, and diminish the power of the individual, this encroachment is not one of the evils which tend spontaneously to disappear, but, on the contrary, to grow more and more formidable. The disposition of mankind, whether as rulers or as fellow-citizens, to impose their own opinions and inclinations as a rule of conduct on others, is so energetically supported by some of the best and by some of the worst feelings incident to human nature, that it is hardly ever kept under restraint by anything but want of power; and as the power is not declining, but growing, unless a strong barrier of moral conviction can be raised against the mischief, we must expect, in the present circumstances of the world, to see it increase.

It will be convenient for the argument, if, instead of at once entering upon the general thesis, we confine ourselves in the first instance to a single branch of it, on which the principle here stated is, if not fully, yet to a certain point, recognised by the current opinions. This one branch is the Liberty of Thought: from which it is impossible to separate the cognate liberty of speaking and of writing. Although these liberties, to some considerable amount, form part of the political morality of all countries which profess religious toleration and free institutions, the grounds, both philosophical and practical, on which they rest, are perhaps not so familiar to the general mind, nor so thoroughly appreciated by many even of the leaders of opinion, as might have been expected. Those grounds, when rightly understood, are of much wider application than to only one division of the subject, and a thorough consideration of this part of the question will be found the best introduction to the remainder. Those to whom nothing which I am about to say will be new, may therefore, I hope, excuse me, if on a subject which for now three centuries has been so often discussed, I venture on one discussion more.

[*_Système de politique positive, ou Traité de sociologie instituant la Religion de l'humanité_, 4 vols. (Paris: Mathias, 1851–54).]

c-c591,592 _Traité [this reference is mistaken; Comte's_ Système _is the work intended.]_

CHAPTER II

Of the Liberty of Thought and Discussion

THE TIME, it is to be hoped, is gone by, when any defence would be necessary of the "liberty of the press" as one of the securities against corrupt or tyrannical government. No argument, we may suppose, can now be needed, against permitting a legislature or an executive, not identified in interest with the people, to prescribe opinions to them, and determine what doctrines or what arguments they shall be allowed to hear. This aspect of the question, besides, has been so often and so triumphantly enforced by preceding writers, that it needs not be specially insisted on in this place. Though the law of England, on the subject of the press, is as servile to this day as it was in the time of the Tudors, there is little danger of its being actually put in force against political discussion, except during some temporary panic, when fear of insurrection drives ministers and judges from their propriety;* and, speak-

---

*These words had scarcely been written, when, as if to give them an emphatic contradiction, occurred the Government Press Prosecutions of 1858. That ill-judged interference with the liberty of public discussion has not, however, induced me to alter a single word in the text, nor has it at all weakened my conviction that, moments of panic excepted, the era of pains and penalties for political discussion has, in our own country, passed away. For, in the first place, the prosecutions were not persisted in; and, in the second, they were never, properly speaking, political prosecutions. The offence charged was not that of criticising institutions, or the acts or persons of rulers, but of circulating what was deemed an immoral doctrine, the lawfulness of Tyrannicide.

If the arguments of the present chapter are of any validity, there ought to exist the fullest liberty of professing and discussing, as a matter of ethical conviction, any doctrine, however immoral it may be considered. It would, therefore, be irrelevant and out of place to examine here, whether the doctrine of Tyrannicide deserves that title. I shall content myself with saying that the subject has been at all times one of the open questions of morals; that the act of a private citizen in striking down a criminal, who, by raising himself above the law, has placed himself beyond the reach of legal punishment or control, has been accounted by whole nations, and by some of the best and wisest of men, not a crime, but an act of exalted virtue; and that, right or wrong, it is not of the nature of assassination, but of civil war. As such, I hold that the instigation to it, in a specific case, may be a proper subject of punishment, but only if an overt act has followed, and at least a probable connexion can be established between the act and the instigation. Even then, it is not a foreign government, but the very government assailed, which alone, in the exercise of self-defence, can legitimately punish attacks directed against its own existence.

ing generally, it is not, in constitutional countries, to be apprehended, that the government, whether completely responsible to the people or not, will often attempt to control the expression of opinion, except when in doing so it makes itself the organ of the general intolerance of the public. Let us suppose, therefore, that the government is entirely at one with the people, and never thinks of exerting any power of coercion unless in agreement with what it conceives to be their voice. But I deny the right of the people to exercise such coercion, either by themselves or by their government. The power itself is illegitimate. The best government has no more title to it than the worst. It is as noxious, or more noxious, when exerted in accordance with public opinion, than when in opposition to it. If all mankind minus one, were of one opinion, and only one person were of the contrary opinion, mankind would be no more justified in silencing that one person, than he, if he had the power, would be justified in silencing mankind. Were an opinion a personal possession of no value except to the owner; if to be obstructed in the enjoyment of it were simply a private injury, it would make some difference whether the injury was inflicted only on a few persons or on many. But the peculiar evil of silencing the expression of an opinion is, that it is robbing the human race; posterity as well as the existing genera- tion; those who dissent from the opinion, still more than those who hold it. If the opinion is right, they are deprived of the opportunity of exchanging error for truth: if wrong, they lose, what is almost as great a benefit, the clearer perception and livelier impression of truth, produced by its collision with error.

It is necessary to consider separately these two hypotheses, each of which has a distinct branch of the argument corresponding to it. We can never be sure that the opinion we are endeavouring to stifle is a false opinion; and if we were sure, stifling it would be an evil still.

First: the opinion which it is attempted to suppress by authority may possibly be true. Those who desire to suppress it, of course deny its truth; but they are not infallible. They have no authority to decide the question for all mankind, and exclude every other person from the means of judging. To refuse a hearing to an opinion, because they are sure that it is false, is to assume that *their* certainty is the same thing as *absolute* certainty. All silencing of discussion is an assumption of infallibility. Its condemnation may be allowed to rest on this common argument, not the worse for being common.

Unfortunately for the good sense of mankind, the fact of their fallibility is far from carrying the weight in their practical judgment, which is always allowed to it in theory; for while every one well knows himself to be fallible, few think it necessary to take any precautions against their own fallibility, or admit the supposition that any opinion, of which they feel very certain, may be one of the examples of the error to which they acknowledge themselves to be liable. Absolute princes, or others who are accustomed to unlimited deference, usually feel this complete confidence in their own opinions on nearly all subjects. People more happily situated, who sometimes hear their opinions disputed, and are not wholly unused to be set right when they are wrong, place the same unbounded reliance only on such of their opinions as are shared by all who surround them, or to whom they habitually defer: for in proportion to a man's want of confidence in his own solitary judgment, does he usually repose, with implicit trust, on the infallibility of "the world" in general. And the world, to each individual, means the part of it with which he comes in contact; his party, his sect, his church, his class of society: the man may be called, by comparison, almost liberal and large-minded to whom it means anything so comprehensive as his own country or his own age. Nor is his faith in this collective authority at all shaken by his being aware that other ages, countries, sects, churches, classes, and parties have thought, and even now think, the exact reverse. He devolves upon his own world the responsibility of being in the right against the dissentient worlds of other people; and it never troubles him that mere accident has decided which of these numerous worlds is the object of his reliance, and that the same causes which make him a Churchman in London, would have made him a Buddhist or a Confucian in Pekin. Yet it is as evident in itself, as any amount of argument can make it, that ages are no more infallible than individuals; every age having held many opinions which subsequent ages have deemed not only false but absurd; and it is as certain that many opinions, now general, will be rejected by future ages, as it is that many, once general, are rejected by the present.

The objection likely to be made to this argument, would probably take some such form as the following. There is no greater assumption of infallibility in forbidding the propagation of error, than in any other thing which is done by public authority on its own judgment and responsibility. Judgment is given to men that they may use it. Because it may be used erroneously, are men to be told that they ought not to use it at all? To prohibit what they think pernicious, is not claiming exemption from error, but fulfilling the duty incumbent on them, although fallible, of acting on their conscientious conviction. If we were never to act on our opinions, because those opinions may be wrong, we should leave all our interests uncared for, and all our duties unperformed. An objection which applies to all conduct, can be no valid objection to any conduct in particular. It is the duty of governments, and of individuals, to form the truest opinions they can; to form them carefully, and never impose them upon others unless they are quite sure of being right. But when they are sure (such reasoners may say), it is not conscientiousness but cowardice to shrink from acting on their opinions, and allow doctrines which they honestly think dangerous to the welfare of mankind, either in this life or in another, to be scattered abroad without restraint, because other people, in less enlightened times, have persecuted opinions now believed to be true. Let us take care, it may be said, not to make the same mistake: but governments and nations have made mistakes in other things, which are not denied to be fit subjects for the exercise of authority: they have laid on bad taxes, made unjust wars. Ought we therefore to lay on no taxes, and, under whatever provocation, make no wars? Men, and governments, must act to the best of their ability. There is no such thing as absolute certainty, but there is assurance sufficient for the purposes of human life. We may, and must, assume our opinion to be true for the guidance of our own conduct: and it is assuming no more when we forbid bad men to pervert society by the propagation of opinions which we regard as false and pernicious.

I answer, that it is assuming very much more. There is the greatest difference between presuming an opinion to be true, because, with every opportunity for contesting it, it has not been refuted, and assuming its truth for the purpose of not permitting its refutation. Complete liberty of contradicting and disproving our opinion, is the very condition which justifies us in assuming its truth for purposes of action; and on no other terms can a being with human faculties have any rational assurance of being right.

When we consider either the history of opinion, or the ordinary conduct of human life, to what is it to be ascribed that the one and the other are no worse than they are? Not certainly to the inherent force of the human understanding; for, on any matter not self-evident, there are ninety-nine persons totally incapable of judging of it, for one who is capable; and the capacity of the hundredth person is only comparative; for the majority of the eminent men of every past generation held many opinions now known to be erroneous, and did or approved numerous things which no one will now justify. Why is it, then, that there is on the whole a preponderance among mankind of rational opinions and rational conduct? If there really is this preponderance—which there must be unless human affairs are, and have always been, in an almost desperate state—it is owing to a quality of the human mind, the source of everything respectable in man either as an intellectual or as a moral being, namely, that his errors are corrigible. He is capable of rectifying his mistakes, by discussion and experience. Not by experience alone. There must be discussion, to show how experience is to be interpreted. Wrong opinions and practices gradually yield to fact and argument: but facts and arguments, to produce any effect on the mind, must be brought before it. Very few facts are able to tell their own story, without comments to bring out their meaning. The whole strength and value, then, of human judgment, depending on the one property, that it can be set right when it is wrong, reliance can be placed on it only when the means of setting it right are kept constantly at hand. In the case of any person whose judgment is really deserving of confidence, how has it become so? Because he has kept his mind open to criticism of his opinions and conduct. Because it has been his practice to listen to all that could be said against him; to profit by as much of it as was just, and expound to himself, and upon occasion to others, the fallacy of what was fallacious. Because he has felt, that the only way in which a human being can make some approach to knowing the whole of a subject, is by hearing what can be said about it by persons of every variety of opinion, and studying all modes in which it can be looked at by every character of mind. No wise man ever acquired his wisdom in any mode but this; nor is it in the nature of human intellect to become wise in any other manner. The steady habit of correcting and completing his own opinion by collating it with those of others, so far from causing doubt and hesitation in carrying it into practice, is the only stable foundation for a just reliance on it: for, being cognisant of all that can, at least obviously, be said against him, and having taken up his position against all gainsayers—knowing that he has sought for objections and difficulties, instead of avoiding them, and has shut out no light which can be thrown upon the subject from any quarter—he has a right to think his judgment better than that of any person, or any multitude, who have not gone through a similar process.

It is not too much to require that what the wisest of mankind, those who are best entitled to trust their own judgment, find necessary to warrant their relying on it, should be submitted to by that miscellaneous collection of a few wise and many foolish individuals, called the public. The most intolerant of churches, the Roman Catholic Church, even at the canonization of a saint, admits, and listens patiently to, a "devil's advocate." The holiest of men, it appears, cannot be admitted to posthumous honours, until all that the devil could say against him is known and weighed. If even the Newtonian philosophy were not permitted to be questioned, mankind could not feel as complete assurance of its truth as they now do. The beliefs which we have most warrant for, have no safeguard to rest on, but a standing invitation to the whole world to prove them unfounded. If the challenge is not accepted, or is accepted and the attempt fails, we are far enough from certainty still; but we have done the best that the existing state of human reason admits of; we have neglected nothing that could give the truth a chance of reaching us: if the lists are kept open, we may hope that if there be a better truth, it will be found when the human mind is capable of receiving it; and in the meantime we may rely on having attained such approach to truth, as is possible in our own day. This is the amount of certainty attainable by a fallible being, and this the sole way of attaining it.

Strange it is, that men should admit the validity of the arguments for free discussion, but object to their being "pushed to an extreme;" not seeing that unless the reasons are good for an extreme case, they are not good for any case. Strange that they should imagine that they are not assuming infallibility, when they acknowledge that there should be free discussion on all subjects which can possibly be *doubtful,* but think that some particular principle or doctrine should be forbidden to be questioned because it is *ᵃsoᵃ certain,* that is, because *they are certain* that it is certain. To call any proposition certain, while there is any one who would deny its certainty if permitted, but who is not permitted, is to assume that we ourselves, and those who agree with us, are the judges of certainty, and judges without hearing the other side.

In the present age—which has been described as "destitute of faith, but terrified at scepticism"[*]—in which people feel sure, not so much that their opinions are true, as that they should not know what to do without them— the claims of an opinion to be protected from public attack are rested not so much on its truth, as on its importance to society. There are, it is alleged, certain beliefs, so useful, not to say indispensable to well-being, that it is as much the duty of governments to uphold those beliefs, as to protect any other of the interests of society. In a case of such necessity, and so directly in the line of their duty, something less than infallibility may, it is maintained, warrant, and even bind, governments, to act on their own opinion, confirmed by the general opinion of mankind. It is also often argued, and still oftener thought, that none but bad men would desire to weaken these salutary beliefs; and there can be nothing wrong, it is thought, in restraining bad men, and prohibiting what only such men would wish to practise. This mode of thinking makes the justification of restraints on discussion not a question of the truth of doctrines, but of their usefulness; and flatters itself by that means to escape the responsibility of claiming to be an infallible judge of opinions. But those who thus satisfy themselves, do not perceive that the assumption of infallibility is merely shifted from one point to another. The usefulness of an opinion is itself matter of opinion: as disputable, as open to discussion, and requiring discussion as much, as the opinion itself. There is the same need of an infallible judge of opinions to decide an opinion to be noxious, as to decide it to be false, unless the opinion condemned has full opportunity of defending itself. And it will not do to say that the heretic may be allowed to maintain the utility or harmlessness of his opinion, though forbidden to maintain its truth. The truth of an opinion is part of its utility. If we would know whether or not it is desirable that a proposition should be believed, is it possible to exclude the consideration of whether or not it is true? In the opinion, not of bad men,

[*Thomas Carlyle, "Memoirs of the Life of Scott," *London and Westminster Review,* VI & XXVIII (Jan., 1838), 315.]

ᵃ⁻ᵃ591, 592   *so [printer's error?]*

but of the best men, no belief which is contrary to truth can be really useful: and can you prevent such men from urging that plea, when they are charged with culpability for denying some doctrine which they are told is useful, but which they believe to be false? Those who are on the side of received opinions, never fail to take all possible advantage of this plea; you do not find *them* handling the question of utility as if it could be completely abstracted from that of truth: on the contrary, it is, above all, because their doctrine is *b*the "truth,"*b* that the knowledge or the belief of it is held to be so indispensable. There can be no fair discussion of the question of usefulness, when an argument so vital may be employed on one side, but not on the other. And in point of fact, when law or public feeling do not permit the truth of an opinion to be disputed, they are just as little tolerant of a denial of its usefulness. The utmost they allow is an extenuation of its absolute necessity, or of the positive guilt of rejecting it.

In order more fully to illustrate the mischief of denying a hearing to opinions because we, in our own judgment, have condemned them, it will be desirable to fix down the discussion to a concrete case; and I choose, by preference, the cases which are least favourable to me—in which the argument against freedom of opinion, both on the score of truth and on that of utility, is considered the strongest. Let the opinions impugned be the belief in a God and in a future state, or any of the commonly received doctrines of morality. To fight the battle on such ground, gives a great advantage to an unfair antagonist; since he will be sure to say (and many who have no desire to be unfair will say it internally), Are these the doctrines which you do not deem sufficiently certain to be taken under the protection of law? Is the belief in a God one of the opinions, to feel sure of which, you hold to be assuming infallibility? But I must be permitted to observe, that it is not the feeling sure of a doctrine (be it what it may) which I call an assumption of infallibility. It is the undertaking to decide that question *for others*, without allowing them to hear what can be said on the contrary side. And I denounce and reprobate this pretension not the less, if put forth on the side of my most solemn convictions. However positive any one's persuasion may be, not only of the falsity but of the pernicious consequences—not only of the pernicious consequences, but (to adopt expressions which I altogether condemn) the immorality and impiety of an opinion; yet if, in pursuance of that private judgment, though backed by the public judgment of his country or his cotemporaries, he prevents the opinion from being heard in its defence, he assumes infallibility. And so far from the assumption being less objectionable or less dangerous because the opinion is called immoral or impious, this is the case of all others in which it is most fatal. These are exactly the occasions on which the men of one generation com-

b-b591, 592, 64   "the truth,"

mit those dreadful mistakes, which excite the astonishment and horror of posterity. It is among such that we find the instances memorable in history, when the arm of the law has been employed to root out the best men and the noblest doctrines; with deplorable success as to the men, though some of the doctrines have survived to be (as if in mockery) invoked, in defence of similar conduct towards those who dissent from *them*, or from their received interpretation.

Mankind can hardly be too often reminded, that there was once a man named Socrates, between whom and the legal authorities and public opinion of his time, there took place a memorable collision. Born in an age and country abounding in individual greatness, this man has been handed down to us by those who best knew both him and the age, as the most virtuous man in it; while *we* know him as the head and prototype of all subsequent teachers of virtue, the source equally of the lofty inspiration of Plato and the judicious utilitarianism of Aristotle, "*i maëstri di color che sanno*,"[*] the two headsprings of ethical as of all other philosophy. This acknowledged master of all the eminent thinkers who have since lived—whose fame, still growing after more than two thousand years, all but outweighs the whole remainder of the names which make his native city illustrious—was put to death by his countrymen, after a judicial conviction, for impiety and immorality. Impiety, in denying the gods recognised by the State; indeed his accuser asserted (see the *Apologia*) that he believed in no gods at all. Immorality, in being, by his doctrines and instructions, a "corrupter of youth."[†] Of these charges the tribunal, there is every ground for believing, honestly found him guilty, and condemned the man who probably of all then born had deserved best of mankind, to be put to death as a criminal.

To pass from this to the only other instance of judicial iniquity, the mention of which, after the condemnation of Socrates, would not be an anti-climax: the event which took place on Calvary rather more than eighteen hundred years ago. The man who left on the memory of those who witnessed his life and conversation, such an impression of his moral grandeur, that eighteen subsequent centuries have done homage to him as the Almighty in person, was ignominiously put to death, as what? As a blasphemer. Men did not merely mistake their benefactor; they mistook him for the exact contrary of what he was, and treated him as that prodigy of impiety, which they themselves are now held to be, for their treatment of him. The feelings with which mankind now regard these lamentable transactions, especially the later of the two, render them extremely unjust

[*See Dante, *Inferno*, Canto IV, 1.131.]

[†Plato, *Apology*, in *Euthyphro, Apology, Crito, Phaedo, Phaedrus* (Greek and English), trans. H. N. Fowler (London: Heinemann; New York: Macmillan, 1914), p. 90 (24b-c). The accuser was Meletus.]

in their judgment of the unhappy actors. These were, to all appearance, not bad men—not worse than men commonly are, but rather the contrary; men who possessed in a full, or somewhat more than a full measure, the religious, moral, and patriotic feelings of their time and people: the very kind of men who, in all times, our own included, have every chance of passing through life blameless and respected. The high-priest who rent his garments when the words were pronounced,[*] which, according to all the ideas of his country, constituted the blackest guilt, was in all probability quite as sincere in his horror and indignation, as the generality of respectable and pious men now are in the religious and moral sentiments they profess; and most of those who now shudder at his conduct, if they had lived in his time, and been born Jews, would have acted precisely as he did. Orthodox Christians who are tempted to think that those who stoned to death the first martyrs must have been worse men than they themselves are, ought to remember that one of those persecutors was Saint Paul.[†]

Let us add one more example, the most striking of all, if the impressiveness of an error is measured by the wisdom and virtue of him who falls into it. If ever any one, possessed of power, had grounds for thinking himself the best and most enlightened among his cotemporaries, it was the Emperor Marcus Aurelius. Absolute monarch of the whole civilized world, he preserved through life not only the most unblemished justice, but what was less to be expected from his Stoical breeding, the tenderest heart. The few failings which are attributed to him, were all on the side of indulgence: while his writings, the highest ethical product of the ancient mind, differ scarcely perceptibly, if they differ at all, from the most characteristic teachings of Christ. This man, a better Christian in all but the dogmatic sense of the word, than almost any of the ostensibly Christian sovereigns who have since reigned, persecuted Christianity. Placed at the summit of all the previous attainments of humanity, with an open, unfettered intellect, and a character which led him of himself to embody in his moral writings the Christian ideal, he yet failed to see that Christianity was to be a good and not an evil to the world, with his duties to which he was so deeply penetrated. Existing society he knew to be in a deplorable state. But such as it was, he saw, or thought he saw, that it was held together, and prevented from being worse, by belief and reverence of the received divinities. As a ruler of mankind, he deemed it his duty not to suffer society to fall in pieces; and saw not how, if its existing ties were removed, any others could be formed which could again knit it together. The new religion openly aimed at dissolving these ties: unless, therefore, it was his duty to adopt that religion, it seemed to be his duty to put it down. Inasmuch then as the

[*Caiaphas; see Matthew, 26:65.]
[†See Acts, 7:58–8:4.]

theology of Christianity did not appear to him true or of divine origin; inasmuch as this strange history of a crucified God was not credible to him, and a system which purported to rest entirely upon a foundation to him so wholly unbelievable, could not be foreseen by him to be that renovating agency which, after all abatements, it has in fact proved to be; the gentlest and most amiable of philosophers and rulers, under a solemn sense of duty, authorized the persecution of Christianity. To my mind this is one of the most tragical facts in all history. It is a bitter thought, how different a thing the Christianity of the world might have been, if the Christian faith had been adopted as the religion of the empire under the auspices of Marcus Aurelius instead of those of Constantine. But it would be equally unjust to him and false to truth, to deny, that no one plea which can be urged for punishing anti-Christian teaching, was wanting to Marcus Aurelius for punishing, as he did, the propagation of Christianity. No Christian more firmly believes that Atheism is false, and tends to the dissolution of society, than Marcus Aurelius believed the same things of Christianity; he who, of all men then living, might have been thought the most capable of appreciating it. Unless any one who approves of punishment for the promulgation of opinions, flatters himself that he is a wiser and better man than Marcus Aurelius—more deeply versed in the wisdom of his time, more elevated in his intellect above it—more earnest in his search for truth, or more single-minded in his devotion to it when found;—let him abstain from that assumption of the joint infallibility of himself and the multitude, which the great Antoninus made with so unfortunate a result.

Aware of the impossibility of defending the use of punishment for restraining irreligious opinions, by any argument which will not justify Marcus Antoninus, the enemies of religious freedom, when hard pressed, occasionally accept this consequence, and say, with Dr. Johnson, that the persecutors of Christianity were in the right;[*] that persecution is an ordeal through which truth ought to pass, and always passes successfully, legal penalties being, in the end, powerless against truth, though sometimes beneficially effective against mischievous errors. This is a form of the argument for religious intolerance, sufficiently remarkable not to be passed without notice.

A theory which maintains that truth may justifiably be persecuted because persecution cannot possibly do it any harm, cannot be charged with being intentionally hostile to the reception of new truths; but we cannot commend the generosity of its dealing with the persons to whom mankind are indebted for them. To discover to the world something which deeply concerns it, and of which it was previously ignorant; to prove to it that it had been mistaken on some vital point of temporal or spiritual interest, is

[*See Boswell, *Life of Johnson*, Vol. II, p. 250 (7 May, 1773); cf. Vol. IV, p. 12 (1780).]

as important a service as a human being can render to his fellow-creatures, and in certain cases, as in those of the early Christians and of the Reformers, those who think with Dr. Johnson believe it to have been the most precious gift which could be bestowed on mankind. That the authors of such splendid benefits should be requited by martyrdom; that their reward should be to be dealt with as the vilest of criminals, is not, upon this theory, a deplorable error and misfortune, for which humanity should mourn in sackcloth and ashes, but the normal and justifiable state of things. The propounder of a new truth, according to this doctrine, should stand, as stood, in the legislation of the Locrians, the proposer of a new law, with a halter round his neck, to be instantly tightened if the public assembly did not, on hearing his reasons, then and there adopt his proposition.[*] People who defend this mode of treating benefactors, cannot be supposed to set much value on the benefit; and I believe this view of the subject is mostly confined to the sort of persons who think that new truths may have been desirable once, but that we have had enough of them now.

But, indeed, the dictum that truth always triumphs over persecution, is one of those pleasant falsehoods which men repeat after one another till they pass into commonplaces, but which all experience refutes. History teems with instances of truth put down by persecution. If not suppressed for ever, it may be thrown back for centuries. To speak only of religious opinions: the Reformation broke out at least twenty times before Luther, and was put down. Arnold of Brescia was put down. Fra Dolcino was put down. Savonarola was put down. The Albigeois were put down. The Vaudois were put down. The Lollards were put down. The Hussites were put down. Even after the era of Luther, wherever persecution was persisted in, it was successful. In Spain, Italy, Flanders, the Austrian empire, Protestantism was rooted out; and, most likely, would have been so in England, had Queen Mary lived, or Queen Elizabeth died. Persecution has always succeeded, save where the heretics were too strong a party to be effectually persecuted. No reasonable person can doubt that Christianity might have been extirpated in the Roman Empire. It spread, and became predominant, because the persecutions were only occasional, lasting but a short time, and separated by long intervals of almost undisturbed propagandism. It is a piece of idle sentimentality that truth, merely as truth, has any inherent power denied to error, of prevailing against the dungeon and the stake. Men are not more zealous for truth than they often are for error, and a sufficient application of legal or even of social penalties will generally succeed

[*See Demosthenes, "Against Timocrates," in *Demosthenes against Meidias, Androtion, Aristocrates, Timocrates, Aristogeiton* (Greek and English), trans. J. H. Vince (London: Heinemann; Cambridge, Mass.: Harvard University Press, 1935), p. 463 (xxiv, 139).]

in stopping the propagation of either. The real advantage which truth has, consists in this, that when an opinion is true, it may be extinguished once, twice, or many times, but in the course of ages there will generally be found persons to rediscover it, until some one of its reappearances falls on a time when from favourable circumstances it escapes persecution until it has made such head as to withstand all subsequent attempts to suppress it.

It will be said, that we do not now put to death the introducers of new opinions: we are not like our fathers who slew the prophets, we even build sepulchres to them. It is true we no longer put heretics to death; and the amount of penal infliction which modern feeling would probably tolerate, even against the most obnoxious opinions, is not sufficient to extirpate them. But let us not flatter ourselves that we are yet free from the stain even of legal persecution. Penalties for opinion, or at least for its expression, still exist by law; and their enforcement is not, even in these times, so unexampled as to make it at all incredible that they may some day be revived in full force. In the year 1857, at the summer assizes of the county of Cornwall, an unfortunate man,* said to be of unexceptionable conduct in all relations of life, was sentenced to twenty-one months' imprisonment, for uttering, and writing on a gate, some offensive words concerning Christianity. Within a month of the same time, at the Old Bailey, two persons, on two separate occasions,† were rejected as jurymen, and one of them grossly insulted by the judge and by one of the counsel, because they honestly declared that they had no theological belief; and a third, a foreigner,‡ for the same reason, was denied justice against a thief. This refusal of redress took place in virtue of the legal doctrine, that no person can be allowed to give evidence in a court of justice, who does not profess belief in a God (any god is sufficient) and in a future state; which is equivalent to declaring such persons to be outlaws, excluded from the protection of the tribunals; who may not only be robbed or assaulted with impunity, if no one but themselves, or persons of similar opinions, be present, but any one else may be robbed or assaulted with impunity, if the proof of the fact depends on their evidence. The assumption on which this is grounded, is that the oath is worthless, of a person who does not believe in a future state; a proposition which betokens much ignorance of history in those who assent to it (since it is historically true that a large proportion of infidels in all ages have been persons of distinguished integrity and honour); and would be maintained by no one who had the smallest conception how many of the persons in greatest repute with the world, both for virtues and for attainments, are

---

*Thomas Pooley, Bodmin Assizes, July 31, 1857. In December following, he received a free pardon from the Crown.

†George Jacob Holyoake, August 17, 1857; Edward Truelove, July, 1857.

‡Baron de Gleichen, Marlborough-street Police Court, August 4, 1857.

well known, at least to their intimates, to be unbelievers. The rule, besides, is suicidal, and cuts away its own foundation. Under pretence that atheists must be liars, it admits the testimony of all atheists who are willing to lie, and rejects only those who brave the obloquy of publicly confessing a detested creed rather than affirm a falsehood. A rule thus self-convicted of absurdity so far as regards its professed purpose, can be kept in force only as a badge of hatred, a relic of persecution; a persecution, too, having the peculiarity, that the qualification for undergoing it, is the being clearly proved not to deserve it. The rule, and the theory it implies, are hardly less insulting to believers than to infidels. For if he who does not believe in a future state, necessarily lies, it follows that they who do believe are only prevented from lying, if prevented they are, by the fear of hell. We will not do the authors and abettors of the rule the injury of supposing, that the conception which they have formed of Christian virtue is drawn from their own consciousness.

These, indeed, are but rags and remnants of persecution, and may be thought to be not so much an indication of the wish to persecute, as an example of that very frequent infirmity of English minds, which makes them take a preposterous pleasure in the assertion of a bad principle, when they are no longer bad enough to desire to carry it really into practice. But unhappily there is no security in the state of the public mind, that the suspension of worse forms of legal persecution, which has lasted for about the space of a generation, will continue. In this age the quiet surface of routine is as often ruffled by attempts to resuscitate past evils, as to introduce new benefits. What is boasted of at the present time as the revival of religion, is always, in narrow and uncultivated minds, at least as much the revival of bigotry; and where there is the strong permanent leaven of intolerance in the feelings of a people, which at all times abides in the middle classes of this country, it needs but little to provoke them into actively persecuting those whom they have never ceased to think proper objects of persecution.*

*Ample warning may be drawn from the large infusion of the passions of a persecutor, which mingled with the general display of the worst parts of our national character on the occasion of the Sepoy insurrection. The ravings of fanatics or charlatans from the pulpit may be unworthy of notice; but the heads of the Evangelical party have announced as their principle for the government of Hindoos and Mahomedans, that no schools be supported by public money in which the Bible is not taught, and by necessary consequence that no public employment be given to any but real or pretended Christians. An Under-Secretary of State [William N. Massey], in a speech delivered to his constituents on the 12th of November, 1857, is reported to have said: "Toleration of their faith" (the faith of a hundred millions of British subjects), "the superstition which they called religion, by the British Government, had had the effect of retarding the ascendancy of the British name, and preventing the salutary growth of Christianity. . . . Toleration was the great corner-stone of the religious liberties of this country;

For it is this—it is the opinions men entertain, and the feelings they cherish, respecting those who disown the beliefs they deem important, which makes this country not a place of mental freedom. For a long time past, the chief mischief of the legal penalties is that they strengthen the social stigma. It is that stigma which is really effective, and so effective is it, that the profession of opinions which are under the ban of society is much less common in England, than is, in many other countries, the avowal of those which incur risk of judicial punishment. In respect to all persons but those whose pecuniary circumstances make them independent of the good will of other people, opinion, on this subject, is as efficacious as law; men might as well be imprisoned, as excluded from the means of earning their bread. Those whose bread is already secured, and who desire no favours from men in power, or from bodies of men, or from the public, have nothing to fear from the open avowal of any opinions, but to be ill-thought of and ill-spoken of, and this it ought not to require a very heroic mould to enable them to bear. There is no room for any appeal *ad misericordiam* in behalf of such persons. But though we do not now inflict so much evil on those who think differently from us, as it was formerly our custom to do, it may be that we do ourselves as much evil as ever by our treatment of them. Socrates was put to death, but the Socratic philosophy rose like the sun in heaven, and spread its illumination over the whole intellectual firmament. Christians were cast to the lions, but the Christian church grew up a stately and spreading tree, overtopping the older and less vigorous growths, and stifling them by its shade. Our merely social intolerance kills no one, roots out no opinions, but induces men to disguise them, or to abstain from any active effort for their diffusion. With us, heretical opinions do not perceptibly gain, or even lose, ground in each decade or generation; they never blaze out far and wide, but continue to smoulder in the narrow circles of thinking and studious persons among whom they originate, without ever lighting up the general affairs of mankind with either a true or a deceptive light. And thus is kept up a state of things very satisfactory to some minds, because, without the unpleasant process of fining or imprisoning anybody, it maintains all prevailing opinions outwardly undisturbed, while it does not absolutely interdict the exercise of reason by dissentients afflicted with the malady of

---

but do not let them abuse that precious word toleration. As he understood it, it meant the complete liberty to all, freedom of worship, *among Christians, who worshipped upon the same foundation.* It meant toleration of all sects and denominations of *Christians who believed in the one mediation.*" [See *The Times*, 14 Nov., 1857, p. 4.] I desire to call attention to the fact, that a man who has been deemed fit to fill a high office in the government of this country, under a liberal Ministry, maintains the doctrine that all who do not believe in the divinity of Christ are beyond the pale of toleration. Who, after this imbecile display, can indulge the illusion that religious persecution has passed away, never to return?

thought. A convenient plan for having peace in the intellectual world, and keeping all things going on therein very much as they do already. But the price paid for this sort of intellectual pacification, is the sacrifice of the entire moral courage of the human mind. A state of things in which a large portion of the most active and inquiring intellects find it advisable to keep the ᶜgeneralᶜ principles and grounds of their convictions within their own breasts, and attempt, in what they address to the public, to fit as much as they can of their own conclusions to premises which they have internally renounced, cannot send forth the open, fearless characters, and logical, consistent intellects who once adorned the thinking world. The sort of men who can be looked for under it, are either mere conformers to commonplace, or time-servers for truth, whose arguments on all great subjects are meant for their hearers, and are not those which have convinced themselves. Those who avoid this alternative, do so by narrowing their thoughts and interest to things which can be spoken of without venturing within the region of principles, that is, to small practical matters, which would come right of themselves, if but the minds of mankind were strengthened and enlarged, and which will never be made effectually right until then: while that which would strengthen and enlarge men's minds, free and daring speculation on the highest subjects, is abandoned.

Those in whose eyes this reticence on the part of heretics is no evil, should consider in the first place, that in consequence of it there is never any fair and thorough discussion of heretical opinions; and that such of them as could not stand such a discussion, though they may be prevented from spreading, do not disappear. But it is not the minds of heretics that are deteriorated most, by the ban placed on all inquiry which does not end in the orthodox conclusions. The greatest harm done is to those who are not heretics, and whose whole mental development is cramped, and their reason cowed, by the fear of heresy. Who can compute what the world loses in the multitude of promising intellects combined with timid characters, who dare not follow out any bold, vigorous, independent train of thought, lest it should land them in something which would admit of being considered ir-religious or immoral? Among them we may occasionally see some man of deep conscientiousness, and subtle and refined understanding, who spends a life in sophisticating with an intellect which he cannot silence, and exhausts the resources of ingenuity in attempting to reconcile the promptings of his conscience and reason with orthodoxy, which yet he does not, perhaps, to the end succeed in doing. No one can be a great thinker who does not recog-nise, that as a thinker it is his first duty to follow his intellect to whatever conclusions it may lead. Truth gains more even by the errors of one who, with due study and preparation, thinks for himself, than by the true opin-

ᶜ⁻ᶜ591, 592   genuine [*printer's error?*]

ions of those who only hold them because they do not suffer themselves to think. Not that it is solely, or chiefly, to form great thinkers, that freedom of thinking is required. On the contrary, it is as much and even more indispensable, to enable average human beings to attain the mental stature which they are capable of. There have been, and may again be, great individual thinkers, in a general atmosphere of mental slavery. But there never has been, nor ever will be, in that atmosphere, an intellectually active people. *When* any people has made a temporary approach to such a character, it has been because the dread of heterodox speculation was for a time suspended. Where there is a tacit convention that principles are not to be disputed; where the discussion of the greatest questions which can occupy humanity is considered to be closed, we cannot hope to find that generally high scale of mental activity which has made some periods of history so remarkable. Never when controversy avoided the subjects which are large and important enough to kindle enthusiasm, was the mind of a people stirred up from its foundations, and the impulse given which raised even persons of the most ordinary intellect to something of the dignity of thinking beings. Of such we have had an example in the condition of Europe during the times immediately following the Reformation; another, though limited to the Continent and to a more cultivated class, in the speculative movement of the latter half of the eighteenth century; and a third, of still briefer duration, in the intellectual fermentation of Germany during the Goethian and Fichtean period. These periods differed widely in the particular opinions which they developed; but were alike in this, that during all three the yoke of authority was broken. In each, an old mental despotism had been thrown off, and no new one had yet taken its place. The impulse given at these three periods has made Europe what it now is. Every single improvement which has taken place either in the human mind or in institutions, may be traced distinctly to one or other of them. Appearances have for some time indicated that all three impulses are well nigh spent; and we can expect no fresh start, until we again assert our mental freedom.

Let us now pass to the second division of the argument, and dismissing the supposition that any of the received opinions may be false, let us assume them to be true, and examine into the worth of the manner in which they are likely to be held, when their truth is not freely and openly canvassed. However unwillingly a person who has a strong opinion may admit the possibility that his opinion may be false, he ought to be moved by the consideration that however true it may be, if it is not fully, frequently, and fearlessly discussed, it will be held as a dead dogma, not a living truth.

There is a class of persons (happily not quite so numerous as formerly)

*d–d*591, 592, 64   Where

who think it enough if a person assents undoubtingly to what they think true, though he has no knowledge whatever of the grounds of the opinion, and could not make a tenable defence of it against the most superficial objections. Such persons, if they can once get their creed taught from authority, naturally think that no good, and some harm, comes of its being allowed to be questioned. Where their influence prevails, they make it nearly impossible for the received opinion to be rejected wisely and considerately, though it may still be rejected rashly and ignorantly; for to shut out discussion entirely is seldom possible, and when it once gets in, beliefs not grounded on conviction are apt to give way before the slightest semblance of an argument. Waving, however, this possibility—assuming that the true opinion abides in the mind, but abides as a prejudice, a belief independent of, and proof against, argument—this is not the way in which truth ought to be held by a rational being. This is not knowing the truth. Truth, thus held, is but one superstition the more, accidentally clinging to the words which enunciate a truth.

If the intellect and judgment of mankind ought to be cultivated, a thing which Protestants at least do not deny, on what can these faculties be more appropriately exercised by any one, than on the things which concern him so much that it is considered necessary for him to hold opinions on them? If the cultivation of the understanding consists in one thing more than in another, it is surely in learning the grounds of one's own opinions. Whatever people believe, on subjects on which it is of the first importance to believe rightly, they ought to be able to defend against at least the common objections. But, some one may say, "Let them be *taught* the grounds of their opinions. It does not follow that opinions must be merely parroted because they are never heard controverted. Persons who learn geometry do not simply commit the theorems to memory, but understand and learn likewise the demonstrations; and it would be absurd to say that they remain ignorant of the grounds of geometrical truths, because they never hear any one deny, and attempt to disprove them." Undoubtedly: and such teaching suffices on a subject like mathematics, where there is nothing at all to be said on the wrong side of the question. The peculiarity of the evidence of mathematical truths is, that all the argument is on one side. There are no objections, and no answers to objections. But on every subject on which difference of opinion is possible, the truth depends on a balance to be struck between two sets of conflicting reasons. Even in natural philosophy, there is always some other explanation possible of the same facts; some geocentric theory instead of heliocentric, some phlogiston instead of oxygen; and it has to be shown why that other theory cannot be the true one: and until this is shown, and until we know how it is shown, we do not understand the grounds of our opinion. But when we turn to subjects infinitely more complicated, to morals, religion, politics, social relations, and the business of life, three-fourths of the arguments for every disputed opinion consist in dispelling the appearances which favour some opinion different from it. The greatest orator, save one,[*] of antiquity, has left it on record that he always studied his adversary's case with as great, if not with still greater, intensity than even his own. What Cicero practised as the means of forensic success, requires to be imitated by all who study any subject in order to arrive at the truth. He who knows only his own side of the case, knows little of that. His reasons may be good, and no one may have been able to refute them. But if he is equally unable to refute the reasons on the opposite side; if he does not so much as know what they are, he has no ground for preferring either opinion. The rational position for him would be suspension of judgment, and unless he contents himself with that, he is either led by authority, or adopts, like the generality of the world, the side to which he feels most inclination. Nor is it enough that he should hear the arguments of adversaries from his own teachers, presented as they state them, and accompanied by what they offer as refutations. That is not the way to do justice to the arguments, or bring them into real contact with his own mind. He must be able to hear them from persons who actually believe them; who defend them in earnest, and do their very utmost for them. He must know them in their most plausible and persuasive form; he must feel the whole force of the difficulty which the true view of the subject has to encounter and dispose of; else he will never really possess himself of the portion of truth which meets and removes that difficulty. Ninety-nine in a hundred of what are called educated men are in this condition; even of those who can argue fluently for their opinions. Their conclusion may be true, but it might be false for anything they know: they have never thrown themselves into the mental position of those who think differently from them, and considered what such persons may have to say; and consequently they do not, in any proper sense of the word, know the doctrine which they themselves profess. They do not know those parts of it which explain and justify the remainder; the considerations which show that a fact which seemingly conflicts with another is reconcilable with it, or that, of two apparently strong reasons, one and not the other ought to be preferred. All that part of the truth which turns the scale, and decides the judgment of a completely informed mind, they are strangers to; nor is it ever really known, but to those who have attended equally and impartially to both sides, and endeavoured to see the reasons of both in the strongest light. So essential is this discipline to a real understanding of moral and human subjects, that if opponents of all important truths do not exist, it is indispensable to imagine them, and supply them with the strongest arguments which the most skilful devil's advocate can conjure up.

[*Demosthenes.]

To abate the force of these considerations, an enemy of free discussion may be supposed to say, that there is no necessity for mankind in general to know and understand all that can be said against or for their opinions by philosophers and theologians. That it is not needful for common men to be able to expose all the misstatements or fallacies of an ingenious opponent. That it is enough if there is always somebody capable of answering them, so that nothing likely to mislead uninstructed persons remains unrefuted. That simple minds, having been taught the obvious grounds of the truths inculcated on them, may trust to authority for the rest, and being aware that they have neither knowledge nor talent to resolve every difficulty which can be raised, may repose in the assurance that all those which have been raised have been or can be answered, by those who are specially trained to the task.

Conceding to this view of the subject the utmost that can be claimed for it by those most easily satisfied with the amount of understanding of truth which ought to accompany the belief of it; even so, the argument for free discussion is no way weakened. For even this doctrine acknowledges that mankind ought to have a rational assurance that all objections have been satisfactorily answered; and how are they to be answered if that which requires to be answered is not spoken? or how can the answer be known to be satisfactory, if the objectors have no opportunity of showing that it is unsatisfactory? If not the public, at least the philosophers and theologians who are to resolve the difficulties, must make themselves familiar with those difficulties in their most puzzling form; and this cannot be accomplished unless they are freely stated, and placed in the most advantageous light which they admit of. The Catholic Church has its own way of dealing with this embarrassing problem. It makes a broad separation between those who can be permitted to receive its doctrines on conviction, and those who must accept them on trust. Neither, indeed, are allowed any choice as to what they will accept; but the clergy, such at least as can be fully confided in, may admissibly and meritoriously make themselves acquainted with the arguments of opponents, in order to answer them, and may, therefore, read heretical books; the laity, not unless by special permission, hard to be obtained. This discipline recognises a knowledge of the enemy's case as beneficial to the teachers, but finds means, consistent with this, of denying it to the rest of the world: thus giving to the *élite* more mental culture, though not more mental freedom, than it allows to the mass. By this device it succeeds in obtaining the kind of mental superiority which its purposes require; for though culture without freedom never made a large and liberal mind, it can make a clever *nisi prius* advocate of a cause. But in countries professing Protestantism, this resource is denied; since Protestants hold, at least in theory, that the responsibility for the choice of a religion must be borne by each for himself, and cannot be thrown off upon teachers. Besides, in the present state of the world, it is practically impossible that writings which are read by the instructed can be kept from the uninstructed. If the teachers of mankind are to be cognisant of all that they ought to know, everything must be free to be written and published without restraint.

If, however, the mischievous operation of the absence of free discussion, when the received opinions are true, were confined to leaving men ignorant of the grounds of those opinions, it might be thought that this, if an intellectual, is no moral evil, and does not affect the worth of the opinions, regarded in their influence on the character. The fact, however, is, that not only the grounds of the opinion are forgotten in the absence of discussion, but too often the meaning of the opinion itself. The words which convey it, cease to suggest ideas, or suggest only a small portion of those they were originally employed to communicate. Instead of a vivid conception and a living belief, there remain only a few phrases retained by rote; or, if any part, the shell and husk only of the meaning is retained, the finer essence being lost. The great chapter in human history which this fact occupies and fills, cannot be too earnestly studied and meditated on.

It is illustrated in the experience of almost all ethical doctrines and religious creeds. They are all full of meaning and vitality to those who originate them, and to the direct disciples of the originators. Their meaning continues to be felt in undiminished strength, and is perhaps brought out into even fuller consciousness, so long as the struggle lasts to give the doctrine or creed an ascendancy over other creeds. At last it either prevails, and becomes the general opinion, or its progress stops; it keeps possession of the ground it has gained, but ceases to spread further. When either of these results has become apparent, controversy on the subject flags, and gradually dies away. The doctrine has taken its place, if not as a received opinion, as one of the admitted sects or divisions of opinion: those who hold it have generally inherited, not adopted it; and conversion from one of these doctrines to another, being now an exceptional fact, occupies little place in the thoughts of their professors. Instead of being, as at first, constantly on the alert either to defend themselves against the world, or to bring the world over to them, they have subsided into acquiescence, and neither listen, when they can help it, to arguments against their creed, nor trouble dissentients (if there be such) with arguments in its favour. From this time may usually be dated the decline in the living power of the doctrine. We often hear the teachers of all creeds lamenting the difficulty of keeping up in the minds of believers a lively apprehension of the truth which they nominally recognise, so that it may penetrate the feelings, and acquire a real mastery over the conduct. No such difficulty is complained of while the creed is still fighting for its existence: even the weaker combatants then know and feel what they are fighting for, and the difference between it and other doctrines; and in

that period of every creed's existence, not a few persons may be found, who
have realized its fundamental principles in all the forms of thought, have
weighed and considered them in all their important bearings, and have
experienced the full effect on the character, which belief in that creed ought
to produce in a mind thoroughly imbued with it. But when it has come to
be an hereditary creed, and to be received passively, not actively—when the
mind is no longer compelled, in the same degree as at first, to exercise its
vital powers on the questions which its belief presents to it, there is a progressive tendency to forget all of the belief except the formularies, or to give it a
dull and torpid assent, as if accepting it on trust dispensed with the necessity
of realizing it in consciousness, or testing it by personal experience; until it
almost ceases to connect itself at all with the inner life of the human being.
Then are seen the cases, so frequent in this age of the world as almost to
form the majority, in which the creed remains as it were outside the mind,
incrusting and petrifying it against all other influences addressed to the
higher parts of our nature; manifesting its power by not suffering any fresh
and living conviction to get in, but itself doing nothing for the mind or heart,
except standing sentinel over them to keep them vacant.

To what an extent doctrines intrinsically fitted to make the deepest impression upon the mind may remain in it as dead beliefs, without being ever
realized in the imagination, the feelings, or the understanding, is exemplified
by the manner in which the majority of believers hold the doctrines of
Christianity. By Christianity I here mean what is accounted such by all
churches and sects—the maxims and precepts contained in the New Testament. These are considered sacred, and accepted as laws, by all professing
Christians. Yet it is scarcely too much to say that not one Christian in a
thousand guides or tests his individual conduct by reference to those laws.
The standard to which he does refer it, is the custom of his nation, his class,
or his religious profession. He has thus, on the one hand, a collection of
ethical maxims, which he believes to have been vouchsafed to him by
infallible wisdom as rules for his government; and on the other, a set of
every-day judgments and practices, which go a certain length with some of
those maxims, not so great a length with others, stand in direct opposition
to some, and are, on the whole, a compromise between the Christian creed
and the interests and suggestions of worldly life. To the first of these
standards he gives his homage; to the other his real allegiance. All Christians
believe that the blessed are the poor and humble, and those who are ill-used
by the world; that it is easier for a camel to pass through the eye of a needle
than for a rich man to enter the kingdom of heaven; that they should judge
not, lest they be judged; that they should swear not at all; that they should
love their neighbour as themselves; that if one take their cloak, they should
give him their coat also; that they should take no thought for the morrow;

that if they would be perfect, they should sell all that they have and give it to the poor.[*] They are not insincere when they say that they believe these things. They do believe them, as people believe what they have always heard lauded and never discussed. But in the sense of that living belief which regulates conduct, they believe these doctrines just up to the point to which it is usual to act upon them. The doctrines in their integrity are serviceable to pelt adversaries with; and it is understood that they are to be put forward (when possible) as the reasons for whatever people do that they think laudable. But any one who reminded them that the maxims require an infinity of things which they never even think of doing, would gain nothing but to be classed among those very unpopular characters who affect to be better than other people. The doctrines have no hold on ordinary believers— are not a power in their minds. They have an habitual respect for the sound of them, but no feeling which spreads from the words to the things signified, and forces the mind to take *them* in, and make them conform to the formula. Whenever conduct is concerned, they look round for Mr. A and B to direct them how far to go in obeying Christ.

Now we may be well assured that the case was not thus, but far otherwise, with the early Christians. Had it been thus, Christianity never wo··d have expanded from an obscure sect of the despised Hebrews into the religion of the Roman empire. When their enemies said, "See how these Christians love one another"[†] (a remark not likely to be made by anybody now), they assuredly had a much livelier feeling of the meaning of their creed than they have ever had since. And to this cause, probably, it is chiefly owing that Christianity now makes so little progress in extending its domain, and after eighteen centuries, is still nearly confined to Europeans and the descendants of Europeans. Even with the strictly religious, who are much in earnest about their doctrines, and attach a greater amount of meaning to many of them than people in general, it commonly happens that the part which is thus comparatively active in their minds is that which was made by Calvin, or Knox, or some such person much nearer in character to themselves. The sayings of Christ coexist passively in their minds, producing hardly any effect beyond what is caused by mere listening to words so amiable and bland. There are many reasons, doubtless, why doctrines which are the badge of a sect retain more of their vitality than those common to all recognised sects, and why more pains are taken by teachers to keep their meaning alive; but one reason certainly is, that the peculiar doctrines are more questioned, and have to be oftener defended against open gainsayers.

[*See, respectively, Luke, 6:20–3 (cf. Matthew, 5:3ff.), and Matthew, 19:24, 7:1, 5:34 (cf. James, 5:12), 19:19, 5:40, 6:34, 19:21.]

[†See Tertullian, *Apology* (Latin and English), trans. T. R. Glover (London: Heinemann; New York: Putnam's Sons, 1931), p. 177 (xxxix, 7).]

Both teachers and learners go to sleep at their post, as soon as there is no enemy in the field.

The same thing holds true, generally speaking, of all traditional doctrines —those of prudence and knowledge of life, as well as of morals or religion. All languages and literatures are full of general observations on life, both as to what it is, and how to conduct oneself in it; observations which everybody knows, which everybody repeats, or hears with acquiescence, which are received as truisms, yet of which most people first truly learn the meaning, when experience, generally of a painful kind, has made it a reality to them. How often, when smarting under some unforeseen misfortune or disappointment, does a person call to mind some proverb or common saying, familiar to him all his life, the meaning of which, if he had ever before felt it as he does now, would have saved him from the calamity. There are indeed reasons for this, other than the absence of discussion: there are many truths of which the full meaning *cannot* be realized, until personal experience has brought it home. But much more of the meaning even of these would have been understood, and what was understood would have been far more deeply impressed on the mind, if the man had been accustomed to hear it argued *pro* and *con* by people who did understand it. The fatal tendency of mankind to leave off thinking about a thing when it is no longer doubtful, is the cause of half their errors. A cotemporary author has well spoken of "the deep slumber of a decided opinion."

But what! (it may be asked) Is the absence of unanimity an indispensable condition of true knowledge? Is it necessary that some part of mankind should persist in error, to enable any to realize the truth? Does a belief cease to be real and vital as soon as it is generally received—and is a proposition never thoroughly understood and felt unless some doubt of it remains? As soon as mankind have unanimously accepted a truth, does the truth perish within them? The highest aim and best result of improved intelligence, it has hitherto been thought, is to unite mankind more and more in the acknowledgment of all important truths: and does the intelligence only last as long as it has not achieved its object? Do the fruits of conquest perish by the very completeness of the victory?

I affirm no such thing. As mankind improve, the number of doctrines which are no longer disputed or doubted will be constantly on the increase: and the well-being of mankind may almost be measured by the number and gravity of the truths which have reached the point of being uncontested. The cessation, on one question after another, of serious controversy, is one of the necessary incidents of the consolidation of opinion; a consolidation as salutary in the case of true opinions, as it is dangerous and noxious when the opinions are erroneous. But though this gradual narrowing of the bounds of diversity of opinion is necessary in both senses of the term, being at once inevitable and indispensable, we are not therefore obliged to conclude that all its consequences must be beneficial. The loss of so important an aid to the intelligent and living apprehension of a truth, as is afforded by the necessity of explaining it to, or defending it against, opponents, though not sufficient to outweigh, is no trifling drawback from, the benefit of its universal recognition. Where this advantage can no longer be had, I confess I should like to see the teachers of mankind endeavouring to provide a substitute for it; some contrivance for making the difficulties of the question as present to the learner's consciousness, as if they were pressed upon him by a dissentient champion, eager for his conversion.

But instead of seeking contrivances for this purpose, they have lost those they formerly had. The Socratic dialectics, so magnificently exemplified in the dialogues of Plato, were a contrivance of this description. They were essentially a negative discussion of the great questions of philosophy and life, directed with consummate skill to the purpose of convincing any one who had merely adopted the commonplaces of received opinion, that he did not understand the subject—that he as yet attached no definite meaning to the doctrines he professed; in order that, becoming aware of his ignorance, he might be put in the way to attain a stable belief, resting on a clear apprehension both of the meaning of doctrines and of their evidence. The school disputations of the middle ages had a somewhat similar object. They were intended to make sure that the pupil understood his own opinion, and (by necessary correlation) the opinion opposed to it, and could enforce the grounds of the one and confute those of the other. These last-mentioned contests had indeed the incurable defect, that the premises appealed to were taken from authority, not from reason; and, as a discipline to the mind, they were in every respect inferior to the powerful dialectics which formed the intellects of the "Socratici viri:"[*] but the modern mind owes far more to both than it is generally willing to admit, and the present modes of education contain nothing which in the smallest degree supplies the place either of the one or of the other. A person who derives all his instruction from teachers or books, even if he escape the besetting temptation of contenting himself with cram, is under no compulsion to hear both sides; accordingly it is far from a frequent accomplishment, even among thinkers, to know both sides; and the weakest part of what everybody says in defence of his opinion, is what he intends as a reply to antagonists. It is the fashion of the present time to disparage negative logic—that which points out weaknesses in theory or errors in practice, without establishing positive truths. Such negative criticism would indeed be poor enough as an ultimate result; but as a means

[*See Cicero, *Letters to Atticus* (Latin and English), trans. E. O. Winstedt, 3 vols. (London: Heinemann; New York: Macmillan, 1912), Vol. III, p. 230 (xiv. 9).]

to attaining any positive knowledge or conviction worthy the name, it cannot be valued too highly; and until people are again systematically trained to it, there will be few great thinkers, and a low general average of intellect, in any but the mathematical and physical departments of speculation. On any other subject no one's opinions deserve the name of knowledge, except so far as he has either had forced upon him by others, or gone through of himself, the same mental process which would have been required of him in carrying on an active controversy with opponents. That, therefore, which when absent, it is so indispensable, but so difficult, to create, how worse than absurd ᵉit isᵉ to forego, when spontaneously offering itself! If there are any persons who contest a received opinion, or who will do so if law or opinion will let them, let us thank them for it, open our minds to listen to them, and rejoice that there is some one to do for us what we otherwise ought, if we have any regard for either the certainty or the vitality of our convictions, to do with much greater labour for ourselves.

It still remains to speak of one of the principal causes which make diversity of opinion advantageous, and will continue to do so until mankind shall have entered a stage of intellectual advancement which at present seems at an incalculable distance. We have hitherto considered only two possibilities: that the received opinion may be false, and some other opinion, consequently, true; or that, the received opinion being true, a conflict with the opposite error is essential to a clear apprehension and deep feeling of its truth. But there is a commoner case than either of these; when the conflicting doctrines, instead of being one true and the other false, share the truth between them; and the nonconforming opinion is needed to supply the remainder of the truth, of which the received doctrine embodies only a part. Popular opinions, on subjects not palpable to sense, are often true, but seldom or never the whole truth. They are a part of the truth; sometimes a greater, sometimes a smaller part, but exaggerated, distorted, and disjoined from the truths by which they ought to be accompanied and limited. Heretical opinions, on the other hand, are generally some of these suppressed and neglected truths, bursting the bonds which kept them down, and either seeking reconciliation with the truth contained in the common opinion, or fronting it as enemies, and setting themselves up, with similar exclusiveness, as the whole truth. The latter case is hitherto the most frequent, as, in the human mind, one-sidedness has always been the rule, and many-sidedness the exception. Hence, even in revolutions of opinion, one part of the truth usually sets while another rises. Even progress, which ought to superadd, for the most part only substitutes, one partial and incomplete truth for another; improvement consisting chiefly in this, that the new fragment of truth is

ᵉ⁻ᵉ591, 592   is it

more wanted, more adapted to the needs of the time, than that which it displaces. Such being the partial character of prevailing opinions, even when resting on a true foundation, every opinion which embodies somewhat of the portion of truth which the common opinion omits, ought to be considered precious, with whatever amount of error and confusion that truth may be blended. No sober judge of human affairs will feel bound to be indignant because those who force on our notice truths which we should otherwise have overlooked, overlook some of those which we see. Rather, he will think that so long as popular truth is one-sided, it is more desirable than otherwise that unpopular truth should have one-sided asserters too; such being usually the most energetic, and the most likely to compel reluctant attention to the fragment of wisdom which they proclaim as if it were the whole.

Thus, in the eighteenth century, when nearly all the instructed, and all those of the uninstructed who were led by them, were lost in admiration of what is called civilization, and of the marvels of modern science, literature, and philosophy, and while greatly overrating the amount of unlikeness between the men of modern and those of ancient times, indulged the belief that the whole of the difference was in their own favour; with what a salutary shock did the paradoxes of Rousseau explode like bombshells in the midst, dislocating the compact mass of one-sided opinion, and forcing its elements to recombine in a better form and with additional ingredients. Not that the current opinions were on the whole farther from the truth than Rousseau's were; on the contrary, they were nearer to it; they contained more of positive truth, and very much less of error. Nevertheless there lay in Rousseau's doctrine, and has floated down the stream of opinion along with it, a considerable amount of exactly those truths which the popular opinion wanted; and these are the deposit which was left behind when the flood subsided. The superior worth of simplicity of life, the enervating and demoralizing effect of the trammels and hypocrisies of artificial society, are ideas which have never been entirely absent from cultivated minds since Rousseau wrote; and they will in time produce their due effect, though at present needing to be asserted as much as ever, and to be asserted by deeds, for words, on this subject, have nearly exhausted their power.

In politics, again, it is almost a commonplace, that a party of order or stability, and a party of progress or reform, are both necessary elements of a healthy state of political life; until the one or the other shall have so enlarged its mental grasp as to be a party equally of order and of progress, knowing and distinguishing what is fit to be preserved from what ought to be swept away. Each of these modes of thinking derives its utility from the deficiencies of the other; but it is in a great measure the opposition of the other that keeps each within the limits of reason and sanity. Unless opinions favourable to democracy and to aristocracy, to property and to equality, to co-operation and to competition, to luxury and to abstinence, to sociality and individuality, to liberty and discipline, and all the other standing antagonisms of practical life, are expressed with equal freedom, and enforced and defended with equal talent and energy, there is no chance of both elements obtaining their due; one scale is sure to go up, and the other down. Truth, in the great practical concerns of life, is so much a question of the reconciling and combining of opposites, that very few have minds sufficiently capacious and impartial to make the adjustment with an approach to correctness, and it has to be made by the rough process of a struggle between combatants fighting under hostile banners. On any of the great open questions just enumerated, if either of the two opinions has a better claim than the other, not merely to be tolerated, but to be encouraged and countenanced, it is the one which happens at the particular time and place to be in a minority. That is the opinion which, for the time being, represents the neglected interests, the side of human well-being which is in danger of obtaining less than its share. I am aware that there is not, in this country, any intolerance of differences of opinion on most of these topics. They are adduced to show, by admitted and multiplied examples, the universality of the fact, that only through diversity of opinion is there, in the existing state of human intellect, a chance of fair play to all sides of the truth. When there are persons to be found, who form an exception to the apparent unanimity of the world on any subject, even if the world is in the right, it is always probable that dissentients have something worth hearing to say for themselves, and that truth would lose something by their silence.

It may be objected, "But *some* received principles, especially on the highest and most vital subjects, are more than half-truths. The Christian morality, for instance, is the whole truth on that subject, and if any one teaches a morality which varies from it, he is wholly in error." As this is of all cases the most important in practice, none can be fitter to test the general maxim. But before pronouncing what Christian morality is or is not, it would be desirable to decide what is meant by Christian morality. If it means the morality of the New Testament, I wonder that any one who derives his knowledge of this from the book itself, can suppose that it was announced, or intended, as a complete doctrine of morals. The Gospel always refers to a pre-existing morality, and confines its precepts to the particulars in which that morality was to be corrected, or superseded by a wider and higher; expressing itself, moreover, in terms most general, often impossible to be interpreted literally, and possessing rather the impressiveness of poetry or eloquence than the precision of legislation. To extract from it a body of ethical doctrine, has never been possible without eking it out from the Old Testament, that is, from a system elaborate indeed, but in many respects barbarous, and intended only for a barbarous people. St. Paul, a declared enemy to this Judaical mode of interpreting the doctrine and filling up the scheme of his Master, equally assumes a pre-existing morality, namely that of the Greeks and Romans; and his advice to Christians is in a great measure a system of accommodation to that; even to the extent of giving an apparent sanction to slavery.[*] What is called Christian, but should rather be termed theological, morality, was not the work of Christ or the Apostles, but is of much later origin, having been gradually built up by the Catholic church of the first five centuries, and though not implicitly adopted by moderns and Protestants, has been much less modified by them than might have been expected. For the most part, indeed, they have contented themselves with cutting off the additions which had been made to it in the middle ages, each sect supplying the place by fresh additions, adapted to its own character and tendencies. That mankind owe a great debt to this morality, and to its early teachers, I should be the last person to deny; but I do not scruple to say of it, that it is, in many important points, incomplete and one-sided, and that unless ideas and feelings, not sanctioned by it, had contributed to the formation of European life and character, human affairs would have been in a worse condition than they now are. Christian morality (so called) has all the characters of a reaction; it is, in great part, a protest against Paganism. Its ideal is negative rather than positive; passive rather than active; Innocence rather than Nobleness; Abstinence from Evil, rather than energetic Pursuit of Good: in its precepts (as has been well said) "thou shalt not" predominates unduly over "thou shalt." In its horror of sensuality, it made an idol of asceticism, which has been gradually compromised away into one of legality. It holds out the hope of heaven and the threat of hell, as the appointed and appropriate motives to a virtuous life: in this falling far below the best of the ancients, and doing what lies in it to give to human morality an essentially selfish character, by disconnecting each man's feelings of duty from the interests of his fellow-creatures, except so far as a self-interested inducement is offered to him for consulting them. It is essentially a doctrine of passive obedience; it inculcates submission to all authorities found established; who indeed are not to be actively obeyed when they command what religion forbids, but who are not to be resisted, far less rebelled against, for any amount of wrong to ourselves. And while, in the morality of the best Pagan nations, duty to the State holds even a disproportionate place, infringing on the just liberty of the individual; in purely Christian ethics, that grand department of duty is scarcely noticed or acknowledged. It is in the *Koran*, not the New Testament, that we read the maxim—"A ruler who appoints any man to an office, when there is in his dominions another man better

[*See, e.g., Colossians, 3:22–4:1.]

qualified for it, sins against God and against the State."[*] What little recognition the idea of obligation to the public obtains in modern morality, is derived from Greek and Roman sources, not from Christian; as, even in the morality of private life, whatever exists of magnanimity, highmindedness, personal dignity, even the sense of honour, is derived from the purely human, not the religious part of our education, and never could have grown out of a standard of ethics in which the only worth, professedly recognised, is that of obedience.

I am as far as any one from pretending that these defects are necessarily inherent in the Christian ethics, in every manner in which it can be conceived, or that the many requisites of a complete moral doctrine which it does not contain, do not admit of being reconciled with it. Far less would I insinuate this of the doctrines and precepts of Christ himself. I believe that the sayings of Christ are all, that I can see any evidence of their having been intended to be; that they are irreconcilable with nothing which a comprehensive morality requires; that everything which is excellent in ethics may be brought within them, with no greater violence to their language than has been done to it by all who have attempted to deduce from them any practical system of conduct whatever. But it is quite consistent with this, to believe that they contain, and were meant to contain, only a part of the truth; that many essential elements of the highest morality are among the things which are not provided for, nor intended to be provided for, in the recorded deliverances of the Founder of Christianity, and which have been entirely thrown aside in the system of ethics erected on the basis of those deliverances by the Christian Church. And this being so, I think it a great error to persist in attempting to find in the Christian doctrine that complete rule for our guidance, which its author intended it to sanction and enforce, but only partially to provide. I believe, too, that this narrow theory is becoming a grave practical evil, detracting greatly from the value of the moral training and instruction, which so many well-meaning persons are now at length exerting themselves to promote. I much fear that by attempting to form the mind and feelings on an exclusively religious type, and discarding those secular standards (as for want of a better name they may be called) which heretofore co-existed with and supplemented the Christian ethics, receiving some of its spirit, and infusing into it some of theirs, there will result, and is even now resulting, a low, abject, servile type of character, which, submit itself as it may to what it deems the Supreme Will, is incapable of rising to or sympathizing in the conception of Supreme Goodness. I believe that other ethics than any which can be evolved from exclusively

[*The passage is not in the *Koran*, but see Charles Hamilton, *The Hedàya or Guide: A Commentary on the Mussulman Laws,* 4 vols. (London: Bensley, 1791), Vol. II, p. 615.]

Christian sources, must exist side by side with Christian ethics to produce the moral regeneration of mankind; and that the Christian system is no exception to the rule, that in an imperfect state of the human mind, the interests of truth require a diversity of opinions. It is not necessary that in ceasing to ignore the moral truths not contained in Christianity, men should ignore any of those which it does contain. Such prejudice, or oversight, when it occurs, is altogether an evil; but it is one from which we cannot hope to be always exempt, and must be regarded as the price paid for an inestimable good. The exclusive pretension made by a part of the truth to be the whole, must and ought to be protested against; and if a reactionary impulse should make the protestors unjust in their turn, this one-sidedness, like the other, may be lamented, but must be tolerated. If Christians would teach infidels to be just to Christianity, they should themselves be just to infidelity. It can do truth no service to blink the fact, known to all who have the most ordinary acquaintance with literary history, that a large portion of the noblest and most valuable moral teaching has been the work, not only of men who did not know, but of men who knew and rejected, the Christian faith.

I do not pretend that the most unlimited use of the freedom of enunciating all possible opinions would put an end to the evils of religious or philosophical sectarianism. Every truth which men of narrow capacity are in earnest about, is sure to be asserted, inculcated, and in many ways even acted on, as if no other truth existed in the world, or at all events none that could limit or qualify the first. I acknowledge that the tendency of all opinions to become sectarian is not cured by the freest discussion, but is often heightened and exacerbated thereby; the truth which ought to have been, but was not, seen, being rejected all the more violently because proclaimed by persons regarded as opponents. But it is not on the impassioned partisan, it is on the calmer and more disinterested bystander, that this collision of opinions works its salutary effect. Not the violent conflict between parts of the truth, but the quiet suppression of half of it, is the formidable evil; there is always hope when people are forced to listen to both sides; it is when they attend only to one that errors harden into prejudices, and truth itself ceases to have the effect of truth, by being exaggerated into falsehood. And since there are few mental attributes more rare than that judicial faculty which can sit in intelligent judgment between two sides of a question, of which only one is represented by an advocate before it, truth has no chance but in proportion as every side of it, every opinion which embodies any fraction of the truth, not only finds advocates, but is so advocated as to be listened to.

We have now recognised the necessity to the mental well-being of mankind (on which all their other well-being depends) of freedom of opinion, and freedom of the expression of opinion, on four distinct grounds; which we will now briefly recapitulate.

First, if any opinion is compelled to silence, that opinion may, for aught we can certainly know, be true. To deny this is to assume our own infallibility.

Secondly, though the silenced opinion be an error, it may, and very commonly does, contain a portion of truth; and since the general or prevailing opinion on any subject is rarely or never the whole truth, it is only by the collision of adverse opinions that the remainder of the truth has any chance of being supplied.

Thirdly, even if the received opinion be not only true, but the whole truth; unless it is suffered to be, and actually is, vigorously and earnestly contested, it will, by most of those who receive it, be held in the manner of a prejudice, with little comprehension or feeling of its rational grounds. And not only this, but, fourthly, the meaning of the doctrine itself will be in danger of being lost, or enfeebled, and deprived of its vital effect on the character and conduct: the dogma becoming a mere formal profession, inefficacious for good, but cumbering the ground, and preventing the growth of any real and heartfelt conviction, from reason or personal experience.

Before quitting the subject of freedom of opinion, it is fit to take some notice of those who say, that the free expression of all opinions should be permitted, on condition that the manner be temperate, and do not pass the bounds of fair discussion. Much might be said on the impossibility of fixing where these supposed bounds are to be placed; for if the test be offence to those whose opinion is attacked, I think experience testifies that this offence is given whenever the attack is telling and powerful, and that every opponent who pushes them hard, and whom they find it difficult to answer, appears to them, if he shows any strong feeling on the subject, an intemperate opponent. But this, though an important consideration in a practical point of view, merges in a more fundamental objection. Undoubtedly the manner of asserting an opinion, even though it be a true one, may be very objectionable, and may justly incur severe censure. But the principal offences of the kind are such as it is mostly impossible, unless by accidental self-betrayal, to bring home to conviction. The gravest of them is, to argue sophistically, to suppress facts or arguments, to misstate the elements of the case, or misrepresent the opposite opinion. But all this, even to the most aggravated degree, is so continually done in perfect good faith, by persons who are not considered, and in many other respects may not deserve to be considered, ignorant or incompetent, that it is rarely possible on adequate grounds conscientiously to stamp the misrepresentation as morally culpable; and still less could law presume to interfere with this kind of controversial misconduct. With regard to what is commonly meant by intemperate discussion, namely invective, sarcasm, personality, and the like, the

denunciation of these weapons would deserve more sympathy if it were
ever proposed to interdict them equally to both sides; but it is only desired
to restrain the employment of them against the prevailing opinion: against
the unprevailing they may not only be used without general disapproval,
but will be likely to obtain for him who uses them the praise of honest zeal
and righteous indignation. Yet whatever mischief arises from their use, is
greatest when they are employed against the comparatively defenceless;
and whatever unfair advantage can be derived by any opinion from this
mode of asserting it, accrues almost exclusively to received opinions. The
worst offence of this kind which can be committed by a polemic, is to
stigmatize those who hold the contrary opinion as bad and immoral men.
To calumny of this sort, those who hold any unpopular opinion are peculiarly exposed, because they are in general few and uninfluential, and nobody but themselves feels much *interested* in seeing justice done them; but
this weapon is, from the nature of the case, denied to those who attack a
prevailing opinion: they can neither use it with safety to themselves, nor,
if they could, would it do anything but recoil on their own cause. In general, opinions contrary to those commonly received can only obtain a hearing by studied moderation of language, and the most cautious avoidance of
unnecessary offence, from which they hardly ever deviate even in a slight
degree without losing ground: while unmeasured vituperation employed on
the side of the prevailing opinion, really does deter people from professing
contrary opinions, and from listening to those who profess them. For the
interest, therefore, of truth and justice, it is far more important to restrain
this employment of vituperative language than the other; and, for example,
if it were necessary to choose, there would be much more need to discourage offensive attacks on infidelity, than on religion. It is, however, obvious
that law and authority have no business with restraining either, while
opinion ought, in every instance, to determine its verdict by the circumstances of the individual case; condemning every one, on whichever side
of the argument he places himself, in whose mode of advocacy either want
of candour, or malignity, bigotry, or intolerance of feeling manifest themselves; but not inferring these vices from the side which a person takes,
though it be the contrary side of the question to our own: and giving merited
honour to every one, whatever opinion he may hold, who has calmness to
see and honesty to state what his opponents and their opinions really are,
exaggerating nothing to their discredit, keeping nothing back which tells,
or can be supposed to tell, in their favour. This is the real morality of public
discussion: and if often violated, I am happy to think that there are many
controversialists who to a great extent observe it, and a still greater number
who conscientiously strive towards it.

*-*59¹, 59²   interest

CHAPTER III

Of Individuality, as One of the Elements of Well-Being

SUCH BEING THE REASONS which make it imperative that human beings should be free to form opinions, and to express their opinions without reserve; and such the baneful consequences to the intellectual, and through that to the moral nature of man, unless this liberty is either conceded, or asserted in spite of prohibition; let us next examine whether the same reasons do not require that men should be free to act upon their opinions—to carry these out in their lives, without hindrance, either physical or moral, from their fellow-men, so long as it is at their own risk and peril. This last proviso is of course indispensable. No one pretends that actions should be as free as opinions. On the contrary, even opinions lose their immunity, when the circumstances in which they are expressed are such as to constitute their expression a positive instigation to some mischievous act. An opinion that corn-dealers are starvers of the poor, or that private property is robbery, ought to be unmolested when simply circulated through the press, but may justly incur punishment when delivered orally to an excited mob assembled before the house of a corn-dealer, or when handed about among the same mob in the form of a placard. Acts, of whatever kind, which, without justifiable cause, do harm to others, may be, and in the more important cases absolutely require to be, controlled by the unfavourable sentiments, and, when needful, by the active interference of mankind. The liberty of the individual must be thus far limited; he must not make himself a nuisance to other people. But if he refrains from molesting others in what concerns them, and merely acts according to his own inclination and judgment in things which concern himself, the same reasons which show that opinion should be free, prove also that he should be allowed, without molestation, to carry his opinions into practice at his own cost. That mankind are not infallible; that their truths, for the most part, are only half-truths; that unity of opinion, unless resulting from the fullest and freest comparison of opposite opinions, is not desirable, and diversity not an evil, but a good, until mankind are much more capable than at present of recognising all sides of the truth, are principles applicable to men's modes of action, not less than to their opinions. As it is useful that while mankind are imperfect there should be different opinions, so is it that there should be different experiments of living; that free scope should be given to varieties of character, short of injury to others; and that the worth of different modes of life should be proved practically, when any one thinks fit to try them. It is desirable, in short, that in things which do not primarily concern others, individuality should assert itself. Where, not the person's own character, but the traditions or customs of other people are the rule of conduct, there is wanting one of the principal ingredients of human happiness, and quite the chief ingredient of individual and social progress.

In maintaining this principle, the greatest difficulty to be encountered does not lie in the appreciation of means towards an acknowledged end, but in the indifference of persons in general to the end itself. If it were felt that the free development of individuality is one of the leading essentials of well-being; that it is not only a co-ordinate element with all that is designated by the terms civilization, instruction, education, culture, but is itself a necessary part and condition of all those things; there would be no danger that liberty should be undervalued, and the adjustment of the boundaries between it and social control would present no extraordinary difficulty. But the evil is, that individual spontaneity is hardly recognised by the common modes of thinking, as having any intrinsic worth, or deserving any regard on its own account. The majority, being satisfied with the ways of mankind as they now are (for it is they who make them what they are), cannot comprehend why those ways should not be good enough for everybody; and what is more, spontaneity forms no part of the ideal of the majority of moral and social reformers, but is rather looked on with jealousy, as a troublesome and perhaps rebellious obstruction to the general acceptance of what these reformers, in their own judgment, think would be best for mankind. Few persons, out of Germany, even comprehend the meaning of the doctrine which Wilhelm Von Humboldt, so eminent both as a *savant* and as a politician, made the text of a treatise—that "the end of man, or that which is prescribed by the eternal or immutable dictates of reason, and not suggested by vague and transient desires, is the highest and most harmonious development of his powers to a complete and consistent whole;" that, therefore, the object "towards which every human being must ceaselessly direct his efforts, and on which especially those who design to influence their fellow-men must ever keep their eyes, is the individuality of power and development;" that for this there are two requisites, "freedom, and *a* variety of situations;" and that from the union of these arise "individual vigour and manifold diversity," which combine themselves in "originality."*

Little, however, as people are accustomed to a doctrine like that of Von

*The Sphere and Duties of Government, from the German of Baron Wilhelm von Humboldt, pp. 11, 13.

aSource, 591, 592   a

Humboldt, and surprising as it may be to them to find so high a value attached to individuality, the question, one must nevertheless think, can only be one of degree. No one's idea of excellence in conduct is that people should do absolutely nothing but copy one another. No one would assert that people ought not to put into their mode of life, and into the conduct of their concerns, any impress whatever of their own judgment, or of their own individual character. On the other hand, it would be absurd to pretend that people ought to live as if nothing whatever had been known in the world before they came into it; as if experience had as yet done nothing towards showing that one mode of existence, or of conduct, is preferable to another. Nobody denies that people should be so taught and trained in youth, as to know and benefit by the ascertained results of human experience. But it is the privilege and proper condition of a human being, arrived at the maturity of his faculties, to use and interpret experience in his own way. It is for him to find out what part of recorded experience is properly applicable to his own circumstances and character. The traditions and customs of other people are, to a certain extent, evidence of what their experience has taught *them*; presumptive evidence, and as such, have a claim to his deference: but, in the first place, their experience may be too narrow; or they may not have interpreted it rightly. Secondly, their interpretation of experience may be correct, but unsuitable to him. Customs are made for customary circumstances, and customary characters; and his circumstances or his character may be uncustomary. Thirdly, though the customs be both good as customs, and suitable to him, yet to conform to custom, merely *as* custom, does not educate or develope in him any of the qualities which are the distinctive endowment of a human being. The human faculties of perception, judgment, discriminative feeling, mental activity, and even moral preference, are exercised only in making a choice. He who does anything because it is the custom, makes no choice. He gains no practice either in discerning or in desiring what is best. The mental and moral, like the muscular powers, are improved only by being used. The faculties are called into no exercise by doing a thing merely because others do it, no more than by believing a thing only because others believe it. If the grounds of an opinion are not conclusive to the person's own reason, his reason cannot be strengthened, but is likely to be weakened, by his adopting it: and if the inducements to an act are not such as are consentaneous to his own feelings and character (where affection, or the rights of others, are not concerned) it is so much done towards rendering his feelings and character inert and torpid, instead of active and energetic.

He who lets the world, or his own portion of it, choose his plan of life for him, has no need of any other faculty than the ape-like one of imitation. He who chooses his plan for himself, employs all his faculties. He must use observation to see, reasoning and judgment to foresee, activity to gather materials for decision, discrimination to decide, and when he has decided, firmness and self-control to hold to his deliberate decision. And these qualities he requires and exercises exactly in proportion as the part of his conduct which he determines according to his own judgment and feelings is a large one. It is possible that he might be guided in some good path, and kept out of harm's way, without any of these things. But what will be his comparative worth as a human being? It really is of importance, not only what men do, but also what manner of men they are that do it. Among the works of man, which human life is rightly employed in perfecting and beautifying, the first in importance surely is man himself. Supposing it were possible to get houses built, corn grown, battles fought, causes tried, and even churches erected and prayers said, by machinery— by automatons in human form—it would be a considerable loss to exchange for these automatons even the men and women who at present inhabit the more civilized parts of the world, and who assuredly are but starved specimens of what nature can and will produce. Human nature is not a machine to be built after a model, and set to do exactly the work prescribed for it, but a tree, which requires to grow and develope itself on all sides, according to the tendency of the inward forces which make it a living thing.

It will probably be conceded that it is desirable people should exercise their understandings, and that an intelligent following of custom, or even occasionally an intelligent deviation from custom, is better than a blind and simply mechanical adhesion to it. To a certain extent it is admitted, that our understanding should be our own: but there is not the same willingness to admit that our desires and impulses should be our own likewise; or that to possess impulses of our own, and of any strength, is anything but a peril and a snare. Yet desires and impulses are as much a part of a perfect human being, as beliefs and restraints: and strong impulses are only perilous when not properly balanced; when one set of aims and inclinations is developed into strength, while others, which ought to co-exist with them, remain weak and inactive. It is not because men's desires are strong that they act ill; it is because their consciences are weak. There is no natural connexion between strong impulses and a weak conscience. The natural connexion is the other way. To say that one person's desires and feelings are stronger and more various than those of another, is merely to say that he has more of the raw material of human nature, and is therefore capable, perhaps of more evil, but certainly of more good. Strong impulses are but another name for energy. Energy may be turned to bad uses; but more good may always be made of an energetic nature, than of an indolent and impassive one. Those who have most natural feeling, are always those whose cultivated feelings may be made the strongest. The same strong susceptibilities which make the personal impulses vivid and powerful, are also the source from whence are generated the most passionate love of virtue, and the sternest self-control. It is through the cultivation of these, that society both does its duty and protects its interests: not by rejecting the stuff of which heroes are made, because it knows not how to make them. A person whose desires and impulses are his own—are the expression of his own nature, as it has been developed and modified by his own culture—is said to have a character. One whose desires and impulses are not his own, has no character, no more than a steam-engine has a character. If, in addition to being his own, his impulses are strong, and are under the government of a strong will, he has an energetic character. Whoever thinks that individuality of desires and impulses should not be encouraged to unfold itself, must maintain that society has no need of strong natures—is not the better for containing many persons who have much character—and that a high general average of energy is not desirable.

In some early states of society, these forces might be, and were, too much ahead of the power which society then possessed of disciplining and controlling them. There has been a time when the element of spontaneity and individuality was in excess, and the social principle had a hard struggle with it. The difficulty then was, to induce men of strong bodies or minds to pay obedience to any rules which required them to control their impulses. To overcome this difficulty, law and discipline, like the Popes struggling against the Emperors, asserted a power over the whole man, claiming to control all his life in order to control his character—which society had not found any other sufficient means of binding. But society has now fairly got the better of individuality; and the danger which threatens human nature is not the excess, but the deficiency, of personal impulses and preferences. Things are vastly changed, since the passions of those who were strong by station or by personal endowment were in a state of habitual rebellion against laws and ordinances, and required to be rigorously chained up to enable the persons within their reach to enjoy any particle of security. In our times, from the highest class of society down to the lowest, every one lives as under the eye of a hostile and dreaded censorship. Not only in what concerns others, but in what concerns only themselves, the individual or the family do not ask themselves—what do I prefer? or, what would suit my character and disposition? or, what would allow the best and highest in me to have fair play, and enable it to grow and thrive? They ask themselves, what is suitable to my position? what is usually done by persons of my station and pecuniary circumstances? or (worse still) what is usually done by persons of a station and circumstances superior to mine? I do not mean that they choose what is customary, in preference to what suits their own inclination. It does not occur to them to have any inclination, except for what is customary. Thus the mind itself is bowed to the yoke: even in what people do for pleasure, conformity is the first thing thought of; they like in crowds; they exercise choice only among things commonly done: peculiarity of taste, eccentricity of conduct, are shunned equally with crimes: until by dint of not following their own nature, they have no nature to follow: their human capacities are withered and starved: they become incapable of any strong wishes or native pleasures, and are generally without either opinions or feelings of home growth, or properly their own. Now is this, or is it not, the desirable condition of human nature?

It is so, on the Calvinistic theory. According to that, the one great offence of man is *b*self-will*b*. All the good of which humanity is capable, is comprised in *c*obedience*c*. You have no choice; thus you must do, and no otherwise: "whatever is not a duty, is a sin." Human nature being radically corrupt, there is no redemption for any one until human nature is killed within him. To one holding this theory of life, crushing out any of the human faculties, capacities, and susceptibilities, is no evil: man needs no capacity, but that of surrendering himself to the will of God: and if he uses any of his faculties for any other purpose but to do that supposed will more effectually, he is better without them. *d*This*d* is the theory of Calvinism; and it is held, in a mitigated form, by many who do not consider themselves Calvinists; the mitigation consisting in giving a less ascetic interpretation to the alleged will of God; asserting it to be his will that mankind should gratify some of their inclinations; of course not in the manner they themselves prefer, but in the way of obedience, that is, in a way prescribed to them by authority; and, therefore, by the necessary conditions of the case, the same for all.

In some such insidious form there is at present a strong tendency to this narrow theory of life, and to the pinched and hidebound type of human character which it patronizes. Many persons, no doubt, sincerely think that human beings thus cramped and dwarfed, are as their Maker designed them to be; just as many have thought that trees are a much finer thing when clipped into pollards, or cut out into figures of animals, than as nature made them. But if it be any part of religion to believe that man was made by a good *e*Being*e*, it is more consistent with that faith to believe, that this Being gave all human faculties that they might be cultivated and unfolded, not rooted out and consumed, and that he takes delight in every nearer approach made by his creatures to the ideal conception embodied in them, every increase in any of their capabilities of comprehension, of action, or of enjoyment. There is a different type of human excellence from the Calvinistic; a conception of humanity as having its nature bestowed on it for other purposes than merely

*b–b*591, 592 Self-will   *c–c*591, 592 Obedience
*d–d*591, 592 That   *e–e*591, 592 being

to be abnegated. "Pagan self-assertion" is one of the elements of human worth, as well as "Christian self-denial."* There is a Greek ideal of self-development, which the Platonic and Christian ideal of self-government blends with, but does not supersede. It may be better to be a John Knox than an Alcibiades, but it is better to be a Pericles than either; nor would a Pericles, if we had one in these days, be without anything good which belonged to John Knox.

It is not by wearing down into uniformity all that is individual in themselves, but by cultivating it and calling it forth, within the limits imposed by the rights and interests of others, that human beings become a noble and beautiful object of contemplation; and as the works partake the character of those who do them, by the same process human life also becomes rich, diversified, and animating, furnishing more abundant aliment to high thoughts and elevating feelings, and strengthening the tie which binds every individual to the race, by making the race infinitely better worth belonging to. In proportion to the development of his individuality, each person becomes more valuable to himself, and is therefore capable of being more valuable to others. There is a greater fulness of life about his own existence, and when there is more life in the units there is more in the mass which is composed of them. As much compression as is necessary to prevent the stronger specimens of human nature from encroaching on the rights of others, cannot be dispensed with; but for this there is ample compensation even in the point of view of human development. The means of development which the individual loses by being prevented from gratifying his inclinations to the injury of others, are chiefly obtained at the expense of the development of other people. And even to himself there is a full equivalent in the better development of the social part of his nature, rendered possible by the restraint put upon the selfish part. To be held to rigid rules of justice for the sake of others, developes the feelings and capacities which have the good of others for their object. But to be restrained in things not affecting their good, by their mere displeasure, developes nothing valuable, except such force of character as may unfold itself in resisting the restraint. If acquiesced in, it dulls and blunts the whole nature. To give any fair play to the nature of each, it is essential that different persons should be allowed to lead different lives. In proportion as this latitude has been exercised in any age, has that age been noteworthy to posterity. Even despotism does not produce its worst effects, so long as ʲindividualityʲ exists under it; and whatever crushes individuality is despotism, by whatever name it may be called, and whether it professes to be enforcing the will of God or the injunctions of men.

*[John] Sterling's *Essays*. ["Simonides," in *Essays and Tales*, ed. Julius Charles Hare, 2 vols. (London: Parker, 1848), Vol. I, p. 190.]

ʲ-ʲ591, 592   Individuality

Having said that Individuality is the same thing with development, and that it is only the cultivation of individuality which produces, or can produce, well-developed human beings, I might here close the argument: for what more or better can be said of any condition of human affairs, than that it brings human beings themselves nearer to the best thing they can be? or what worse can be said of any obstruction to good, than that it prevents this? Doubtless, however, these considerations will not suffice to convince those who most need convincing; and it is necessary further to show, that these developed human beings are of some use to the undeveloped—to point out to those who do not desire liberty, and would not avail themselves of it, that they may be in some intelligible manner rewarded for allowing other people to make use of it without hindrance.

In the first place, then, I would suggest that they might possibly learn something from them. It will not be denied by anybody, that originality is a valuable element in human affairs. There is always need of persons not only to discover new truths, and point out when what were once truths are true no longer, but also to commence new practices, and set the example of more enlightened conduct, and better taste and sense in human life. This cannot well be gainsaid by anybody who does not believe that the world has already attained perfection in all its ways and practices. It is true that this benefit is not capable of being rendered by everybody alike: there are but few persons, in comparison with the whole of mankind, whose experiments, if adopted by others, would be likely to be any improvement on established practice. But these few are the salt of the earth; without them, human life would become a stagnant pool. Not only is it they who introduce good things which did not before exist; it is they who keep the life in those which already existed. If there were nothing new to be done, would human intellect cease to be necessary? Would it be a reason why those who do the old things should forget why they are done, and do them like cattle, not like human beings? There is only too great a tendency in the best beliefs and practices to degenerate into the mechanical; and unless there were a succession of persons whose ever-recurring originality prevents the grounds of those beliefs and practices from becoming merely traditional, such dead matter would not resist the smallest shock from anything really alive, and there would be no reason why civilization should not die out, as in the Byzantine Empire. Persons of genius, it is true, are, and are always likely to be, a small minority; but in order to have them, it is necessary to preserve the soil in which they grow. Genius can only breathe freely in an *atmosphere* of freedom. Persons of genius are, *ex vi termini, more* individual than any other people—less capable, consequently, of fitting themselves, without hurtful compression, into any of the small number of moulds which society provides in order to save its members the trouble of forming their own character. If from timidity they consent to be forced into one of these moulds, and to let all that part of themselves which cannot expand under the pressure remain unexpanded, society will be little the better for their genius. If they are of a strong character, and break their fetters, they become a mark for the society which has not succeeded in reducing them to commonplace, to point at with solemn warning as "wild," "erratic," and the like; much as if one should complain of the Niagara river for not flowing smoothly between its banks like a Dutch canal.

I insist thus emphatically on the importance of genius, and the necessity of allowing it to unfold itself freely both in thought and in practice, being well aware that no one will deny the position in theory, but knowing also that almost every one, in reality, is totally indifferent to it. People think genius a fine thing if it enables a man to write an exciting poem, or paint a picture. But in its true sense, that of originality in thought and action, though no one says that it is not a thing to be admired, nearly all, at heart, think that they can do very well without it. Unhappily this is too natural to be wondered at. Originality is the one thing which unoriginal minds cannot feel the use of. They cannot see what it is to do for them: how should they? If they could see what it would do for them, it would not be originality. The first service which originality has to render them, is that of opening their eyes: which being once fully done, they would have a chance of being themselves original. Meanwhile, recollecting that nothing was ever yet done which some one was not the first to do, and that all good things which exist are the fruits of originality, let them be modest enough to believe that there is something still left for it to accomplish, and assure themselves that they are more in need of originality, the less they are conscious of the want.

In sober truth, whatever homage may be professed, or even paid, to real or supposed mental superiority, the general tendency of things throughout the world is to render mediocrity the ascendant power among mankind. In ancient history, in the middle ages, and in a diminishing degree through the long transition from feudality to the present time, the individual was a power in himself; and if he had either great talents or a high social position, he was a considerable power. At present individuals are lost in the crowd. In politics it is almost a triviality to say that public opinion now rules the world. The only power deserving the name is that of masses, and of governments while they make themselves the organ of the tendencies and instincts of masses. This is as true in the moral and social relations of private life as in public transactions. Those whose opinions go by the name of public opinion, are not always the same sort of public: in America they are the whole white population; in England, chiefly the middle class. But they are always a mass, that is to say, collective mediocrity. And what is a still greater novelty, the mass do not now take their opinions from dignitaries in Church or

State, from ostensible leaders, or from books. Their thinking is done for them by men much like themselves, addressing them or speaking in their name, on the spur of the moment, through the newspapers. I am not complaining of all this. I do not assert that anything better is compatible, as a general rule, with the present low state of the human mind. But that does not hinder the government of mediocrity from being mediocre government. No government by a democracy or a numerous aristocracy, either in its political acts or in the opinions, qualities, and tone of mind which it fosters, ever did or could rise above mediocrity, except in so far as the sovereign Many have let themselves be guided (which in their best times they always have done) by the counsels and influence of a more highly gifted and instructed One or Few. The initiation of all wise or noble things, comes and must come from individuals; generally at first from some one individual. The honour and glory of the average man is that he is capable of following that initiative; that he can respond internally to wise and noble things, and be led to them with his eyes open. I am not countenancing the sort of "hero-worship" which applauds the strong man of genius for forcibly seizing on the government of the world and making it do his bidding in spite of itself.[*] All he can claim is, freedom to point out the way. The power of compelling others into it, is not only inconsistent with the freedom and development of all the rest, but corrupting to the strong man himself. It does seem, however, that when the opinions of masses of merely average men are everywhere become or becoming the dominant power, the counterpoise and corrective to that tendency would be, the more and more pronounced individuality of those who stand on the higher eminences of thought. It is in these circumstances most especially, that exceptional individuals, instead of being deterred, should be encouraged in acting differently from the mass. In other times there was no advantage in their doing so, unless they acted not only differently, but better. In this age, the mere example of nonconformity, the mere refusal to bend the knee to custom, is itself a service. Precisely because the tyranny of opinion is such as to make eccentricity a reproach, it is desirable, in order to break through that tyranny, that people should be eccentric. Eccentricity has always abounded when and where strength of character has abounded; and the amount of eccentricity in a society has generally been proportional to the amount of genius, mental vigour, and moral courage which it contained. That so few now dare to be eccentric, marks the chief danger of the time.

I have said that it is important to give the freest scope possible to uncustomary things, in order that it may in time appear which of these are fit to be converted into customs. But independence of action, and disregard of

[*Undoubtedly a reference to Thomas Carlyle, *On Heroes, Hero-Worship, and the Heroic in History* (London: Fraser, 1841).]

custom, are not solely deserving of encouragement for the chance they afford that better modes of action, and customs more worthy of general adoption, may be struck out; nor is it only persons of decided mental superiority who have a just claim to carry on their lives in their own way. There is no reason that all human ^{g}existence^g should be constructed on some one or some small number of patterns. If a person possesses any tolerable amount of common sense and experience, his own mode of laying out his existence is the best, not because it is the best in itself, but because it is his own mode. Human beings are not like sheep; and even sheep are not undistinguishably alike. A man cannot get a coat or a pair of boots to fit him, unless they are either made to his measure, or he has a whole warehouseful to choose from: and is it easier to fit him with a life than with a coat, or are human beings more like one another in their whole physical and spiritual conformation than in the shape of their feet? If it were only that people have diversities of taste, that is reason enough for not attempting to shape them all after one model. But different persons also require different conditions for their spiritual development; and can no more exist healthily in the same moral, than all the variety of plants can in the same physical, atmosphere and climate. The same things which are helps to one person towards the cultivation of his higher nature, are hindrances to another. The same mode of life is a healthy excitement to one, keeping all his faculties of action and enjoyment in their best order, while to another it is a distracting burthen, which suspends or crushes all internal life. Such are the differences among human beings in their sources of pleasure, their susceptibilities of pain, and the operation on them of different physical and moral agencies, that unless there is a corresponding diversity in their modes of life, they neither obtain their fair share of happiness, nor grow up to the mental, moral, and aesthetic stature of which their nature is capable. Why then should tolerance, as far as the public sentiment is concerned, extend only to tastes and modes of life which extort acquiescence by the multitude of their adherents? Nowhere (except in some monastic institutions) is diversity of taste entirely unrecognised; a person may, without blame, either like or dislike rowing, or smoking, or music, or athletic exercises, or chess, or cards, or study, because both those who like each of these things, and those who dislike them, are too numerous to be put down. But the man, and still more the woman, who can be accused either of doing "what nobody does," or of not doing "what everybody does," is the subject of as much depreciatory remark as if he or she had committed some grave moral delinquency. Persons require to possess a title, or some other badge of rank, or of the consideration of people of rank, to be able to indulge somewhat in the luxury of doing as they like without detriment to their estimation. To indulge somewhat, I repeat: for whoever allow themselves much

$^{g\text{-}g}$591, 592   existences

of that indulgence, incur the risk of something worse than disparaging speeches—they are in peril of a commission *de lunatico*, and of having their property taken from them and given to their relations.*

There is one characteristic of the present direction of public opinion, peculiarly calculated to make it intolerant of any marked demonstration of individuality. The general average of mankind are not only moderate in intellect, but also moderate in inclinations: they have no tastes or wishes strong enough to incline them to do anything unusual, and they consequently do not understand those who have, and class all such with the wild and intemperate whom they are accustomed to look down upon. Now, in addition to this fact which is general, we have only to suppose that a strong movement has set in towards the improvement of morals, and it is evident what we have to expect. In these days such a movement has set in; much has actually been effected in the way of increased regularity of conduct, and discouragement of excesses; and there is a philanthropic spirit abroad, for the exercise of which there is no more inviting field than the moral and prudential improvement of our fellow-creatures. These tendencies of the times cause the public to be more disposed than at most former periods to prescribe general rules of conduct, and endeavour to make every one conform to the approved standard. And that standard, express or tacit, is to desire nothing strongly. Its ideal of character is to be without any marked character; to maim by compression, like a Chinese lady's foot, every part of

*There is something both contemptible and frightful in the sort of evidence on which, of late years, any person can be judicially declared unfit for the management of his affairs; and after his death, his disposal of his property can be set aside, if there is enough of it to pay the expenses of litigation—which are charged on the property itself. All the minute details of his daily life are pried into, and whatever is found which, seen through the medium of the perceiving and describing faculties of the lowest of the low, bears an appearance unlike absolute commonplace, is laid before the jury as evidence of insanity, and often with success; the jurors being little, if at all, less vulgar and ignorant than the witnesses; while the judges, with that extraordinary want of knowledge of human nature and life which continually astonishes us in English lawyers, often help to mislead them. These trials speak volumes as to the state of feeling and opinion among the vulgar with regard to human liberty. So far from setting any value on individuality—so far from respecting the *h*right*h* of each individual to act, in things indifferent, as seems good to his own judgment and inclinations, judges and juries cannot even conceive that a person in a state of sanity can desire such freedom. In former days, when it was proposed to burn atheists, charitable people used to suggest putting them in a mad-house instead: it would be nothing surprising now-a-days were we to see this done, and the doers applauding themselves, because, instead of persecuting for religion, they had adopted so humane and Christian a mode of treating these unfortunates, not without a silent satisfaction at their having thereby obtained their deserts.

*h–h*591, 592   rights

human nature which stands out prominently, and tends to make the person markedly dissimilar in outline to commonplace humanity.

As is usually the case with ideals which exclude one-half of what is desirable, the present standard of approbation produces only an inferior imitation of the other half. Instead of great energies guided by vigorous reason, and strong feelings strongly controlled by a conscientious will, its result is weak feelings and weak energies, which therefore can be kept in outward conformity to rule without any strength either of will or of reason. Already energetic characters on any large scale are becoming merely traditional. There is now scarcely any outlet for energy in this country except business. The energy expended in *this* may still be regarded as considerable. What little is left from that employment, is expended on some hobby; which may be a useful, even a philanthropic hobby, but is always some one thing, and generally a thing of small dimensions. The greatness of England is now all collective: individually small, we only appear capable of anything great by our habit of combining; and with this our moral and religious philanthropists are perfectly contented. But it was men of another stamp than this that made England what it has been; and men of another stamp will be needed to prevent its decline.

The despotism of custom is everywhere the standing hindrance to human advancement, being in unceasing antagonism to that disposition to aim at something better than customary, which is called, according to circumstances, the spirit of liberty, or that of progress or improvement. The spirit of improvement is not always a spirit of liberty, for it may aim at forcing improvements on an unwilling people; and the spirit of liberty, in so far as it resists such attempts, may ally itself locally and temporarily with the opponents of improvement; but the only unfailing and permanent source of improvement is liberty, since by it there are as many possible independent centres of improvement as there are individuals. The progressive principle, however, in either shape, whether as the love of liberty or of improvement, is antagonistic to the sway of Custom, involving at least emancipation from that yoke; and the contest between the two constitutes the chief interest of the history of mankind. The greater part of the world has, properly speaking, no history, because the despotism of Custom is complete. This is the case over the whole East. Custom is there, in all things, the final appeal; justice and right mean conformity to custom; the argument of custom no one, unless some tyrant intoxicated with power, thinks of resisting. And we see the result. Those nations must once have had originality; they did not start out of the ground populous, lettered, and versed in many of the arts of life; they made themselves all this, and were then the greatest and most powerful nations *of* the

*i-i*591, 592   that
*j-j*591, 592   in

world. What are they now? The subjects or dependents of tribes whose fore-fathers wandered in the forests when theirs had magnificent palaces and gorgeous temples, but over whom custom exercised only a divided rule with liberty and progress. A people, it appears, may be progressive for a certain length of time, and then stop: when does it stop? When it ceases to possess individuality. If a similar change should befall the nations of Europe, it will not be in exactly the same shape: the despotism of custom with which these nations are threatened is not precisely stationariness. It proscribes singularity, but it does not preclude change, provided all change together. We have discarded the fixed costumes of our forefathers; every one must still dress like other people, but the fashion may change once or twice a year. We thus take care that when there is change it shall be for change's sake, and not from any idea of beauty or convenience; for the same idea of beauty or convenience would not strike all the world at the same moment, and be simultaneously thrown aside by all at another moment. But we are progressive as well as changeable: we continually make new inventions in mechanical things, and keep them until they are again superseded by better; we are eager for improvement in politics, in education, even in morals, though in this last our idea of improvement chiefly consists in persuading or forcing other people to be as good as ourselves. It is not progress that we object to; on the contrary, we flatter ourselves that we are the most progressive people who ever lived. It is individuality that we war against: we should think we had done wonders if we had made ourselves all alike; forgetting that the unlikeness of one person to another is generally the first thing which draws the attention of either to the imperfection of his own type, and the superiority of another, or the possibility, by combining the advantages of both, of producing something better than either. We have a warning example in China—a nation of much talent, and, in some respects, even wisdom, owing to the rare good fortune of having been provided at an early period with a particularly good set of customs, the work, in some measure, of men to whom even the most enlightened European must accord, under certain limitations, the title of sages and philosophers. They are remarkable, too, in the excellence of their apparatus for impressing, as far as possible, the best wisdom they possess upon every mind in the community, and securing that those who have appropriated most of it shall occupy the posts of honour and power. Surely the people who did this have discovered the secret of human progressiveness, and must have kept themselves steadily at the head of the movement of the world. On the contrary, they have become stationary—have remained so for thousands of years; and if they are ever to be farther improved, it must be by foreigners. They have succeeded beyond all hope in what English philanthropists are so industriously working at—in making a people all alike, all governing their thoughts and conduct by the same maxims and rules; and these are the fruits. The modern *régime* of public opinion is, in an unorganized form, what the Chinese educational and political systems are in an organized; and unless individuality shall be able successfully to assert itself against this yoke, Europe, notwithstanding its noble antecedents and its professed Christianity, will tend to become another China.

What is it that has hitherto preserved Europe from this lot? What has made the European family of nations an improving, instead of a stationary portion of mankind? Not any superior excellence in them, which, when it exists, exists as the effect, not as the cause; but their remarkable diversity of character and culture. Individuals, classes, nations, have been extremely unlike one another: they have struck out a great variety of paths, each leading to something valuable; and although at every period those who travelled in different paths have been intolerant of one another, and each would have thought it an excellent thing if all the rest could have been compelled to travel his road, their attempts to thwart each other's development have rarely had any permanent success, and each has in time endured to receive the good which the others have offered. Europe is, in my judgment, wholly indebted to this plurality of paths for its progressive and many-sided development. But it already begins to possess this benefit in a considerably less degree. It is decidedly advancing towards the Chinese ideal of making all people alike. M. de Tocqueville, in his last important work, remarks how much more the Frenchmen of the present day resemble one another, than did those even of the last generation.[*] The same remark might be made of Englishmen in a far greater degree. In a passage already quoted from Wilhelm von Humboldt,[†] he points out two things as necessary conditions of human development, because necessary to render people unlike one another; namely, freedom, and variety of situations. The second of these two conditions is in this country every day diminishing. The circumstances which surround different classes and individuals, and shape their characters, are daily becoming more assimilated. Formerly, different ranks, different neighbourhoods, different trades and professions, lived in what might be called different worlds; at present, to a great degree in the same. Comparatively speaking, they now read the same things, listen to the same things, see the same things, go to the same places, have their hopes and fears directed to the same objects, have the same rights and liberties, and the same means of asserting them. Great as are the differences of position which remain, they are nothing to those which have ceased. And the assimilation is still proceeding. All the political changes of the age promote it, since they all tend to raise the low and to lower the high. Every extension of education promotes it, because education brings people under common influences, and gives them access to the general stock

[*See Alexis de Tocqueville, *L'Ancien régime* (Paris: Lévy, 1856), p. 119.]
[†See above, p. 261.]

of facts and sentiments. Improvements in the means of communication promote it, by bringing the inhabitants of distant places into personal contact,
and keeping up a rapid flow of changes of residence between one place and
another. The increase of commerce and manufactures promotes it, by diffusing more widely the advantages of easy circumstances, and opening all
objects of ambition, even the highest, to general competition, whereby the
desire of rising becomes no longer the character of a particular class, but of
all classes. A more powerful agency than even all these, in bringing about a
general similarity among mankind, is the complete establishment, in this and
other free countries, of the ascendancy of public opinion in the State. As the
various social eminences which enabled persons entrenched on them to
disregard the opinion of the multitude, gradually become levelled; as the
very idea of resisting the will of the public, when it is positively known that
they have a will, disappears more and more from the minds of practical
politicians; there ceases to be any social support for nonconformity—any
substantive power in society, which, itself opposed to the ascendancy of
numbers, is interested in taking under its protection opinions and tendencies
at variance with those of the public.

The combination of all these causes forms so great a mass of influences
hostile to Individuality, that it is not easy to see how it can stand its ground.
It will do so with increasing difficulty, unless the intelligent part of the public
can be made to feel its value—to see that it is good there should be differences, even though not for the better, even though, as it may appear to them,
some should be for the worse. If the claims of Individuality are ever to be
asserted, the time is now, while much is still wanting to complete the
enforced assimilation. It is only in the earlier stages that any stand can be
successfully made against the encroachment. The demand that all other
people shall resemble ourselves, grows by what it feeds on. If resistance waits
till life is reduced *nearly* to one uniform type, all deviations from that type
will come to be considered impious, immoral, even monstrous and contrary
to nature. Mankind speedily become unable to conceive diversity, when they
have been for some time unaccustomed to see it.

CHAPTER IV

Of the Limits to the Authority of Society over the Individual

WHAT, THEN, is the rightful limit to the sovereignty of the individual over himself? Where does the authority of society begin? How much of human life should be assigned to individuality, and how much to society?

Each will receive its proper share, if each has that which more particularly concerns it. To individuality should belong the part of life in which it is chiefly the individual that is interested; to society, the part which chiefly interests society.

Though society is not founded on a contract, and though no good purpose is answered by inventing a contract in order to deduce social obligations from it, every one who receives the protection of society owes a return for the benefit, and the fact of living in society renders it indispensable that each should be bound to observe a certain line of conduct towards the rest. This conduct consists first, in not injuring the interests of one another; or rather certain interests, which, either by express legal provision or by tacit understanding, ought to be considered as rights; and secondly, in each person's bearing his share (to be fixed on some equitable principle) of the labours and sacrifices incurred for defending the society or its members from injury and molestation. These conditions society is justified in enforcing at all costs to those who endeavour to withhold fulfilment. Nor is this all that society may do. The acts of an individual may be hurtful to others, or wanting in due consideration for their welfare, without going the length of violating any of their constituted rights. The offender may then be justly punished by opinion, though not by law. As soon as any part of a person's conduct affects prejudicially the interests of others, society has jurisdiction over it, and the question whether the general welfare will or will not be promoted by interfering with it, becomes open to discussion. But there is no room for entertaining any such question when a person's conduct affects the interests of no persons besides himself, or needs not affect them unless they like (all the persons concerned being of full age, and the ordinary amount of understanding). In all such cases there should be perfect freedom, legal and social, to do the action and stand the consequences.

It would be a great misunderstanding of this doctrine to suppose that it is one of selfish indifference, which pretends that human beings have no business with each other's conduct in life, and that they should not concern themselves about the well-doing or well-being of one another, unless their own interest is involved. Instead of any diminution, there is need of a great increase of disinterested exertion to promote the good of others. But disinterested benevolence can find other instruments to persuade people to their good, than whips and scourges, either of the literal or the metaphorical sort. I am the last person to undervalue the self-regarding virtues; they are only second in importance, if even second, to the social. It is equally the business of education to cultivate both. But even education works by conviction and persuasion as well as by compulsion, and it is by the former only that, when the period of education is past, the self-regarding virtues should be inculcated. Human beings owe to each other help to distinguish the better from the worse, and encouragement to choose the former and avoid the latter. They should be for ever stimulating each other to increased exercise of their higher faculties, and increased direction of their feelings and aims towards wise instead of foolish, elevating instead of degrading, objects and contemplations. But neither one person, nor any number of persons, is warranted in saying to another human creature of ripe years, that he shall not do with his life for his own benefit what he chooses to do with it. He is the person most interested in his own well-being: the interest which any other person, except in cases of strong personal attachment, can have in it, is trifling, compared with that which he himself has; the interest which society has in him individually (except as to his conduct to others) is fractional, and altogether indirect: while, with respect to his own feelings and circumstances, the most ordinary man or woman has means of knowledge immeasurably surpassing those that can be possessed by any one else. The interference of society to overrule his judgment and purposes in what only regards himself, must be grounded on general presumptions; which may be altogether wrong, and even if right, are as likely as not to be misapplied to individual cases, by persons no better acquainted with the circumstances of such cases than those are who look at them merely from without. In this department, therefore, of human affairs, Individuality has its proper field of action. In the conduct of human beings towards one another, it is necessary that general rules should for the most part be observed, in order that people may know what they have to expect; but in each person's own concerns, his individual spontaneity is entitled to free exercise. Considerations to aid his judgment, exhortations to strengthen his will, may be offered to him, even obtruded on him, by others; but he himself is the final judge. All errors which he is likely to commit against advice and warning, are far outweighed by the evil of allowing others to constrain him to what they deem his good.

I do not mean that the feelings with which a person is regarded by others, ought not to be in any way affected by his self-regarding qualities or deficiencies. This is neither possible nor desirable. If he is eminent in any of the qualities which conduce to his own good, he is, so far, a proper object of admiration. He is so much the nearer to the ideal perfection of human nature. If he is grossly deficient in those qualities, a sentiment the opposite of admiration will follow. There is a degree of folly, and a degree of what may be called (though the phrase is not unobjectionable) lowness or depravation of taste, which, though it cannot justify doing harm to the person who manifests it, renders him necessarily and properly a subject of distaste, or, in extreme cases, even of contempt: a person could not have the opposite qualities in due strength without entertaining these feelings. Though doing no wrong to any one, a person may so act as to compel us to judge him, and feel to him, as a fool, or as a being of an inferior order: and since this judgment and feeling are a fact which he would prefer to avoid, it is doing him a service to warn him of it beforehand, as of any other disagreeable consequence to which he exposes himself. It would be well, indeed, if this good office were much more freely rendered than the common notions of politeness at present permit, and if one person could honestly point out to another that he thinks him in fault, without being considered unmannerly or presuming. We have a right, also, in various ways, to act upon our unfavourable opinion of any one, not to the oppression of his individuality, but in the exercise of ours. We are not bound, for example, to seek his society; we have a right to avoid it (though not to parade the avoidance), for we have a right to choose the society most acceptable to us. We have a right, and it may be our duty, to caution others against him, if we think his example or conversation likely to have a pernicious effect on those with whom he associates. We may give others a preference over him in optional good offices, except those which tend to his improvement. In these various modes a person may suffer very severe penalties at the hands of others, for faults which directly concern only himself; but he suffers these penalties only in so far as they are the natural, and, as it were, the spontaneous consequences of the faults themselves, not because they are purposely inflicted on him for the sake of punishment. A person who shows rashness, obstinacy, self-conceit—who cannot live within moderate means—who cannot restrain himself from hurtful indulgences—who pursues animal pleasures at the expense of those of feeling and intellect—must expect to be lowered in the opinion of others, and to have a less share of their favourable sentiments; but of this he has no right to complain, unless he has merited their favour by special excellence in his social relations, and has thus established a title to their good offices, which is not affected by his demerits towards himself.

What I contend for is, that the inconveniences which are strictly inseparable from the unfavourable judgment of others, are the only ones to which a person should ever be subjected for that portion of his conduct and character which concerns his own good, but which does not affect the interests of others in their relations with him. Acts injurious to others require a totally different treatment. Encroachment on their rights; infliction on them of any loss or damage not justified by his own rights; falsehood or duplicity in dealing with them; unfair or ungenerous use of advantages over them; even selfish abstinence from defending them against injury—these are fit objects of moral reprobation, and, in grave cases, of moral retribution and punishment. And not only these acts, but the dispositions which lead to them, are properly immoral, and fit subjects of disapprobation which may rise to abhorrence. Cruelty of disposition; malice and ill-nature; that most anti-social and odious of all passions, envy; dissimulation and insincerity; irascibility on insufficient cause, and resentment disproportioned to the provocation; the love of domineering over others; the desire to engross more than one's share of advantages (the πλεονεξια of the Greeks); the pride which derives gratification from the abasement of others; the egotism which thinks self and its concerns more important than everything else, and decides all doubtful questions in its own favour;—these are moral vices, and consti-tute a bad and odious moral character: unlike the self-regarding faults pre-viously mentioned, which are not properly immoralities, and to whatever pitch they may be carried, do not constitute wickedness. They may be proofs of any amount of folly, or want of personal dignity and self-respect; but they are only a subject of moral reprobation when they involve a breach of duty to others, for whose sake the individual is bound to have care for himself. What are called duties to ourselves are not socially obligatory, unless cir-cumstances render them at the same time duties to others. The term duty to oneself, when it means anything more than prudence, means self-respect or self-development; and for none of these is any one accountable to his fellow creatures, because for none of them is it for the good of mankind that he be held accountable to them.

The distinction between the loss of consideration which a person may rightly incur by defect of prudence or of personal dignity, and the reproba-tion which is due to him for an offence against the rights of others, is not a merely nominal distinction. It makes a vast difference both in our feelings and in our conduct towards him, whether he displeases us in things in which we think we have a right to control him, or in things in which we know that we have not. If he displeases us, we may express our distaste, and we may stand aloof from a person as well as from a thing that displeases us; but we shall not therefore feel called on to make his life uncomfortable. We shall reflect that he already bears, or will bear, the whole penalty of his error; if he spoils his life by mismanagement, we shall not, for that reason, desire to spoil it still further: instead of wishing to punish him, we shall rather endeavour to alleviate his punishment, by showing him how he may avoid or cure the evils his conduct tends to bring upon him. He may be to us an object of pity, perhaps of dislike, but not of anger or resentment; we shall not treat him like an enemy of society: the worst we shall think ourselves justified in doing is leaving him to himself, if we do not interfere benevolently by showing interest or concern for him. It is far otherwise if he has infringed the rules necessary for the protection of his fellow-creatures, individually or collectively. The evil consequences of his acts do not then fall on himself, but on others; and society, as the protector of all its members, must retaliate on him; must inflict pain on him for the express purpose of punishment, and must take care that it be sufficiently severe. In the one case, he is an offender at our bar, and we are called on not only to sit in judgment on him, but, in one shape or another, to execute our own sentence: in the other case, it is not our part to inflict any suffering on him, except what may incidentally follow from our using the same liberty in the regulation of our own affairs, which we allow to him in his.

The distinction here pointed out between the part of a person's life which concerns only himself, and that which concerns others, many persons will refuse to admit. How (it may be asked) can any part of the conduct of a member of society be a matter of indifference to the other members? No person is an entirely isolated being; it is impossible for a person to do anything seriously or permanently hurtful to himself, without mischief reaching at least to his near connexions, and often far beyond them. If he injures his property, he does harm to those who directly or indirectly derived support from it, and usually diminishes, by a greater or less amount, the general resources of the community. If he deteriorates his bodily or mental faculties, he not only brings evil upon all who depended on him for any portion of their happiness, but disqualifies himself for rendering the services which he owes to his fellow-creatures generally; perhaps becomes a burthen on their affection or benevolence; and if such conduct were very frequent, hardly any offence that is committed would detract more from the general sum of good. Finally, if by his vices or follies a person does no direct harm to others, he is nevertheless (it may be said) injurious by his example; and ought to be compelled to control himself, for the sake of those whom the sight or knowledge of his conduct might corrupt or mislead.

And even (it will be added) if the consequences of misconduct could be confined to the vicious or thoughtless individual, ought society to abandon to their own guidance those who are manifestly unfit for it? If protection against themselves is confessedly due to children and persons under age, is not society equally bound to afford it to persons of mature years who are equally incapable of self-government? If gambling, or drunkenness, or incontinence, or idleness, or uncleanliness, are as injurious to happiness, and as great a hindrance to improvement, as many or most of the acts prohibited by law, why (it may be asked) should not law, so far as is consistent with practicability and social convenience, endeavour to repress these also? And as a supplement to the unavoidable imperfections of law, ought not opinion at least to organize a powerful police against these vices, and visit rigidly with social penalties those who are known to practise them? There is no question here (it may be said) about restricting individuality, or impeding the trial of new and original experiments in living. The only things it is sought to prevent are things which have been tried and condemned from the beginning of the world until now; things which experience has shown not to be useful or suitable to any person's individuality. There must be some length of time and amount of experience, after which a moral or prudential truth may be regarded as established: and it is merely desired to prevent generation after generation from falling over the same precipice which has been fatal to their predecessors.

I fully admit that the mischief which a person does to himself may seriously affect, both through their sympathies and their interests, those nearly connected with him, and in a minor degree, society at large. When, by conduct of this sort, a person is led to violate a distinct and assignable obligation to any other person or persons, the case is taken out of the self-regarding class, and becomes amenable to moral disapprobation in the proper sense of the term. If, for example, a man, through intemperance or extravagance, becomes unable to pay his debts, or, having undertaken the moral responsibility of a family, becomes from the same cause incapable of supporting or educating them, he is deservedly reprobated, and might be justly punished; but it is for the breach of duty to his family or creditors, not for the extravagance. If the resources which ought to have been devoted to them, had been diverted from them for the most prudent investment, the moral culpability would have been the same. George Barnwell murdered his uncle to get money for his mistress, but if he had done it to set himself up in business, he would equally have been hanged.[*] Again, in the frequent case of a man who causes grief to his family by addiction to bad habits, he deserves reproach for his unkindness or ingratitude; but so he may for cultivating habits not in themselves vicious, if they are painful to those with whom he passes his life, or who from personal ties are dependent on him for their comfort. Whoever fails in the consideration generally due to the interests and feelings of others, not being compelled by some more imperative duty, or justified by allowable self-preference, is a subject of moral disapprobation for that failure, but not for the cause of it, nor for the errors, merely personal to himself, which may have remotely led to it. In like

[*See George Lillo, *The London Merchant: or, the History of George Barnwell* (London: Gray, 1731).]

manner, when a person disables himself, by conduct purely self-regarding, from the performance of some definite duty incumbent on him to the public, he is guilty of a social offence. No person ought to be punished simply for being drunk; but a soldier or a policeman should be punished for being drunk on duty. Whenever, in short, there is a definite damage, or a definite risk of damage, either to an individual or to the public, the case is taken out of the province of liberty, and placed in that of morality or law.

But with regard to the merely contingent, or, as it may be called, constructive injury which a person causes to society, by conduct which neither violates any specific duty to the public, nor occasions perceptible hurt to any assignable individual except himself; the inconvenience is one which society can afford to bear, for the sake of the greater good of human freedom. If grown persons are to be punished for not taking proper care of themselves, I would rather it were for their own sake, than under pretence of preventing them from impairing their capacity of rendering to society benefits which society does not pretend it has a right to exact. But I cannot consent to argue the point as if society had no means of bringing its weaker members up to its ordinary standard of rational conduct, except waiting till they do something irrational, and then punishing them, legally or morally, for it. Society has had absolute power over them during all the early portion of their existence: it has had the whole period of childhood and nonage in which to try whether it could make them capable of rational conduct in life. The existing generation is master both of the training and the entire circumstances of the generation to come; it cannot indeed make them perfectly wise and good, because it is itself so lamentably deficient in goodness and wisdom; and its best efforts are not always, in individual cases, its most successful ones; but it is perfectly well able to make the rising generation, as a whole, as good as, and a little better than, itself. If society lets any considerable number of its members grow up mere children, incapable of being acted on by rational consideration of distant motives, society has itself to blame for the consequences. Armed not only with all the powers of education, but with the ascendancy which the authority of a received opinion always exercises over the minds who are least fitted to judge for themselves; and aided by the *natural* penalties which cannot be prevented from falling on those who incur the distaste or the contempt of those who know them; let not society pretend that it needs, besides all this, the power to issue commands and enforce obedience in the personal concerns of individuals, in which, on all principles of justice and policy, the decision ought to rest with those who are to abide the consequences. Nor is there anything which tends more to discredit and frustrate the better means of influencing conduct, than a resort to the worse. If there be among those whom it is attempted to coerce into prudence or temperance, any of the material of which vigorous and independent characters are made, they will infallibly rebel against the yoke. No such person will ever feel that others have a right to control him in his concerns, such as they have to prevent him from injuring them in theirs; and it easily comes to be considered a mark of spirit and courage to fly in the face of such usurped authority, and do with ostentation the exact opposite of what it enjoins; as in the fashion of grossness which succeeded, in the time of Charles II, to the fanatical moral intolerance of the Puritans. With respect to what is said of the necessity of protecting society from the bad example set to others by the vicious or the self-indulgent; it is true that bad example may have a pernicious effect, especially the example of doing wrong to others with impunity to the wrong-doer. But we are now speaking of conduct which, while it does no wrong to others, is supposed to do great harm to the agent himself: and I do not see how those who believe this, can think otherwise than that the example, on the whole, must be more salutary than hurtful, since, if it displays the misconduct, it displays also the painful or degrading consequences which, if the conduct is justly censured, must be supposed to be in all or most cases attendant on it.

But the strongest of all the arguments against the interference of the public with purely personal conduct, is that when it does interfere, the odds are that it interferes wrongly, and in the wrong place. On questions of social morality, of duty to others, the opinion of the public, that is, of an overruling majority, though often wrong, is likely to be still oftener right; because on such questions they are only required to judge of their own interests; of the manner in which some mode of conduct, if allowed to be practised, would affect themselves. But the opinion of a similar majority, imposed as a law on the minority, on questions of self-regarding conduct, is quite as likely to be wrong as right; for in these cases public opinion means, at the best, some people's opinion of what is good or bad for other people; while very often it does not even mean that; the public, with the most perfect indifference, passing over the pleasure or convenience of those whose conduct they censure, and considering only their own preference. There are many who consider as an injury to themselves any conduct which they have a distaste for, and resent it as an outrage to their feelings; as a religious bigot, when charged with disregarding the religious feelings of others, has been known to retort that they disregard his feelings, by persisting in their abominable worship or creed. But there is no parity between the feeling of a person for his own opinion, and the feeling of another who is offended at his holding it; no more than between the desire of a thief to take a purse, and the desire of the right owner to keep it. And a person's taste is as much his own peculiar concern as his opinion or his purse. It is easy for any one to imagine an ideal public, which leaves the freedom and choice of individuals in all uncertain matters undisturbed, and only requires them to abstain from modes of conduct which universal experience has condemned. But where has there been seen a public which set any such limit to its censorship? or when does the public trouble itself about universal experience? In its interferences with personal conduct it is seldom thinking of anything but the enormity of acting or feeling differently from itself; and this standard of judgment, thinly disguised, is held up to mankind as the dictate of religion and philosophy, by nine-tenths of all moralists and speculative writers. These teach that things are right because they are right; because we feel them to be so. They tell us to search in our own minds and hearts for laws of conduct binding on ourselves and on all others. What can the poor public do but apply these instructions, and make their own personal feelings of good and evil, if they are tolerably unanimous in them, obligatory on all the world?

The evil here pointed out is not one which exists only in theory; and it may perhaps be expected that I should specify the instances in which the public of this age and country improperly invests its own preferences with the character of moral laws. I am not writing an essay on the aberrations of existing moral feeling. That is too weighty a subject to be discussed parenthetically, and by way of illustration. Yet examples are necessary, to show that the principle I maintain is of serious and practical moment, and that I am not endeavouring to erect a barrier against imaginary evils. And it is not difficult to show, by abundant instances, that to extend the bounds of what may be called moral police, until it encroaches on the most unquestionably legitimate liberty of the individual, is one of the most universal of all human propensities.

As a first instance, consider the antipathies which men cherish on no better grounds than that persons whose religious opinions are different from theirs, do not practise their religious observances, especially their religious abstinences. To cite a rather trivial example, nothing in the creed or practice of Christians does more to envenom the hatred of Mahomedans against them, than the fact of their eating pork. There are few acts which Christians and Europeans regard with more unaffected disgust, than Mussulmans regard this particular mode of satisfying hunger. It is, in the first place, an offence against their religion; but this circumstance by no means explains either the degree or the kind of their repugnance; for wine also is forbidden by their religion, and to partake of it is by all Mussulmans accounted wrong, but not disgusting. Their aversion to the flesh of the "unclean beast" is, on the contrary, of that peculiar character, resembling an instinctive antipathy, which the idea of uncleanness, when once it thoroughly sinks into the feelings, seems always to excite even in those whose personal habits are anything but scrupulously cleanly, and of which the sentiment of religious impurity, so intense in the Hindoos, is a remarkable example. Suppose now that in a people, of whom the majority were Mussulmans, that majority should insist upon not permitting pork to be eaten within the limits of the country. This would be nothing new in Mahomedan countries.* Would it be a legitimate exercise of the moral authority of public opinion? and if not, why not? The practice is really revolting to such a public. They also sincerely think that it is forbidden and abhorred by the Deity. Neither could the prohibition be censured as religious persecution. It might be religious in its origin, but it would not be persecution for religion, since nobody's religion makes it a duty to eat pork. The only tenable ground of condemnation would be, that with the personal tastes and self-regarding concerns of individuals the public has no business to interfere.

To come somewhat nearer home: the majority of Spaniards consider it a gross impiety, offensive in the highest degree to the Supreme Being, to worship him in any other manner than the Roman Catholic; and no other public worship is lawful on Spanish soil. The people of all Southern Europe look upon a married clergy as not only irreligious, but unchaste, indecent, gross, disgusting. What do Protestants think of these perfectly sincere feelings, and of the attempt to enforce them against non-Catholics? Yet, if mankind are justified in interfering with each other's liberty in things which do not concern the interests of others, on what principle is it possible consistently to exclude these cases? or who can blame people for desiring to suppress what they regard as a scandal in the sight of God and man? No stronger case can be shown for prohibiting anything which is regarded as a personal immorality, than is made out for suppressing these practices in the eyes of those who regard them as impieties; and unless we are willing to adopt the logic of persecutors, and to say that we may persecute others because we are right, and that they must not persecute us because they are wrong, we must beware of admitting a principle of which we should resent as a gross injustice the application to ourselves.

The preceding instances may be objected to, although unreasonably, as drawn from contingencies impossible among us: opinion, in this country, not being likely to enforce abstinence from meats, or to interfere with people for worshipping, and for either marrying or not marrying, according to

---

*The case of the Bombay Parsees is a curious instance in point. When this industrious and enterprising tribe, the descendants of the Persian fire-worshippers, flying from their native country before the Caliphs, arrived in Western India, they were admitted to toleration by the Hindoo sovereigns, on condition of not eating beef. When those regions afterwards fell under the dominion of Mahomedan conquerors, the Parsees obtained from them a continuance of indulgence, on condition of refraining from pork. What was at first obedience to authority became a second nature, and the Parsees to this day abstain both from beef and pork. Though not required by their religion, the double abstinence has had time to grow into a custom of their tribe; and custom, in the East, is a religion.

their creed or inclination. The next example, however, shall be taken from an interference with liberty which we have by no means passed all danger of. Wherever the Puritans have been sufficiently powerful, as in New England, and in Great Britain at the time of the Commonwealth, they have endeavoured, with considerable success, to put down all public, and nearly all private, amusements: especially music, dancing, public games, or other assemblages for purposes of diversion, and the theatre. There are still in this country large bodies of persons by whose notions of morality and religion these recreations are condemned; and those persons belonging chiefly to the middle class, who are the ascendant power in the present social and political condition of the kingdom, it is by no means impossible that persons of these sentiments may at some time or other command a majority in Parliament. How will the remaining portion of the community like to have the amusements that shall be permitted to them regulated by the religious and moral sentiments of the stricter Calvinists and Methodists? Would they not, with considerable peremptoriness, desire these intrusively pious members of society to mind their own business? This is precisely what should be said to every government and every public, who have the pretension that no person shall enjoy any pleasure which they think wrong. But if the principle of the pretension be admitted, no one can reasonably object to its being acted on in the sense of the majority, or other preponderating power in the country; and all persons must be ready to conform to the idea of a Christian commonwealth, as understood by the early settlers in New England, if a religious profession similar to theirs should ever succeed in regaining its lost ground, as religions supposed to be declining have so often been known to do.

To imagine another contingency, perhaps more likely to be realized than the one last mentioned. There is confessedly a strong tendency in the modern world towards a democratic constitution of society, accompanied or not by popular political institutions. It is affirmed that in the country where this tendency is most completely realized—where both society and the government are most democratic—the United States—the feeling of the majority, to whom any appearance of a more showy or costly style of living than they can hope to rival is disagreeable, operates as a tolerably effectual sumptuary law, and that in many parts of the Union it is really difficult for a person possessing a very large income, to find any mode of spending it, which will not incur popular disapprobation. Though such statements as these are doubtless much exaggerated as a representation of existing facts, the state of things they describe is not only a conceivable and possible, but a probable result of democratic feeling, combined with the notion that the public has a right to a veto on the manner in which individuals shall spend their incomes. We have only further to suppose a considerable diffusion of Socialist opinions, and it may become infamous in the eyes of the majority to possess more property than some very small amount, or any income not earned by manual labour. Opinions similar in principle to these, already prevail widely among the artizan class, and weigh oppressively on those who are amenable to the opinion chiefly of that class, namely, its own members. It is known that the bad workmen who form the majority of the operatives in many branches of industry, are decidedly of opinion that bad workmen ought to receive the same wages as good, and that no one ought to be allowed, through piecework or otherwise, to earn by superior skill or industry more than others can without it. And they employ a moral police, which occasionally becomes a physical one, to deter skilful workmen from receiving, and employers from giving, a larger remuneration for a more useful service. If the public have any jurisdiction over private concerns, I cannot see that these people are in fault, or that any individual's particular public can be blamed for asserting the same authority over his individual conduct, which the general public asserts over people in general.

But, without dwelling upon supposititious cases, there are, in our own day, gross usurpations upon the liberty of private life actually practised, and still greater ones threatened with some expectation of success, and opinions *propounded* which assert an unlimited right in the public not only to prohibit by law everything which it thinks wrong, but in order to get at what it thinks wrong, to prohibit any number of things which it admits to be innocent.

Under the name of preventing intemperance, the people of one English colony, and of nearly half the United States, have been interdicted by law from making any use whatever of fermented drinks, except for medical purposes: for prohibition of their sale is in fact, as it is intended to be, prohibition of their use. And though the impracticability of executing the law has caused its repeal in several of the States which had adopted it, including the one from which it derives its name, an attempt has notwithstanding been commenced, and is prosecuted with considerable zeal by many of the professed philanthropists, to agitate for a similar law in this country. The association, or "Alliance" as it terms itself, which has been formed for this purpose, has acquired some notoriety through the publicity given to a correspondence between its Secretary and one of the very few English public men who hold that a politician's opinions ought to be founded on principles.[*] Lord Stanley's share in this correspondence is calculated to strengthen the hopes already built on him, by those who know how rare such qualities as are manifested in some of his public appearances, un-

[*See "Lord Stanley, M.P., and The United Kingdom Alliance," *The Times*, 2 Oct., 1856, pp. 9–10.]

*a–a*591, 592   proposed

happily are among those who figure in political life. The organ of the Alliance, who would "deeply deplore the recognition of any principle which could be wrested to justify bigotry and persecution," undertakes to point out the "broad and impassable barrier" which divides such principles from those of the association. "All matters relating to thought, opinion, conscience, appear to me," he says, "to be without the sphere of legislation; all pertaining to social act, habit, relation, subject only to a discretionary power vested in the State itself, and not in the individual, to be within it." No mention is made of a third class, different from either of these, viz. acts and habits which are not social, but individual; although it is to this class, surely, that the act of drinking fermented liquors belongs. Selling fermented liquors, however, is trading, and trading is a social act. But the infringement complained of is not on the liberty of the seller, but on that of the buyer and consumer; since the State might just as well forbid him to drink wine, as purposely make it impossible for him to obtain it. The Secretary, however, says, "I claim, as a citizen, a right to legislate whenever my social rights are invaded by the social act of another." And now for the definition of these "social rights." "If anything invades my social rights, certainly the traffic in strong drink does. It destroys my primary right of security, by constantly creating and stimulating social disorder. It invades my right of equality, by deriving a profit from the creation of a misery I am taxed to support. It impedes my right to free moral and intellectual development, by surrounding my path with dangers, and by weakening and demoralizing society, from which I have a right to claim mutual aid and intercourse."[*] A theory of "social rights," the like of which probably never before found its way into distinct language: being nothing short of this—that it is the absolute social right of every individual, that every other individual shall act in every respect exactly as he ought; that whosoever fails thereof in the smallest particular, violates my social right, and entitles me to demand from the legislature the removal of the grievance. So monstrous a principle is far more dangerous than any single interference with liberty; there is no violation of liberty which it would not justify; it acknowledges no right to any freedom whatever, except perhaps to that of holding opinions in secret, without ever disclosing them: for, the moment an opinion which I consider noxious passes any one's lips, it invades all the "social rights" attributed to me by the Alliance. The doctrine ascribes to all mankind a vested interest in each other's moral, intellectual, and even physical perfection, to be defined by each claimant according to his own standard.

Another important example of illegitimate interference with the rightful liberty of the individual, not simply threatened, but long since carried into

[*Samuel Pope, letter to Lord Stanley, *ibid.*, p. 9.]

triumphant effect, is Sabbatarian legislation.[*] Without doubt, abstinence on one day in the week, so far as the exigencies of life permit, from the usual daily occupation, though in no respect religiously binding on any except Jews, is a highly beneficial custom. And inasmuch as this custom cannot be observed without a general consent to that effect among the industrious classes, therefore, in so far as some persons by working may impose the same necessity on others, it may be allowable and right that the law should guarantee to each the observance by others of the custom, by suspending the greater operations of industry on a particular day. But this justification, grounded on the direct interest which others have in each individual's observance of the practice, does not apply to the self-chosen occupations in which a person may think fit to employ his leisure; nor does it hold good, in the smallest degree, for legal restrictions on amusements. It is true that the amusement of some is the day's work of others; but the pleasure, not to say the useful recreation, of many, is worth the labour of a few, provided the occupation is freely chosen, and can be freely resigned. The operatives are perfectly right in thinking that if all worked on Sunday, seven days' work would have to be given for six days' wages: but so long as the great mass of employments are suspended, the small number who for the enjoyment of others must still work, obtain a proportional increase of earnings; and they are not obliged to follow those occupations, if they prefer leisure to emolument. If a further remedy is sought, it might be found in the establishment by custom of a holiday on some other day of the week for those particular classes of persons. The only ground, therefore, on which restrictions on Sunday amusements can be defended, must be that they are religiously wrong; a motive of legislation which never can be too earnestly protested against. "Deorum injuriæ Diis curæ."[†] It remains to be proved that society or any of its officers holds a commission from on high to avenge any supposed offence to Omnipotence, which is not also a wrong to our fellow creatures. The notion that it is one man's duty that another should be religious, was the foundation of all the religious persecutions ever perpetrated, and if admitted, would fully justify them. Though the feeling which breaks out in the repeated attempts to stop railway travelling on Sunday, in the resistance to the opening of Museums, and the like, has not the cruelty of the old persecutors, the state of mind indicated by it is fundamentally the same. It is a determination not to tolerate others in doing what is permitted by their religion, because it is not permitted by the persecutor's religion. It is a belief that God not only abominates the act of the misbeliever, but will not hold us guiltless if we leave him unmolested.

[*See, e.g., 13 & 14 Victoria, c. 23 (1850).]
[†Tacitus, *The Annals*, Vol. I, p. 368 (I, lxxiii).]

I cannot refrain from adding to these examples of the little account commonly made of human liberty, the language of downright persecution which breaks out from the press of this country, whenever it feels called on to notice the remarkable phenomenon of Mormonism. Much might be said on the unexpected and instructive fact, that an alleged new revelation, and a religion founded on it, the product of palpable imposture, not even supported by the *prestige* of extraordinary qualities in its founder, is believed by hundreds of thousands, and has been made the foundation of a society, in the age of newspapers, railways, and the electric telegraph. What here concerns us is, that this religion, like other and better religions, has its martyrs; that its prophet and founder[*] was, for his teaching, put to death by a mob; that others of its adherents lost their lives by the same lawless violence; that they were forcibly expelled, in a body, from the country in which they first grew up; while, now that they have been chased into a solitary recess in the midst of a desert, many in this country openly declare that it would be right (only that it is not convenient) to send an expedition against them, and compel them by force to conform to the opinions of other people. The article of the Mormonite doctrine which is the chief provocative to the antipathy which thus breaks through the ordinary restraints of religious tolerance, is its sanction of polygamy; which, though permitted to Mahomedans, and Hindoos, and Chinese, seems to excite unquenchable animosity when practised by persons who speak English, and profess to be a kind of Christians. No one has a deeper disapprobation than I have of this Mormon institution; both for other reasons, and because, far from being in any way countenanced by the principle of liberty, it is a direct infraction of that principle, being a mere rivetting of the chains of one-half of the community, and an emancipation of the other from reciprocity of obligation towards them. Still, it must be remembered that this relation is as much voluntary on the part of the women concerned in it, and who may be deemed the sufferers by it, as is the case with any other form of the marriage institution; and however surprising this fact may appear, it has its explanation in the common ideas and customs of the world, which teaching women to think marriage the one thing needful, make it intelligible that many a woman should prefer being one of several wives, to not being a wife at all. Other countries are not asked to recognise such unions, or release any portion of their inhabitants from their own laws on the score of Mormonite opinions. But when the dissentients have conceded to the hostile sentiments of others, far more than could justly be demanded; when they have left the countries to which their doctrines were unacceptable, and established themselves in a remote corner of the earth, which they have been the first to render habitable to human beings; it is difficult to see on what principles but those of tyranny

[*Joseph Smith.]

they can be prevented from living there under what laws they please, provided they commit no aggression on other nations, and allow perfect freedom of departure to those who are dissatisfied with their ways. A recent writer, in some respects of considerable merit, proposes (to use his own words) not a crusade, but a *civilizade*, against this polygamous community, to put an end to what seems to him a retrograde step in civilization. It also appears so to me, but I am not aware that any community has a right to force another to be civilized. So long as the sufferers by the bad law do not invoke assistance from other communities, I cannot admit that persons entirely unconnected with them ought to step in and require that a condition of things with which all who are directly interested appear to be satisfied, should be put an end to because it is a scandal to persons some thousands of miles distant, who have no part or concern in it. Let them send missionaries, if they please, to preach against it; and let them, by any fair means (of which silencing the teachers is not one,) oppose the progress of similar doctrines among their own people. If civilization has got the better of barbarism when barbarism had the world to itself, it is too much to profess to be afraid lest barbarism, after having been fairly got under, should revive and conquer civilization. A civilization that can thus succumb to its vanquished enemy, must first have become so degenerate, that neither its appointed priests and teachers, nor anybody else, has the capacity, or will take the trouble, to stand up for it. If this be so, the sooner such a civilization receives notice to quit, the better. It can only go on from bad to worse, until destroyed and regenerated (like the Western Empire) by energetic barbarians.

CHAPTER V

Applications

THE PRINCIPLES asserted in these pages must be more generally admitted as the basis for discussion of details, before a consistent application of them to all the various departments of government and morals can be attempted with any prospect of advantage. The few observations I propose to make on questions of detail, are designed to illustrate the principles, rather than to follow them out to their consequences. I offer, not so much applications, as specimens of application; which may serve to bring into greater clearness the meaning and limits of the two maxims which together form the entire doctrine of this Essay, and to assist the judgment in holding the balance between them, in the cases where it appears doubtful which of them is applicable to the case.

The maxims are, first, that the individual is not accountable to society for his actions, in so far as these concern the interests of no person but himself. Advice, instruction, persuasion, and avoidance by other people if thought necessary by them for their own good, are the only measures by which society can justifiably express its dislike or disapprobation of his conduct. Secondly, that for such actions as are prejudicial to the interests of others, the individual is accountable, and may be subjected either to social or to legal *punishment*, if society is of opinion that the one or the other is requisite for its protection.

In the first place, it must by no means be supposed, because damage, or probability of damage, to the interests of others, can alone justify the interference of society, that therefore it always does justify such interference. In many cases, an individual, in pursuing a legitimate object, necessarily and therefore legitimately causes pain or loss to others, or intercepts a good which they had a reasonable hope of obtaining. Such oppositions of interest between individuals often arise from bad social institutions, but are unavoidable while those institutions last; and some would be unavoidable under any institutions. Whoever succeeds in an overcrowded profession, or in a competitive examination; whoever is preferred to another in any contest for an object which both desire, reaps benefit from the loss of others, from their wasted exertion and their disappointment. But it is, by common

*a–a*591,592 punishments

admission, better for the general interest of mankind, that persons should pursue their objects undeterred by this sort of consequences. In other words, society admits no right, either legal or moral, in the disappointed competitors, to immunity from this kind of suffering; and feels called on to interfere, only when means of success have been employed which it is contrary to the general interest to permit—namely, fraud or treachery, and force.

Again, trade is a social act. Whoever undertakes to sell any description of goods to the public, does what affects the interest of other persons, and of society in general; and thus his conduct, in principle, comes within the jurisdiction of society: accordingly, it was once held to be the duty of governments, in all cases which were considered of importance, to fix prices, and regulate the processes of manufacture. But it is now recognised, though not till after a long struggle, that both the cheapness and the good quality of commodities are most effectually provided for by leaving the producers and sellers perfectly free, under the sole check of equal freedom to the buyers for supplying themselves elsewhere. This is the so-called doctrine of Free Trade, which rests on grounds different from, though equally solid with, the principle of individual liberty asserted in this Essay. Restrictions on trade, or on production for purposes of trade, are indeed restraints; and all restraint, *quâ* restraint, is an evil: but the restraints in question affect only that part of conduct which society is competent to restrain, and are wrong solely because they do not really produce the results which it is desired to produce by them. As the principle of individual liberty is not involved in the doctrine of Free Trade, so neither is it in most of the questions which arise respecting the limits of that doctrine; as for example, what amount of public control is admissible for the prevention of fraud by adulteration; how far sanitary precautions, or arrangements to protect workpeople employed in dangerous occupations, should be enforced on employers. Such questions involve considerations of liberty, only in so far as leaving people to themselves is always better, *cæteris paribus*, than controlling them: but that they may be legitimately controlled for these ends, is in principle undeniable. On the other hand, there are questions relating to interference with trade, which are essentially questions of liberty; such as the Maine Law, already touched upon; the prohibition of the importation of opium into China; the restriction of the sale of poisons;[*] all cases, in short, where the object of the interference is to make it impossible or difficult to obtain a particular commodity. These interferences are objectionable, not as infringements on the liberty of the producer or seller, but on that of the buyer.

One of these examples, that of the sale of poisons, opens a new question; the proper limits of what may be called the functions of police; how far

[*See 14 & 15 Victoria, c. 13 (1851).]

liberty may legitimately be invaded for the prevention of crime, or of accident. It is one of the undisputed functions of government to take precautions against crime before it has been committed, as well as to detect and punish it afterwards. The preventive function of government, however, is far more liable to be abused, to the prejudice of liberty, than the punitory function; for there is hardly any part of the legitimate freedom of action of a human being which would not admit of being represented, and fairly too, as increasing the facilities for some form or other of delinquency. Nevertheless, if a public authority, or even a private person, sees any one evidently preparing to commit a crime, they are not bound to look on inactive until the crime is committed, but may interfere to prevent it. If poisons were never bought or used for any purpose except the commission of murder, it would be right to prohibit their manufacture and sale. They may, however, be wanted not only for innocent but for useful purposes, and restrictions cannot be imposed in the one case without operating in the other. Again, it is a proper office of public authority to guard against accidents. If either a public officer or any one else saw a person attempting to cross a bridge which had been ascertained to be unsafe, and there were no time to warn him of his danger, they might seize him and turn him back, without any real infringement of his liberty; for liberty consists in doing what one desires, and he does not desire to fall into the river. Nevertheless, when there is not a certainty, but only a danger of mischief, no one but the person himself can judge of the sufficiency of the motive which may prompt him to incur the risk: in this case, therefore, (unless he is a child, or delirious, or in some state of excitement or absorption incompatible with the full use of the reflecting faculty) he ought, I conceive, to be only warned of the danger; not forcibly prevented from exposing himself to it. Similar considerations, applied to such a question as the sale of poisons, may enable us to decide which among the possible modes of regulation are or are not contrary to principle. Such a precaution, for example, as that of labelling the drug with some word expressive of its dangerous character, may be enforced without violation of liberty: the buyer cannot wish not to know that the thing he possesses has poisonous qualities. But to require in all cases the certificate of a medical practitioner, would make it sometimes impossible, always expensive, to obtain the article for legitimate uses. The only mode apparent to me, in which difficulties may be thrown in the way of crime committed through this means, without any infringement, worth taking into account, upon the liberty of those who desire the poisonous substance for other purposes, consists in providing what, in the apt language of Bentham, is called "preappointed evidence."[*] This provision is familiar to every one

[*See, e.g., *An Introductory View of the Rationale of Evidence*, in *Works*, Vol. VI, p. 60.]

in the case of contracts. It is usual and right that the law, when a contract is entered into, should require as the condition of its enforcing performance, that certain formalities should be observed, such as signatures, attestation of witnesses, and the like, in order that in case of subsequent dispute, there may be evidence to prove that the contract was really entered into, and that there was nothing in the circumstances to render it legally invalid: the effect being, to throw great obstacles in the way of fictitious contracts, or contracts made in circumstances which, if known, would destroy their validity. Precautions of a similar nature might be enforced in the sale of articles adapted to be instruments of crime. The seller, for example, might be required to enter in a register the exact time of the transaction, the name and address of the buyer, the precise quality and quantity sold; to ask the purpose for which it was wanted, and record the answer he received. When there was no medical prescription, the presence of some third person might be required, to bring home the fact to the purchaser, in case there should afterwards be reason to believe that the article had been applied to criminal purposes. Such regulations would in general be no material impediment to obtaining the article, but a very considerable one to making an improper use of it without detection.

The right inherent in society, to ward off crimes against itself by antecedent precautions, suggests the obvious limitations to the maxim, that purely self-regarding misconduct cannot properly be meddled with in the way of prevention or punishment. Drunkenness, for example, in ordinary cases, is not a fit subject for legislative interference; but I should deem it perfectly legitimate that a person, who had once been convicted of any act of violence to others under the influence of drink, should be placed under a special legal restriction, personal to himself; that if he were afterwards found drunk, he should be liable to a penalty, and that if when in that state he committed another offence, the punishment to which he would be liable for that other offence should be increased in severity. The making himself drunk, in a person whom drunkenness excites to do harm to others, is a crime against others. So, again, idleness, except in a person receiving support from the public, or except when it constitutes a breach of contract, cannot without tyranny be made a subject of legal punishment; but if, either from idleness or from any other avoidable cause, a man fails to perform his legal duties to others, as for instance to support his children, it is no tyranny to force him to fulfil that obligation, by compulsory labour, if no other means are available.

Again, there are many acts which, being directly injurious only to the agents themselves, ought not to be legally interdicted, but which, if done publicly, are a violation of good manners, and coming thus within the category of offences against others, may rightfully be prohibited. Of this kind are offences against decency; on which it is unnecessary to dwell, the rather as they are only connected indirectly with our subject, the objection to publicity being equally strong in the case of many actions not in themselves condemnable, nor supposed to be so.

There is another question to which an answer must be found, consistent with the principles which have been laid down. In cases of personal conduct supposed to be blameable, but which respect for liberty precludes society from preventing or punishing, because the evil directly resulting falls wholly on the agent; what the agent is free to do, ought other persons to be equally free to counsel or instigate? This question is not free from difficulty. The case of a person who solicits another to do an act, is not strictly a case of self-regarding conduct. To give advice or offer inducements to any one, is a social act, and may, therefore, like actions in general which affect others, be supposed amenable to social control. But a little reflection corrects the first impression, by showing that if the case is not strictly within the definition of individual liberty, yet the reasons on which the principle of individual liberty is grounded, are applicable to it. If people must be allowed, in whatever concerns only themselves, to act as seems best to themselves at their own peril, they must equally be free to consult with one another about what is fit to be so done; to exchange opinions, and give and receive suggestions. Whatever it is permitted to do, it must be permitted to advise to do. The question is doubtful, only when the instigator derives a personal benefit from his advice; when he makes it his occupation, for subsistence or pecuniary gain, to promote what society and the *b*State*b* consider to be an evil. Then, indeed, a new element of complication is introduced; namely, the existence of classes of persons with an interest opposed to what is considered as the public weal, and whose mode of living is grounded on the counteraction of it. Ought this to be interfered with, or not? Fornication, for example, must be tolerated, and so must gambling; but should a person be free to be a pimp, or to keep a gambling-house? The case is one of those which lie on the exact boundary line between two principles, and it is not at once apparent to which of the two it properly belongs. There are arguments on both sides. On the side of toleration it may be said, that the fact of following anything as an occupation, and living or profiting by the practice of it, cannot make that criminal which would otherwise be admissible; that the act should either be consistently permitted or consistently prohibited; that if the principles which we have hitherto defended are true, society has no business, *as* society, to decide anything to be wrong which concerns only the individual; that it cannot go beyond dissuasion, and that one person should be as free to persuade, as another to dissuade. In opposition to this it may be contended, that although the public, or the State, are

*b–b*591   state

not warranted in authoritatively deciding, for purposes of repression or punishment, that such or such conduct affecting only the interests of the individual is good or bad, they are fully justified in assuming, if they regard it as bad, that its being so or not is at least a disputable question: That, this being supposed, they cannot be acting wrongly in endeavouring to exclude the influence of solicitations which are not disinterested, of instigators who cannot possibly be impartial—who have a direct personal interest on one side, and that side the one which the State believes to be wrong, and who confessedly promote it for personal objects only. There can surely, it may be urged, be nothing lost, no sacrifice of good, by so ordering matters that persons shall make their election, either wisely or foolishly, on their own prompting, as free as possible from the arts of persons who stimulate their inclinations for interested purposes of their own. Thus (it may be said) though the statutes respecting unlawful games are utterly indefensible— though all persons should be free to gamble in their own or each other's houses, or in any place of meeting established by their own subscriptions, and open only to the members and their visitors—yet public gambling-houses should not be permitted. It is true that the prohibition is never effectual, and that, whatever amount of tyrannical power ᶜmay beᶜ given to the police, gambling-houses can always be maintained under other pretences; but they may be compelled to conduct their operations with a certain degree of secrecy and mystery, so that nobody knows anything about them but those who seek them; and more than this, society ought not to aim at. There is considerable force in these ᵈarguments. Iᵈ will not venture to decide whether they are sufficient to justify the moral anomaly of punishing the accessary, when the principal is (and must be) allowed to go free; of fining or imprisoning the procurer, but not the fornicator, the gambling-house keeper, but not the gambler. Still less ought the common operations of buying and selling to be interfered with on analogous grounds. Almost every article which is bought and sold may be used in excess, and the sellers have a pecuniary interest in encouraging that excess; but no argument can be founded on this, in favour, for instance, of the Maine Law; because the class of dealers in strong drinks, though interested in their abuse, are indispensably required for the sake of their legitimate use. The interest, however, of these dealers in promoting intemperance is a real evil, and justifies the State in imposing restrictions and requiring guarantees which, but for that justification, would be infringements of legitimate liberty.

A further question is, whether the State, while it permits, should nevertheless indirectly discourage conduct which it deems contrary to the best interests of the agent; whether, for example, it should take measures to

c-c591,592 is
d-d591 arguments; I

render the means of drunkenness more costly, or add to the difficulty of procuring them by limiting the number of the places of sale. On this as on most other practical questions, many distinctions require to be made. To tax stimulants for the sole purpose of making them more difficult to be obtained, is a measure differing only in degree from their entire prohibition; and would be justifiable only if that were justifiable. Every increase of cost is a prohibition, to those whose means do not come up to the augmented price; and to those who do, it is a penalty laid on them for gratifying a particular taste. Their choice of pleasures, and their mode of expending their income, after satisfying their legal and moral obligations to the State and to individuals, are their own concern, and must rest with their own judgment. These considerations may seem at first sight to condemn the selection of stimulants as special subjects of taxation for purposes of revenue. But it must be remembered that taxation for fiscal purposes is absolutely inevitable; that in most countries it is necessary that a considerable part of that taxation should be indirect; that the State, therefore, cannot help imposing penalties, which to some persons may be prohibitory, on the use of some articles of consumption. It is hence the duty of the State to consider, in the imposition of taxes, what commodities the consumers can best spare; and à fortiori, to select in preference those of which it deems the use, beyond a very moderate quantity, to be positively injurious. Taxation, therefore, of stimulants, up to the point which produces the largest amount of revenue (supposing that the State needs all the revenue which it yields) is not only admissible, but to be approved of.

The question of making the sale of these commodities a more or less exclusive privilege, must be answered differently, according to the purposes to which the restriction is intended to be subservient. All places of public resort require the restraint of a police, and places of this kind peculiarly, because offences against society are especially apt to originate there. It is, therefore, fit to confine the power of selling these commodities (at least for consumption on the spot) to persons of known or vouched-for respectability of conduct; to make such regulations respecting hours of opening and closing as may be requisite for public surveillance, and to withdraw the licence if breaches of the peace repeatedly take place through the connivance or incapacity of the keeper of the house, or if it becomes a rendez-vous for concocting and preparing offences against the law. Any further restriction I do not conceive to be, in principle, justifiable. The limitation in number, for instance, of beer and spirit houses, for the express purpose of rendering them more difficult of access, and diminishing the occasions of temptation, not only exposes all to an inconvenience because there are some by whom the facility would be abused, but is suited only to a state of society in which the labouring classes are avowedly treated as children or savages, and placed under an education of restraint, to fit them for future admission to the privileges of freedom. This is not the principle on which the labouring classes are professedly governed in any free country; and no person who sets due value on freedom will give his adhesion to their being so governed, unless after all efforts have been exhausted to educate them for freedom and govern them as freemen, and it has been definitively proved that they can only be governed as children. The bare statement of the alternative shows the absurdity of supposing that such efforts have been made in any case which needs be considered here. It is only because the institutions of this country are a mass of inconsistencies, that things find admittance into our practice which belong to the system of despotic, or what is called paternal, government, while the general freedom of our institutions precludes the exercise of the amount of control necessary to render the restraint of any real efficacy as a moral education.

It was pointed out in an early part of this Essay,[*] that the liberty of the individual, in things wherein the individual is alone concerned, implies a corresponding liberty in any number of individuals to regulate by mutual agreement such things as regard them jointly, and regard no persons but themselves. This question presents no difficulty, so long as the will of all the persons implicated remains unaltered; but since that will may change, it is often necessary, even in things in which they alone are concerned, that they should enter into engagements with one another; and when they do, it is fit, as a general rule, that those engagements should be kept. Yet, in the laws, probably, of every country, this general rule has some exceptions. Not only persons are not held to engagements which violate the rights of third parties, but it is sometimes considered a sufficient reason for releasing them from an engagement, that it is injurious to themselves. In this and most other civilized countries, for example, an engagement by which a person should sell himself, or allow himself to be sold, as a slave, would be null and void; neither enforced by law nor by opinion. The ground for thus limiting his power of voluntarily disposing of his own lot in life, is apparent, and is very clearly seen in this extreme case. The reason for not interfering, unless for the sake of others, with a person's voluntary acts, is consideration for his liberty. His voluntary choice is evidence that what he so chooses is desirable, or at the least endurable, to him, and his good is on the whole best provided for by allowing him to take his own means of pursuing it. But by selling himself for a slave, he abdicates his liberty; he foregoes any future use of it beyond that single act. He therefore defeats, in his own case, the very purpose which is the justification of allowing him to dispose of himself. He is no longer free; but is thenceforth in a position which has no longer the presumption in its favour, that would be afforded by his volun-

[*See p. 226 above.]

tarily remaining in it. The principle of freedom cannot require that he should be free not to be free. It is not freedom, to be allowed to alienate his freedom. These reasons, the force of which is so conspicuous in this peculiar case, are evidently of far wider application; yet a limit is everywhere set to them by the necessities of life, which continually require, not indeed that we should resign our freedom, but that we should consent to this and the other limitation of it. The principle, however, which demands uncontrolled freedom of action in all that concerns only the agents themselves, requires that those who have become bound to one another, in things which concern no third party, should be able to release one another from the engagement: and even without such voluntary release, there are perhaps no contracts or engagements, except those that relate to money or money's worth, of which one can venture to say that there ought to be no liberty whatever of retractation. Baron Wilhelm von Humboldt, in the excellent essay from which I have already quoted, states it as his conviction, that engagements which involve personal relations or services, should never be legally binding beyond a limited duration of time; and that the most important of these engagements, marriage, having the peculiarity that its objects are frustrated unless the feelings of both the parties are in harmony with it, should require nothing more than the declared will of either party to dissolve it.[*] This subject is too important, and too complicated, to be discussed in a parenthesis, and I touch on it only so far as is necessary for purposes of illustration. If the conciseness and generality of Baron Humboldt's dissertation had not obliged him in this instance to content himself with enunciating his conclusion without discussing the premises, he would doubtless have recognised that the question cannot be decided on grounds so simple as those to which he confines himself. When a person, either by express promise or by conduct, has encouraged another to rely upon his continuing to act in a certain way—to build expectations and calculations, and stake any part of his plan of life upon that supposition—a new series of moral obligations arises on his part towards that person, which may possibly be overruled, but cannot be ignored. And again, if the relation between two contracting parties has been followed by consequences to others; if it has placed third parties in any peculiar position, or, as in the case of marriage, has even called third parties into existence, obligations arise on the part of both the contracting parties towards those third persons, the fulfilment of which, or at all events the mode of fulfilment, must be greatly affected by the continuance or disruption of the relation between the original parties to the contract. It does not follow, nor can I admit, that these obligations extend to requiring the fulfilment of the contract at all costs to the happiness of the reluctant party; but they are a necessary element in the question; and even if, as Von Hum-

[*The Sphere and Duties of Government, p. 34.]

boldt maintains, they ought to make no difference in the *legal* freedom of the parties to release themselves from the engagement (and I also hold that they ought not to make *much* difference), they necessarily make a great difference in the *moral* freedom. A person is bound to take all these circumstances into account, before resolving on a step which may affect such important interests of others; and if he does not allow proper weight to those interests, he is morally responsible for the wrong. I have made these obvious remarks for the better illustration of the general principle of liberty, and not because they are at all needed on the particular question, which, on the contrary, is usually discussed as if the interest of children was everything, and that of grown persons nothing.

I have already observed that, owing to the absence of any recognised general principles, liberty is often granted where it should be withheld, as well as withheld where it should be granted; and one of the cases in which, in the modern European world, the sentiment of liberty is the strongest, is a case where, in my view, it is altogether misplaced. A person should be free to do as he likes in his own concerns; but he ought not to be free to do as he likes in acting for another, under the pretext that the affairs of ᵉthe otherᵉ are his own affairs. The State, while it respects the liberty of each in what specially regards himself, is bound to maintain a vigilant control over his exercise of any power which it allows him to possess over others. This obligation is almost entirely disregarded in the case of the family relations, a case, in its direct influence on human happiness, more important than all others taken together. The almost despotic power of husbands over wives needs not be enlarged upon here, because nothing more is needed for the complete removal of the evil, than that wives should have the same rights, and should receive the protection of law in the same manner, as all other persons; and because, on this subject, the defenders of established injustice do not avail themselves of the plea of liberty, but stand forth openly as the champions of power. It is in the case of children, that misapplied notions of liberty are a real obstacle to the fulfilment by the State of its duties. One would almost think that a man's children were supposed to be literally, and not metaphorically, a part of himself, so jealous is opinion of the smallest interference of law with his absolute and exclusive control over them; more jealous than of almost any interference with his own freedom of action: so much less do the generality of mankind value liberty than power. Consider, for example, the case of education. Is it not almost a self-evident axiom, that the State should require and compel the education, up to a certain standard, of every human being who is born its citizen? Yet who is there that is not afraid to recognise and assert this truth? Hardly any one indeed will deny that it is one of the most sacred duties of the parents (or, as law and usage now stand, the

ᵉ⁻ᵉ591,592   another

father), after summoning a human being into the world, to give to that being an education fitting him to perform his part well in life towards others and towards himself. But while this is unanimously declared to be the father's duty, scarcely anybody, in this country, will bear to hear of obliging him to perform it. Instead of his being required to make any exertion or sacrifice for securing education to the child, it is left to his choice to accept it or not when it is provided gratis! It still remains unrecognised, that to bring a child into existence without a fair prospect of being able, not only to provide food for its body, but instruction and training for its mind, is a moral crime, both against the unfortunate offspring and against society; and that if the parent does not fulfil this obligation, the State ought to see it fulfilled, at the charge, as far as possible, of the parent.

Were the duty of enforcing universal education once admitted, there would be an end to the difficulties about what the State should teach, and how it should teach, which now convert the subject into a mere battle-field for sects and parties, causing the time and labour which should have been spent in educating, to be wasted in quarrelling about education. If the government would make up its mind to *require* for every child a good education, it might save itself the trouble of *providing* one. It might leave to parents to obtain the education where and how they pleased, and content itself with helping to pay the school fees of the poorer *fclasses* of children, and defraying the entire school expenses of those who have no one else to pay for them. The objections which are urged with reason against State education, do not apply to the enforcement of education by the State, but to the State's taking upon itself to direct that education: which is a totally different thing. That the whole or any large part of the education of the people should be in State hands, I go as far as any one in deprecating. All that has been said of the importance of individuality of character, and diversity in opinions and modes of conduct, involves, as of the same unspeakable importance, diversity of education. A general State education is a mere contrivance for moulding people to be exactly like one another: and as the mould in which it casts them is that which pleases the predominant power in the government, whether this be a monarch, a priesthood, an aristocracy, or the majority of the existing generation, in proportion as it is efficient and successful, it establishes a despotism over the mind, leading by natural tendency to one over the body. An education established and controlled by the State should only exist, if it exist at all, as one among many competing experiments, carried on for the purpose of example and stimulus, to keep the others up to a certain standard of excellence. Unless, indeed, when society in general is in so backward a state that it could not or would not provide for itself any proper institutions of education, unless the government undertook the task: then,

*f-f*591   class

indeed, the government may, as the less of two great evils, take upon itself
the business of schools and universities, as it may that of joint stock companies, when private enterprise, in a shape fitted for undertaking great works
of industry, does not exist in the country. But in general, if the country contains a sufficient number of persons qualified to provide education under
government auspices, the same persons would be able and willing to give an
equally good education on the voluntary principle, under the assurance of
remuneration afforded by a law rendering education compulsory, combined
with State aid to those unable to defray the expense.

The instrument for enforcing the law could be no other than public examinations, extending to all children, and beginning at an early age. An
age might be fixed at which every child must be examined, to ascertain if he
(or she) is able to read. If a child proves unable, the father, unless he has
some sufficient ground of excuse, might be subjected to a moderate fine, to be
worked out, if necessary, by his labour, and the child might be put to school
at his expense. Once in every year the examination should be renewed, with
a gradually extending range of subjects, so as to make the universal acquisition, and what is more, retention, of a certain minimum of general knowledge, virtually compulsory. Beyond that minimum, there should be voluntary examinations on all subjects, at which all who come up to a certain
standard of proficiency might claim a certificate. To prevent the State from
exercising, through these arrangements, an improper influence over opinion,
the knowledge required for passing an examination (beyond the merely instrumental parts of knowledge, such as languages and their use) should, even
in the higher *classes* of examinations, be confined to facts and positive
science exclusively. The examinations on religion, politics, or other disputed topics, should not turn on the truth or falsehood of opinions, but on
the matter of fact that such and such an opinion is held, on such grounds, by
such authors, or schools, or churches. Under this system, the rising generation would be no worse off in regard to all disputed truths, than they are at
present; they would be brought up either churchmen or dissenters as they
now are, the *State* merely taking care that they should be instructed churchmen, or instructed dissenters. There would be nothing to hinder them from
being taught religion, if their parents chose, at the same schools where they
were taught other things. All attempts by the *State* to bias the conclusions
of its citizens on disputed subjects, are evil; but it may very properly offer
to ascertain and certify that a person possesses the knowledge, requisite to
make his conclusions, on any given subject, worth attending to. A student
of philosophy would be the better for being able to stand an examination

g-g591,592   class
h-h591,592   state
i-i591,592   state

both in Locke and in Kant, whichever of the two he takes up with, or even if with neither: and there is no reasonable objection to examining an atheist in the evidences of Christianity, provided he is not required to profess a belief in them. The examinations, however, in the higher branches of knowledge should, I conceive, be entirely voluntary. It would be giving too dangerous a power to governments, were they allowed to exclude any one from professions, even from the profession of teacher, for alleged deficiency of qualifications: and I think, with Wilhelm von Humboldt,[*] that degrees, or other public certificates of scientific or professional acquirements, should be given to all who present themselves for examination, and stand the test; but that such certificates should confer no advantage over competitors, other than the weight which may be attached to their testimony by public opinion.

It is not in the matter of education only, that misplaced notions of liberty prevent moral obligations on the part of parents from being recognised, and legal obligations from being imposed, where there are the strongest grounds for the former always, and in many cases for the latter also. The fact itself, of causing the existence of a human being, is one of the most responsible actions in the range of human life. To undertake this responsibility—to bestow a life which may be either a curse or a blessing—unless the being on whom it is to be bestowed will have at least the ordinary chances of a desirable existence, is a crime against that being. And in a country either overpeopled, or threatened with being so, to produce children, beyond a very small number, with the effect of reducing the reward of labour by their competition, is a serious offence against all who live by the remuneration of their labour. The laws which, in many countries on the Continent, forbid marriage unless the parties can show that they have the means of supporting a family, do not exceed the legitimate powers of the *j*State*j*: and whether such laws be expedient or not (a question mainly dependent on local circumstances and feelings), they are not objectionable as violations of liberty. Such laws are interferences of the *k*State*k* to prohibit a mischievous act—an act injurious to others, which ought to be a subject of reprobation, and social stigma, even when it is not deemed expedient to superadd legal punishment. Yet the current ideas of liberty, which bend so easily to real infringements of the freedom of the individual in things which concern only himself, would repel the attempt to put any restraint upon his inclinations when the consequence of their indulgence is a life or lives of wretchedness and depravity to the offspring, with manifold evils to those sufficiently within reach to be in any way affected by their actions. When we compare the strange respect of mankind for liberty, with their strange want of respect for it, we might imagine that a

[*See *The Sphere and Duties of Government*, p. 123.]
*j-j*591,592   state
*k-k*591,592   state

man had an indispensable right to do harm to others, and no right at all to please himself without giving pain to any one.

I have reserved for the last place a large class of questions respecting the limits of government interference, which, though closely connected with the subject of this Essay, do not, in strictness, belong to it. These are cases in which the reasons against interference do not turn upon the principle of liberty: the question is not about restraining the actions of individuals, but about helping them: it is asked whether the government should do, or cause to be done, something for their benefit, instead of leaving it to be done by themselves, individually, or in voluntary combination.

The objections to government interference, when it is not such as to involve infringement of liberty, may be of three kinds.

The first is, when the thing to be done is likely to be better done by individuals than by the government. Speaking generally, there is no one so fit to conduct any business, or to determine how or by whom it shall be conducted, as those who are personally interested in it. This principle condemns the interferences, once so common, of the legislature, or the officers of government, with the ordinary processes of industry. But this part of the subject has been sufficiently enlarged upon by political economists, and is not particularly related to the principles of this Essay.

The second objection is more nearly allied to our subject. In many cases, though individuals may not do the particular thing so well, on the average, as the officers of government, it is nevertheless desirable that it should be done by them, rather than by the government, as a means to their own mental education—a mode of strengthening their active faculties, exercising their judgment, and giving them a familiar knowledge of the subjects with which they are thus left to deal. This is a principal, though not the sole, recommendation of jury trial (in cases not political); of free and popular local and municipal institutions; of the conduct of industrial and philanthropic enterprises by voluntary associations. These are not questions of liberty, and are connected with that subject only by remote tendencies; but they are questions of development. It belongs to a different occasion from the present to dwell on these things as parts of national education; as being, in truth, the peculiar training of a citizen, the practical part of the political education of a free people, taking them out of the narrow circle of personal and family selfishness, and accustoming them to the comprehension of joint interests, the management of joint concerns—habituating them to act from public or semi-public motives, and guide their conduct by aims which unite instead of isolating them from one another. Without these habits and powers, a free constitution can neither be worked nor preserved; as is exemplified by the too-often transitory nature of political freedom in countries where it does not rest upon a sufficient basis of local liberties. The management of purely local business by the localities, and of the great enterprises of industry by the union of those who voluntarily supply the pecuniary means, is further recommended by all the advantages which have been set forth in this Essay as belonging to individuality of development, and diversity of modes of action. Government operations tend to be everywhere alike. With individuals and voluntary associations, on the contrary, there are varied experiments, and endless diversity of experience. What the State can usefully do, is to make itself a central depository, and active circulator and diffuser, of the experience resulting from many trials. Its business is to enable each experimentalist to benefit by the experiments of others; instead of tolerating no experiments but its own.

The third, and most cogent reason for restricting the interference of government, is the great evil of adding unnecessarily to its power. Every function superadded to those already exercised by the government, causes its influence over hopes and fears to be more widely diffused, and converts, more and more, the active and ambitious part of the public into hangers-on of the government, or of some party which aims at becoming the government. If the roads, the railways, the banks, the insurance offices, the great joint-stock companies, the universities, and the public charities, were all of them branches of the government; if, in addition, the municipal corporations and local boards, with all that now devolves on them, became departments of the central administration; if the employés of all these different enterprises were appointed and paid by the government, and looked to the government for every rise in life; not all the freedom of the press and popular constitution of the legislature would make this or any other country free otherwise than in name. And the evil would be greater, the more efficiently and scientifically the administrative machinery was constructed—the more skilful the arrangements for obtaining the best qualified hands and heads with which to work it. In England it has of late been proposed that all the members of the civil service of government should be selected by competitive examination, to obtain for those employments the most intelligent and instructed persons procurable; and much has been said and written for and against this proposal.[*] One of the arguments most insisted on by its opponents, is that the occupation of a permanent official servant of the State does not hold out sufficient prospects of emolument and importance to attract the highest talents, which will always be able to find a more inviting career in the professions, or in the service of companies and other public bodies. One would not have been surprised if this argument had been used by the friends of the proposition, as an answer to its principal difficulty. Coming from the opponents it is strange enough. What is urged as an objection is the safety-valve of the proposed system. If indeed all the high talent of the country *could* be

[*See, e.g., J. S. Mill, "Reform of the Civil Service," pp. 205–11 above.]

drawn into the service of the government, a proposal tending to bring about that result might well inspire uneasiness. If every part of the business of society which required organized concert, or large and comprehensive views, were in the hands of the government, and if government offices were universally filled by the ablest men, all the enlarged culture and practised intelligence in the country, except the purely speculative, would be concentrated in a numerous bureaucracy, to whom alone the rest of the community would look for all things: the multitude for direction and dictation in all they had to do; the able and aspiring for personal advancement. To be admitted into the ranks of this bureaucracy, and when admitted, to rise therein, would be the sole objects of ambition. Under this régime, not only is the outside public ill-qualified, for want of practical experience, to criticize or check the mode of operation of the bureaucracy, but even if the accidents of despotic or the natural working of popular institutions occasionally raise to the summit a ruler or rulers of reforming inclinations, no reform can be effected which is contrary to the interest of the bureaucracy. Such is the melancholy condition of the Russian empire, as [1] shown in the accounts of those who have had sufficient opportunity of observation. The Czar himself is powerless against the bureaucratic body; he can send any one of them to Siberia, but he cannot govern without them, or against their will. On every decree of his they have a tacit veto, by merely refraining from carrying it into effect. In countries of more advanced civilization and of a more insurrectionary spirit, the public, accustomed to expect everything to be done for them by the State, or at least to do nothing for themselves without asking from the State not only leave to do it, but even how it is to be done, naturally hold the State responsible for all evil which befals them, and when the evil exceeds their amount of patience, they rise against the government and make what is called a revolution; whereupon somebody else, with or without legitimate authority from the nation, vaults into the seat, issues his orders to the bureaucracy, and everything goes on much as it did before; the bureaucracy being unchanged, and nobody else being capable of taking their place.

A very different spectacle is exhibited among a people accustomed to transact their own business. In France, a large part of the people having been engaged in military service, many of whom have held at least the rank of non-commissioned officers, there are in every popular insurrection several persons competent to take the lead, and improvise some tolerable plan of action. What the French are in military affairs, the Americans are in every kind of civil business; let them be left without a government, every body of Americans is able to improvise one, and to carry on that or any other public business with a sufficient amount of intelligence, order, and decision. This is what every free people ought to be: and a people capable of this is certain to

[1]591,592 is

be free; it will never let itself be enslaved by any man or body of men because these are able to seize and pull the reins of the central administration. No bureaucracy can hope to make such a people as this do or undergo anything that they do not like. But where everything is done through the bureaucracy, nothing to which the bureaucracy is really adverse can be done at all. The constitution of such countries is an organization of the experience and practical ability of the nation, into a disciplined body for the purpose of governing the rest; and the more perfect that organization is in itself, the more successful in drawing to itself and educating for itself the persons of greatest capacity from all ranks of the community, the more complete is the bondage of all, the members of the bureaucracy included. For the governors are as much the slaves of their organization and discipline, as the governed are of the governors. A Chinese mandarin is as much the tool and creature of a despotism as the humblest cultivator. An individual Jesuit is to the utmost degree of abasement the slave of his order, though the order itself exists for the collective power and importance of its members.

It is not, also, to be forgotten, that the absorption of all the principal ability of the country into the governing body is fatal, sooner or later, to the mental activity and progressiveness of the body itself. Banded together as they are— working a system which, like all systems, necessarily proceeds in a great measure by fixed rules—the official body are under the constant temptation of sinking into indolent routine, or, if they now and then desert that mill-horse round, of rushing into some half-examined crudity which has struck the fancy of some leading member of the corps: and the sole check to these closely allied, though seemingly opposite, tendencies, the only stimulus which can keep the ability of the body itself up to a high standard, is liability to the watchful criticism of equal ability outside the body. It is indispensable, therefore, that the means should exist, independently of the government, of forming such ability, and furnishing it with the opportunities and experience necessary for a correct judgment of great practical affairs. If we would possess permanently a skilful and efficient body of functionaries—above all, a body able to originate and willing to adopt improvements; if we would not have our bureaucracy degenerate into a pedantocracy, this body must not engross all the occupations which form and cultivate the faculties required for the government of mankind.

To determine the point at which evils, so formidable to human freedom and advancement, begin, or rather at which they begin to predominate over the benefits attending the collective application of the force of society, under its recognised chiefs, for the removal of the obstacles which stand in the way of its well-being; to secure as much of the advantages of centralized power and intelligence, as can be had without turning into governmental channels too great a proportion of the general activity—is one of the most difficult and complicated questions in the art of government. It is, in a great measure, a question of detail, in which many and various considerations must be kept in view, and no absolute rule can be laid down. But I believe that the practical principle in which safety resides, the ideal to be kept in view, the standard by which to test all arrangements intended for overcoming the difficulty, may be conveyed in these words: the greatest dissemination of power consistent with efficiency; but the greatest possible centralization of information, and diffusion of it from the centre. Thus, in municipal administration, there would be, as in the New England States, a very minute division among separate officers, chosen by the localities, of all business which is not better left to the persons directly interested; but besides this, there would be, in each department of local affairs, a central superintendence, forming a branch of the general government. The organ of this superintendence would concentrate, as in a focus, the variety of information and experience derived from the conduct of that branch of public business in all the localities, from everything analogous which is done in foreign countries, and from the general principles of political science. This central organ should have a right to know all that is done, and its special duty should be that of making the knowledge acquired in one place available for others. Emancipated from the petty prejudices and narrow views of a locality by its elevated position and comprehensive sphere of observation, its advice would naturally carry much authority; but its actual power, as a permanent institution, should, I conceive, be limited to compelling the local officers to obey the laws laid down for their guidance. In all things not provided for by general rules, those officers should be left to their own judgment, under responsibility to their constituents. For the violation of rules, they should be responsible to law, and the rules themselves should be laid down by the legislature; the central administrative authority only watching over their execution, and if they were not properly carried into effect, appealing, according to the nature of the case, to the *m*tribunals*m* to enforce the law, or to the constituencies to dismiss the functionaries who had not executed it according to its spirit. Such, in its general conception, is the central superintendence which the Poor Law Board is intended to exercise over the administrators of the Poor Rate throughout the country. Whatever powers the Board exercises beyond this limit, were right and necessary in that peculiar case, for the cure of rooted habits of maladministration in matters deeply affecting not the localities merely, but the whole community; since no locality has a moral right to make itself by mismanagement a nest of pauperism, necessarily overflowing into other localities, and impairing the moral and physical condition of the whole labouring community. The powers of administrative coercion and subordinate legislation possessed by the

*m–m*591,592   tribunal

Poor Law Board (but which, owing to the state of opinion on the subject, are very scantily exercised by them), though perfectly justifiable in a case of first-rate national interest, would be wholly out of place in the superintendence of interests purely local. But a central organ of information and instruction for all the localities, would be equally valuable in all departments of administration. A government cannot have too much of the kind of activity which does not impede, but aids and stimulates, individual exertion and development. The mischief begins when, instead of calling forth the activity and powers of individuals and bodies, it substitutes its own activity for theirs; when, instead of informing, advising, and, upon occasion, denouncing, it makes them work in fetters, or bids them stand aside and does their work instead of them. The worth of a State, in the long run, is the worth of the individuals composing it; and a State which postpones the interests of *their* mental expansion and elevation, to a little more of administrative skill, or of that semblance of it which practice gives, in the details of business; a State which dwarfs its men, in order that they may be more docile instruments in its hands even for beneficial purposes—will find that with small men no great thing can really be accomplished; and that the perfection of machinery to which it has sacrificed everything, will in the end avail it nothing, for want of the vital power which, in order that the machine might work more smoothly, it has preferred to banish.

38373192R00228

Made in the USA
Middletown, DE
18 December 2016